# THE ISGAP PAPERS
## ANTISEMITISM IN COMPARATIVE PERSPECTIVE
### VOLUME THREE

# THE ISGAP PAPERS

## ANTISEMITISM IN COMPARATIVE PERSPECTIVE

### VOLUME THREE

Charles Asher Small

*Editor*

ISGAP

*New York · Montreal · Kyiv · Tel Aviv · Paris · Rome · Oxford · Vienna*

Cover design and layout by AETS
Cover image by ariadne de raadt/Shutterstock

# Table of Contents

# Introduction

## Charles Asher Small[*]

History teaches that antisemitism affects all of society. It is neither a Jewish nor an Israeli parochial issue. As Elie Wiesel warned repeatedly, antisemitism begins with the Jews, but it never ends with them. Once this virulent form of hatred is unleashed, it attacks all of society, as well as the very institutions that are fundamental to the protection of democratic practice, citizenship, and basic human rights. Antisemitism knows no boundaries. The very forces that demonize and attack Jews also target women, religious minorities, various gendered identities, and those with unconventional political beliefs who are deemed to be impure by reactionary forces. In the contemporary context, we are witnessing reactionary social movements that attempt to delegitimize the State of Israel and notions of Jewish peoplehood. Simultaneously, this hatred is tolerated and even supported by some who claim to be "progressive" and "liberal," including a number of leading Western policy-makers. It is this amalgamation of hatred—contemporary antisemitism—that needs to be mapped, decoded, and examined at the highest levels of scholarship.

Antisemitism is a highly complex and, at times, perplexing form of hatred. It spans history and has infected many societies, religious and philosophical movements, and even civilizations. In the aftermath of the Holocaust, some contend that antisemitism illustrates the limitations of humanity itself. Manifestations of antisemitism emerge in numerous ideologically-based narratives and in the constructed identities of belonging and otherness such as race and ethnicity, nationalisms, and anti-nationalisms. The investigation of antisemitism has a long and impressive intellectual and research history. It remains a topic of ongoing political importance and scholarly engagement. However, when it comes to the formal study of antisemitism, especially in its contemporary manifestations, such as extreme anti-Israel practice and sentiment and the growth of Islamist antisemitism in the West and the Middle East, there is an

---

* Founder and Executive Director, Institute for the Study of Global Antisemitism and Policy (ISGAP); Goldman Fellow at the Harold Hartog School of Government and Policy and Senior Research Fellow at the Moshe Dayan Center for Middle Eastern and African Studies, Tel Aviv University; Visiting Scholar at St Antony's College, Oxford.

unwillingness within the academy to address the topic in accordance with its traditions of serious and unfettered intellectual inquiry. In fact, some might argue that, in this politically correct, postmodern moment, the academy in general has actually been guilty of antisemitism as a result of its refusal to engage with these important issues in an open and honest manner and its attempts to silence those who seek to challenge the new status quo. In other words, the academy itself has become a purveyor of antisemitism in contemporary society.

The rise of political Islam, which incorporates antisemitism at the core of its ideology, has been largely met with acquiescence in the West. As a result, this reactionary social movement has wreaked havoc across the Middle East and beyond, including the ongoing genocide in Syria and a refugee crisis that has spilled over from the Middle East into Europe. In spite of this, the West's response to criticism of its tolerance of political Islam is itself becoming increasingly intolerant, with the emergence of nationalist and xenophobic tendencies becoming more mainstream, as the vacuum created by denial and inaction is filled.

In 2004, the Institute for the Study of Global Antisemitism and Policy (ISGAP) was established with the aim of promoting the interdisciplinary study of antisemitism—with a focus on the contemporary context—and publishing high-caliber academic research in this area. ISGAP's mission encompasses the study of such subjects as the changing historical phases of antisemitism, regional variations, and how hatred of the Jewish people relates to other forms of hate. From the outset, the aims and objectives of ISGAP have been supported by scholars from many disciplines and countries and by a group of dedicated philanthropists initially led by the great humanitarian William (Bill) Prusoff. ISGAP is committed to countering efforts to sweep antisemitism under the carpet by providing scholarly research, academic programming, curriculum development, and publications of unassailable quality. It is also the only international interdisciplinary research organization that is seeking to confront and combat antisemitism within the academy on a practical and ideological level. ISGAP aims to ensure that future generations of scholars and professionals are both aware of the destructive nature of antisemitism and determined to eradicate it from society.

Between 2006 and 2011, ISGAP sponsored and operated the Yale Initiative for the Interdisciplinary Study of Antisemitism (YIISA), the first academic research center dedicated to the study of antisemitism based at a North American university. During this period, YIISA hosted a successful graduate and postgraduate fellowship program, research projects, conferences, and a high-level interdisciplinary seminar series at Yale University. A selection of the papers presented in the framework of this seminar series, as well as several other working papers, conference papers, and lectures commissioned by or submitted to YIISA by eminent scholars and researchers from around the world, was published in 2015 in *The Yale Papers: Antisemitism in Comparative Perspective*. In addition to providing a fascinating overview and scholarly analysis of some of the many facets of historical and contemporary antisemitism around the globe, this substantial volume stands as a solid and incontrovertible testament to the abundant—and, above all, productive—academic activity that characterized YIISA's truncated tenure at Yale, despite the prevailing political and academic environment that often suppresses the study of this important subject matter.

Since parting ways with Yale, ISGAP has continued to flourish as an independent academic institute that works closely with leading scholars and top tier universities in the United States and around the world. Among its many activities, ISGAP continues to host its "Antisemitism in Comparative Perspective" seminar series at Harvard University, McGill University, Stanford University, Columbia University Law School, and the University of Miami. As part of its international efforts, moreover, ISGAP has established seminar series at Rome's Sapienza University (2013), at the Sorbonne University and the Centre National de la Recherche Scientifique (CNRS) in Paris (2014), at the National University of Kyiv-Mohyla Academy in Kiev (2015), and at the American College of Greece in Athens (2016). In June 2016, ISGAP also cosponsored a conference at Sapienza University on the Dynamics and Policies of Prejudice from the Eighteenth to the Twenty-First Century. In September 2017, ISGAP held three consecutive international conferences at the Vatican, the Parliament of Italy, and La Sapienza University. These conferences were entitled, respectively, "Antisemitism and Minority Rights in the Middle East: Regional and International Implications," "Antisemitism as a Strategic Threat to Europe," and "Antisemitism as a Gateway to Terrorism." Hundreds of scholars, policymakers and public intellectuals from around the world were in attendance, while ISGAP representatives met with Pope Francis, Tony Blair, and other world leaders.

Another major ISGAP project is the Summer Institute for Curriculum Development in Critical Antisemitism Studies, a workshop-based program aimed primarily at professors with full-time college or university positions. Under the guidance of leading international scholars, participants in the program design a course syllabus and curriculum for the interdisciplinary study of contemporary antisemitism, which they subsequently implement at their home universities by teaching courses for credit. The first Summer Institute, which took place at the University of Oxford's Hertford College in July 2015, was a resounding success. Now in its fourth year, the Summer Institute will take place at St John's College, Oxford, in July 2018. This is just one of the many ways in which ISGAP is encouraging and supporting the study of antisemitism within academia.

ISGAP has an active publishing program that includes published collections of conference and seminar papers as well as co-publications with leading international academic publishers. Recent titles include *Global Antisemitism: A Crisis of Modernity* (2013), *The Yale Papers: Antisemitism in Comparative Perspective* (2015), *The First Shall Be The Last: Rethinking Antisemitism* (2015), *The ISGAP Papers: Antisemitism In Comparative Perspective—Volume Two* (2016), *Industry of Lies: Media, Academia, and the Israeli-Arab Conflict* (2017), and *The Caliph and the Ayatollah: Our World Under Siege* (2018). In addition to providing information and updates about its various activities, ISGAP's website provides access to a database of academic papers, a large video library of seminar and conference presentations, and the new *Flashpoint* series (2015), which disseminates up-to-date comments and articles on antisemitism, extremism, and global politics. A printed collection of *Flashpoint* articles is scheduled to appear in the near future.

As mentioned above, ISGAP's "Antisemitism in Comparative Perspective" seminar series continues to generate a steady flow of interesting presentations and papers on a wide range of topics relating to antisemitism. The present volume contains a selection of papers presented during the seminar series. Like the seminars on which they are based, these papers cover a range of topics that have profound implications for our understanding of historical and contemporary antisemitism, its impact on Jews and non-Jews, and our efforts to combat this irrational yet enduring prejudice. Although originally presented at different times and without an underlying thematic connection, the papers in this volume can be divided into two broad categories.

The papers in the first category examine various forms of classic and contemporary antisemitism from an academic perspective, analyzing how this phenomenon can be understood (or explained) at an intellectual level, how it is studied, and why it appears to be enjoying a revival in academic circles and among the intelligentsia. The papers in the second category analyze manifestations of antisemitism in various parts of the world, including the Middle East, Latin America and Eastern Europe. In particular, they show how various new and old ideologies and prejudices feed into contemporary antisemitism—sometimes in unexpected ways.

Kicking off the first category, Adam Katz examines various aspects of classic and contemporary antisemitism and observes that both are rooted in opposition to what he describes as "Jewish firstness," namely the idea that the ancient Jews invented or discovered monotheism. While acknowledging that this claim is perhaps somewhat overstated, he also observes that it can never be completely erased, since originality (or "going first") generates resentment on the part of those who subsequently adopt the invention or discovery for themselves. In this case, going first also creates a paradox, as Judaism models a universal community from which it exempts itself, as if the Jews refuse to play according to the rules that they have laid down for others. Antisemitism thus derives in part from an attempt to resolve this paradox by reducing it to Jewish particularism, exploitativeness, subversiveness, manipulation, and so on. Another example of "Jewish firstness" relates to the way in which Jews have gone first in terms of victimhood, as a result of the unprecedented horror of the Holocaust. The virulence of contemporary antisemitism thus derives in part from a sense that the Jews have monopolized victimhood in the modern world and used it to victimize another people. The Holocaust has left a terrible burden of guilt in Europe, and the powerful desire to be rid of that burden is expressed, paradoxically, in the insistence that Israel itself has become so evil, so Nazi-like, as to cancel that earlier guilt—and to transform what is left into guilt for Europe's indirect contribution to what Israel is doing to the Palestinians.

Examining the other side of the coin, as it were, Alon Segev notes that the term "Jewish self-hatred," which was coined and introduced into the academic and political discourse on antisemitism by Theodor Lessing in 1930, actually goes back many centuries. In fact, it long ago became a label attached by Jews of one political hue to Jews of another political hue. In recent decades, the question of Jewish self-hatred has often been raised and discussed in the context of the Israeli-Palestinian conflict, especially in relation to the Boycott, Divestment and Sanctions (BDS) movement, which draws support from Israelis and Jews abroad. People with Jewish ancestry—Israeli and non-Israeli—who criticize Israel and blame it for the conflict and the misery of the Palestinians are often tagged as "self-hating" Jews. Although the distinction between self-critique and self-hatred seems fairly obvious at first sight, it is actually quite difficult to draw clear lines between self-critique, self-hatred, Jewish self-hatred, and antisemitism—and their underlying motives—on a conceptual level. In this paper, Segev critically analyzes Theodor Lessing's book on this phenomenon, which marked Lessing's personal conversion from self-hatred to Zionism.

Turning to the study of antisemitism, Neil Kressel and Samuel Kressel review evidence bearing on whether antisemitism has recently reemerged as a dangerous and global sociopolitical problem. They present two empirical studies that explore how psychologists and other social scientists have investigated anti-Jewish bigotry. The first looks at research trends in major social scientific databases since the 1940s. The second is a content analysis of abstracts of psychological studies on antisemitism since 1990. The two empirical studies enable the authors to address (a) whether critics are correct about the neglect of contemporary antisemitism; (b) which aspects of the topic, to date, have been most studied; and (c) whether current research trends make it likely that we will learn what we need to know about this potentially dangerous sociopolitical phenomenon. They conclude, among other findings, that while social scientific aspects of the Holocaust have been studied in some detail, contemporary anti-Jewish hostility has been underestimated, and antisemitism from the Muslim/Arab world has been largely ignored. One reason for this may be that there persists among many social scientists a belief that all bigotry and prejudice is fundamentally similar, arising from the same spots in the human psyche and drawing strength from the same ideological, sociopolitical, and economic sources. To the extent that researchers believe this to be true, they may assume that antisemitism can be understood through extrapolations from general theories of prejudice. However, such an assumption would seem inconsistent with historical arguments why Jew-hatred is to a large extent sui generis.

Still on the subject of the study of antisemitism, Susanna Schrafstetter and Alan Steinweis note that scholars and students of historical events must always remain conscious of the strengths and limitations of their sources, but that special vigilance is in order when examining key questions relating to the response of ordinary Germans to the persecution and mass murder of the Jews between 1933 and 1945. From the time of the Holocaust until the present day, these questions have generated intense and often emotional disagreements. When carried out in the public arena, such disagreements have often been based more on emotion and the received wisdom of collective memory than on a sober examination of the historical evidence. Communities of memory in many countries and across several generations have had a strong emotional stake in the question, and their perceptions have often been shaped by anger, guilt, and shame. As the Nazi period recedes into the past, however, the passing of generations offers the opportunity for a more nuanced appreciation of this difficult history. The discrepancy between the historical significance of the topic, on the one hand, and the fragmentary nature of the evidence that is available to analyze it, on the other, has posed a continual challenge to scholars. Fortunately, historians have persisted in their efforts to find new and previously overlooked sources. In fact, serious scholarship in this area has accelerated, rather than slowed, in recent years. In their paper, Schrafstetter and Steinweis summarize some of these recent findings and present some new, original work that is still in progress, revealing the enormous sophistication with which contemporary scholars have been approaching this controversial subject.

Turning now to the rise of antisemitism within academic circles, Barry Kosmin examines the history and recent resurgence of antisemitism in the academy and among the intelligentsia. As regards its latest incarnation, in particular, he identifies several contributing factors. For the past century, Jews have been over-represented in Western universities and have made outstanding achievements in the academic and intellectual arena. This success has led to certain predictable yet unwelcome consequences. At present, moreover, higher education in the West, particularly in the humanities and social sciences, is under threat, and its future looks uncertain. History shows—and psychology predicts—that such insecurity gives rise to prejudice and a search for moral absolutes. A competitive, disorderly, insecure, and fearful environment will almost inevitably make antisemitism attractive, particularly to the kind of utopian idealists who are over-represented in university and intellectual circles. Their individual careerist ambitions, combined with their psychological anxieties and political orientations, seem to predispose a large fraction of academics and intellectuals to embrace boycotts, divestment, and sanctions against Israel and Jews, while the transgressions of states like Russia, Syria, Iran, China, and Saudi Arabia are largely ignored.

In a similar vein, Martin Kramer asks what purpose Holocaust inversion— the claim that Israel acts toward the Palestinians as the Nazis acted toward the Jews—actually serves. That it flourishes on crackpot websites or in the alleyways of Karachi is of scant interest. More interesting are situations where it gains traction among people whom we assume to be sophisticated about history and politics, especially in Western academia and journalism. After all, it is highly unlikely that anyone in these settings really believes that Israel conducts itself as Nazi Germany did. According to Kramer, "inverters" know that by making this analogy they compel those who defend Israel to spell out all the differences between Gaza and Auschwitz, for example, thus implying that they belong in the same moral category. The second reason Holocaust inversion persists, despite its supposedly self-defeating excess, is that it makes lesser but still preposterous analogies sound more reasonable. Having exhausted their outrage against the Nazi analogy, defenders of Israel will be a tad less vociferous in expressing their outrage against these other analogies, which are also specious but now appear "reasonable" and worthy of debate. In other words, Holocaust inversion is a rhetorical softening up. Those who use it don't seek to make the Israel-Nazi analogy credible—an impossible task—but to make other analogies seem like debatable propositions.

In the final paper in this category, Richard Landes examines the relationship between anti-Zionism and Jihad's cognitive war on the Western world. He argues that, of all the battlefields in the cognitive war taking place in the Western public sphere, none reveals both the weakness of the West and the apocalyptic dimension of the conflict so much as the issue of Israel. In the jihadi apocalyptic narrative, Israel is the entity that threatens Islam with annihilation and whose elimination opens up the road for Islamism to impose the Caliphate upon all infidels. For jihadis to win this war, they need to get their enemy to adopt this narrative and make choices that will strengthen their cause and weaken the West. And what they want—and have wanted since they first realized they could not accomplish it themselves—is to have the West help them destroy Israel. In order to get the West to comply without realizing that it is also a target, jihadis have acted as if Muslim anger against Israel, so at variance with the democratic ethos of the West, arises from a secular drama, namely the plight of the Palestinians. If the West can be convinced to sacrifice Israel on these grounds, Landes warns, the jihadis will be able to avenge the most painful of the humiliations inflicted on Islam by the modern world and advance to the next stage of global sharia.

In the first paper of the second category, which analyzes manifestations of antisemitism around the world, David Gurevich and Yisca Harani examine the facts and implications of the violent murder of Greek Orthodox monk Philoumenos Hasapis in Jacob's Well Church in Nablus in 1979. Despite the absence of any factual evidence to this effect, Philoumenos' death was immediately depicted as a ritual murder performed by a fanatical Jewish-Israeli group, and he was later sanctified by the Greek Orthodox Patriarchate in Jerusalem. This narrative gained publicity in Orthodox Christian communities around the world and was even endorsed by various NGOs and scholars. In their paper, Gurevich and Harani compare the development of this popular narrative to similar accusations levied against medieval Jewish communities in Europe, as well as to the contemporary framing of the Israeli-Palestinian conflict. They observe that the publicity granted to the narrative is connected to the cultural context of its target audience, the interests of the Orthodox Church, and the role of the political actors involved. In particular, they conclude that the leveraging of the popular narrative by various actors is indicative of the link between medieval Christian antisemitism and the "new antisemitism" of the twenty-first century.

Maintaining the focus on the Middle East, Eran Lerman examines a broad but often misunderstood or understated aspect of the Palestinian-Israeli conflict, which he refers to as the totalitarian temptation. From the beginning of the twentieth century, the Palestinians felt that they were up against a powerful rival and that they therefore needed the help of equally powerful historical forces that could offer them what the West, even when sympathetic to their cause, could not. This was the tempting promise of a revolutionary change in world affairs that would include the destruction or annihilation of the Zionist project. First came the appeal of Nazism, due to what prominent Palestinians perceived as a promise to rid them of both the British and the Jews. This was followed by a gradual shift to a full-fledged Soviet orientation, which was consistent with the radical Palestinian vision of destroying Western imperialism, Zionism, and conservative Arab regimes. By the time this alliance also failed, there was in place a third, home-grown promise of a future in which there would be no Israel and no Zionism, in the form of modern Islamist totalitarianism. Although certain elements in the Palestinian leadership have abandoned these three temptations, Lerman points out that the need to latch on to a strong, deterministic current in world affairs that removes the need for painful compromise at the negotiating table still exists in a different (far more benign but still dangerous) form, namely the strong preference, particularly within the BDS movement, to paint Zionism as a colonialist project and Israel as an apartheid state. According to Lerman, this attitude is perhaps the most immediate and powerful impediment to peace today, side by side with the still active threat of Islamism.

Moving across the globe, Luis Fleischman discusses the rise of negative attitudes toward Israel in Latin America. He observes that, although initially supportive of Israel, many Latin America countries shifted allegiance to the Arab and Palestinian cause as a direct result of the Arab oil embargo. In the following years, as many of them began their transition to democracy, they showed a lack of interest in issues related to the Middle East. However, things began to change again in the early 2000s, as the Left triumphed in national elections in a number of countries. As a result, Fleischman notes, Latin American countries are now looking to pursue a foreign policy that is independent from that of the United States and closer to the interests of the Third World. This has led them to be sympathetic to the Palestinian cause for ideological reasons, such as anti-colonialism and opposition to US influence in the region, rather than for reasons related to Arab oil. In fact, the Palestinians have come to symbolize and even justify the existence of the Left in Latin America. In their eyes, they are both freedom fighters opposing a powerful Western enemy. Although the liberal parties and the media traditionally adopt pro-Israel positions, Fleischman concludes that anti-Israel prejudice is now so deeply embedded in the system that counteracting it will require hard work.

The final four papers in this collection examine the causes, motives, and ideologies behind the resurgence of antisemitism in Eastern Europe. Dovid Katz focuses on the relationship between Holocaust inversion and antisemitism in Eastern Europe. He notes that, while antisemitism in Western Europe is nowadays overwhelmingly a product of the (Far) Left, whose members focus on Middle Eastern affairs and the Israeli-Palestinian conflict, antisemitism in the "nationalist" parts of Eastern Europe is overwhelmingly a product of the (Far) Right. Its practitioners tend to be positive toward Israel and have little or nothing against Jews abroad. Instead, their antisemitism focuses on the Holocaust and those who do not share the state's official historical narrative concerning the war years. Right-wing antisemites in Eastern Europe are determined to "fix" this narrative, often supported by generous government financing. In a worrying development, however, the trend in "acceptable" Holocaust revisionism is drifting from the equalization of Nazi and Soviet crimes in the framework of the "double genocide" paradigm to a form of inversion that praises the perpetrators and defames the victims of the Holocaust in a pseudo-postmodernist reversal of the narrative. Katz call on scholars and politicians to challenge such deliberate distortions of history, which undermine human rights, the struggle against antisemitism, and key values of democratic societies.

According to Vladimir (Ze'ev) Khanin, any effort to understand contemporary antisemitism should focus not only on Western Europe, the United States, and the Muslim world, but also on the former communist countries. In his paper, he therefore analyses the real picture and structure of antisemitism in the post-Soviet space, with an emphasis on Russia and Ukraine. In particular, he examines whether post-communist antisemitism is a manifestation of traditional (classic) antisemitism or a new form of antisemitism, what implications it has for the Jewish population in Russia and Ukraine, and whether it is possible to define Ukrainian and Russian society as inherently antisemitic. Based on his findings, Khanin concludes that the observed decline in antisemitic violence in Russia and Ukraine does not mean that antisemitism has disappeared. In fact, long-term political and ideological campaigns launched by the Russian government since the turn of the century have led to an increase in Russian chauvinistic nationalism and a decrease in ethnic, national, and religious tolerance, especially since 2012. Russian society still enjoys a "hard core" of antisemites who have not disappeared, despite the general decline in levels of xenophobia. In Ukraine, the number of "hard-core" antisemites may be smaller, but it is still visible. In addition, the majority of xenophobic groups in FSU society feature "latent" or "sleeping" antisemitism. Thus, according to Khanin, the general trend toward a decline in classic antisemitic attitudes will not necessarily prevent their resurgence in the future.

In his paper, Samuel Sokol reports that one of the lesser reported aspects of the Ukrainian conflict is the propaganda war that has been waged between Moscow and Kiev regarding the treatment of the country's Jews. Much has been reported regarding hybrid warfare, the distortion of history for political ends, and the rise and fall of the Far Right in Ukraine, but little has been done thus far to integrate such research and reporting into a unified history of the Jewish experience in post-revolutionary Ukraine, especially as it relates to allegations of a rise in antisemitism. In this paper, Sokol details the Ukrainian conflict as perceived by Jewish observers, offering a fresh perspective. His fact-based account is based on a wealth of first-hand research and interviews conducted in Ukraine during the period under discussion. Based on his findings, Sokol concludes that the Ukrainian state is not overtly antisemitic but that its tolerance of historical revisionism regarding Ukraine's complicity in the Holocaust is unacceptable (if unremarkable when placed alongside similar practices in Hungary and the Baltic states) and that its willingness to overlook the neo-Nazi affiliations of those involved in the ongoing conflict with Russia is worrying indeed.

Finally, Zbyněk Tarant shakes up the old "enemy of my enemy" paradigm by exploring the complicated attitude of the Czech antisemitic scene to Islam and Muslims from a fresh perspective. Based on his analysis of a sample of anti-semitic websites, Tarant concludes that the prevailing discourse on Islam and Muslims is dominated by two conflicting stereotypes: the image of Islam as an authentic culture that resists Western influence and the image of Muslim immigration as a threat to Europe. Members of the antisemitic scene tend to resolve this conflict by stating that Islam can be tolerated as long as it stays in the Muslim world. In fact, Czech neo-Nazis support Iran and the Ba'athist establishment in Syria and previously defended Gaddafi's Libya. Tarant also notes that the Jews are accused of encouraging Muslim immigration, on the one hand, and hijacking the anti-immigration agenda for "Zionist purposes," on the other. In other words, they are blamed for promoting Islamization as well as Islamophobia. Rather than promoting naively philosemitic attitudes, as one might expect, Tarant warns that anti-Muslim attitudes may thus actually encourage antisemitism.

* * *

ISGAP's core mission is to encourage high-caliber academic research that seeks to map, decode, and combat antisemitism. As well as serving an important purpose in its own right, we believe that such scholarship will spur the academy to accept and encourage the study of this unique and timeless hatred—particularly its contemporary manifestations. It is the hope of all those connect-ed with ISGAP that the papers in this volume will stimulate and inspire readers, help them understand the changing realities of contemporary antisemitism, and encourage them to develop policies and strategies to combat and defeat this and other destructive hatreds. With the publication of this latest volume, as well as all its other academic efforts, ISGAP continues to fight antisemitism on the battlefield of ideas.

# Antisemitism and the Problem of Jewish Firstness

## Adam Katz*

Many discussions of antisemitism begin by distinguishing between its "old" and "new" varieties. This discussion will be no exception, although I think the distinctions I make differ from most in resisting the urge to frame antisemitism exclusively in terms of victimizers and victims, as the next few paragraphs will make clear.

First, while Jews were generally (even if rarely completely) powerless during the persecutions they underwent in Christian, Muslim and, more recently, fascist and Communist societies and were, indeed, completely innocent of the vast and colorful array of crimes of which they were accused, contemporary antisemitism focuses primarily on the state of Israel, which, whatever your view of it, is far from powerless—nor is it innocent in general, even if it is guiltless of the more extravagant accusations made against it from various points within the international community. At the very least, the Jews targeted today take action, defend themselves effectively, employ various levers of power, sometimes succeed in their enterprises, make allies and enemies, and so on. Antisemitism, in that case, cannot be discussed solely in unidirectional terms, as what others do to the Jews; we must also take interaction into account.

Second, the major player in the specific form of antisemitism directed toward the state of Israel, and Zionism more generally, is the pro-Palestinian Left. It is the secular Left that accuses Israel of genocide, that stigmatizes Israeli self-defense as war crimes, that fabricates Israeli massacres of innocent Palestinians, that toys on occasion with modern blood libels regarding Jewish theft of Palestinian organs, and so on. And, we must acknowledge, a major player within the Left consists of secular Jews, participating not just as leftists or anti-imperialists of no particular ethnic or religious identity, but often specifically as Jews who ostentatiously claim to reject or redefine Jewish identities that to their mind have been hijacked by Zionism. To call a movement heavily populated with Jews "antisemitic" is somewhat counterintuitive, to say the least. We can call leftist defamers of Israel "self-hating," and draw upon a whole social scientific

---

* Associate Teaching Professor of English, Quinnipiac Universtity.

and therapeutic vocabulary to do so, but I think we would thereby make things too easy for ourselves by avoiding part of the reality of the situation. Certainly the people we would therefore be diagnosing often evince, if anything, rather excessive self-love, a kind of righteous narcissism. And why should they be self-hating? We are not speaking of marginalized, tormented members of a minority group that would have internalized various stigmas directed at them from childhood; on the contrary, we are speaking, very often, of wealthy, pampered products of the richest suburbs and best universities. The simpler explanation might be that their leftism is more important to them than their Jewishness. Or that this is how they interpret their Jewishness.

Third, and this is connected to the first two, charges of antisemitism have, to use the term made famous by the French deconstructionist Jacques Derrida, "always already" been tagged as political. Going back to the 1980s, pro-Palestinian activists began mocking charges of antisemitism, pointing out that they advanced the interests of Israel. And could we deny that they do? Of course less antisemitism would be good for Israel!

So, we clearly cannot model any critique of antisemitism today on the kind of liberal, consensual campaigns directed against the Nazis during the 1930s and 1940s or the kind of self-evident exposures of Czarist pogroms that enraged enlightened opinion around the turn of the last century. We cannot assume a shared definition of antisemitism or even a shared assumption that it's bad. For the pro-Palestinian Left, for example, instances of Jew-hatred propagated by the Palestinian Authority are just further evidence of how badly the Israeli occupation has damaged its victims and represent an understandable if not justifiable expression of resentment. Even more, "debunking" of various "Jewish myths" (regarding the history of Jewish existence in ancient Israel or even the biological continuity of the Jewish people) may be seen as a necessary part of the struggle against the legitimation of Zionism, although such debunking will often be indistinguishable from antisemitism. All of this further means that antisemitism will not be isolatable as an issue—to put it a bit simplistically, to talk about anti-semitism is to talk about everything else. It means that we will not be able to talk about antisemitism as a pathology that really has nothing to do with Jews because it can be located within the antisemite, as Sartre proposed. It means, finally, that the Jews are actors in the "drama" of antisemitism, not passive victims, and that studying antisemitism will involve studying Jews as protago-nists as well as antagonists in that drama, and opposing antisemitism will involve defending and criticizing all kind of things that all kinds of different Jews do. This is a "messy" approach, because the protocols of discussing modern forms of racism and discrimination more generally involve a strict prohibition on "blaming the victim," on suggesting that hatred and victimization are in any way elicited by actions of the victimized, and with good reason—the line between offering reasons for why a particular group may be hated and offering a justification for that hatred is a thin one. A great many liberal (in the broadest sense) assumptions are invested here. But I think we have to do it because those liberal assumptions and desires will blind us and disable us in too many ways.

In a book I have written together with Eric Gans (well, he actually did most of the writing), we develop a way of thinking about antisemitism that, let's say, implicates the Jews without exculpating the antisemites. First of all, it seems useful to have a definition, or at least a description, of antisemitism available, especially since we will always have to explain the difference between criticism of and even hostility toward Israel (which, let's assume, is possible for non-anti-semites), on the one hand, and antisemitism on the other. Quite a few people today define antisemitism, in this connection, as a kind of double standard toward Israel—if you only condemn Israeli human rights abuses and ignore far worse abuses by other countries, there is good reason to suspect antisemitism. My own definition would overlap with that approach, but the problem with it is that there is no a priori standard determining which standards to apply to which countries. I would myself hold the Connecticut police to a higher standard than the Moscow police, and that doesn't make me anti-Connecticut. Higher standards applied more insistently to Israel might actually mean that the complainants see Israel as more "like us" than they would, say, Saudi Arabia or Uganda. I prefer a more narratological and hermeneutic approach—in other words, I propose looking at how people tell stories about Jews. Stories have agents or actors—it's a functional role in a story, someone has to be doing something. More complex stories have a few, or many, people, doing lots of things, the things they do affect one another, characters change, there are various and debatable attributions of responsibility, and so on. In antisemitic narratives, these roles are fixed: Jews (all Jews, or a subsection, like Zionists) are the agents driving the action, controlling and benefiting from the result, while all other agents are either dupes or victims of the Jews. All responsibility can be attributed to the Jews. If we read anti-Israel discourses in these terms we can see what makes them antisemitic—in each conflict with Hamas, for example, we can see that protests against Israel's actions are completely abstracted from anything the Palestinians have done. If the firing of rockets by Hamas must be mentioned, well, the rockets are harmless, much like the stone throwing by teenagers in the Intifada of the late 1980s; or it's a response to previous Israeli aggressions; or they have every right to do it. In no way can it be acknowledged that Israel's response is reasonable or understandable—rather, Israel's actions are simply an integral part of what Israel always does and Israel is—the genocid-al dispossessor of the Palestinians. If one observes that this must be the slowest genocide in human history, one is referred to some mysterious property of the Palestinians or the magical power of world public opinion that somehow enables them to evade total obliteration, despite the worst Israeli intentions. Ultimately, the victims of the Jews must become martyrs, saints, or both. Antisemitism places Jews at the center, the place of God in sacred orders, albeit in this case a Gnostic god that has usurped the true one.

The problem here is that the antisemite has a point. There is a very important sense in which Jews are at the center and have been for a very long time. Jewish monotheism is a discovery to which Christianity, Islam, the Enlightenment, and post-Enlightenment ideological and political forces like liberalism, nationalism, and socialism/communism are all indebted and which therefore had to be displaced for those successor forms of thought and social order to install themselves. To put it simply, without Judaism and Jews, there is no Christianity, Islam, Enlightenment, and so on; but, as long as there is Judaism and there are Jews, Christianity et al. are not irrefutable. The continued existence of Jews refutes the universality of Christianity and Islam, the Jews' adherence to their "superstitions" interferes with the spread of Enlightenment, the particularism of Jews disturbs liberalism, and the nationalist transnationalism of Judaism ensures the incompleteness of any nation within whose borders Jews reside. The continuation of this Jewish anomaly is easily read as defiance (since the Jews should have been the first to recognize the superiority of the new mode of being) and, even more, attempts by Jews at assimilation and normalization, especially when Jews become privileged interpreters and expert reformers of the "host" culture, are likely to appear to be sophisticated efforts at subversion and robbery of the "native"—or what Yuri Slezkine, in his *The Jewish Century*, calls the "Apollonian"—culture. At the very least, then, Jews are caught in an unavoidable feedback loop with antisemitism.

This relationship between Jews and the cultures that have remade themselves on and against the Jewish model is what Gans and I have called "Jewish firstness." We live in a postmodern world that has deconstructed originality out of existence, and with good reason: we have been discovering over the past several decades that cross-cultural and intra-cultural borrowing goes far deeper than had been previously imagined, and, when it comes to the arts, sciences, and other fields, claims to originality are usually overstated. And that may be the case with the invention or discovery of monotheism by the ancient Jews as well—the discovery of, in Gans's words, God's name as the declarative sentence "I am that/what I am," as announced to Moses at the burning bush. But originality can never be completely erased, especially since originality—going first—generates resentment on the part of those who adopt the invention or discovery for themselves (perhaps this resentment is in part responsible for the pervasive deconstruction of originality). This is especially the case with a moral invention, which is persuasive to the extent that it extracts a community from a self-destructive or at least self-limiting circle of violence. If God's name can no longer be invoked through sacrificial ritual and God's actions no longer compelled on one's behalf, the organization of the community in accordance with shared rules replaces the organization of the community through the supply of sacrificial victims. Going first in such moral inventions involves a paradox, fully on display in the relation between Judaism and its others—a community organized around rules rather than imperatives issued to and received from an exclusive god is implicitly universal, but can only be exemplified in a particular community. Judaism models a universal community from which it exempts itself, as if the Jews refused to play according to the rules they laid down for others. The antisemitic imagination can be derived from the attempt to resolve this paradox by reducing it to Jewish particularism, Jewish exploitativeness, Jewish subversiveness, Jewish manipulation, and so on. The maturity needed to reject the antisemitic imagination would involve accepting this paradox, or anomaly, as constitutive of human being and sociality itself—all of the values and ideals we would like to universalize, from fairness to equality to freedom, presuppose particular models that are irreducible to the value or ideal.

The virulence of the hatred directed toward Israel results from a new way in which Jews have been first in the contemporary world—victimhood—as a result of the unprecedented horror of the Nazi extermination. By now it is very clear that we live in a victimary era, in which the prime value is the defense of victims of a presumptive and presumptuous normative center. Jewish firstness in the realm of victimhood is a direct result of their monotheistic firstness, as resentment of that firstness is what drove the Nazi extermination project: the master race had to displace the chosen people, and the systematic degradation of Jews, an intrinsic part of the extermination process, can be seen as the determination to ensure that this episode of Jewish suffering could not be recouped within a redemptive theological narrative. In the wake of the Shoah, which momentarily unified the world around an absolute disavowal of Nazism, all forms of victimization have been modeled on the Nazi-Jew dichotomy, and all social inequalities figured as modes of victimization. Racism became the primary evil in the United States, national domination the primary evil in the European colonial powers, and passive obedience in the face of atrocities committed by one's own government (being a "good German") became the antithesis of responsible citizenship as a result of mass and international opposition to the Vietnam War.

The results of the first wave of victimary politics have become thoroughly consensual (no one argues for a return to colonialism or Jim Crow segregation), so it is easy to ignore the connection between those long-assimilated victories and more contentious recent events in the realm of gender, sexual, environmental, and other politics, along with intensified attention to micro-aggressions on the racial front. I don't mean to get into these issues here, except to make the point that they continue to be modeled on the Nazi-Jew binary, involving an completely evil oppressor desiring the subjugation or extermination of the Other over whom those oppressors have absolute power. The model might be invoked figuratively—perhaps in their "war on women" Republicans don't want to literally exterminate or even subjugate all women, but they do want to "cleanse" the public sphere of all trace of what might be called women's concerns. To concede that some of these issues might involve complex questions of institutional reform, which cannot be undertaken without consideration of possibly unintended consequences is to "once again" sacrifice the rights of the Other to some fictional "common good" or "social stability"; to argue that inequalities and conflicts along racial and sexual lines might better be addressed gradually and dialogically rather than through the ratcheting up of "rights talk," resistance, and retribution is to make one "complicit" with exclusionary practices—implicitly, a "good German."

All this is relevant insofar as it brings us back to what Bernard-Henri Lévy has recently called the "time bomb" of contemporary antisemitism, which derives its virulence from its claim that the Jews have monopolized victimization in the modern world and have used that monopolization to victimize, presumably with impunity, another people, the Palestinians. We have a classic double bind here: the Jews are accused of monopolizing the very mode of victimization that is now deployed against them by their accusers. The more we assume that the Shoah has left a terrible burden of guilt upon the European countries, in particular those complicit with Nazism to some extent, the more we must assume a powerful desire to be rid of that burden. This desire is expressed in the attempt to abandon European nationhood altogether, but above all, paradoxically, in the insistence that Israel itself has become so evil, so Nazi-like, as to cancel that earlier guilt—and to transform what is left into guilt for Europe's indirect contribution to what the Israelis have done to the Palestinians. Meanwhile, those on the Left who have found the Nazi-Jew binary an unparalleled weapon in their campaign on behalf of the aggrieved are caught in a double bind of their own: the event that generated the model must be preserved in political memory but freed of all its specifically Jewish characteristics—otherwise, its use as a model will always be limited by what the Jews have to say about it. The South Africanization and ultimately Nazification of Israel accomplishes this liberation of the victimary model, by placing the Jews at the center of it. To be against the continuation of the spirit of racial genocide represented by the Nazis is, now, first of all to be against Israel—not only against Israel politically, but against all ways of talking about the Shoah that might lend legitimacy to the Zionist project. At the very least, a kind of soft Holocaust denial is implicit here.

This brings me to an even more disturbing element in this equation. The revision of the Shoah so as to make it, rather than a radicalization of European antisemitism, an instance of extreme "discrimination," on the one hand, and the revision of views of Israel, so as to make it, rather than the restoration of an ancient people or even a haven for a homeless and persecuted minority, the most egregious contemporary example of said "discrimination," on the other, put a premium on a certain kind of Jewishness. The Jew who is proud of Judaism's "traditions of social justice" while repudiating its particularism, who disavows Israel and that nation's claim to speak in "his or her name," the Jew who, in fact, lends support to attacks on Israel in order to immunize the attackers against charges of antisemitism—such Jews have an honored place in today's media, academy, and activist movements. But this is also an old story, as Yuri Slezkine shows in *The Jewish Century*.

No doubt Jewish firstness is a burden for Jews as well. Slezkine frames his study of the entrance of Jews into modern Europe in terms of the distinction between "Mercurian" Jews (experts in middleman activities and the "liminal" more generally) and the "Apollonian" nations they sought to enter as equal participants. Along with formal equality there are a whole range of informal inequalities and, once those inequalities reach, or are perceived to reach, a threshold that cannot be determined in advance, the formal equalities come to be seen as a "mask" covering up the inequalities. How, we might ask, will a despised minority, with a highly literate population, a habit of urban living, and a history of working within finance and commerce, assimilate into societies that those very characteristics are coming to define? They will bypass traditional occupations, and, while perhaps making a brief stop in the new industrial professions, will find their way into the quintessential modern professions: finance, trade, media, entertainment, the academy, etc. These professions, some more than others, of course, come to be perceived as the source of power, often hidden power, and of subversion of traditional ways of life.

Even more, from within those positions, that minority will find it necessary to make those societies more livable by weakening traditional prejudices and "rewriting" the national character along more liberal lines. Slezkine speaks, for example, of the role Jewish scholars took in devising national literary and cultural canons that promoted the understanding of the nation as an ideal community rather than a community of blood. (At the same time, insofar as these efforts are concerted, the Jews must, without necessarily realizing it, maintain a solidarity among themselves that does not quite fit the ideal they have figured for others.) The rant that Philip Roth puts in the mouth of his character, "Philip Roth," in his novel *Operation Shylock* captures Slezkine's point perfectly:

I heard myself next praising the greatest Diasporist of all, the father of the new Diasporist movement, Irving Berlin. "People ask where I got the idea. Well, I got it listening to the radio." The radio was playing "Easter Parade" and I thought, But this is Jewish genius on a par with the Ten Commandments. God gave Moses the Ten Commandments and then He gave to Irving Berlin "Easter Parade" and "White Christmas." The two holidays that celebrate the divinity of Christ—the divinity that's the very heart of the Jewish rejection of Christianity—and what does Irving Berlin brilliantly do? He de-Christs them both! Easter he turns into a fashion show and Christmas into a holiday about snow. Gone is the gore and the murder of Christ—down with the crucifix and up with the bonnet! *He turns their religion into schlock.* But nicely! Nicely! So nicely the goyim don't even know what hit 'em. They love it. *Everybody* loves it.

The furthest end of this assimilationist impulse is, again paradoxically, social reform, including revolution, deploying the principles of one's society against its reality. Slezkine documents carefully the disproportion of Jews on the Left, which continues undiminished today. Indeed, one of Slezkine's most provocative discussions is his enumeration of the enormous influx of Jews in the Soviet Union's ruling Communist Party during the 1930s, and, consequentially, their role in its worst atrocities. We can say that all these attempts to minimize or abolish one's Jewishness have only restored a new kind of Jewish firstness, generated the same reaction-formations on the part of Jews and antisemites alike. Indeed, I think there are good reasons to anticipate a resurgence of anti-semitism on the Right, focused, in particular, on the longstanding support of Jewish organizations (and, I believe, Jewish public opinion) for the liberal immigration policies of the West (aimed, one could imagine, at diluting the "Apollonian" national stock) that are now a source of so much contention.

Lévy calls this new antisemitism a "time bomb." What, exactly, would its explosion involve? There is something irreal about today's antisemitism—in Europe it is taking recognizable and "traditional" forms, such as physical violence against Jews and Jewish institutions, to the point where it is reasonable to ask whether Jewish life will continue to be viable in countries like France and Great Britain. Much of this is connected with Muslim immigrants into those countries who do not seem much interested in the subtle distinctions between "Israeli" and "Jew." However terrible that is, though, does it count as a "giant time bomb," especially since it's already happening? Lévy does not say, but I must assume he means that antisemitism will be a catalyst of some larger, uncontrollable, violence. What does all the talk about the delegitimation and destruction of Israel amount to, though? Supporters of the Palestinians often find their unconcealed hatred of Jews and destructive fury against Israel (not just the "occupation") unpleasant but dismiss it as the pained outcry of the powerless. At any rate, the Palestinians and their allies don't have anywhere near the power of the Nazis to fulfill their fantasies. The assumption that we should keep pushing the "peace process," aimed at creating a Palestinian state alongside Israel, regardless of the pervasive genocidal hatred of Jews broadcast even by the "moderate" Palestinian Authority, operates in accordance with another assumption, namely that the more grounded the Palestinians become in reality, in dealing with the responsibilities of statehood, the more common peaceful, normal interactions between Palestinians and Jews will become and the more these fantasies will dissipate. But the desire for a two-state solution is no less phantasmal than antisemitism itself, resting upon a desire for a kind of symbolic completion of the process of violence that culminated in the Shoah, but included the dispossession of the Palestinians as one of its after-effects. Still, it is possible that the antisemitism of the Palestinians and many of their supporters is simply a part of a new status quo, a new pathology within a larger pathological, but sustainable, situation that nobody really imagines changing all that much.

The time bomb, though, lies in the acquisition by the Iranian regime of atomic weapons. The fantasy that the achievement of a two-state solution would resolve the broader set of conflicts and crises comprising the modern Middle East (and the antisemitic corollary that it is therefore Israel's recalcitrance that, once again, prevents the emergence of a new, salvational dispensation) has inhibited the West from consistently confronting the Iranians. The logic of the new antisemitism would lead us to the conclusion that the Iranians must be permitted to have nuclear weapons—why should the Israelis be the only regime in the area to have such weapons? But if the Iranians get the bomb, will not the Saudis want one; or even, for that matter, a little way down the road, a somewhat domesticated Islamic State? And will the competition among these newly empowered radical Islamic states resolve itself into a test regarding which of them is daring enough to take on Israel and eliminate this festering wound in the Islamic world once and for all? And will there not be voices, indeed powerful and accredited voices, in the West arguing that the Jews are once again standing in the way of some grand bargain or of the United States finally extricating itself once and for all from the Middle East?

But there is an even bigger time bomb inherent in antisemitism today. It might be said that the main victim of antisemitism, aside from the Jews, is thinking—that is, the capacity to accept paradoxes, asymmetries, and anomalies as part of the world. For example, to accept that liberal societies may have illiberal elements that are nevertheless constitutive of those societies; that violence can be deferred, but never eliminated once and for all; that the same goes for inequality; and, furthermore, that attempts to eradicate violence and inequality once and for all only lead to more monstrous forms of violence and inequality. To even consider such concepts as equality, fairness, peace, justice, and so on is to presuppose a world in which these concepts must be preserved and testified to at all costs, but do not rule, because otherwise the concepts would have no meaning. The Western "anti-Jewish tradition," as David Nirenberg calls it, is that part of Western thought and culture that imagines abolishing these anomalies and paradoxes and to some extent rightly associates their continuance with the continued existence of the Jews or, more abstractly, "Jewishness." A very good example of this is what has happened to the legal concept of "proportionality" in war at the hands of defamers of Israel: a legal concept meant to tie means to ends (you use only as much force as you need to achieve legitimate military goals) has been transformed into a bizarre pseudo-concept implying that it is "unfair" to use more force than your opponent. In this way, the basic concepts that we need in order to think about law, politics, and social life are emptied of intellectual content and become mere epithets.

My co-inquirer, Eric Gans, is the inventor of a hypothesis regarding language origin that sees the origin of language in an "aborted gesture of appropriation," that is, a shared renunciation of some commonly desired object by the newly human community. Gans's claim is that representation is the deferral of violence—insofar as signs mean something, some possible form of violence has been deferred. Gans's hypothesis involves a foundational paradox, which he has borrowed from René Girard: those whom we take as models and strive to imitate become rivals, because it is through them that we arrive at our desires, and it is they who become obstacles to our desires. Language and culture are the ongoing efforts at mediating these rivalries and the violence to which they lead, and they do so by converting singular objects that can only be possessed by one to the exclusion of the other into symbolic objects that can be shared and that are, in principle, inexhaustible. If we dare to resist antisemitism by positing a "Jewish" cultural principle, I would suggest it be the assertion that a more inclusive social form must always be initiated in some exclusive manner, and that it must always be sustained in that manner as well—whoever discovers or, really, stumbles upon a sign or gesture that arrests some violent imperative is first of all obliged to preserve and refine that sign or gesture, even at the risk of being accused of secrecy, conspiracy, and greed by those who derive their very accusations from their appropriation of that sign or gesture. With enough people willing to take on the burden of "firstness" so as to slow and ultimately reverse the resentment directed toward that firstness, civilization and sociality are impossible. Today, both the refusal to indulge in antisemitic fantasies and the willingness to reveal and represent the inevitable resentments driving those fantasies are part of the acceptance of that burden.

*Works cited*

Katz, Adam and Eric Gans. *The First Shall Be the Last: Rethinking Antisemitism.* Martinus Nijhoff, 2015.

Lévy, Bernard-Henri. "Today's Anti-Semitism is a Ticking Time Bomb," *New Republic*, October 8, 2014.

Roth, Philip. *Operation Shylock: A Confession.* Vintage, 1994.

Slezkine, Yuri. *The Jewish Century.* Princeton University Press, 2006.

# Theodor Lessing and Jewish Self-Hatred

## Alon Segev[*]

In 1931, when Theodor Lessing visited Palestine, he was amazed that he could find a copy of his book *Jewish Self-Hatred* on sale in Jerusalem and that he was recognized and called by name by strangers while visiting the Wailing Wall.[1] Among the admiring readers of Lessing's book were Gershom Scholem[2] and Max Brod.[3] Today his work is completely forgotten, and Lessing would definitely not be recognized by anyone at the Wall. Lessing coined and introduced into the discourse on antisemitism the term "Jewish self-hatred." His book on the topic marked his personal conversion from self-hatred to Zionism. In this book, Lessing analyzed the phenomenon he defined as "Jewish self-hatred" and offered a cure. His method was psychoanalysis, and his attitude toward the Jewish question was Nietzschean. The present paper critically analyzes Lessing's text, showing his debt to Nietzsche, Freud and Husserl. It concludes with Lessing's discussion of Maximilian Harden—a converted Jew in whom Lessing saw an illustrative example of a self-hating Jew.

## I

The term "Jewish self-hatred" was coined and introduced into academic and political discourse by Theodor Lessing in 1930,[4] although, as has been demonstrated by Sander Gilman, we can relate the term back many centuries to expressions and writings by converted Jews regarding non-converted Jews. "Jewish self-hater" long ago became a label attached by Jews of one political hue to Jews of another political hue. Thus, for example, Israel's prime minister, Benjamin Netanyahu, has called Rahm Emanuel and David Axelrod "self-hating Jews."[5] In recent decades, the question of Jewish self-hatred has very often been

---

[*] Adjunct Assistant Professor of Philosophy, University of Illinois at Springfield.

[1] Paul Reitter, *On the Origins of Jewish Self-Hatred* (Princeton: Princeton University Press, 2012), 5.

[2] Id., 75.

[3] Id., 5.

[4] Theodor Lessing, *Der jüdische Selbsthaß* (Berlin: Jüdischer Verlag, 1930).

[5] See Reitter, *Origins of Jewish Self-Hatred*, 13.

raised and discussed following suggestions (and accusations) made by Jews in Israel and abroad that Israel is responsible for at least part of Palestinian suffering and misery. Lately, the question of Jewish self-hatred has often been raised in relation to the Boycott, Divestment and Sanctions (BDS) movement, which draws support from Israelis and Jews abroad. The distinction between self-critique and self-hatred seems to be unproblematic and clear at the level of common sense, but once we try to tackle it at higher level it is difficult to draw clear lines between self-critique, self-hatred, Jewish self-hatred, and anti-semitism. Descending from that higher level, we see the peril in automatically dubbing any criticism leveled at Israel's body politic as an expression of self-hatred. Most importantly, as can be inferred from Shulamit Volkov's description of Theodor Lessing's negative attitude toward the *Ostjuden*, not all expressions of Jewish-hatred by Jews imply *self*-hatred. A Jewish person does not have to identify with the Jewish people or nation. Thus, in hating Jews, he does not necessarily hate himself.

> The criticism of Eastern European Jewry by people like Lessing was not *self*-hatred in this milieu; it was a critique from the outside, from a position of aloofness and distance.[6]

The meaning of a given term is contingent upon coherent use and implementation in a circumscribed context. The difficulties implicit in the term "Jewish (self-)hatred" emerge once we attempt to implement it. For example, Rahel Varnhagen's Jewish (self-)hatred should be discussed in the context of the social milieu and literary salon culture into which she apparently fit, but deep inside she felt her Jewish origin barred her from belonging there.[7] Otto Weininger's Jewish (self-)hatred should be discussed in the context of his theory that portrays the Jew as feminine and lacking a personal center. (For Weininger, women also lacked such a personal center, but, contrary to the Jew, they could find it in their husbands.) Likewise, Karl Marx's Jewish (self-)hatred should be discussed in the context of his critique of capitalism, according to which, as developed in *On the Jewish Question*, "Judaism" is the idea of capitalism and egoism—an idea that reached its full realization under Christians and within a Christian state.[8] Quite differently, Karl Kraus's and Anton Kuh's Jewish (self-)

---

6 Shulamit Volkov, *Germans, Jews and Antisemites—Trials in Emancipation* (Cambridge: Cambridge University Press, 2006), 43.

7 "Rahels Leben ist an die Minderwertigkeit, an ihre 'infarne Geburt' von Jugend an fixiert. Was kommt, ist nur Bestätigung, 'Verblutung'. Also jeden Anlaß der Bestätigung meiden, nicht handeln, nicht lieben, sich nicht mit der Welt einlassen." Hannah Arendt, *Rahel Varnhagen—Lebensgeschichte einer deutschen Jüdin aus der Romantik* (Munich: Piper, 1959), 20.

8 "Das Judentum erreicht seinen Höhepunkt mit der Vollendung der bürgerlichen Gesellschaft; aber die bürgerliche Gesellschaft vollendet sich erst in der *christlichen* Welt.

hatred should be discussed in the context of the Zionist movement that began in the late nineteenth century.[9]

In a broad study, entitled *Jewish Self-Hatred—Anti-Semitism and the Hidden Language of the Jews*,[10] which focuses on antisemitism and Jewish self-hatred in German speaking areas in Europe from the twelfth century until the period after the Holocaust, Sander Gilman suggests *language* as the key to understanding Jewish self-hatred. Thus, any occurrence of antisemitism and Jewish self-hatred should be traced back to the peculiar language spoken by the Jews or to the relationships between different spoken languages or jargons. According to Gilman, Hebrew was conceived as a secret language of witchery and corruption that molded and formed the personality of the Jew, and Yiddish as an inferior German dialect spoken by inferior humans. Hence, both were regarded as a suitable means for thieves to communicate surreptitiously.

Gilman's framework may enable us to map different expressions of anti-Judaism voiced by Jews, but the ambition to trace all these expressions to language or to the relationships between different languages turns out to be an unjustified theoretical projection, and thus the outcome may look farfetched. Rahel Varnhagen talked about the "shame" (*Scham*) of being a Jew as the core of her resentment toward herself.[11] Likewise, Jakob Wassermann talks about "shame" as the essence of his Jewish (self-)hatred.[12] It is worth noting that Varn-

---

Nur unter der Herrschaft des Christentums, welches *alle* nationalen, natürlichen, sittlichen, theoretischen Verhältnisse dem Menschen *äußerlich* macht, konnte die bürgerliche Gesellschaft sich vollständig vom Staatsleben trennen, alle Gattungsbande des Menschen zerreißen, den Egoismus, das eigennützige Bedürfnis an die Stelle dieser Gattungsbande setzen, die Menschenwelt in eine Welt atomistischer, feindlich sich gegenüberstehender Individuen auflösen." Karl Marx, "Zur Judenfrage," in Karl Marx and Friedrich Engels, *Werke* (Berlin: Karl Dietz Verlag, 1976), 1:347-377 at 376.

[9] For a discussion on Krauss and Kuh, see Reitter, *Origins of Jewish Self-Hatred*.

[10] Sander L. Gilman, *Jewish Self Hatred—Anti-Semitism and the Hidden Language of the Jews* (Baltimore: Johns Hopkins University Press, 1990).

[11] See Arendt, *Rahel Varnhagen*, 201-211. "Wenn es für die Unerfüllbarkeit des zentralen Wunsches ihres Lebens, aus dem Judentum herauszukommen, noch einen Grund gibt, außer der von außen bestimmten Unmöglichkeit, als Jude ein normaler Mensch zu werden, außer dem Judenhaß ihrer Umgebung, so liegt er in dieser Scham." Id., 201.

[12] "Mein Verhältnis zu ihnen [i.e. den Juden], innerlich wie äußerlich, war von Anfang an ein höchst zwiespältiges. Um aufrichtig zu sein, muß ich gestehen, daß ich mir bisweilen wie in Verbannung geraten unter ihnen erschien. Ich war bei den deutschen Juden mehr an bürgerliche Abgeschliffenheit und soziale Unauffälligkeit gewöhnt. Hier wurde ich eine gewisse Scham nie ganz los. Ich schämte mich ihrer Manieren, ich schämte mich ihrer Haltung. Die Scham für den andern ist ein ungemein quälendes Gefühl, am quälendsten natürlich, wo Blut- und Rasseverwandtschaft im Spiel ist, und man durch ein unabwälzbares inneres Gebot wie infolge moralischer Selbsterziehung verpflichtet ist, für jede Äußerung und jede Handlung von ihm in irgendwelcher Weise einzustehen." Jakob Wassermann, *Mein Weg als Deutscher und Jude* (Berlin: Fischer Verlag, 1921), 103.

hagen was born into an orthodox family and that Yiddish was her first language, whereas Wasserman was born into an entirely assimilated family and German was his first language. Their *shame* consisted of various components and cannot be explained away by reducing it to language.

Moreover, in the case of Fritz Mauthner, who is probably best known today for his contribution to the philosophy of language and his influence on Ludwig Wittgenstein's and Samuel Beckett's attitudes toward language (the futility of and contradiction in attempting to surpass language and "metaphysically" refer to reality outside the realm of language), Gilman's attempt to trace back the Jewish otherness to special "Jewish" use of language seems to me unfounded.[13] The "materialistic" aspect of language (according to Mauthner in his *Memoirs*) is an essential fact of language as such and not of any specific language.[14] Mauthner, who grew up with Czech, German, Hebrew, and *Mauscheldeutsch*,[15] wondered about the "contamination" of language (i.e. the use of foreign words and the formation of words in one language according to their usage in a different language), but initially without a direct reference to his being a Jew or to the Jews as speaking a peculiar language.

Language turns out to be *too broad* a framework to subsume under different corporeal manifestations such as skin or hair color, differences in costume, or economic status, to name but a few factors to which Gilman refers. Secondly, the juxtaposition of German and the similar yet different language of the Jews (i.e. Yiddish) did not exist everywhere. Likewise, because of Jewish resettlement in Palestine, and later in the State of Israel, Hebrew was no longer just an exotic, dead language of prayer but an official, spoken language.

In what follows, I will discuss some aspects of Theodor Lessing's study of Jewish self-hatred. My discussion belongs in the broader discipline known as *Begriffsgeschichte* ("conceptual history" or "history of terms"). I make no pretense to being able to distinguish between self-hatred, self-critique, Jewish self-hatred, and antisemitism. I also do not suggest that the term "Jewish self-hatred" refers to related phenomena, as Gilman does in claiming that the various

---

[13] See Gilman, *Jewish Self Hatred*, 230.

[14] "Die Sprache ist ein Werkzeug, mit dem sich die Wirklichkeit nicht fassen läßt. Im besten Fall sind die Worte orientierende Erinnerungen an Sinneseindrücke. Darum ist die Sprache in ihrem Wesen materialistisch, kann bestenfalls in den einzelnen Naturwissenschaften dem Ordnungstrieb der Menschen dienen, kann bestenfalls der Weltanschauung des Materialismus genügen, kann aber über den Materialismus hinaus dem unausrottbaren metaphysischen Bedürfnis nicht helfen. Weil unser Denken nur Sprechen ist, darum müssen wir uns in allen Wissenschaften auf das Beschreiben beschränken und gelangen nicht zum Erklären." Fritz Mauthner, *Erinnerungen* (Munich: Georg Müller, 1918), 217-218.

[15] "Mauscheldeutsch," meaning Moses or Moishe German, is a pejorative term for Yiddish.

phenomena he classifies as expressions of Jewish self-hatred are inherently related by language or by relationships between languages. Instead, I suggest that we must consider Lessing's recurring references, above all, to Nietzsche's philosophy of *amor fati*, Freud's psychoanalysis, and Husserl's phenomenology in order to understand the tenor of his theory. Paul Reitter, who dedicated a volume to Lessing's and Kuh's use of and reference to "Jewish self-hatred," classifies Lessing's *Jewish Self-Hatred* as a "self-help book."[16] It seems to me that this attitude toward the text is possible only by overlooking Lessing's references to Nietzsche and Husserl, which results in a deficient and superficial interpretation of the text. The scope of the present paper merely allows me to point out Lessing's debt to Husserl and Nietzsche but not to expand on this topic.

## II

The question of Jewish self-hatred has been discussed intensively over the last few decades. The context of this discussion is above all the ongoing Palestinian-Israeli conflict. People with Jewish ancestry—Israeli and non-Israeli—who criticize Israel and blame it for the conflict and the misery of the Palestinians are often tagged as "self-hating" Jews. Such discussions have been fueled by calls from Israelis and Jews who support the BDS movement to boycott Israel for its policies beyond the 1967 borders.

The use of the term "self-hating Jew" is not new and not confined to discussions about the Israeli-Palestinian conflict. Theodor Herzl referred to Zionists who opposed or did not see the necessity of founding a Jewish state as "disguised antisemites of Jewish origin."[17] The term also surfaced in the debate between assimilated Jews and Zionists in Europe, each accusing the other of self-hatred.

The question concerning Jewish self-hatred and its motives is intimately related to the question of antisemitism and its motives—with the difference that in the case of antisemitism the agent of hatred is a non-Jew and in the case of Jewish self-hatred it is a Jew who has internalized the negative judgments of the antisemitic environment. Both judgments—those made by non-Jews and directed against Jews and those made by Jews and directed toward themselves or other Jews—are rooted in abstraction of both the hater and the hated. The subject and the object of these negative judgments lack individuality and serve as specimens of abstract general groups of people. Thus, I do not hate the individual person but rather the *Jewish* person. In this statement, the individual person evaporates and vanishes in the general predicate "Jewish."

---

[16] Reitter, *Origins of Jewish Self-Hatred*, 35-37.
[17] Id., 23.

Thus, following the publication of Hannah Arendt's *Eichmann in Jerusalem*, Gershom Scholem wrote her a letter in which he accused her of lacking *Ahavat Yisrael* (love of Israel or the Jewish people).[18] Arendt's reply was that she had neither love nor lack of love toward this or that people, but rather toward *individuals*, that is, individual people (friends and enemies).[19] Arendt's response bears truth as far as love and hatred go, for such sentiments primarily refer to relationships between individuals and only secondarily or metaphorically to relations between groups.

What seems to make Jewish self-hatred so hard to grasp is the "internalization" of the generalization of the hated Jew, that is, the projection of the hatred upon one's self. In other words, the hated person internalizes a general idea or image of the Jew that the particular person hates. Thus, "Jewish self-hatred" implies the problematic assumption that all self-hating Jews have nearly the same self-image that they hate. In this framework, the particular self-hatred of whatever kind it may be, such as self-underestimation or self-critique, is reduced to one hated self-image. It is clear that, in his study, Lessing holds the following assumption to be true, despite its problematic nature: "There's no person of Jewish origin ["*Blut*," i.e. race] in whom we couldn't find at least signs of Jewish self-hatred."[20]

Traditionally, we find three general motives underlying Jew-hatred or anti-semitism: metaphysical, racial, and economic. The metaphysical motive implies a *religious worldview* in which the Jews are the Messiah's murderer, the obstacle to salvation, deniers of the message of Christ or Muhammad, cursed by birth, rootless, and nationless. On the other hand, the racial and economic motives imply a *secular worldview*. From the racial perspective, the Jew is seen as belonging to an inferior race that threatens the existence of a superior race. From the economic perspective, the Jew is seen as owning money, not sharing in productive activity, living off the back of other people, exploiting the workers, and so forth.

Theodor Lessing (1872-1933) was born into a middle-class, assimilated Jewish family in Hanover. He studied medicine, and then switched to philosophy,

---

[18] "There is something in the Jewish language that is completely indefinable, yet fully concrete—what the Jews call ahavath Israel, or love for the Jewish people. With you, my dear Hannah, as with so many intellectuals coming from the German left, there is no trace of it." Gershom Scholem, *A Life in Letters: 1914-1982* (Cambridge: Harvard University Press, 2002), 396.

[19] "How right you are that I have no such love, and for two reasons: first, I have never in my life 'loved' some nation or collective—not the German, French or American nation, or the working class, or whatever else might exist. The fact is that I love only my friends and am quite incapable of any other sort of love." Id., 399.

[20] "Es lebt kein Mensch aus jüdischem Blut, bei dem wir nicht wenigstens Ansätze zum 'jüdischen Selbsthasse' fänden." Lessing, *Der jüdische Selbsthaß*, 40.

psychology, and literature. By that time, he had converted to Christianity and, as he later admitted, become a self-hating Jew.[21] As Shulamit Volkov notes:

> In 1909 Lessing published a series of articles in the *Allgemeine Zeitung des Judentums* entitled "Impressions from Galicia" and containing an appalling account of Jewish life in this province. Despite his preference for "life" over "intellect," Lessing was shocked at what he saw. In a synagogue in a small town he suddenly found himself amidst loud crying, mad gestures, general excitement, and restlessness: "I was practically shaking with fear at this prayer," he recounted. "I got sick. I forced my way out and fled away." Lessing's articles provoked sharp criticism. His unabashed nausea at the sight of his brethren was shocking even for some of the regular, often similarly disposed readers of the *Allgemeine Zeitung des Judentums*. Nevertheless, they were published in full in this respectable journal and were apparently not entirely unacceptable to the Jewish readership at that time.[22]

Following an antisemitic incident he experienced at the school where he taught, Lessing returned to Judaism and became an ardent Zionist, and even visited Palestine in 1931. In 1925, he published a critical study on the president of the Weimar Republic, Paul von Hindenburg, dealing with his weak personality and warning that such weakness of character could open the door to radical forces seeking to ascend to power. These claims gave rise to a wave of resentment and protest against Lessing. His lectures at the university were interrupted by students, and in the end he was no longer allowed to teach. After the Nazis came to power, Lessing and his wife fled to Czechoslovakia, where he continued to publish in German magazines. Shortly after that, a reward was offered to anyone who would deliver Lessing into the hands of the Nazis. In August 1933, at the age of 61, he was assassinated in his home in Czechoslovakia.

Lessing's works include studies of Nietzsche, Schopenhauer, and Hindenburg, as well as on noise (*Lärm*). The most obvious influences on his writing and method are Nietzsche's philosophy of *amor fati*, Freud's psychoanalysis, and Husserl's phenomenology. His book *Jewish Self-Hatred* contains a long introductory essay in which he tries to account for Jewish self-hatred and provide a cure. Lessing then explains his understanding of Jewish self-hatred, applying it to the biographies of six prominent German Jews who denied their Jewish roots in their striving to succeed and ascend in society: Paul Reé—philosopher and physician, and a close friend of Nietzsche; Otto Weininger—the author of the influential book *Sex and Character* (1903); Arthur Trebitsch—writer, philosopher, and an ardent antisemite; Max Steiner—scientist and intellectual; Walter Calé—a German poet; and Maximilian Harden—a prominent journalist, a close friend of Bismarck, and the editor of the journal *Die Zukunft*.

---

21 Id.
22 Volkov, *Germans, Jews and Antisemites*, 44.

Reading Lessing's treatise on Jewish self-hatred, we should bear in mind that, following Nietzsche, Freud, and Husserl, Lessing rejects any realistic, objective, and metaphysical ascription of meaning. That is to say, meaning stems neither from objective reality nor from any metaphysical realm. Reality as such lacks any meaning and is thus indifferent to human beings. Meaning is rather a subjective projection on a naked reality. Thus, Jewish self-hatred (as well as anti-semitism) can be understood neither metaphysically nor economically nor racially—self-hatred is rather a subjective projection. Self-hatred was first systematically explained by Freud in *Mourning and Melancholia* (1917). The question then becomes about the cause of such neurosis, of neurotic self-hatred. And further, we should ask what steps should be taken according to Lessing to heal this neurosis. Lessing's attitude toward assimilated and self-hating Jews was very negative. By contrast, his attitude toward the Jews living in Palestine and striving to build their own nation was always very positive:

> Disgrace on all sons who, in order to have the worldly luxury of the Western cosmopolitan cities, prefer to dedicate themselves to literature or to pursue an academic career, instead of carrying stones on the road to Jerusalem.[23]

This creates the impression that Lessing had answers to questions about the cause of this neurotic self-hatred as well as the ability to offer a cure. This impression will turn out to be misleading.

III

Lessing starts his discussion of self-hatred by focusing on the feeling of *guilt*. According to Lessing, reality is bereft of objective meaning. Meaning stems from a rather subjective projection carried out by the individual upon reality. Bad things that befall me have no meaning as such—neither destiny nor intention to afflict me; they rather gain their meaning through my subjective projection of meaning upon reality: I project or ascribe guilt or fault to something or some-body else, and thus I give them meaning and account for their occurrence. For example, I explain my suffering by ascribing it to other people to whom I attribute the source of my suffering and cause of my grief. It is also possible that I may project guilt or fault upon myself—it is my own fault that something bad has befallen me, although one's human nature mainly tends to blame others for bad things that befall oneself.

With the Jews, Lessing claims, it is a different story. Following two millennia of persecution and suffering, they always project guilt upon themselves: we

---

[23] "Schmach allen Söhnen, die es vorziehen, für die Luxuswelt westlicher Weltstädte 'sich der Literatur zu widmen' oder 'die akademische Laufbahn einzuschlagen', statt Steine zu tragen zu der Landstraße nach Jeruschalajim." Lessing, *Der jüdische Selbsthaß*, 26.

suffer, are tortured and killed because we are guilty and thus deserve it.[24] Self-hatred relates to the Jewish-Christian practice of confession (*Vidduy*) and thus reflects a universal phenomenon.[25] And yet, Lessing claims, the Jews exemplify this phenomenon more than any other people on earth.[26]

From the projection of guilt, Lessing continues to a deeper level that triggers the projection of guilt. Lessing utilizes psychoanalysis in order to penetrate behind the projection of guilt. The projection of guilt takes place in the highest part of the personality, at the level of the super-ego. The super-ego is a late differentiation between my own ego and the alter ego. This stage of sublimation emanates from the prime level of the ego in which there is no sublimation and no differentiation between my own ego and the alter ego.[27] Self-hatred is founded in this differentiation, and it turns against its source at the prime level of the ego, the level at which there is as yet no differentiation between the ego and the alter-ego. The first and lower level can be retrieved in experience of art and religion.[28] Lessing calls this retrieval "religious aesthetical experience." At the higher level, where the differentiation appears, Lessing identifies two kinds of experience: "logical experience" and "moral experience."[29]

The higher level, the sublimation, runs counter to and strives to annihilate the lower level. In the case of Jews, evaluating moral experience and evaluating logical and perceptual experience—which both take place in the upper level of the personality—are not equal. Instead, moral experience outweighs logical perceptual experience. This is the lot of the minority living among a hostile majority, namely the minority's need to continuously adapt itself to its surroundings and to look around and ensure that the minority is not conspicuous and is acceptable in the eyes of the majority.[30]

The Jew's excessive sublimation can always produce a "perfect" imitation of the non-Jew, of the hateful surrounding majority. Thus, the Jew can emulate and excel in the surrounding society. But the more the Jew succeeds—the more he adopts and internalizes the viewpoint and norms of his hater and the better

---

[24] Id., 12-13.

[25] Id., 13.

[26] Id., 27.

[27] Id., 27-28.

[28] Id., 32.

[29] "Wir haben sonach zwei Erlebnisgruppen zu unterscheiden. Solche, welche jenseits der 'Selbstentfremdung' (d.h. der Subjekt-Objekt-Relation) liegen. Und solche, welche auf dem Fundamente der Selbstverdoppelung (der Subjekt-Objekt-Relation) sich erheben. Die erste Gruppe bezeichnen wir als die religiös-ästhetischen Erlebnisse. Die zweite als die logisch-ethischen. Nur die letzteren sind im engeren Sinn die 'menschlichen' Erlebnisse." Id., 32.

[30] Id., 34-35.

his deception—the more he is afflicted by self-hatred and the more his personality demands he take revenge on himself.[31]

IV

Assuming that the source of meaning can be neither metaphysical nor economical, the cure for Jewish self-hatred can be found neither in adapting Jewish religion and rites to their surroundings nor in changing the economic or social status of the Jew and emancipating him. Rather, the solution should be of a psychological kind that lies in affirming life and affirming one's own destiny, albeit the hardest life to live. Lessing writes:

> Don't deceive your destiny. Love your destiny. Follow your destiny. And follow it to death. Take heart. Through all the hells of our human-self you always come into the heaven of yourself. To your eternal people.[32]

Affirming one's life and destiny is the only way to bestow meaning on life, live it fully, and thus overcome the disease of self-hatred. Lessing writes:

> If we were asked, "Why do you thus still want to continue to exist?" then, if we are honest, we could not reply otherwise than "because we exist."[33]

This is by no means *self-help language*, as Paul Reitter claims, but rather *Nietzschean language*. Lessing echoes Zarathustra's call to the cripples and invalids to affirm their miserable life. Contrary to Christ, who came to heal and redeem from life's misery, Zarathustra came to call people to affirm their life, albeit the most miserable and wretched life:

> When one taketh his hump from the hunchback, then doth one take from him his spirit—so do the people teach. And when one giveth the blind man eyes, then doth he see too many bad things on the earth: so that he curseth him who healed him. He, however, who maketh the lame man run, inflicteth upon him the greatest injury ...
>
> *To redeem what is past, and to transform every "It was" into "Thus would I have it!"—that only do I call redemption!*[34]

---

[31] Id., 41-42.

[32] "Betrüge nicht dein Schicksal. Liebe dein Schicksal. Folge dem Schicksal. Und folge auch in den Tod. Getrost! Durch alle Höllen unsres menschlichen Ich gelangst du immer wieder in den Himmel deines Selbst. Zu deinem ewigen Volke." Id., 51.

[33] "Würde man uns fragen: "Warum wollt ihr denn noch dauern?" so könnten wir darauf, wenn wir ehrlich sind, gar nicht anders antworten, als wie alle Wesen antworten: "Weil wir sind." Id., 214.

[34] Friedrich Nietzsche, "Redemption," in Friedrich Nietzsche, *Thus Spake Zarathustra*, trans. Thomas Common (Virginia: Wilder Publications, 2009), 94-95 [emphasis added].

Affirmation of life is achieved by a free decision (*Entschluss*) that should not be derived from any interest or different motive other than to live one's destiny.[35]

At this point we can already see part of the problem of Lessing's theory surface. If, as he argues, reality in itself has no meaning, it follows that destiny as such—which Lessing calls upon us to submit to—is likewise bereft of meaning. It is rather our subjective projection of the self-hatred. Accordingly, the solution to the problem should have been thought through by means of psychological introspection *into* the sick soul. However, Lessing sends us *outside*, to the transcendental destiny, to search for the cure. It seems to me that Lessing must have run into this obvious contradiction, because he does not tell us where meaning stems from. As we have noted, Lessing regards meaning as a subjective projection onto a bare and meaningless reality. But where does this meaning come from? As we have seen, the lower level of the self—the *id*, according to Lessing—is also a bare reality with no differentiation between subject and object, between me and you. Thus, the source of the self also lacks any meaning. Hence, the self must also get meaning from outside itself. At the end of the long and complicated intellectual journey on which Lessing has taken us, we are therefore left with no explanation as to the origin of the self-hatred and, likewise, with no cure.

V

Of all the six biographies in Lessing's book of German Jewish intellectuals who were haunted by self-hatred, I find the last one, that of Maximilian Harden, the most interesting. It is also the most detailed one of the six. Lessing was friendly with Harden, and thus had greater access to his biography.

Maximilian Harden was born in Switzerland in 1861 as Felix Ernst Witkowski. Harden was born to a Jewish father who was a silk handler. His brother was the influential banker and politician Richard Witting. When he was twelve years old, Harden's father forced him to leave the French Gymnasium in Berlin. At the age of thirteen, in 1874, he completed training as a theatrical actor and joined a wandering theater group, leaving no clue to his family of his whereabouts. He changed his name to Maximilian Harden and converted to Protestantism. Beginning in 1884, he worked as a theater critic and published under the pseudonym *Apostata*. He was co-founder of the Free Stage Association and reorganized the German Theater in Berlin. In 1892 he founded the magazine *Die Zukunft*, in which he published art and political critiques. He became friends with Bismarck and directed most of his sharp critique against Bismarck's successor, Wilhelm II, exposing homosexuality among his advisors in order to discredit his reign. These publications caused great damage to the

---

[35] Lessing, *Der jüdische Selbsthaß*, 222-223.

imperial house and led to lawsuits and proceedings against Harden. Most importantly, for our purpose, Harden published antisemitic articles in *Die Zukunft*, the most famous of which being Walther Rathenau's article *Höre Israel! (Shma Israel)*. Rathenau was himself a Jew, and later became the foreign minister of the Weimar Republic. In this article, in which he admitted that he was a Jew, Rathenau wrote of the Jews:

> Strange sight! Within German life an isolated foreign human kind, glaring and ostensibly dressed, with a nimble hot-blooded conduct. On the sand of Mark Brandenburg an Asian mob.[36]

Goebbels's *Völkischer Beobachter* and Streicher's *Der Stürmer* always returned to this statement by the Jewish Rathenau whenever they wanted to portray a distorted picture of the Jew, as it stemmed from a Jewish pen. In 1920 the friendship between Rathenau and Harden broke down. Harden began criticizing Rathenau in *Die Zukunft*. He continued criticizing Rathenau even after his assassination, wondering why his death still drew so much attention. Thus, for example, he wrote concerning Rathenau:

> Cagliostro. Bright, witty, prototype of the Jewish upper class. However, entirely sterile. No single lasting achievement. And his writings? Overmorrow will be forgotten, being already today outdated.[37]

Judaism, according to Rathenau, was reminiscent of meaningless old oriental rites in the middle of a modern Western culture. Thus, the Jews should give up these practices in order to remove the tension between themselves and their surroundings.[38] According to Lessing, Rathenau's attitude characterized the mindset of the Jewish majority. It would win and lead to the dissolution of the entire Jewish religion in Germany, unless Zionism became so influential and attracted to itself the young generation.[39] On the fifth anniversary of *Die Zukunft*, Harden wrote to his 100,000 readers, promising that throughout his entire life he would serve the well-being of the German people to the best of his capacity and knowledge. Then he turned to the subject of the Jews and the Jewish question: "What do you really want," he said to the Jews, "do say it clearly, whose business are you promoting, the business of Germany or Zion?"[40]

---

[36] Cited in Julius Schoeps, "Haß auf die eigene jüdische Herkunft—Zur Biographie zweier Repräsentanten und Außenseiter im Wilhelminischen Deutschland," *Die Zeit*, January 25, 1987.

[37] Id.

[38] Lessing, *Der jüdische Selbsthaß*, 189.

[39] Id.

[40] "'Was wollt Ihr denn eigentlich,' rief er in der 'Zukunft' den Juden zu, 'sagt doch klar, wessen Geschäfte besorgt Ihr, die Geschäfte Deutschlands oder die Geschäfte Zions?'" Id., 190.

At the beginning of World War I, Harden voiced enthusiastic support for the war and annexation in *Die Zukunft*. When the war was lost, he changed his mind and spoke out against it. From around 1916 onwards, Harden wrote in favor of peace and about rescuing Germany. After the war, he was among the very few Germans who supported the Treaty of Versailles. Then came the revolution, and two months after the Treaty of Versailles had been signed, Rathenau was assassinated. A few days after the assassination of Rathenau, an attempt was made on Harden's life in which he was severely injured.

As Lessing concludes, many saw in this attempted murder an appropriate act by faithful servants of the Fatherland. In the end, then, it turned out that Harden had always been a foreigner in his land.[41] His assassins were exculpated by the court on the grounds that they were acting out of the conviction that they were ridding the country of vermin. Everything was done, according to Lessing, to depict the murderous act as stemming from noble intentions.[42] In contemporary publications, Harden was referred to as Isidor Witkowski of Galicia, who was brought in by Bismarck as a writing assistant. Harden was never called Isidor, and he did not come to Germany from Galicia.[43] Although abroad Harden was regarded as a German fanatic, in Germany he was now referred to as dirty Jew.[44] The judge at the trial was a converted Jew, the son of a rabbi, and the two lawyers who represented and defended the claim that Harden's would-be assassins had acted out of noble motivations were also converted Jews—Bloch and Schiff. Regarding this, Lessing says:

> A German court in which converted Jews sit favors the murderers of another converted Jew, because these murderers ascertain that they wanted to murder in the name and out of the spirit of the German state of mind.[45]

Harden thus found himself in a strange situation. He stood, as a Jew, trying to defend himself against two converted lawyers who represented and defended his would-be murderers in a trial conducted by a converted judge, and. And thus, in addressing the court, Harden said that if he were not a Jew, the court would decide the case differently and would not acquit his almost assassins.[46] Harden also said in his speech that he did understand antisemitism, and yet he regretted that in Germany people did not realize that the very attributes they ascribed to the Jews in Germany people abroad ascribed to the Germans.[47]

---

[41] Id., 199.

[42] Id., 200.

[43] Id.

[44] Id., 201.

[45] Id., 204.

[46] Id., 202.

[47] Id., 203

Shortly before his death, following a sympathetic article that Lessing published about him, Harden told Lessing:

> I'm a fighter, and to what extent I am, will emerge in a few weeks, as *Die Zukunft* will appear again, which is nowadays more important to Germany than ever before.[48]

Thus, according to Lessing, the story of Maximilian Harden illustrates the fate of a self-hating Jew who admits his Judaism—to himself and to the public—only when forced to do so by the pressure of hostile surroundings, but once such pressures diminishes reverts to being a self-hating Jew.

---

[48] "Ich bin ein Kämpfer, und wie lebendig, das wird sich in einigen Wochen zeigen, wo die 'Zukunft' wiedererscheinen wird, die für Deutschland notwendiger ist als je." Id., 207.

# Trends in the Psychological Study
# of Contemporary Antisemitism:
# Conceptual Issues and Empirical Evidence*

Neil J. Kressel[a] and Samuel W. Kressel[b]

## Abstract

*This article reviews evidence bearing on whether antisemitism has recently reemerged as a dangerous and global sociopolitical problem. Two empirical studies then explore how psychologists and other social scientists have investigated anti-Jewish bigotry. The first looks at research trends in major social scientific databases since the 1940s. The second is a content analysis of abstracts of psychological studies on antisemitism since 1990. The article concludes, among other findings, that while social scientific aspects of the Holocaust have been studied in some detail, contemporary anti-Jewish hostility has been underestimated, and antisemitism from the Muslim/Arab world has been largely ignored.*

During the past 15 years, several journalists and scholars from various disciplines have contended that antisemitism has reemerged as a dangerous sociopolitical problem, despite widespread expectations among social scientists that Jew-hatred would continue a decline perceived in the decades following the Second World War. According to a budding literature, virulent anti-Jewish bigotry is now most prevalent in several Muslim-majority countries, but the trend is nearly global and even affects some liberal democracies (Bard, 2014; Berenbaum, 2008; Bostom, 2008; Chesler, 2003; B. Cohen, 2014; F. Cohen, 2013; F. Cohen, Jussim, Harber, & Bhasin, 2009; Fatah, 2010; Fineberg, Samuels, & Weitzman, 2007; Foxman, 2003, 2007, 2010; Harrison, 2006; Heni, 2013; Iganski & Kosmin, 2003; Jaspal, 2014; Kressel, 2007a, 2007b, 2012; Küntzel, 2007;

---

* This article was first published as Neil J. Kressel and Samuel W. Kressel, "Trends in the Psychological Study of Contemporary Antisemitism: Conceptual Issues and Empirical Evidence," *Basic and Applied Social Psychology* 38, no. 2 (2016): 111-126. It is reprinted here by permission of the publisher (Taylor & Francis, Ltd).

a William Paterson University.
b Brandeis University.

Nirenstein, 2005; Rickman, 2011; Schoenfeld, 2004; Simon & Schaler, 2007; Small, 2013; Taguieff, 2004b; Timmerman, 2003; Wistrich, 2010). Denis MacShane (2008), a political scientist and the British Minister for Europe under Prime Minister Tony Blair, writes that "antisemitism has been called a light sleeper. It is wide awake now" (p. 159). Several writers have further charged that, for the most part, social scientists, journalists, policymakers, and human rights activists in the West have failed to understand and react to the intensity of the trend toward greater antisemitism, or, at least, to certain manifestations of that trend (Berman, 2010; Chesler, 2003; Cohen, 2007; Fine, 2009; Harrison, 2006; Kressel, 2004, 2012; Norwood, 2013; Tobin & Ybarra, 2008; Wistrich, 2012).

This article starts with a brief overview of empirical evidence bearing on these topics, along with a summary of the central elements in the journalistic and scholarly debate about the significance of contemporary antisemitism. From this overview, the article identifies several important and researchable questions that social scientists might answer about contemporary antisemitism. The article next presents the results of two empirical studies of trends in research on Jew-hatred. The first analyzes major social scientific research databases since the 1940s. The second is a content analysis of abstracts of psychological research on antisemitism that have appeared since 1990. The two empirical studies enable us to address (a) whether critics are correct about the neglect of contemporary antisemitism; (b) which aspects of the topic, to date, have been most studied; and (c) whether current research trends make it likely that we will learn what we need to know about this potentially dangerous sociopolitical phenomenon.

## LITERATURE REVIEW

### The neglect debate

Various reasons have been offered in journalistic, scholarly, and political writings for the purported neglect of contemporary antisemitism by most researchers, policymakers, journalists, and human rights activists. The simplest explanation, perhaps, comes from Alvin Rosenfeld, Director of the Institute for the Study of Contemporary Antisemitism at Indiana University; he suggested that most people in enlightened circles continue to believe, wrongly, that although "residual passions of this ugly sort might linger for a while on the fringes of society … within mainstream Western opinion anti-Semitism … [is] morally and politically discredited—a spent force without personal or cultural appeal" (as cited in Harrison, 2006, p. vii). Others have suggested that the postulated neglect or downplaying of contemporary anti-Jewish bigotry may stem from a variety of political biases (Berman, 2010; Chesler, 2003; Cohen, 2007; Norwood, 2013; Wistrich, 2012), methodological proclivities (Kressel,

2004), and/or cultural norms common among social scientists (Kressel, 2012). For example, Charles Small (2013) the former director of the now-defunct Yale Initiative for the Interdisciplinary Study of Antisemitism, maintained that

> certain members of the academic community, especially those who claim to espouse progressive and/or postmodernist views, often perceive the study of antisemitism as an attempt to undermine criticism of the state of Israel and accuse those engaged in this study of being political advocates rather than pursuers of real scholarship. (pp. 7-8; see also Wistrich, 2012)

According to another argument, there are instances of historical anti-semitism—for example, the Holocaust—that have been well studied by academics and widely acknowledged by most policymakers and journalists, whereas there are other manifestations of more recent anti-Jewish bigotry that, for complex reasons, receive far less attention. Yet another argument holds that even the Holocaust, when discussed, is sometimes divorced from its particular antisemitic components and viewed instead as the embodiment of evil in general (Fine, 2009). Small (2013) made the more general point that "if one looks at the history of antisemitism, it was never acceptable to study or examine contemporary forms of antisemitism at the time in which they occurred" (p. 10).

If social scientists have in fact produced relatively few studies on contemporary antisemitism, one reason might be that they are simply failing to focus on what may be residual aspects of a social problem that once rose to devastating dimensions but that nowadays really is a "spent force"—in any case, one less dangerous than many other forms of bigotry. If this is the case, the critics who were just noted may be regarded as needlessly alarmist and overstating the scale of the problem, either earnestly or for ulterior motives. It has, many times, been suggested that some Jews and, vicariously, some others may be hypersensitive to relatively minor instances of anti-Jewish prejudice and discrimination, owing to the traumatic consequences of Jew-hatred in the past (Dershowitz, 1997; Tobin & Sassler, 1988). In addition, numerous writers have suggested that those who support the state of Israel may have an interest in overstating the prevalence of antisemitism in order to garner favor for their cause (Brownfeld, 2005; Cohen, 2009; Ginsberg, 2011; Khalidi, 2006). Political scientists Mearsheimer and Walt (2008) go even further, writing, "No discussion of how the [Israel] lobby operates would be complete without examining one of its most powerful weapons: the charge of anti-Semitism." They accordingly proceed to describe early 21st-century claims about a resurgent antisemitism as unjustifiably "alarmist" (p. 188).

Despite the vitriol of these debates, we possess little empirical data on how social scientists are actually approaching questions about contemporary anti-semitism. A preliminary search of psychological and sociological research databases in 2003 suggested that social scientists, despite their long history of studying antisemitism in other contexts (e.g., Ackerman & Jahoda, 1950; Adorno, Frenkel-Brunswick, Levinson, & Sanford, 1950; Allport, 1954; Arendt, 1951; Glock & Stark, 1966; Stember, Sklare, & Salomon, 1966), had, until then, produced almost no studies on Jew-hatred in the contemporary Muslim world (Kressel, 2003, 2007b). The extent to which social scientists in the years since 2003 have increased their attention to Muslim Jew-hatred remains unknown. Another study (Kressel, in press) examined syllabi and textbooks in English-language courses dealing with racism, bigotry, and prejudice, tentatively concluding that antisemitism rarely figures as a prominent topic in such courses, except when the courses focus specifically on the Holocaust or geno-cide. Even then, contemporary antisemitism is frequently not discussed. When Jew-hatred is studied in psychological, sociological, or other social scientific courses on racism and prejudice, it tends to be treated as a problem from the past; sources published after the 1990s—such as those previously listed—are almost never mentioned. In syllabi as well as textbooks, the study of anti-semitism in the Muslim and Arab world is nearly always omitted altogether. Still, existing research did not employ random sampling of texts or syllabi and should therefore be treated as preliminary rather than conclusive.

*Empirical evidence concerning contemporary global antisemitism*

Ultimately, how one assesses the efforts and performance of social scientists with regard to contemporary antisemitism depends very much on how one assesses the danger of antisemitism itself as a sociopolitical force in the world today. In the view of the authors, those who attempt to defend the "antisemitism is a spent force" theory need to explain a great deal of data to the contrary. For example, in 2014, the Anti-Defamation League (ADL)—a century-old activist organization that fights antisemitism, as well as many other forms of bigotry—released the results of a well-funded and extensive survey dealing with anti-semitism around the world (ADL, 2014). Respondents included 53,100 people, ages 18 and older, from 101 countries as well as the Palestinian Territories in the West Bank and Gaza. In-person and telephone interviews were conducted in 96 languages and—although a genuinely random sample was impossible for such a broad study—researchers devoted much effort to obtaining full national coverage in the countries that were studied and close-to-random samples whenever possible. The study assessed agreement with 11 aspects of traditional antisemitic stereotypes, including items such as "Jews have too much power in international financial markets," "People hate Jews because of the way Jews behave," and "Jews have too much control over the global media." The ADL summarized its findings by classifying a person as an antisemite if he or she said that at least six of the 11 negative stereotypical items were "probably true."

Using this approach, the ADL classified 1.09 billion people worldwide as antisemites. According to the data, Middle Eastern and Muslim-majority countries score2d highest in self-reported antisemitic opinions; for example, 92% of Iraqis and 69% of Turks scored above the antisemitism threshold. However, antisemitic belief systems were also common in many non-Muslim, non-Middle Eastern countries with, for example, 69% of Greeks scoring anti-semitic, 53% of South Koreans, 52% of Panamanians, 45% of Poles, 44% of Bulgarians, 38% of Peruvians, 37% of the French, 30% of Russians, 27% of Germans, and 20% of the Chinese. Relatively good news came from the United States (9%), the United Kingdom (8%), the Netherlands (5%), and the Philip-pines (3%) Overall, 26% of the respondents in the study qualified as antisemitic using the ADL criteria.

It is worth noting that the United States Department of State (2008) and some other organizations have incorporated various aspects of extreme hostility to the state of Israel into their definition of antisemitism, but the ADL measures generally avoided items tapping directly into such attitudes and relied mainly on measures of traditional anti-Jewish stereotypes. Still, some critics have objected to elements of the ADL methodology. Some reject the dichotomous classifica-tion of antisemites and non-antisemites, arguing that a continuous spectrum of hostility would be more reflective of reality (Singal, 2014). Others suggest that the study might have included additional target groups for assessment in order to provide a comparative perspective. Still others objected to inclusion of particular items in the antisemitism scale. The belief that "Jews have too much power in international financial markets" may, for example, be a measure first and foremost of attitudes toward the power of international financial markets. The belief that "Jews still talk too much about what happened to them in the Holocaust" need not, in itself, indicate hostility toward Jews and may even, in fact, be expressed by many who are concerned about contemporary anti-semitism. Finally, the notion that Jews are more loyal to Israel than to countries they live in may also tap beliefs other than antisemitism. Of course, the ADL has not advanced any of these items individually as a definitive indicator of anti-Jewish bigotry; it is when they are assessed in conjunction with other beliefs that a pattern emerges. Moreover, even if one agrees with some criticism of the study, it would seem that the scope and pattern of responses broadly support the contention that antisemitism is currently a very popular form of bigotry with a uniquely global reach. Critics like Shapiro (2015) reasonably call attention to the survey's measurement of prejudiced attitudes as opposed to bigoted behaviors; nonetheless, it is hard to dismiss the ADL findings as insignificant, even with the focus on attitudes and the possible overstatement of the prevalence of these attitudes. (See, also, ADL, 2015, for an update.)

A multinational survey conducted by the Pew Global Attitudes Project (2008) employed different methodology but yielded results fairly consistent with the ADL's 2014 and 2015 findings. Samples from around the world were asked whether they had a very favorable, somewhat favorable, somewhat unfavorable, or very unfavorable opinion of the Jews. A varying percentage of respondents in every country refrained from offering an opinion, but many people were willing to provide their views. As in the ADL study, there was again relatively good news concerning the United States with only 2% saying they held very unfavorable opinions about the Jews and only 5% holding somewhat unfavorable opinions. Australians, British, and French were not far behind the Americans in their generally benign attitudes toward the Jews. However, in Muslim-majority countries or countries with substantial Muslim minorities, large numbers of respondents were willing to share with researchers that they held very unfavorable or somewhat unfavorable opinions of the Jews. The percentages reporting very unfavorable views of the Jews were 68% in Turkey, 92% in Egypt, 94% in Jordan, 65% in Pakistan, 36% in Indonesia, 22% in Nigeria, and 21% in India. Even in countries with relatively few Muslims, the numbers indicated a considerable amount of negative feeling regarding the Jews. The percentages admitting to either very unfavorable or somewhat unfavorable opinions about the Jews were as follows: 44% for Japan, 41% for South Korea, 50% for Brazil, 46% for Mexico, 55% for China, 46% for Spain, 34% for Russia, and 25% for Germany. One possibility is that some of those who report unfavorable views of Jews are not specifically hard-core antisemites; some people, for example, may hold similarly negative views concerning a variety of outside groups. Or they may dislike groups with which they are unfamiliar. Some may be primarily hostile toward Jewish Israelis and not understand the distinction between Jewish citizens of Israel and other Jews. The distinction between attitudes and behaviors remains key. Nonetheless, it is hard to conclude from either the ADL or Pew data that antisemitism has during the past half century lost its once widely acknowledged status as a preeminent, durable, and potentially destructive global problem.

It is beyond our scope here to review all the evidence supporting the resurgence argument, but it should be noted that the case generally emerges not from empirical studies alone but rather from (a) an examination of antisemitic incidents and (b) an analysis of the frequency and virulence with which powerful leaders in the worlds of politics, religion, academia, and journalism have voiced sentiments that most reasonable people would deem bigoted.

The evidence for an intensive and growing Jew-hatred in the Muslim world is hard to deny, although there are many possible explanations for the origins of this hatred (Kressel, 2012). Documentation of Jew-hatred in the Muslim world falls into 12 categories:

1. Antisemitic assertions by heads of state, political leaders, former political leaders, government officials, religious figures, and scholars.
2. Lack of general outrage or even significant, well-publicized challenge in response to these antisemitic assertions.
3. Antisemitic articles and images in print media, broadcast media, and the Internet.
4. Antisemitic textbooks and other instruments for socialization of the young.
5. Public opinion data showing highly prevalent negative and stereotypical attitudes toward Jews.
6. Video documentation of bigotry in very young children.
7. Terrorist targeting of Jews and Jewish institutions.
8. Vicious denunciations of those Muslims who defend Jews.
9. Denunciations of all sorts of political, personal, and theological opponents as Jews, or as friends of the Jews.
10. Excerpts from religious texts—the Koran, Hadith, Sira, and so forth—that plausibly appear to sustain or reinforce hostility toward Jews (especially when coupled with anti-Jewish interpretations by contemporary religious leaders and theologians in contrast to more moderate or tolerant interpretations).
11. Laws and organizational policies that discriminate against Jews.
12. Reports by Jews that they feel uncomfortable or unsafe practicing Judaism or displaying signs of Jewish identity in Muslim countries or regions with high percentages of Muslim residents (Kressel, 2012).

Within Europe, numerous surveys have documented the disproportionate presence of antisemitism among Muslim Europeans. A 2015 review of these studies concluded that this bigotry could not be readily explained away by reference to demographic and socioeconomic variables. According to Günther Jikeli (2015), the author of the review,

> educational level, age, gender, social disadvantage, discrimination, and legal restrictions of Islamic practice—cannot explain the differences between Muslims and non-Muslims. This refutes the widespread assumption that Muslim antisemitism is a reaction to discrimination or suppression. The surveys considered are strong evidence that current interpretations of Muslim identity and belief are major sources for hatred against Jews. … A distinction between Islamism and Islam is surely important, but might be insufficient: although antisemitism is particularly strong among fundamentalist as well as believing and practicing Muslims, the level of antisemitism among less religious Muslims is still higher than in the general population. (pp. 19-20)

For similar findings, see also the study by the Anti-Defamation League (2015).

In Egypt, Syria, Iran and other parts of the Muslim world, viewers in recent years have watched multipart television series based on the blood libel and on the antisemitic classic, *The Protocols of the Elders of Zion*. Years ago, scholars and courts determined this document to be a forgery, almost certainly penned by agents of the Czarist secret police (Ben-Itto, 2005). Yet, for many in the Muslim world, *The Protocols of the Elders of Zion* displays the facts of the past and present (Taguieff, 2004a). In many places, the epithet "sons of pigs and apes" is widely understood by Muslims to mean "Jews" (though, on occasion, it is extended to include Christians as well). The phrase comes from the Koran, though its use in reference to contemporary Jews (or Christians) requires some stretching; this stretching may not be theologically justified, but there has been no shortage of Muslim clerics eager to argue that the nasty appellation is wholly appropriate (Kressel, 2012). Finally, as the 2015 attack by Muslim extremists on the Hyper Cacher (kosher) market in Paris and other recent violent attacks on Jews and Jewish institutions suggest, the consequences of antisemitic defamation are potentially bloody.

It is, of course, possible to question the methodologies of the studies just cited, as well as the other evidence. That is what academics should do. However, it is hard to question the prima facie case that antisemitism in the Muslim world is a problem worthy of serious research.

The topic might reasonably command considerable attention from scholars of racism and prejudice, as well as from those who deal with human rights and the Middle East. After all, the global antisemitic movement is centered in a political region of unquestioned strategic importance. It is the latest manifestation of a bigotry that has poisoned diverse cultures for millennia and driven genocide. Also, the social sciences in the United States and elsewhere include many scholars of Jewish origin, and these scholars have played a prominent role in developing social scientific theory and research on prejudice. Thus, if there is truly a lack of social science research on contemporary antisemitism, the inattention would require an explanation.

Some authors have accepted the empirical proposition that many people around the world—Muslims, Arabs, and others—hold negative opinions about Jews but insist for various reasons that these opinions do not constitute antisemitism or prejudice. Arguments of this sort assume many forms and some of them—in particular cases—may have merit. Critics have also contended that most of what the surveys detect, most of the incidents, and most of the remarks actually involve a form of political protest against the perceived misdeeds of the state of Israel (e.g., Mearsheimer & Walt, 2008). Whatever one's position on the Arab-Israeli conflict, however, this position is implausible. The problem is that so much of the evidence addresses Jews per se, and not Israelis. Moreover, much of the bigotry has historical continuity with source material predating the Arab-Israeli conflict. Bigotries of many forms may rest upon a "kernel of truth," and target groups may, indeed, misbehave (Allport, 1954). But social scientists do not as a rule accept any of this as justification or evidence that a problem is not a problem.

*Key research questions*

The literature review suggests many questions that social scientists might want to answer about the historical, political, economic, anthropological, and social psychological roots of contemporary antisemitism in its various forms and locales. In addition, social scientists might reasonably want to shed light on the relationship between antisemitic *attitudes* and anti-Jewish *behaviors* ranging from antilocution to extermination (Allport, 1954). Moreover, much remains to be learned about the connection between behavioral and attitudinal antisemitism, on one hand, and a host of sociopolitical and social psychological opinions and actions, on the other; for example, our understanding could benefit from empirical studies exploring interrelationships among antisemitic, antizionist, racist, anti-Arab, anti-Muslim, religious, leftist, rightist, authoritarian, and other mind-sets. It would also be important to gather data on antisemitism in the many regions where Jew-hatred manifests, partly so we could grasp more clearly the similarities and differences among antisemitic movements in these various locales; historically, antisemitism has always borrowed from previous eruptions and always reinvented itself to fit cultural surroundings. Finally, given the utility of social psychologically grounded antiracist interventions in many contexts, we might wish for significant research exploring the potential value of various prosocial activities designed to lessen contemporary Jew-hatred.

However, this ambitious agenda requires as a precondition social scientists who are motivated to understand, and—ultimately—combat, contemporary antisemitism, and it requires disciplinary infrastructures receptive to their work. Thus, a preliminary set of questions includes the following:

– To what extent have psychologists and other social scientists brought their talents to bear on the problem of contemporary antisemitism?
– To what extent has Jew-hatred in the Islamic and Arab world been addressed by studies over the years?
– To what extent has research on past hostility, especially the Holocaust, dominated the social scientific study of antisemitism? In other words, have researchers shown a predilection for researching past antisemitism instead of current antisemitism?
– Has the volume of research on contemporary antisemitism increased in response to the upsurge in Jew-hatred during the past quarter century that has been identified by some writers?

- Has research focused on those locations where antisemitism seems to have the widest acceptance and the greatest intensity?
- Have there been any clear and discernible biases in the way antisemitism researchers have framed their questions?

The two empirical studies that follow have been designed to increase our empirical knowledge concerning these questions. Beyond assessing the merits of the "neglect" criticism just discussed, the two projects seek to identify gaps and blind spots that might exist in recent social scientific work, especially in the field of psychology. This, in turn, might facilitate a better informed and more comprehensive agenda for research on contemporary Jew-hatred—something that would seem a constructive component of any effort to address the problem.

## Study 1: Database Searches

### *Goals and methodology*

The database searches were designed to answer three main questions. First, to what extent have researchers in the social sciences attended to anti-Semitism, and how has their attentiveness varied over the years? Second, how much attention have social scientific researchers paid to antisemitism in the Muslim and Arab world, and have research trends regarding this matter been influenced by the reported increase in recent years in this form of anti-Jewish hostility? Third, to what extent has the Holocaust dominated research on antisemitism? This last question is of theoretical interest because of arguments that discussions of the Holocaust have, in some instances, become increasingly divorced from discussions of antisemitism (Bromley & Russell, 2010; Fine, 2009; Riley & Totten, 2002).

Title fields and abstract fields were searched in four important research databases in the social sciences: PsycINFO, Sociological Abstracts, ProQuest Social Science Journals, and Worldwide Political Science Abstracts. All the searches went up to the end of 2014, though the starting dates varied due to differing coverage of the databases. For PsycINFO, we went back to 1940, for Sociological Abstracts to 1950, for ProQuest Social Science Journals to 1990, and for Worldwide Political Science Abstracts to 1970.

Owing to the varied content of the databases and different search engine functionality, the methods used for the database searches were not identical, but they were very similar. We always searched for English-language sources only, and we conducted identical searches of the title and abstract fields. (Roughly similar results were obtained using searches of the subject fields, but ultimately we chose not to rely on these results due to our inability to determine precisely how items were classified by subject in the four databases.)

We first searched by decade for all references to antisemitism using numerous spellings of "antisemitism" and "antisemite," supplemented by the terms "Jew-hatred," "prejudice against Jews," and "anti-Jewish." We then conducted the searches again, adding the term "Holocaust." Finally, we conducted the searches a third time, adding the terms "Nazi," "Hitler," and "Nazism." Next, we took the results of the first antisemitism search, the one that did not use the terms dealing specifically with the Holocaust or Nazism, and searched those results for mentions of the terms "Muslim," "Islam," "Islamic," or "Arab." We redid these searches concerning the Arab and Islamic world using a much longer list of search terms, including the names of many major Muslim and Arab countries. Ultimately, however, we chose to rely on the first set of results, for two reasons. First, the broader list of search terms yielded a number of items that—upon further examination—were obviously misclassified, that is, they had nothing to do with Muslim or Arab antisemitism. Second, the results of the latter search produced results that were similar in all essentials to the results of the simpler search based on the shorter list of search terms.

In our view, the title field searches ended up producing the most convincing indicator of trends in coverage. This is because—as our subsequent in-depth examination of a sample of search results revealed—references in the abstract field were occasionally superficial or misleading. Thus, an abstract might contain the word *antisemitism*, but the article or book may really be dealing almost entirely with another matter. Still, as the following results indicate, there were few occasions where an analysis of the abstract field led to conclusions different from those stemming from an analysis of the title field.

*References to antisemitism and the Holocaust*

Table 1 shows the number of references to antisemitism found by searching the title and abstract fields of the four social science research databases. As noted, these searches were conducted using several spellings of "antisemite" and "antisemitism" as well as the terms "Jew-hatred," "anti-Jewish," and "prejudice against Jews." In PsycINFO, the number of items referring to antisemitism was somewhat higher in the 1940s than in the 1950s, 1960s, 1970s, or 1980s, when the number remained consistently low. From the 1990s through the end of 2014, however, the number of items dealing with antisemitism increased substantially. In Sociological Abstracts, no data are available for the 1940s, but the number of references to antisemitism increases in each decade from the 1950s through the present. A similar upward trend in coverage of antisemitism is evident in the Worldwide Political Science Abstracts database for the period from the 1970s through the present. ProQuest Social Science Journals also follows an upward trend from the 1990s through the present, except for a slight dip in title references during the most recent years.

*Table 1. References to antisemitism in titles and abstracts in four social science research databases (items per decade).*

| | 1940s | 1950s | 1960s | 1970s | 1980s | 1990s | 2000s | 2010s[a] |
|---|---|---|---|---|---|---|---|---|
| **Number of entries per decade** | | | | | | | | |
| **PsycINFO** | | | | | | | | |
| Title | 37 | 20 | 17 | 14 | 35 | 34 | 73 | 88 |
| Abs | 75 | 48 | 28 | 38 | 53 | 111 | 193 | 194 |
| **Sociological Abstracts** | | | | | | | | |
| Title | | 20 | 34 | 41 | 82 | 126 | 132 | 168 |
| Abs | | 29 | 104 | 100 | 110 | 269 | 346 | 332 |
| **ProQuest Social Science Journals** | | | | | | | | |
| Title | | | | | | 67 | 84 | 70 |
| Abs | | | | | | 83 | 173 | 226 |
| **Worldwide Political Science Abstracts** | | | | | | | | |
| Title | | | | 11 | 51 | 61 | 135 | 156 |
| Abs | | | | 35 | 85 | 117 | 319 | 342 |

*Note.* The terms used for these searches included various spellings of antisemitism and antisemite, as well as "Jew-hatred," "anti-Jewish," and "prejudice against Jews." Abs = abstracts.

[a] For purposes of comparison with earlier decades, the number shown in the 2010s column is a heuristic projection obtained by doubling the actual number of entries obtained in database searches covering the 5-year period from January 1, 2010, through December 31, 2014.

The time trends, however, cannot be unambiguously interpreted as an indication of an increased focus by social scientists on the matter of anti-Semitism, as all of the databases have grown substantially over time. For example, PsycINFO includes only about 4,000 items in total (on all topics) for 1945, but it includes about 110,000 for 2005. Sociological Abstracts includes about 2,500 total entries for 1955 but about 31,000 for 2005. In light of such tremendous growth, we would predict that the absolute number of entries on many topics would increase, even without commanding a greater portion of a discipline's attention.

To address this concern, Table 2 shows references to antisemitism in titles and abstracts "per 10,000 items in the database" for each decade for which data were available. Using these figures, we see that relative attentiveness to antisemitism in PsycINFO declined from a high in the 1940s to a low in the present decade; most of this decline, however, seems to have taken place during the 1950s. Since then, the numbers seem to have been fairly stable. No clear time trends emerge for Sociological Abstracts or ProQuest Social Science Journals. For Worldwide Political Science Abstracts, there seems to have been a slight but consistent increase in coverage of antisemitism from the 1970s through the 2000s.

A somewhat different picture emerges when the word "Holocaust" is added to the title and abstract searches. Table 3 shows items referring to the "Holocaust" without also referring to antisemitism. It is important to note that the term "Holocaust" was not widely used in reference to the Nazi genocide until the 1970s. When Table 3 is compared with Table 1, it becomes apparent that by

*Table 2. References to antisemitism in titles and abstracts in four social science research databases (items per 10,000 entries in database by decade).*

| | 1940s | 1950s | 1960s | 1970s | 1980s | 1990s | 2000s | 2010s[a] |
|---|---|---|---|---|---|---|---|---|
| **Number of entries per 10,000 items in database** | | | | | | | | |
| **PsycINFO** | | | | | | | | |
| Title | 7.4 | 2.7 | 1.4 | .7 | 1.0 | .7 | .8 | .6 |
| Abs | 15.0 | 6.4 | 2.3 | 1.9 | 1.6 | 2.2 | 2.0 | 1.3 |
| **Sociological Abstracts** | | | | | | | | |
| Title | | 8.0 | 6.3 | 5.2 | 5.0 | 4.0 | 4.2 | 5.8 |
| Abs | | 11.6 | 19.3 | 12.7 | 6.7 | 8.5 | 11.0 | 11.5 |
| **ProQuest Social Science Journals** | | | | | | | | |
| Title | | | | | | 1.8 | 1.9 | 1.3 |
| Abs | | | | | | 2.2 | 4.0 | 4.3 |
| **Worldwide Political Science Abstracts** | | | | | | | | |
| Title | | | | .9 | 2.3 | 2.7 | 4.3 | 4.0 |
| Abs | | | | 2.7 | 3.9 | 5.1 | 10.2 | 8.7 |

*Note.* The terms used for these searches included various spellings of antisemitism and antisemite, as well as "Jew-hatred," "anti-Jewish," and "prejudice against Jews." Abs = abstracts.

[a] The number shown in the 2010s column is based on database searches covering the 5-year period from January 1, 2010, through December 31, 2014.

*Table 3. Items mentioning "Holocaust"(but not antisemitism) in titles and abstracts in four social science research databases.*

| | 1940s | 1950s | 1960s | 1970s | 1980s | 1990s | 2000s | 2010s[a] |
|---|---|---|---|---|---|---|---|---|
| **Number of items per decade** | | | | | | | | |
| **PsycINFO** | | | | | | | | |
| Title | 0 | 0 | 4 | 14 | 177 | 241 | 334 | 348 |
| Abs | 0 | 1 | 2 | 24 | 369 | 531 | 671 | 824 |
| **Sociological Abstracts** | | | | | | | | |
| Title | | 0 | 1 | 12 | 95 | 296 | 249 | 292 |
| Abs | | 0 | 8 | 29 | 73 | 304 | 436 | 600 |
| **ProQuest Social Science Journals** | | | | | | | | |
| Title | | | | | | 217 | 251 | 208 |
| Abs | | | | | | 210 | 358 | 386 |
| **Worldwide Political Science Abstracts** | | | | | | | | |
| Title | | | | 9 | 54 | 106 | 243 | 232 |
| Abs | | | | 9 | 100 | 111 | 341 | 394 |

*Note.* This table shows the number of items in the database that used the word "Holocaust" but did not also refer to antisemitism (using various spellings of the terms "Jew-hatred," "anti-Jewish," or "prejudice against Jews"). Abs = abstracts.

[a] For purposes of comparison with earlier decades, the number shown in the 2010s column is a heuristic projection obtained by doubling the actual number of entries obtained in database searches covering the 5-year period from January 1, 2010, through December 31, 2014.

the 1980s, items dealing specifically with the Holocaust outnumber items dealing with antisemitism per se. Thus, for example, in PsycINFO, in the decade from 2000 to 2009, there were 334 items that mentioned "Holocaust" in the title (without also mentioning antisemitism) and 73 items that mentioned antisemitism (three of which also mentioned the Holocaust).

Table 4 shows for each decade items mentioning the Holocaust (but not antisemitism per se) as a percentage of total items on the Holocaust and antisemitism. This table shows a clear and dramatic upward time trend in the PsycINFO and Sociological Abstracts data. The trend is also present, but less dramatic, in Worldwide Political Science Abstracts. More important than the time trend, however, is the fact that for the past few decades, especially in PsycINFO, the number of studies dealing with the Holocaust greatly outnumbers studies of all other antisemitism combined. It is also worth noting that this tendency to focus on the Holocaust has mainly been increasing as we get further and further away from that event and in the face of contentions of growing present-day antisemitism.

*Table 4. Percentage of total antisemitism items in four social science research databases included because "Holocaust" was mentioned.*

| | **Number of entries per decade** | | | | | | | |
|---|---|---|---|---|---|---|---|---|
| | 1940s | 1950s | 1960s | 1970s | 1980s | 1990s | 2000s | 2010s[a] |
| **PsycINFO** | | | | | | | | |
| Title | 0 | 0 | 19 | 50 | 83 | 88 | 82 | 80 |
| Abs | 0 | 2 | 7 | 39 | 87 | 83 | 73 | 81 |
| **Sociological Abstracts** | | | | | | | | |
| Title | | 0 | 3 | 23 | 54 | 70 | 65 | 63 |
| Abs | | 0 | 7 | 22 | 40 | 53 | 56 | 64 |
| **ProQuest Social Science Journals** | | | | | | | | |
| Title | | | | | | 76 | 75 | 75 |
| Abs | | | | | | 72 | 67 | 63 |
| **Worldwide Political Science Abstracts** | | | | | | | | |
| Title | | | | 45 | 51 | 63 | 64 | 60 |
| Abs | | | | 20 | 54 | 49 | 52 | 54 |

*Note.* Abs = abstracts.
[a] The percentages shown in the 2010s column are based on database searches covering the 5-year period from January 1, 2010, through December 31, 2014.

Another calculation supports this conclusion. In addition to searches for antisemitism and for the "Holocaust," title searches were conducted for mentions of Nazism using words other than "Holocaust"; these terms included "Hitler," "Nazi," and "Nazism." The results of all three were combined to yield the total number of times that items mentioned antisemitism, the Holocaust, Hitler, Nazis, or Nazism. In the period from 1950 through 1989, PsycINFO items mentioning antisemitism accounted for 22.5% of these entries. For the period from 1990 to the end of 2014, that percentage had dropped to 12.9%. Similarly, in Sociological Abstracts, items mentioning antisemitism accounted for 33.5% in the 1950 to 1989 period. From 1990 to the end of 2014, the percentage had dropped to 23.4%. (The calculation was not made for the other databases, as they did not cover the earlier period.)

*References to antisemitism in the Muslim and Arab world*

Table 5 shows the number of items in the four social science research databases referring to antisemitism in the Muslim and Arab world. The results indicate very clearly that that was virtually no social scientific interest at all in the topic in any of the databases until the 2000s. An examination of the few items that were found shows that the abstract searches, which yielded a high of five items per decade, probably overstated the degree of interest in the topic, as most of these entries seemed only peripherally concerned about antisemitism in the Muslim and Arab world. Since 2000, there has been a small but clear increase in the number of items dealing with the topic. During recent years, the automated searches returned numbers that were slightly higher than those reported in the table; a few entries were removed upon individual inspection when it was apparent that they had been wrongly classified. In other words, they may have mentioned "antisemitism" and "Islam" in the same abstract without dealing in any way with antisemitism in the Islamic world. In any case, the actual number of items removed on these grounds amounted to only a handful. Inasmuch as the absolute number of entries dealing with Muslim and Arab antisemitism was so small, no attempt was made to formally take into account the size of the databases in each decade by calculating the numbers on a "per 10,000 entries in

*Table 5. References to antisemitism in the Islamic and Arab world in titles and abstracts in four social science research databases.*

| | 1940s | 1950s | 1960s | 1970s | 1980s | 1990s | 2000s | 2010s[a] |
|---|---|---|---|---|---|---|---|---|
| | | | | **Number of entries per decade** | | | | |
| | | | | **PsycINFO** | | | | |
| Title | 0 | 0 | 0 | 0 | 0 | 0 | 7 | 6 |
| Abs | 1 | 1 | 1 | 0 | 0 | 0 | 29 | 20 |
| | | | | **Sociological Abstracts** | | | | |
| Title | | 0 | 0 | 0 | 0 | 1 | 2 | 8 |
| Abs | | 0 | 5 | 5 | 1 | 5 | 27 | 24 |
| | | | | **ProQuest Social Science Journals** | | | | |
| Title | | | | | | 0 | 1 | 6 |
| Abs | | | | | | 3 | 34 | 50 |
| | | | | **Worldwide Political Science Abstracts** | | | | |
| Title | | | | 0 | 1 | 0 | 8 | 12 |
| Abs | | | | 2 | 5 | 5 | 49 | 50 |

[a] For purposes of comparison with earlier decades, the number shown in the 2010s column is a heuristic projection obtained by doubling the actual number of entries obtained in database searches covering the 5-year period from January 1, 2010, through December 31, 2014.

the database" basis. However, it is clear that even in recent years when the databases were huge, the topic of Muslim antisemitism commanded little interest among social scientists who published their works in outlets covered by the major research databases. The topic has been virtually ignored by the major American Psychological Association-sponsored journals.

There is no simple answer to the question of how much research on any given topic is enough, and regarding antisemitism this issue is especially complex and controversial. We return to this matter later, but Table 6 presents some relevant data concerning the PsycINFO database. This table shows the total number of items by decade that were returned by a search of the subject field for "prejudice OR racism OR discrimination." This broad search no doubt includes a number of irrelevant items and excludes others that belong. But an examination of search results shows it to be a reasonable indicator of the interest of psychologists in racism and prejudice over the decades. Table 6 shows three types of antisemitism entries—antisemitism, antisemitism plus the Holocaust, and Muslim and Arab anti-Semitism—as a fraction of the total number of social scientific studies of racism, prejudice, and discrimination. The results indicate that about two to five of every 1,000 items on prejudice in PsycINFO focus on antisemitism, except during the 1940s and 1950s when there was somewhat more interest. When we add the word "Holocaust" to the searches, the number rises substantially, starting in the 1980s. The number of items reaches the 27 or 28 out of every 1,000. Table 6 also shows, again, that interest in Muslim anti-semitism has been close to nonexistent among psychologists.

*Table 6. Antisemitism items as a fraction of overall items dealing with prejudice, racism, and discrimination (by decades).*

| | PRD items (subject field) | AS items (title field) | AS/PRD | AS + H items (title field) | AS + H/PRD | MAS (title field) | MAS/PRD |
|---|---|---|---|---|---|---|---|
| 1940-1949 | 527 | 37 | .070 | 37 | .070 | 0 | .0000 |
| 1950-1959 | 1028 | 20 | .019 | 20 | .019 | 0 | .0000 |
| 1960-1969 | 3985 | 17 | .004 | 21 | .005 | 0 | .0000 |
| 1970-1979 | 7153 | 14 | .002 | 28 | .004 | 0 | .0000 |
| 1980-1989 | 7526 | 35 | .005 | 212 | .028 | 0 | .0000 |
| 1990-1999 | 10197 | 34 | .003 | 275 | .027 | 0 | .0000 |
| 2000-2009 | 14658 | 73 | .005 | 407 | .028 | 7 | .0005 |
| 2010-2014 | 8841 | 44 | .005 | 174 | .020 | 3 | .0000 |

*Note.* AS = antisemitism; PRD = prejudice, racism, and discrimination; AS + H = antisemitism and Holocaust; MAS = Muslim and Arab antisemitism.

## STUDY 2: CONTENT ANALYSIS OF PSYCHOLOGICAL STUDIES

### Goals and methodology

Some questions of interest could not be answered by computerized searches of the research databases. We wanted to know more about the content of recent items that dealt with antisemitism—specifically, whether antisemitism was the focus of the item, a significant concern, or simply something mentioned in passing. We also wanted to determine which aspects of antisemitism were covered, which eras, and which regions. We additionally hoped to gain some insight into which psychological and intellectual approaches were employed and which explanations of antisemitic phenomena were favored.

Table 1 shows that from 1990 until the end of 2014, 401 items in the PsycINFO database mentioned antisemitism in their abstracts. The present study used a similar and overlapping sample identified by searching the subject field of PsycINFO for the term "antisemitism" during the period from 1990 through the end of June 2014. This search produced an initial listing of 314 entries. Thirty-six entries were removed from the sample because they were missing abstracts, they were duplicates, or for some other reason they obviously didn't belong. When the term "Holocaust" was added to the subject field search, the total number of items rose to 1,808, again confirming the extent to which the Holocaust dominates research on antisemitism. Thus, about 83% of total items covering the Holocaust and antisemitism are included because they mention the Holocaust; this percentage is comparable to the percentages reported in Table 4 from the title and abstract searches. The Holocaust items were omitted from the present content analytic study because our primary goal was to understand coverage of contemporary Jew-hatred.

The sample included 278 items, which were coded by the authors. To assess intercoder reliability, a random subsample of 20 abstracts was coded by both coders. All of the variables included in the study had agreements on at least 17 of the items (85%), except for whether the abstract dealt with "antisemitism in literature or intellectual life" (80%), whether antisemitism was a current problem (80%), primary era of focus (70%), and whether a social psychological approach was mentioned or obviously implied (60%). On abstracts where there was disagreement, subsequent analysis generally revealed that it was a close judgment call where both coders saw merit in the other choice. Problems in classifying the era of the item stemmed from incomplete information in abstracts, as well as a tendency for some authors to mention briefly eras that were not important to their studies.

## Description of the abstract sample

Sixty percent of studies focused on antisemitism, 27% had antisemitism as a significant concern but not the central focus, and 13% mentioned it only in passing. These 13% were dropped from subsequent analyses, leaving a sample of 242 abstracts to be analyzed. Seventy-two percent of the PsycINFO items were journal articles; the remainder included books (7%), book reviews (6%), book chapters (9%), and other formats. *Patterns of Prejudice* published significantly more articles on antisemitism than any other journal indexed in PsycINFO. *The International Journal of Applied Psychoanalytic Studies* and *Current Psychology* each dedicated an issue to antisemitism. Other journals publishing at least three articles on antisemitism from 1990 through the end of July 2014 were *American Behavioral Scientist, American Ethnologist, American Imago, Ethnic and Racial Studies, International Journal of Psychoanalysis, Journal of Analytical Psychology,*

*Journal of Counseling and Development, Journal of Psychohistory, Journal for the Scientific Study of Religion, Pastoral Psychology, Political Psychology, Psychoanalysis and History, Psychological Reports, Scandinavian Psychoanalytic Review*, and *Women and Therapy*. It is worth noting that psychoanalytic journals are fairly well represented on this list, but most social psychology journals are absent.

Sixty-nine percent of entries in the final sample, or 166 journal articles, books, chapters, and other items, had antisemitism as their main concern; for the remainder, antisemitism was a significant concern among other equally important or more important concerns. Sixty-three items appeared in the 1990s, 135 in the 2000s, and 44 from 2010 through the end of June 2014. When the frequency of articles is analyzed by year, we note that 2007 had many more items (34) than any other year—double the next closest. This can be explained partly by the previously noted appearance of two special issues on the topic in that year (Kressel, 2007b; Ostow, 2007; Simon & Schaler, 2007). As the absolute number of items appearing each year is very low, year-by-year fluctuations are highly subject to influence by dedicated journal issues, edited books, and authored books, which generate multiple reviews in the journals. The years 2003 and 2005 tied for the second highest number of yearly items, so it is also possible—given publication time lags—that the wave of interest in Islamic extremism following 9/11 and the Second Intifada led to some increase in the number of studies on antisemitism.

It is important to recall that the term "Holocaust" was not used to locate items for this study. Still, some items in the sample did examine or, at least, mention the Holocaust. About 58% of items in the sample mentioned antisemitism as a contemporary, post-1970 issue, whereas 42% were limited to discussions of pre-1970 antisemitism. Another way of classifying the era under discussion found that 41% dealt more with post-1970 antisemitism, 43% dealt more with pre-1970 antisemitism, and 16% dealt with both periods equally, or the coder could not determine which era was dealt with more. Yet another method of determining the era of focus found that 3% dealt with the pre-1900 era, 31% the era from 1900-1970, 34% the post-1970 period; the remainder dealt with multiple periods, the period was unspecified, or the coder couldn't determine the period under study. The coding scheme did not permit us to determine whether studies of the contemporary period focused on the most recent decades or the period from 1970 through the end of the 20th century. The data show clearly that there has been little emphasis on studying pre-1900 antisemitism. Of course, it would have been surprising if psychologists, given their methods and interests, had focused heavily on the distant past. Still, one main finding is that when psychologists have studied antisemitism, they very often have been looking to the past rather than analyzing contemporary attitudes and behaviors.

Although the lion's share of research on the "Holocaust" was not included in the sample, still about 30% of the abstracts on antisemitism mentioned the Holocaust or Nazi antisemitism. Seventy percent did not. We must recall that this analysis is based only on what is in the abstract, and it is likely that some of those items also mentioned the Holocaust in the text. Another category scored the number of abstracts dealing with antisemitism in Germany and Austria, now and in the past. Twenty-eight percent of the items mentioned antisemitism in these places.

The data provide some information about which other regions received the most attention from psychologically oriented researchers. Twenty-four percent of abstracts mentioned antisemitism in Southern or Western Europe, 13% in the Communist world or the countries that formerly were Communist, 3% in Canada, and 21% in the United States. This latter figure is noteworthy, as research shows the United States to have among the lowest levels of anti-semitism in the world. The research emphasis on America, of course, may be explained partly as a consequence of the interests of American psychologists and their access to research subjects in the United States.

Two percent of items—a handful—dealt with Black, African American, or African antisemitism; here it is worth noting that surveys consistently show both that (a) African Americans score higher that other Americans on most measures of antisemitism, and (b) most African Americans do not display anti-semitic attitudes (Anti-Defamation League, 2013; Sigelman, 1995). Only nine items made any reference to antisemitism coming from the left, although this has been identified by major antisemitism scholars as one locus of contemporary hostility to Jews (see Norwood, 2013; Wistrich, 2012).

Twelve percent of the sample, or 30 items, dealt with some aspect of anti-semitism in the Arab world or the world of Islam. Most of these (24) dealt with the post-1970 period. The year of publication was positively associated with the likelihood of mentioning antisemitism in the world of Islam or the Arab world ($r = .21$).

An unexpectedly large percentage (26%) of the items covered antisemitism in literary or intellectual life. Many of these pieces had to do with antisemitic proclivities or suspected proclivities among noted psychologists or intellectuals, mainly from the past. Twelve percent of the items treated antisemitism in some context related to psychotherapy. There was no immediately apparent theme or focus to these items; some dealt with approaches to handling the emergence of antisemitism in therapy sessions, some dealt with the impact of antisemitism on the life experiences of noted therapists, and some explored charges of anti-semitism directed against various therapists.

Classifying the explanatory frameworks used by authors was not a simple matter. About 29% of the works made some reference to psychoanalytic explanations of Jew-hatred. The relative prominence of these theories is con-sistent with the presence of several psychoanalytically oriented journals among those journals publishing research on antisemitism during the period under study. Our category for assessing social psychological and/or sociological explanations of antisemitism was intended to be a broadly conceived measure, and it did not achieve adequate intercoder reliability. We included all explanations based on theories in sociology or social psychology, mentioned or implied, excluding psychoanalytic theories. This admittedly flawed category appeared in about 43% of the works.

Overall, 77% of works made no reference at all to the religious roots of anti-semitism, but 12% made some mention of origins in some aspect of Christianity and 4% made some reference to origins in Islam. An additional 7% made references to religious origins that were either unspecified or related to both Christianity and Islam. It should be noted that our coding scheme here aimed at being inclusive; if there was any way one might infer that the author saw a religious root to the bigotry, the coder marked the category. Thus, we think that the numbers we found probably overstate the degree of researcher interest in the religious roots of Jew-hatred.

Very few works (12) referred to the "new antisemitism" by name; the "new antisemitism" refers to Jew-hatred based on extreme and disproportionate hostility to the state of Israel (e.g., Chesler, 2003; Nirenstein, 2005). Only eight items made reference to antisemitism as an inappropriate label for criticism of the state of Israel. Thus, debates on these matters in the mass media do not show up prominently in the psychological research literature.


## Discussion

The results of the two empirical studies enable us to address some of the questions raised by the literature review. The major ADL study of global anti-semitism, the Pew studies, and other research all point to the Muslim world as the epicenter of contemporary global antisemitism, yet social scientists have devoted very little of their attention to understanding this problem. The United States, a relatively tolerant place for Jews (Kressel, 2016), has been studied far more frequently than many nations where Jew-hatred has reached in recent years what might arguably be described as epidemic proportions. Although there has been some growth since 2000 in the number of studies dealing with contemporary antisemitism in the Muslim world, the absolute number of studies remains small. Many non-Muslim countries with high levels of anti-semitism (according to work done by the ADL and others)—for example, Greece and South Korea—have also been ignored by researchers.

Still, the topic of antisemitism in general has not been ignored, especially if we count research on the Holocaust. In a general sense, all research on the Holocaust can be viewed as research on antisemitism; however, analyzed on a case-by-case basis, much of this body of work may attend little to antisemitism per se, focusing instead on more general matters (Bromley & Russell, 2010). The authors, in any event, regard the body of research on the Holocaust (and other genocides) as tremendously important; in fact, one of us wrote a book and several articles on the topic (Kressel, 1996). We also believe that much work remains to be done in educating present and future generations about the Nazi destruction of European Jewry. However, with so few social scientists researching antisemitism, we wonder whether it is wise to devote so much research and teaching effort to this topic, if it comes at the expense of ignoring massive contemporary antisemitism.

We further think it is important to link discussions of the Holocaust to assessments of contemporary Jew-hatred. In our view, the Holocaust certainly can be conceptualized as an instance of "man's inhumanity to man," but it also cannot reasonably be divorced from its particular lessons regarding antisemitism. We also wonder whether the lessons of the Holocaust have truly been learned if a current generation of social scientists is neglecting the study of Jew-hatred where it is presently most widespread and intense—in the Muslim and Arab world.

Moreover, the lack of research attention to contemporary Jew-hatred has other consequences. Preliminary empirical studies have shown that English-language textbooks on prejudice and discrimination tend to treat antisemitism as a phenomenon of the past; this is not surprising, as such books draw upon the research literature for source material. Similarly, a wide range American college courses on prejudice and racism tend to devote little attention to antisemitism in the contemporary world, especially when it comes from Muslim and Arab sources (Kressel, in press).


## CONCLUSION

Of course, any study of this sort faces the question of how much research attention is enough. One argument is that it is hard to escape the conclusion that much more research on contemporary antisemitism, especially in the Muslim world, is needed when considers three things: (a) the tiny percentage of studies on racism and prejudice that have addressed the topic, (b) the abundant empirical evidence that such prejudice exists in copious amounts and considerable intensity, and (c) the history of the destructive potential of Jew-hatred, not only for Jews but for everyone whom it touches.

Viewed against the death toll of the Holocaust or other recent genocides, the body count from contemporary antisemitism has been relatively small. But there have been many violent incidents nonetheless, including numerous and ongoing terrorist attacks on Jews. Some Jewish residents have reported that they do not feel comfortable remaining in some parts of Western Europe, especially if they wear visible signs of their religious or ethnic affiliation (Bremner, 2015). Clearly, Jews are not comfortable in many Muslim-majority countries. If the Iranian regime obtains nuclear weapons, one can certainly imagine many more Jewish causalities as an outgrowth of that regime's officially sanctioned Jew-hatred. The social psychology of genocide and the social psychology of terrorism both teach that murderous movements develop step by step along a continuum of destruction (Kressel, 1996; Staub, 1989). It does not make sense to ignore a bubbling cauldron of hatred on grounds that its contents still remain mostly in the pot. Genocidal antisemitism, in the past, was a consequence of well-intentioned (and not-so-well-intentioned) people ignoring lesser forms of prejudice, and American academia in the 1930s has been criticized for playing a significant part in perpetuating this blindness (Norwood, 2009).

In our view, the "spent force" theory persists partly because there are far lower levels of antisemitism in countries where most English-language social scientific research is conducted. In the United States—the largest single source of social science research—not only do most Americans show little evidence of overt antisemitism, but Jews are generally well regarded. Religion researchers indeed have documented empirically that Judaism may not be the not best liked religion in the United States, but it may well be the least detested (Putnam & Campbell, 2010). Researchers may to some degree infer from their immediate experiences in their local surroundings that antisemitism in the United States is continuing its decline and this conclusion may not be incorrect (Kressel, 2016). However, the situation outside the United States is very different.

Trying to decide which variety of bigotry is the worst is a fool's game—or a scoundrel's. However, contemporary antisemitism is an understudied and poorly understood phenomenon. More research is needed, and more attention is needed in courses and textbooks on racism, prejudice, and social injustice. If college courses and texts do not address the problem of Jew-hatred as a contemporary global phenomenon, many students will likely assume that the problem does not persist.

Although antisemitism in the United States and Canada survives with real consequences (e.g., Gold, 2004; Marcus, 2007; Saxe, Sasson, Wright, & Hecht, 2015), researchers should probably focus more on places where manifestations of the bigotry are more severe and more common. These places are harder to study and require more innovative and flexible research strategies. But such approaches exist, and new ones can be devised. See, for example, Jaspal (2014) for interesting and innovative methods for studying Jew-hatred in the Muslim world.

To conclude, although the Holocaust can be the source of many lessons, one of its most basic must surely be the danger of antisemitism run amok. To the extent that the Holocaust is becoming a general metaphor for extreme evil and man's inhumanity to man, that lesson may be lost. The scarcity of studies addressing humanity's "longest hatred" and its "lethal obsession" (Wistrich, 1991, 2010) in the pre-Holocaust period may also have deleterious consequences. As the 2,000-year history of Jew-hatred is forgotten, the attention of scholars and students may move away from understanding its roots in two of world's major religions—Christianity and Islam (Gilbert, 2010; Perry & Schweitzer, 2002). As we have seen, these religious sources are understudied by most contemporary researchers. Perhaps, more generally, on all matters regarding antisemitism, the problem is less the lack of good research and more the lack of *attention* to the pockets of good research that exist in psychology and the other social sciences.

One more subtle factor lies at the root of the neglect of contemporary antisemitism by researchers and teachers in the social sciences. There may persist among many social scientists a belief that all bigotry and prejudice is fundamentally similar, arising from the same spots in the human psyche and drawing strength from the same ideological, sociopolitical, and economic sources. To the extent that researchers believe this to be true, they may assume that antisemitism can be understood through extrapolations from general theories of prejudice. However, such an assumption would seem inconsistent with historical arguments why Jew-hatred is to a large extent sui generis.

Jews, after all, have been accused of deicide in the Christian tradition and of perpetual treachery in the Islamic tradition; such charges may disappear for a while, but they have an unfortunate tendency to reemerge after periods of dormancy when circumstances are ripe (Perry & Schweitzer, 2002). Many admired Christian saints and leaders have argued for the doctrinal necessity of keeping Jews down; in Islam, the founding tradition includes official approval of the mass murder of the Banu Qurayza Jews as well as expulsion of other Jewish tribes from Arabia (Bostom, 2008; Fatah, 2010). It is especially hard to erase justifications for discrimination when they come from sacred leaders. At another level, the very fact that Jew-hatred has existed for so long in so many cultures has contributed to its perceived credibility in the eyes of many; thus, antisemites often make the point that so many people with different outlooks in different times and civilizations could not possibly all have been wrong. This argument reemerges with every new wave of antisemitism, even when the phenomenon has undergone fundamental metamorphosis. Finally, unlike many (but not all) other targets of prejudice, Jews more often have been hated not because they are seen as inferior but because of their perceived potency and cleverness. Envy has been a critical source of Jew-hatred in many contexts. Thus, Jews have been hated for their religion, race, social status, politics, and national state, yet each new incarnation of antisemitism builds upon the old. The phenomenon is complex. Clearly, mere extrapolations from general theories of prejudice and racism will not do.

## ACKNOWLEDGMENT

An earlier version of this article was presented on July 5, 2015, at the 38th Annual Meeting of the International Society of Political Psychology, in San Diego, CA.

## REFERENCES

Ackerman, N.W., & Jahoda, M. (1950). *Anti-semitism and emotional disorder, a psychoanalytic interpretation.* New York, NY: Harper.

Adorno, T.W., Frenkel-Brunswick, E., Levinson, D.J., & Sanford, R.N. (1950). The authoritarian personality.

Allport, G.W. (1954). *The nature of prejudice.* Cambridge, MA: Addison-Wesley.

Anti-Defamation League. (2013). *ADL poll: Anti-semitic attitudes in America decline 3 percent but deep-seated anti-semitic beliefs linger [press release].* Retrieved from http://www.adl.org/press-center/press-releases/anti-semitism-usa/adl-poll-anti-semitic-attitudes-america-decline-3-percent.html.

Anti-Defamation League. (2014). *ADL global 100: An index of antisemitism.* Retrieved from http://global100.adl.org/public/ADL-Global-100-Executive-Summary.pdf.

Anti-Defamation League. (2015). *New ADL poll finds dramatic decline in anti-Semitic attitudes in France; significant drops in Germany and Belgium: Update of ADL global 100 Poll shows anti-Semitism markedly higher among Muslims in six European countries [press release].* Retrieved July 1, 2015, from http://www.adl.org.

Arendt, H. (1951). *The origins of totalitarianism.* New York, NY: Harcourt, Brace.

Bard, M. (2014). *Death to the infidel: Radical Islam's war against the Jews.* New York, NY: Palgrave-Macmillan.

Ben-Itto, H. (2005). *The lie that wouldn't die: The protocols of the elders of zion.* Portland, OR: Vallentine Mitchell.

Berenbaum, M. (Ed.). (2008). *Not your father's antisemitism: Hatred of the Jews in the twenty-first century.* St. Paul, MN: Paragon House.

Berman, P. (2010). *The flight of the intellectuals.* Brooklyn, NY: Melville House.

Bostom, A.G. (Ed.). (2008). *The legacy of Islamic antisemitism: From sacred texts to solemn history.* Amherst, NY: Prometheus Books.

Bremner, C. (2015, January 3). *Jews flee France in record numbers to escape anti-semitism.* The Times (London). Retrieved from www.lexisnexis.com/hot topics/lnacademic.

Bromley, P., & Russell, S.G. (2010). The Holocaust as history and human rights: A cross-national analysis of Holocaust education in social science textbooks, 1970-2008. *Prospects, 40,* 153-173. doi:10.1007/s11125-010-9139-5.

Brownfeld, A.C. (2005, April). Playing the Holocaust card: Are charges of anti-semitism used to silence debate? *Washington Report of Middle East Affairs,* 58-59. Retrieved from http://www.wrmea.org/2005-april/israel-and-judaism.html.

Chesler, P. (2003). *The new anti-semitism: The current crisis and what we must do about it.* San Francisco, CA: Jossey-Bass.

Cohen, B. (2014). *Some of my best friends: A journey through twenty-first century antisemitism.* Berlin, Germany: Edition Critic.

Cohen, F. (2013). Muslim anti-semitism: The by-product of existential fear: A review of the sons of pigs and apes: Muslim antisemitism and the conspiracy of silence. *Peace and Conflict, 19,* 425-426. doi:10.1037/a0034842.

Cohen, F., Jussim, L., Harber, K.D., & Bhasin, G. (2009). Modern anti-semitism and anti-Israeli attitudes. *Journal of Personality and Social Psychology, 97,* 290-306. doi:10.1037/a0015338.

Cohen, J. (2009). The accusation of anti-semitism as moral blackmail: Con-servative Jews in France and the Israel-Palestinian conflict. *Human Architecture, 7* (2), 23-33.

Cohen, N. (2007). *What's left? How the left lost its way.* New York, NY: Harper Perennial.

Dershowitz, A. (1997). *The vanishing American Jew.* Boston, MA: Little Brown.

Fatah, T. (2010). *The Jew is not my enemy: Unveiling the myths that fuel Muslim anti-semitism.* Plattsburgh, NY: McClelland & Stewart.

Fine, R. (2009). Fighting with phantoms: A contribution to the debate on anti-semitism in Europe. *Patterns of Prejudice, 43,* 459-479. doi:10.1080/0031 3220903339006.

Fineberg, M., Samuels, S., & Weitzman, M. (2007). *Antisemitism, the generic hatred: Essays in memory of Simon Wiesenthal.* Portland, OR: Vallentine Mitchell.

Foxman, A.H. (2003). *Never again? The threat of the new anti-semitism.* San Francisco, CA: HarperSanFrancisco.

Foxman, A.H. (2007). *The deadliest lies: The Israel lobby and the myth of Jewish control.* New York, NY: Palgrave Macmillan.

Foxman, A.H. (2010). *Jews and money: The story of a stereotype.* New York, NY: Palgrave Macmillan.

Gilbert, M. (2010). *In Ishmael's house: A history of Jews in Muslim lands.* New Haven, CT: Yale University Press.

Ginsberg, T. (2011). The deployment of "anti-semitism," "controversy," and "neutrality" in Ginsberg v. NCSU. *Arab Studies Quarterly, 33* (3/4), 228-243.

Glock, C.Y., & Stark, R. (1966). *Christian beliefs and antisemitism.* New York, NY: Harper & Row.

Gold, N. (2004). Sexism and antisemitism as experienced by Canadian Jewish women: Results of a national study. *Women's Studies International Forum, 27* (1), 55-74. doi:10.1016/j.wsif.2003.12.005.

Harrison, B. (2006). *The resurgence of anti-semitism: Jews, Israel, and liberal opinion.* Lanham, MD: Rowman & Littlefield.

Heni, C. (2013). *Antisemitism, a specific phenomenon: Holocaust trivialization, Islamism, post-colonial and cosmopolitan anti-Zionism.* Berlin, Germany: Edition Critic.

Iganski, P., & Kosmin, B.A. (Eds.) (2003). *The new antisemitism? Debating Judeophobia in 21st-century Britain.* London, UK: Profile.

Jaspal, R. (2014). *Antisemitism and anti-Zionism: Representation, cognition, and everyday talk.* Farnham, UK: Ashgate.

Jikeli, G. (2015). *Antisemitic attitudes among Muslims in Europe: A survey review.* New York, NY: Institute for the Study of Global Antisemitism and Policy. Retrieved from http://isgap.org.

Khalidi, R. (2006). *The iron cage: The story of the Palestinian struggle for statehood.* Boston, MA: Beacon Press.

Kressel, N.J. (1996). *Mass hate: The global rise of genocide and terror.* New York, NY: Plenum.

Kressel, N.J. (2003). Antisemitism, social science, and the Muslim and Arab world. *Judaism, 207/208,* 225-245.

Kressel, N.J. (2004). The urgent need to study Islamic antisemitism. *Chronicle of Higher Education, 50* (27), B14-B15.

Kressel, N.J. (2007a). *Bad faith: The danger of religious extremism.* Amherst, NY: Prometheus Books.

Kressel, N.J. (2007b). Mass hatred in the Muslim and Arab world: The neglected problem of anti-semitism. *International Journal of Applied Psychoanalytic Studies, 4,* 197-215. doi:10.1002/aps.140.

Kressel, N.J. (2012). *The sons of pigs and apes: Muslim antisemitism and the conspiracy of silence.* Dulles, VA: Potomac Books.

Kressel, N.J. (2016). How to interpret American poll data on Jews, Israel and anti-semitism. In S.K. Baum, N.J. Kressel, F. Cohen-Abady, & S.L. Jacobs (Eds.), *New world, old hate: North American antisemitism* (pp. 3-32). Boston, MA: Brill.

Kressel, N.J. (in press). The great failure of the antiracist community: How and why Muslim antisemitism has been neglected in English-language textbooks, research and the classroom. In E.G. Pollock (Ed.), *Antisemitism and anti-Zionism: Past and present.* Boston, MA: Academic Studies Press.

Küntzel, M. (2007). *Jihad and Jew-hatred: Islamism Nazism and the roots of 9/11.* New York, NY: Telos Press.

MacShane, D. (2008). *Globalising hatred: The new antisemitism.* London, England: Weidenfeld & Nicolson.

Marcus, K.L. (2007). The resurgence of anti-semitism on American college campuses. *Current Psychology: A Journal for Diverse Perspectives on Diverse Psychological Issues, 26* (3-4), 206-212. doi:10.1007/s12144-007-9014-6.

Mearsheimer, J.J., & Walt, S.M. (2008). *The Israel lobby and U.S. foreign policy.* New York, NY: Farrar, Straus and Giroux.

Nirenstein, F. (2005). *Terror: The new anti-semitism and the war against the west.* Hanover, NH: Smith and Kraus.

Norwood, S.H. (2009). *The Third Reich in the ivory tower: Complicity and conflict on American campuses.* New York, NY: Cambridge University Press.

Norwood, S.H. (2013). *Antisemitism and the American far left.* New York, NY: Cambridge University Press.

Ostow, M. (2007). Commentary on "mass hatred in the Muslim and Arab world: The neglected problem of anti-semitism" by Neil Kressel. *International Journal of Applied Psychoanalytic Studies, 4,* 221-234. doi:10.1002/aps.152.

Perry, M., & Schweitzer, F.M. (2002). *Antisemitism: Myth and hate from antiquity to the present.* New York, NY: Palgrave Macmillan.

Pew Global Attitudes Project. (2008). *Unfavorable views of Jews and Muslims on the increase in Europe.* Retrieved from http://www.pewglobal.org.

Putnam, R.D., & Campbell, D.E. (2010). *American grace.* New York, NY: Simon & Schuster.

Rickman, G.J. (2011). *Hating the Jews: The rise of antisemitism in the 21st century.* Boston, MA: Academic Studies Press.

Riley, K.L., & Totten, S. (2002). Understanding matters: Holocaust curricula and the social studies classroom. *Theory and Research in Social Education, 30,* 541-562. doi:10.1080/00933104.2002.10473210.

Saxe, L., Sasson, T., Wright, G., and Hecht, S. (2015). *Antisemitism on the college campus: Perceptions and realities.* Maurice and Marilyn Cohen Center for Modern Jewish Studies, Brandeis University. Retrieved from http://www.brandeis.edu/cmjs/pdfs/birthright/AntisemitismCampus072715.pdf.

Schoenfeld, G. (2004). *The return of anti-semitism.* San Francisco, CA: Encounter Books.

Shapiro, E.S. (2015, February). Global antisemitism? *First Things, 250,* 19-21.

Sigelman, L. (1995). Blacks, whites, and anti-semitism. *Sociological Quarterly, 36*, 649-656. doi:10.1111/j.1533-8525.1995.tb00458.x.

Simon, R.J., & Schaler, J.A. (2007). Anti-semitism the world over in the twenty-first century. *Current Psychology: A Journal for Diverse Perspectives on Diverse Psychological Issues, 26*, 152-182.

Singal, J. (2014, May 14). *The ADL's Flawed anti-semitism survey.* New York Magazine. Retrieved from http://nymag.com/scienceofus/2014/05/adls-flawed-anti-semitism-survey.html.

Small, C. (2013). *Global antisemitism: A crisis of modernity* (Vol. 5). New York, NY: Institute for the Study of Global Antisemitism and Policy.

Staub, E. (1989). *The roots of evil: The origins of genocide and other group violence.* New York, NY: Cambridge.

Stember, C.H., Sklare, M., & Salomon, G. (1966). *Jews in the mind of America.* New York, NY: Basic Books.

Taguieff, P. (2004a). *Les protocols des sages de sion: Faux et usages d'un faux.* Paris: Berg International Fayard.

Taguieff, P. (2004b). *Rising from the muck: The new antisemitism in Europe.* Chicago: Ivan R. Dee.

Timmerman, K.R. (2003). *Preachers of hate: Islam and the war on America.* New York, NY: Crown.

Tobin, G.A., & Sassler, S.L. (1988). *Jewish perceptions of antisemitism.* New York, NY: Plenum.

Tobin, G.A., & Ybarra, D.R. (2008). *The trouble with textbooks: Distorting history and religion.* Lanham, MD: Lexington Books. United States Department of State. (2008). *Contemporary global anti-semitism.* Washington, DC: U.S. Department of State.

United States Department of State. (2008). *Contemporary global anti-semitism.* Washington, DC: U.S. Department of State.

Wistrich, R.S. (1991). *Antisemitism: The longest hatred.* New York, NY: Schocken Books.

Wistrich, R.S. (2010). *A lethal obsession: Anti-semitism from antiquity to the global jihad.* New York, NY: Random House. Wistrich, R.S. (2012). *From ambivalence to betrayal.* Lincoln: University of Nebraska Press.

Wistrich, R.S. (2012). *From ambivalence to betrayal.* Lincoln: University of Nebraska Press.

# The German People and the Holocaust:
# New Sources, New Insights

Susanna Schrafstetter and Alan E. Steinweis*

On 14 November 1938, four days after the nationwide "Kristallnacht" pogrom had wrought devastation on the Jews of Germany, the chief of the Gestapo office of the northwest city of Bielefeld circulated a memorandum to the local secret police offices in the region. He was interested in collecting key pieces of information about the pogrom and its consequences.[1] Which synagogues had been destroyed by fire? Which had suffered severe damage? Which Jewish-owned businesses had been destroyed or damaged, and what was the financial extent of the damages? Which homes of Jews had been vandalized? Which Jews had been killed or injured? What property had been plundered from Jews? In all, the inquiry listed fourteen sets of questions. The last of these related to "responses to the action in the population." The Gestapo wanted to know who had uttered criticism of the pogrom, where they lived, and precisely what it was that they had said. Scientific surveys of popular opinion of the sort that we take for granted today did not exist in Germany in 1938. But this did not mean that the Nazi regime made no effort to keep track of what the population was thinking about a wide variety of questions, including the persecution of the Jews.

---

* Susanna Schrafstetter is Associate Professor of History at the University of Vermont. Alan E. Steinweis is the L & C Miller Distinguished Professor of Holocaust Studies at the University of Vermont, where he also serves as Director of the Miller Center for Holocaust Studies. The following text has been adapted from the Introduction to *The Germans and the Holocaust: Popular Responses to the Persecution and Murder of the Jews*, eds. Susanna Schrafstetter and Alan E. Steinweis (New York: Berghahn Books, 2016). The authors are grateful to Berghahn Books for permission to republish the text here.

[1] Stapostelle Bielefeld, "Rundverfügung, 14 November 1938," in *Die Juden in den geheimen NS-Stimmungsberichten, 1933-1945*, ed. Otto Dov Kulka and Eberhard Jäckel (Düsseldorf: Droste Verlag, 2004), document 357 (document 2558 on the accompanying CD-ROM). A translation of the printed collection is available as Otto Dov Kulka and Eberhard Jäckel, eds., *The Jews in the Secret Nazi Reports on Popular Opinion in Germany, 1933-1945*, trans. William Templer (New Haven: Yale University Press, 2010). It should be noted that both editions are accompanied by a CD-ROM containing a much more extensive collection of documents only in German.

One of the responses to the inquiry from the Bielefeld Gestapo office came from the mayor of Amt Borgentreich, an administrative district consisting of several communities located in the triangle between Paderborn, Kassel, and Göttingen.[2] Writing on November 17, the mayor summarized the situation in the following way:

> Large segments of the population did not understand the operation, or rather, they did not want to understand it. Some people felt sorry for the Jews. In particular, they felt sorry for them because their property was damaged and because male Jews were sent to concentration camps. To be sure, these sentiments were not shared by the entire population, but I would estimate that around here at least 60 percent of the population thought in this way.

On its surface, this document provides a useful piece of information in a fairly straightforward way. But there are several respects in which the document points up the difficulty of assessing the responses of "ordinary Germans" to the persecution of the Jews. First, it is probably impossible to ascertain whether the mayor's quantitative estimate rested on shoot-from-the-hip speculation or from a more serious consideration of the facts. Second, it is extremely difficult to adjust for the possible biases that lay behind the mayor's estimate. Was he understating the extent of popular criticism of the pogrom to avoid creating the impression that he had failed to instill sufficient enthusiasm for Nazism in his population? Or was he exaggerating the extent of the criticism because he had considered the pogrom a foolish mistake by the regime's leadership? If we were to presume that his estimate was accurate, then what are we to make of it? Do we emphasize the 60 percent majority of the population that reacted to the pogrom disapprovingly, or do we focus on the very sizable 40 percent minority that did not respond negatively? Then there is the question of whether and to what extent Borgentreich may be considered typical, and, if not, what peculiarities of the community may account for the actions and attitudes of its citizens? Even when we have a detailed, contemporary document purporting to report systematically on public opinion, historians remain confronted by perplexing questions of interpretation.

At the time of the Kristallnacht, Lore Walb was a nineteen-year-old woman living in Alzey, a town located about thirty-five miles southwest of Frankfurt. Walb, who possessed literary and journalistic ambitions, kept a diary in which she recorded her impressions of the major events of her day. She was an admirer of the Nazi regime. Decades later she would observe that she had been convinced that "everything the Nazis did is correct, the National Socialist behaves

---

2 Bürgermeister Amt Borgentreich, "Betrifft: Aktion gegen die Juden am 10.11.1938," November 17, 1938, in Kulka and Jäckel, *Stimmungsberichten*, document 357 (2624 on the CD-ROM).

honorably, is a good person, righteous, reliable, truthful." She had embraced the truth of the Nazi slogan "The Jews are our misfortune" and had acknowledged the necessity of marginalizing and persecuting them.

After World War II, Walb became a journalist, retiring in 1979 after twenty years as director of the Women and Family Department of Bavarian State Radio. She published her diary in 1997.[3] Rather than let the document speak for itself, Walb engaged critically with her own record of events from the Nazi era. One question she put to herself almost sixty years after the event was why her diary from 1938 ended with an entry for November 6. In retrospect she recognized what had been her inability at the time to confront the "the terror against the German Jews." She had possessed full knowledge of what had taken place during Kristallnacht and sensed that a great crime had been committed, but she could not process the information lest it undermine her "entire orientation system," which had been based on a positive attitude toward Nazism.[4] The dissonance between her ideology and her instinctive grasp of the wrongness of the pogrom generated feelings of shame, and the shame, in turn, resulted in silence. The momentous events of November 1938 simply remained absent from her diary.

The Walb diary offers important lessons for historians. Even such a so-called ego document, which was not intended for publication at the time it was created, can contain significant discrepancies between what was witnessed and what was recorded. People withhold the truth not only from others, but also from themselves. And when they report on events in their diaries, correspondence, or memoirs, they can do so in ways that are distorting, self-serving, or based on faulty memory.

The reliability and biases of source materials arises time and again in the academic research. Scholars and students of all historical events should, of course, remain conscious of the strengths and limitations of their sources. But special vigilance is in order when examining key questions relating to the response of ordinary Germans to the persecution and mass murder of the Jews between 1933 and 1945. What did they know, when did they know it, and how did they react? From the time of the Holocaust into the present day, these questions have generated intense and often emotional disagreements. When carried out in the public arena, such disagreements have often been based more on emotion and the received wisdom of collective memory than on a sober examination of the historical evidence.[5] Communities of memory in many countries and across several generations have had a strong emotional stake in

---

[3] Lore Walb, *Ich, die Alte—ich, die Junge: Konfrontation mit meinen Tagebüchern 1933-1945* (Berlin: Aufbau-Verlag, 1997).

[4] Id., 118-121.

[5] Geoff Eley, ed., *The "Goldhagen Effect": History, Memory, Nazism; Facing the German Past* (Ann Arbor: University of Michigan Press, 2000).

the question, and their perceptions have often been shaped by anger, guilt, and shame. As the Nazi period recedes into the past, however, the passing of generations offers the opportunity for a soberer and more nuanced appreciation of this difficult history.

The discrepancy between the historical significance of the topic, on the one hand, and the fragmentary nature of the evidence that is available to analyze it, on the other, has posed a continual challenge to scholars. Fortunately, historians have persisted in their efforts to find new and previously overlooked sources. Serious scholarship in this area has accelerated, rather than slowed, in the past few years.[6] The aim of this essay is to encapsulate some of these recent findings and to present some new, original work that is still in progress. The summaries that follow reflect the enormous sophistication with which contemporary scholars have been approaching a controversial subject.

When considering German responses to the persecution and mass murder of the Jews, it is important to remain very cognizant of the chronology and geography of the Holocaust. Between January 1933 and September 1939, Nazi measures directly affected only German Jews as well as those who lived in areas annexed by the Reich in 1938—Austria and the Sudetenland region of Czechoslovakia—and in the Reich "Protectorate" established over the Czech lands of Bohemia and Moravia in 1939. Accounting both for the emigration of German Jews as well as for the acquisition of these new territories, the number of Jews subjected to direct Nazi control hovered at around half a million throughout the prewar period. It was only with the advent of World War II in Europe in September 1939 that the number of Jews under German control grew from hundreds of thousands into millions.

During the prewar period, Nazi Jewish policy radicalized over time. After the Nazi takeover of the German government in 1933, Jews were subjected to economic boycotts, expelled from a variety of professions, deprived of their

---

6 Key works have included (listed in order of publication): Otto Dov Kulka, "'Public Opinion' in National Socialist Germany and the 'Jewish Question,'" *Zion: Quarterly for Research in Jewish History* 40 (1975): 186-290 (in Hebrew, with English summary and German-language documents); a condensed version of the Kulka article published entirely in English can be found in *Jerusalem Quarterly* (1982), no. 25, 121-44, and no. 26, 34-45; Ian Kershaw, *Popular Opinion and Political Dissent in the Third Reich, Bavaria 1933-1945* (Oxford: Clarendon Press, 1983); Sarah Gordon, *Hitler, Germans, and the "Jewish Question"* (Princeton: Princeton University Press, 1984); David Bankier, *The Germans and the Final Solution: Public Opinion under Nazism* (Oxford: Wiley-Blackwell, 1992); Peter Longerich, *"Davon haben wir nichts gewusst!" Die Deutschen und die Judenverfolgung 1933-45* (Munich: Siedler Verlag, 2006); Frank Bajohr and Dieter Pohl, *Der Holocaust als offenes Geheimnis. Die Deutschen, die NS-Führung und die Alliierten* (Munich: C.H. Beck, 2006); Bernward Dörner, *Die Deutschen und der Holocaust. Was niemand wissen wollte, aber jeder wissen konnte* (Berlin: Propyläen Verlag, 2007).

citizenship, and placed under pressure to have their property Aryanized, that is, transferred to non-Jewish Germans. This process of marginalization was carried out in a legal and bureaucratic fashion, although it was accompanied by a good deal of humiliation, intimidation, and waves of genuine violence.[7] The Kristallnacht pogrom saw violence on an unprecedented level, with the mass destruction of synagogues and Jewish-owned businesses, widespread physical attacks on Jews in their homes and on the streets, and the arrest of about 30,000 Jewish men, who were transferred to concentration camps.

After the outbreak of war in September 1939, the Jews who remained in Germany were removed from their homes and compelled to live in segregated apartment buildings or other facilities. They were also subjected to forced labor. Beginning in 1941 and extending into the following year, the majority of German Jews were deported to ghettos and camps in Poland and the Baltic region, where most of them died or were murdered. German Jews who survived the Holocaust fell mainly into one of several categories: those who lived in mixed-marriages with their so-called Aryan spouses and could thereby avoid deportation; those who managed to go underground and escape deportation; those who were deported initially to the Theresienstadt (Terezin) ghetto but managed to avoid subsequent deportation to Auschwitz; and those who were selected for forced labor in the east and remained fortunate enough to escape the gas chambers. The deportation of most of Germany's Jews was common knowledge throughout the German population.

The measures targeted at German Jews after the onset of the war unfolded roughly in parallel with the persecution of Jews in countries occupied by or allied with Germany. By the early summer of 1941, about two million Jews were subjected to compulsory ghettoization and forced labor in German-occupied Poland. Policies of persecution were implemented across German-dominated Europe. Information about these developments was by no means kept secret from the German population.

The Nazi regime initiated the systematic mass murder of Jews upon its invasion of the Soviet Union in June 1941. These killings took the form of mass shootings carried out by mobile killing units across a large swath of territory in eastern Poland, the western Soviet Union (Ukraine and White Russia), and the Baltic States. In this first phase of the Final Solution, German special task forces organized and carried out the killings, often receiving significant assistance from local militias whose members were motivated by a combination of antisemitism and an eagerness to ingratiate themselves with their new German overlords. These killings were officially carried out in secret, but it has been well docu-

---

7 Michael Wildt, *Hitler's Volksgemeinschaft and the Dynamics of Racial Exclusion: Violence against Jews in Provincial Germany, 1919-1939* (New York: Berghahn Books, 2012).

mented that information about them leaked back into Germany. This was recently confirmed again dramatically by the publication of the wartime diary of Friedrich Kellner,[8] a court civil servant in the small Hessian town of Laubach. On 28 October 1941, Kellner made the following entry in his diary:

> A soldier on leave reports to have been an eyewitness to horrible atrocities in the occupied region of Poland. He watched as naked Jewish men and women, who were lined up in front of a long, deep ditch, were shot at the base of their skulls by Ukrainians at the order of the SS and fell into the ditch. The ditch was then shoveled closed. Screams still came out of the ditch!

Kellner was convinced that "99 percent of the German population bears indirect or direct guilt for the present situation. One may only conclude: 'it will serve us right' [*mitgegangen – mitgefangen*]."

The information about the massacres that was available to Kellner, who lived in a small, provincial town, was also available to millions of other Germans. So the debate revolves not around whether German *could* have known, but more around other questions: How widespread was such knowledge? Did the information suffice for Germans to understand that the massacres were part of a systematic program of mass murder? To what extent were Germans distracted by other war-related issues? Through what kinds of psychological mechanisms did Germans avoid, repress, or deny such information?

In 1942 the mass murder program expanded to include all of the Jews of Europe. In this new phase of the Final Solution, the killing was shifted from mass shooting by mobile task forces to a more centralized, industrialized process, based at extermination camps in German-occupied Poland. A team of German officials, coordinated by Adolf Eichmann, organized the deportations of Jews from their home countries to the killing sites. Deportations on such a scale could hardly be carried out in secret, and knowledge about them was widespread across Europe. The key question for historians is not whether ordinary Germans knew of these deportations—they obviously did—but rather whether they comprehended the ultimate fate of the deported Jews and, to the extent that they did, how they reacted. In Germany after World War II, the refrain "Davon haben wir nichts gewusst" ("We didn't know about that") was often invoked when the subject of the mass murder of the Jews was raised. This assertion can be assessed on the basis of concrete historical evidence.

These questions were the focus of a symposium convened by the Center for Holocaust Studies at the University of Vermont on April 22, 2012. Under the title "The German People and the Persecution of the Jews," the symposium brought together a group of internationally recognized experts on the social

---

8 Friedrich Kellner, *"Vernebelt, verdunkelt sind alle Hirne." Tagebücher 1939-1945*, 2 vols., eds. Sascha Feuchert et al. (Göttingen: Wallstein Verlag, 2011).

history of Nazi Germany. Revised versions of the papers were collected into the volume *The Germans and the Holocaust: Popular Responses to the Persecution and Murder of the Jews*, eds. Susanna Schrafstetter and Alan E. Steinweis (New York: Berghahn Books, 2016). The remainder of this essay will summarize the most important argument of the contributions to this volume.

Four of the six essays in the volume focus on the period from 1933 to 1945, while the other two frame the Nazi period within the broader context of modern German history. The first essay, written by Richard S. Levy, is titled "Anti-Semitism in Germany, 1890-1933: How Popular Was It?" Levy's definition of antisemitism will strike some readers as unconventional. Levy distinguishes between anti-Jewish prejudice, on the one hand, and antisemitism, on the other—the latter, in his opinion, being an actual willingness to act on the basis of anti-Jewish animus, politically or even through acts of violence. According to Levy, from the 1890s through about the midpoint of World War I, anti-semitism—as he defines it—was not especially widespread in Germany. To be sure, "most Germans did not like Jews," but few Germans were prepared to act on that sentiment. German Jews enjoyed legal equality and prospered economically and professionally, even though they suffered under various forms of social exclusion.

World War I, Levy argues, and especially the German defeat in 1918, consti-tuted the turning point. After November 1918, there was a significant increase in the number of Germans willing to join or support political movements that advocated concrete anti-Jewish measures. Levy cites evidence for this transfor-mation in a variety of places, including growing membership in the Nazi Party and other right-wing political associations, as well as a dramatic rise in the desecrations of synagogues and Jewish cemeteries. There was also a notable intensification of rhetorical attacks against Jews in public, which must be considered as part and parcel of the coarsening of Germany's political culture during the Weimar Republic. As Levy points out, when fourteen million Germans voted Nazi in July 1932, they lent their support to a political party that had quite openly advocated antisemitic positions since 1919. While not all of these voters were antisemites, they were also not willing to defend the rights or the dignity of Germany's Jewish citizens. By the time of the Nazi takeover in January 1933, a large number of Germans had abandoned any commitment to the equality of Jews.

The first of the volume's four contributions on the Nazi era is Frank Bajohr's analysis of "German Responses to the Persecution of the Jews as Reflected in Three Collections of Secret Reports." Bajohr compares and contrasts three published collections of documents that are indispensable to historians working in this area. The first, which Bajohr refers to as the "regime-internal reports," is a set of slightly under four thousand documents collected from a large number of German archives as part of a joint German-Israeli project and made available in 2003.[9] The second collection consists of reports on the persecution of the Jews filed by foreign diplomats stationed in Germany. Bajohr himself led the project that collected and published these consular reports in 2011.[10] The third collection, published in 1980, is composed of reports produced during the Nazi era by the German Social Democratic Party (SPD) in exile.[11]

The regime-internal reports, according to Bajohr, distinguish mainly between Germans and Jews, while the diplomatic and SPD reports "present a more complex structure" of German society, differentiating among Jews, Germans, and Nazis. Bajohr also contends that the diplomatic reports tended to offer a "functionalistic" rather than ideological interpretation of Nazi anti-Jewish measures. The diplomats often pointed to the use of antisemitism as a nationalistic mobilization strategy, believing that it had to be understood within the context of the regime's other priorities. Despite such differences, all three sets of reports converged with respect to the prewar period. They agreed on the existence of "a general antisemitic consensus" in German society and at the same time agreed that there was widespread rejection of anti-Jewish violence.

For the war years, Bajohr explains, the comparison among the three sets of documents is more difficult. The SPD collection ends in 1940, and the number of consular reports dwindled as countries broke diplomatic relations with Germany. Only the regime-internal reports offer a substantial body of relevant documentation. From there it emerges, as Bajohr observes, that "many Germans were speaking about the treatment of the Jews in a kind of mélange of bad conscience, fears of future retribution, and projection of guilt." Many interpreted the bombardment of their cities by the Allies as punishment for the persecution of the Jews. Bajohr concludes his essay by noting that the Nazi regime did not require a popular consensus in favor of mass murder. The general antisemitic consensus in German society provided the regime with the room for maneuver it needed in order to plan and carry out the Final Solution.

The third essay, by Wolf Gruner, is also focused on documentation, although in this case on a single, unpublished archival source. Titled "Indifference? Participation and Protest as Individual Responses to the Persecution of the Jews as Revealed in Berlin Police Logs and Trial Records, 1933-45," Gruner's contribution offers a detailed, richly textured portrait of how non-Jewish Berliners interacted with their Jewish neighbors during the Nazi era. The article

---

[9] See note 1 above.

[10] Frank Bajohr and Christoph Strupp, eds., *Fremde Blicke auf das "Dritte Reich." Berichte ausländischer Diplomaten über Herrschaft und Gesellschaft in Deutschland 1933-1945* (Göttingen: Wallstein Verlag, 2011).

[11] Klaus Behnken, ed., *Deutschland-Berichte der Sozialdemokratischen Partei Deutschlands (Sopade), 1934-1940*, 7 vols. (Frankfurt: Petra Nettelbeck/Zweitausendeins, 1980).

is based on research in the log books of almost three hundred police precincts in Berlin, which was both Germany's largest city and the site of the country's largest Jewish population. The chapter is also based on an analysis of a large number of cases of *Heimtücke* (literally: malice), the term used by the Nazi regime to designate the crime of maligning the national leadership and its policies. In view of Berlin's status as the national capital, the country's largest city, the focal point of Germany's Jewish community, and the center of progressive politics and culture, Berlin was, it must be emphasized, by no means a typical German community.

Gruner examines two waves of organized attacks against Jewish-owned businesses in Berlin in 1933 and 1935. These attacks, he contends, created social space and legitimacy for further anti-Jewish violence and contributed to the gradual marginalization of Jews in German society. But, as Gruner emphasizes, the attacks were greeted with disapproval and disgust by a great many Berliners. The Berlin police recorded numerous instances in which residents of the city expressed compassion for the Jews and outrage over their treatment. This was true not only in 1933 and 1935, but also applied to reactions to the Kristallnacht pogrom in November 1938. Negative reactions to the pogrom within the German population have been well documented, but often with an emphasis on popular objections to the destruction of property.[12] In contrast, Gruner argues that the condemnations recorded by the Berlin police did not focus on property, but rather on moral outrage and humanitarian concerns for the Jewish victims of the pogrom. At the same time, Gruner explains, a significant number of Berliners profited from the misfortune of their Jewish neighbors and did what they could to exploit the situation to their own advantage.

Gruner provides a detailed analysis of the Berliners' reactions to the deportation of the city's Jews in 1941 and 1942. "No one in Berlin could overlook the deportation of tens of thousands of Jews." Here again, the response was complex. On the one hand, some Berliners were happy to take possession of property and dwellings left behind by the deported Jews. Others denounced Jews who had tried to escape deportation by going underground. On the other hand, many expressed concern about the fate of the Jews and responded very negatively to information about mass murder that had leaked back to Berlin. It is precisely this last issue that lies at the heart of Peter Fritzsche's contribution, "Babi Yar, but not Auschwitz: What Did Germans Know about the Final Solution?" Through a careful reading of the diaries kept by Germans during the

---

[12] For example, Bankier, *Germans and the Final Solution*, and Kershaw, *Popular Opinion*. Gruner's argument in this volume supports the assertion in Longerich, *"Davon haben wir nichts gewusst,"* that the moral outrage of the German population at the pogrom has probably been underestimated.

Nazi era,[13] Fritzsche offers a detailed analysis of popular responses to Nazi Jewish policy against the chronologies of deportation, mass murder, and the Allied bombing of German cities.

Fritzsche grounds his argument in an analysis of the complex interrelationship among four distinct categories of knowledge. The first of these was the widespread knowledge within Germany of the massacres of Jews that took place in Eastern Europe in the second half of 1941. The second was the even more widespread knowledge of the mass deportation of German Jews to that region in late 1941 and 1942. The third was the experience of the Allied bombing of Germany, which over time "eroded knowledge of the Final Solution" and fueled Germans' fantasies of Jewish revenge. And the fourth was the official propaganda campaign of 1943, in which the mass murder of the Jews was tacitly acknowledged in the regime's warnings about the potential catastrophic consequences of a German defeat.

Fritzsche arrives at the conclusion that ordinary Germans possessed extensive knowledge of the Final Solution but that this knowledge was incomplete and "deformed" by the convergence of factors described above. Germans, he argues, knew more about the mass executions of Jews by the *Einsatzgruppen* in 1941 and 1942 than they would learn about the subsequent killings in the extermination camps.

In the volume's final contribution devoted to the Nazi period, "Submergence into Illegality: Hidden Jews in Munich, 1941-45," Susanna Schrafstetter shifts the focus to *Rettungswiderstand*, or resistance through rescue. This term originated from the impulse to recognize those few Germans who came to the aid of Jews as resisters against Nazism. But the term is also problematic inasmuch as it obscures the actions of the hidden Jews as active agents who helped determine their own destinies. The concept of *Rettungswiderstand* also deflects attention away from the fact that hidden Jews also encountered ordinary Germans as traitors, blackmailers, or robbers.

While stories of hidden Jews have been well documented in Berlin, other regions in Germany have received far less attention. Schrafstetter examines several cases in which Jews from the Bavarian capital of Munich survived the Holocaust in hiding with support from non-Jews. For her sources, she relies on memoirs, compensation claims by Jewish survivors, de-Nazification files, and applications to Yad Vashem for inclusion of rescuers as "Righteous among the Nations." Individual compensation claims, in particular, form a hitherto underused set of sources for the study of German-Jewish experiences, as survivors had to account for their whereabouts during the war in their applications.

---

[13] See also Peter Fritzsche, *Life and Death in the Third Reich* (Cambridge, MA: Harvard University Press, 2008), which relies mainly on memoirs and published diaries.

Schrafstetter explains the peculiarities of Munich that determined the patterns of underground life and prospects for its success. When the deportations of German Jews began in the fall of 1941, there were about 3,400 Jews still living in Munich, amounting to only a small fraction of the remaining Jewish population in Berlin. Of these 3,400, about one hundred survived in hiding inside the city of Munich, in the city's rural hinterland, or on an odyssey through the entire country. For each of these Jews to remain in hiding successfully, the active support of several non-Jews was necessary. Some of these acted out of altruism, others acted out of greed, while still others acted out of a complex combination of these motivations. Even though the absolute number of Jews who survived underground was relatively small, the cases do underscore the existence of non-Jewish Germans who were prepared to run the considerable risk of lending assistance. Unlike in Berlin, the overall number of Jews left in Munich in 1941 was small, and therefore organized structures designed both to aid and to exploit fleeing Jews did not develop to the same degree as in Berlin.

The volume concludes with Atina Grossmann's chapter "Where Did All 'Our' Jews Go? Germans and Jews in Post-Nazi Germany." Any assessment of German popular responses to the Holocaust must also consider the extent to which antisemitism persisted in German society after the defeat of the Nazi regime. Grossmann's contribution examines German attitudes toward Jewish Holocaust survivors, mainly from Eastern Europe, who lived as displaced persons (DPs) in postwar Germany. Most, although not all, lived in camps administered by the United Nations Relief and Rehabilitation Administration (UNRRA), concentrated primarily in the American and British zones of occupation. Despite their status as refugees whose presence in Germany was intended to remain temporary, the Jewish DPs came into close contact with the German population. They interacted on a variety of levels: economic, personal, and even sexual.

Grossmann describes how these interactions were influenced by "lingering stereotypes and renovated traditional prejudices against *Ostjuden*" in German society. Given the nature of their situation, many of the DPs were compelled to engage in black-market commerce, which reinforced antisemitic stereotypes about Jewish dishonesty and lack of respect for honest labor. When the American military government extended a protective hand over the DPs, some Germans took this as a validation of their suspicion that the Allies had been in the hands of the Jews.

Resentment toward the perceived alliance between Americans and Jews intensified as a result of American support of Jewish reparations claims. Many Germans regarded such claims as further evidence of Jewish "money-grubbing," which in this case they saw as threatening the normalization of postwar German society and undermining the nation's economic recovery. To be sure, Gross-

mann points out, most postwar Germans denied harboring antisemitic prejudice. But, she concludes, "there should be no doubt that the philo-Semitism or
shamed silence that tabooized anti-Jewish acts or utterances often attributed to
postwar Germany not only coexisted with, but was often overwhelmed by, a
strong and entirely acceptable anti-Semitism."

Taken together, the contributions to this volume convey a broad picture of
how antisemitism functioned in German society during the first half of the
twentieth century. A broadly based set of prejudices was endowed with political
potency by the trauma of war and defeat between 1914 and 1918. Antisemitism
became a central tenet of the German Right during the Weimar Republic, and a
large segment of German society, even if not actively antisemitic, was not
repelled by the Nazi movement's obsession with Jews. Between 1933 and 1939,
the Nazi regime consolidated an antisemitic consensus in German society. The
consensus did not extend to include anti-Jewish violence, but it did provide the
hard-core antisemites who governed Germany with the room for maneuver that
they needed to pursue their maximalist agenda. Once that regime had been
destroyed through external intervention, politically organized antisemitism
ceased to be a factor, but many of the foundational prejudices persisted in the
German population.

More than twice as much time has elapsed between the end of World War II
and today than between World War I and 1945. How German attitudes toward
Jews have developed since the immediate postwar period is a question that lies
beyond the scope of this essay. But we should note that Germany today is a far
different—and better—place today than it was in 1945.

# Resentment, Anxiety, and Careerism:
## Accounting for Antisemitism in the Academy and among the Intelligentsia

Barry A. Kosmin*

INTRODUCTION

Recently I have been professionally involved in surveys of two very different Jewish populations—one of Jewish university students on fifty-five American campuses and the other of Jewish leaders in twenty-eight European countries. Yet a majority of respondents in both surveys reported great concern about antisemitism.

A 2013 Pew Survey of US Jews revealed that older American Jews are unlikely to meet antisemitism, but young Jews do meet it.[1] Where in the United States today is one most likely to find antisemitism? Where do swastikas appear? Not on shop windows, at railroad stations, or at sports stadiums but on university campuses on Jewish fraternity houses and on banners at campus demonstrations.

And what of the situation in Europe? In 2015, on behalf of the Joint Distribution Committee, we surveyed several hundred European Jewish community leaders in five languages. They were asked who their allies were in the struggle against antisemitism "always or most of the time." A majority of 54 percent said their national governments were supportive, while only 13 percent said intellectuals and academics acted as friends of the Jews. Conversely when asked who they saw as a threat to Jewish communities "always or sometimes," 33 percent of Western European leaders cited intellectuals and academics compared to 18 percent in former Soviet bloc nations.[2] This hostility to Jews, particularly among

---

* Research Professor of Public Policy and Law and Founding Director of the Institute for the Study of Secularism in Society and Culture (ISSSC) at Trinity College, Hartford, Connecticut.

[1] *A Portrait of Jewish Americans: Findings from a Pew Research Center Survey of U.S. Jews* (Washington, DC: Pew Research Center, 2013).

[2] Barry A. Kosmin, *Third Survey of European Jewish Leaders and Opinion Formers, 2015* (Paris: JDC International Centre for Community Development, 2016), 22.

"

Western European intellectuals, requires explanation, for it is not a new phenomenon. My task here is to try to explain why Jews have a problem in the Academy and at universities.


## I. THE INTELLIGENTSIA

The author Tom Wolfe made a distinction between intellectuals and people of intellectual achievement. In his definition, "an intellectual feeds on indignation" and is "a person who is knowledgeable in one field but speaks only in others."[3] As we shall see, history reveals that Jews are disproportionately the targets of such indignation.

Jewish history in the modern period has been dominated by the experience and fate of Jews in Germany and Russia—countries of intellectual pretensions and powerful ideas. The intelligentsia in nineteenth-century Russia was the first to be aware of itself as such. It created an astonishing high culture of writers and thinkers, painters, and musicians that became the admiration of Europe. But certain elements had a messianic twist, drawing on monkish notions of the "Third Rome" and folk memories of Holy Rus and the Slav soul, to give Russia a universal mission to redeem the fallen, materialist world with a higher spirit of Christian Orthodox truth and justice. Dostoevsky—no friend of the Jews—was the exemplar of this movement. When Tsarism fell, mystical memories of Russia as moral savior of mankind were transferred to the new Soviet Union in the official formula "the fatherland of the international proletariat and the toilers of the world."[4] This gave Russia, transformed into the USSR, another universal mission as the worker's fatherland that would lead the world to socialism and finally the nirvana of communism. History records that Jews became victims of both the materialistic and the spiritual versions of Russia's forays into utopian idealism. One result of this Russian-Soviet connection was that antisemitism— in the form of Marxist-Leninist anti-capitalism and anti-Zionism—found a place in leftist ideology and progressive anti-colonialist politics worldwide. Historic antisemitism produced the anti-Zionism we see today.

One of the fallacies under which many Jews and other well-meaning people suffer is that educated people are inherently less prejudiced than the uneducated. Racism and nastiness, like crime generally, is commonly associated with the so-called "lower orders." Conventional wisdom holds that prejudice equals ignorance and therefore can be fought—and ultimately eradicated—through education. More education begets more enlightenment.

---

[3] "Notable & Quotable: Tom Wolfe," *Wall Street Journal*, November 1, 2015.

[4] *Programme of the Communist International* (Moscow: Comintern Sixth Congress, 1929).

In 1776, Adam Smith postulated that "an instructed and intelligent people ... are always more decent and orderly than an ignorant stupid one."[5] This belief is a twin version of a worldview that contrasts the physicality and boorishness of the benighted with the refinement and sophistication of the learned class. Both relate to a theory of individual pathology and the mob's proclivity to violence. The frustrated, inarticulate, alienated, and angry simpleton is juxtaposed with the balanced and mentally healthy scholar.

The problem with this psychological construct is that it relies on class prejudice rather than historical facts. It is a liberal myth. The educated clergy in Europe were not always less cruel than the illiterate peasants. Architects are not necessarily morally superior or better behaved than truck drivers. The focus of this paper is the realm of ideas and the world of the intellect. Ideas are crucial to explaining the problem of the efficacy of hate. Ideas are what people have always been prepared to live, kill, and die for. The famous economist, John Maynard Keynes suggested that:

> Ideas ... both when they are right and when they are wrong, are more powerful than is commonly understood. Indeed the world is ruled by little else. I am sure the power of vested interests is vastly exaggerated compared to the gradual encroachment of ideas.[6]

Nietzsche claimed the root of political psychology is resentment—*ressentiment*—and that it was the distinguishing social emotion of modern societies.[7] His thesis was that the success of other people or groups breeds resentment and that resentment in turn breeds hate. It is a passion bound up with the identity of the one who feels it, who rejoices in damaging others by virtue of their membership of the targeted group. Moreover, particularly in insecure epochs, hatred brings order out of chaos and decision out of uncertainty.

Once we understand that ideas are both freestanding and powerful, we gain an indispensable tool for combating the insidious argument that victims cause the hatred they receive. Jewish behavior or actions can—and do—affect the arguments and narratives of enemies. Yet this recognition does not mean that the actions and behavior of Jews, rather than their simple existence, causes antisemitism. In the 1930s, it was the individual economic or racial Jew who was the claimed cause of German, European, and global misery. Biological antisemitism logically requires a genocidal solution. Anti-Zionism offers a very different—and theoretically less murderous—prospect. The logical targets for eradication are Zionist political institutions and the leadership, rather than the whole

---

5 Adam Smith, *The Wealth of Nations* (1776), Book V, Chapter 1, Part 3, Article II.

6 John Maynard Keynes, *The General Theory of Employment, Interest and Money* (London: Palgrave Macmillan, 1936), 384.

7 Friedrich Nietzsche, *On the Genealogy of Morals* (London: T. Fisher Unwin, 1899).

population. The assault on these political institutions may involve violence and death, but it is not inevitable. Hence the proponents claim neither to be racist nor genocidal.

This argument is particularly relevant to the contemporary university campus in North America and Western Europe. The current atmosphere in many arts and social science departments requires one to revisit the thesis of the attack of French essayist Julien Benda in *La Trahison des clercs* (1927). Benda accused the intelligentsia of his day of:

> abandoning their attachment to the traditional panoply of philosophical and scholarly ideals [whereby] for centuries [they] had exhorted men … to deaden the feeling of their differences [and instead had come to support and favor] the intellectual organization of political hatreds.[8]

This distinguished French writer once defined intellectuals as people whose function was to defend eternal and disinterested values like justice and reason. Events in twentieth century Europe were to disappoint him.

One fact often ignored about interwar Europe and the build-up to the Holocaust is that in Germany and Austria the Nazis controlled the universities before they controlled the streets or the organs of government. Looking back at the history of the Third Reich, what stands out is the conspicuous absence of resistance by means of faculty strikes or student protests to the mass expulsions of Jewish staff and students from universities. One result, as Daniel Goldhagen showed in his controversial book *Hitler's Willing Executioners*, was that the *Einsatzgruppen*, the mobile killing squads of the Eastern Front in 1941-1942,[9] were definitely a "better class of German." There was a surprisingly high proportion of university graduates among these fanatics and psychopaths.

All this makes prescient the words of that leading light of the *Aufklärung*, the German Enlightenment, Georg Christoph Lichtenberg (1742-1799), who suggested:

> Today we are trying to spread knowledge everywhere. Who knows if in centuries to come there will not be universities for re-establishing our former ignorance?[10]

Lichtenberg, one of the most famous scientists of the eighteenth century, might just as aptly be describing today's postmodernist academics. Education, after all, has two core aspects: the cognitive and the affective. Thus I would suggest that

---

[8] Roger Kimball, "The Treason of the Intellectuals and the 'Undoing of Thought,'" introduction to Julien Benda, *The Treason of the Intellectuals*, trans. Richard Aldington (London and New York: Routledge, 2017), x-xi.

[9] Daniel Goldhagen, *Hitler's Willing Executioners* (New York: Alfred Knopf, 1996).

[10] Georg Christoph Lichtenberg, *Aphorisms*, trans. R.J. Hollingdale (London: Penguin Classics, 1990), 58.

knowledge is essentially a good thing. By themselves, ideas are neither good nor bad. It is through their application—and combination—that the two become deleterious. This is the problem—and danger—of modernity: the linkage of knowledge with bad ideas. One could claim that the most dangerous people have not been soldiers or scientists but political philosophers and ideologues.

The problem here resides in the unenlightened or retrograde center of higher education. In fact, this phenomenon emerged much earlier—and in the highest echelons of academia—than even Lichtenberg could have imagined. For it was the greatest German historian of his age, Heinrich von Treitschke, professor of history at the University of Berlin, who in 1879 recoined and endorsed the slogan "Die Juden sind unser Unglück" (the Jews are our misfortune) first used by Martin Luther.[11] While von Treitschke died in 1896, his idea lived on. Fifty years later this identical phrase became both a slogan and a rallying cry, as it was to be incorporated into the banner of the Nazi Party newspaper *Der Stürmer* in order to inspire Hitler's stormtroopers. Postmodern fashion would classify such things as coincidences. Yet it is significant that that the editor and publisher of this newspaper, Julius Streicher, was to be tried at Nuremberg and executed for crimes against humanity. Why? In the words of the prosecution, Streicher was convicted of "poisoning the minds of a generation."[12] It is a resounding endorsement of Keynes's axiom about the power of ideas. It is equally important for us to note this innovation in international law. Ideas and words have consequences: The incitement to hatred and advocacy of murder and genocide is as much a crime as the act itself.

The issue of antisemitism in higher education is important because of the crucial role universities play in society, culture, and the modern economy. They control access to the professions and act as gatekeepers to positions of power and authority, as well as most high-paying occupations. For the past 150 years, the key to socioeconomic advancement in most countries has been access to higher education. In order to understand the problem, let us examine the historical record in detail.


## II. JEWS AND THE UNIVERSITY PROBLEM

Historically, universities in the Christian West and in the Muslim lands were founded and run by religious bodies. Theology was the preeminent discipline and other subjects were only slowly added to the syllabus. Thus Jews were

---

[11] Martin Luther, *Von den Juden und Ihren Lügen* [On the Jews and their lies] (1543).

[12] Ben S. Austin, "The Nuremberg Trials: Brief Overview of Defendants and Verdicts," n.d., http://www.jewishvirtuallibrary.org/brief-overview-of-defendants-and-verdicts-at-nuremberg-trials.

excluded on religious grounds from most European universities from the Middle Ages until the era of Jewish civil emancipation in the nineteenth century. The main exception was Italy's medical schools, especially in Padua. The Protestant Reformation did not change this exclusion policy. The Protestants maintained a strong commitment to replacement theology—the belief in the transfer of the Covenant from the Jewish people to the Christian Church, which has become the "New Israel." In addition, Martin Luther was fiercely anti-semitic. In 1543, Luther published *On the Jews and Their Lies*, in which he wrote that the Jews are a "base, whoring people, that is, no people of God, and their boast of lineage, circumcision, and law must be accounted as filth." They are full of the "devil's feces … which they wallow in like swine."[13] Tolerance was slow in emerging across Europe. In England, the universities of Oxford, Cambridge, and Durham operated religious Test Acts for admission until 1871. It was no accident that in the 1820s leading supporters of Jeremy Bentham's new secular University College London were prominent Jews.

Russia had the world's largest Jewish population from the 1790s to the 1930s, but they faced severe educational barriers. During the late nineteenth century, Tsar Alexander III introduced a policy that only a tiny percentage of Jews could receive a higher education.

After the 1917 Communist revolution, large numbers of Jews enrolled in institutions of higher education, and professors and research workers won signal recognition in the universities, institutes, and academies. During Stalin's "black years" (1948-1953), however, a drastic reduction of their number took place, when Jewish scholars were dismissed in great numbers from their posts and many of them arrested or exiled. After Stalin's death, the situation improved, but restrictions on those of Jewish nationality (in the Soviet parlance) were reintroduced during the anti-Zionist campaign of the late 1970s—under the slogan "Zionism is racism"—and the battle over freedom of emigration. Thus, prestigious academic institutions such as Moscow State University introduced a 2 percent quota for Jewish students. There was a kind of "back to the future" irony in Soviet President Leonid Brezhnev's reintroduction of the public policies of Tsar Alexander III. It certainly suggested that the Communist experiment of international brotherhood and solidarity was failing and that the end was nigh for the Soviet Union.

In other states with large Jewish communities, similar constraints on Jewish social advancement operated. In the 1920s, Poland, Hungary, and Romania introduced the *numerus clausus* to limit Jewish student enrolment. In Poland, particularly, Jews were relegated to the "ghetto benches" in university lecture

---

[13] Martin Luther, *Von den Juden und Ihren Lügen* (1543), cited in Robert Michael, *Holy Hatred: Christianity, Antisemitism, and the Holocaust* (New York: Palgrave Macmillan, 2006), 111, 113.

halls, while periodic riots were organized by antisemitic students. The United States was not immune to this discriminatory trend. In 1922, Harvard president A. Lawrence Lowell defended the existence of a 10 percent quota for Jews at Harvard by expressing concern about "the large and increasing proportion of Jewish students in Harvard College." This policy was supported by Harvard undergraduates who claimed that "Jews do not mix [and] they destroy the unity of the college."[14] In 1945, Dartmouth College president E.M. Hopkins justified a quota for Jewish students by emphasizing that "Dartmouth is a Christian college founded for the Christianization of its students."[15] In 1947, President Truman's Commission on Higher Education charged that quota systems and policies of exclusion had prevented young people of many religious and racial groups, but particularly Jews and blacks, from obtaining a higher education and professional training. A 1949 study by the American Council on Education showed that the average Jewish applicant for college admission had considerably less chance of acceptance than a Catholic or Protestant of comparable scholastic ability. In the same year, application forms of 518 colleges and universities and eighty-eight schools of medicine and dentistry were still found to contain at least one and usually several potentially discriminatory questions. Even after Jewish students were admitted in most countries there remained barriers to hiring Jewish faculty.

Of course, the classic example of civilization morphing into barbarism with the active assistance of large sections of the intelligentsia is Germany, the country which most of the world admired for its scientific and cultural leadership. Its prestigious university system was the model for modern institutions of higher education. Germany established the multidisciplinary research university with its doctoral programs, graduate schools, and scholarship across the natural sciences, humanities, and the new social and behavioral sciences. In 1922, the famous German economist and sociologist, Max Weber, wrote an essay entitled *Wissenschaft als Beruf* (Science as a vocation). Here he put his finger, ten years before Hitler came to power, on one of the major reasons for the eventual displacement of the scholar by Nazi demagogues as proponents of academic values and goals. Without reference to the Nazis or any other political party, Weber revealed how the value void arose, which would permit totalitarian dictators and other fanatics to impose their iron rule over the universities. In the late 1920s, during the later years of the Weimar Republic, German university students began to harass Jewish students and put pressure on Jewish professors,

---

[14] *Harvard Graduates' Magazine*, September 1922.

[15] Robert G. Spivak and Leo M. Swaim, Jr., "Dartmouth Limits Jews to Stop Anti-Semitism, Says Its Prexy," *New York Post*, August 7, 1945, cited in Tamar Buchsbaum, "A Note on Antisemitism in Admissions at Dartmouth," *Jewish Social Studies* 49, no. 1 (1987): 82.

thus preparing for the academic repression characteristic of the Nazi regime. It is important to note here that the Nazis controlled the universities, both student unions and the faculty clubs, before they controlled the streets or the government. In the 1920s, there was continuing demand for the removal of Jews from the German Student Federation (*Deutsche Studentenschaft*). This evidence suggests that the majority of students supported at least a drastic reduction in the number of Jewish teachers at institutions of higher learning.

The publication in 1914, nineteen years before the Hitler regime took power, of Philipp Lenard's *England und Deutschland zur Zeit des großen Krieges* (England and Germany at the time of the great war) is a prime example of academic and intellectual antisemitism and conspiracy thinking. As a Nobel Prize winner in physics before World War I, Lenard's views were quite influential. He not only believed that Jewish-controlled "England nearly always was a political monster" but also that Albert Einstein practiced "Jewish physics," which somehow differed from "German physics."[16] Similar views were held by the famous German physicist Johannes Stark, the zoologist Arthur Golf, the theologian Emanuel Hirsch, the art historian Wilhelm Pinder, the surgeon Ferdinand Sauerbruch and countless other German intellectuals.

On the Nazi take-over in January 1933, famous philosopher Martin Heidegger delivered a speech entitled "Die Idee der Politischen Universität," in which he stated:

> The National Socialist revolution is not merely the taking over of an already existing power in the state by another party sufficiently large to do so; this revolution means a complete revolution of our German existence. ... Hail Hitler![17]

Heidegger and eight of his colleagues published a "Vow of Allegiance of the Professors of the German Universities and High-Schools to Adolf Hitler and the National Socialistic [sic] State."[18] Thus began the so-called "cleansing process" at German universities. All German professors were public employees, responsible to the Minister of Science, Art, and Public Education at Berlin. On April 7, 1933, regulations were issued designed to exclude from the German Civil Service, and hence from all universities, those persons who in the view of the Nazi party were unfit to hold office—"non-Aryans," that is to say, Jews. As a consequence of these policies, the dismissals of professors at German universi-

---

16 Philip Ball, *Serving the Reich: The Struggle for the Soul of Physics under Hitler* (Chicago: University of Chicago Press, 2014).

17 Anson Rabinach and Sander L. Gilman, eds., *The Third Reich Sourcebook* (Berkeley: University of California Press, 2013), 275-276.

18 Wolfgang Bialas and Anson Rabinbach, eds., *Nazi Germany and the Humanities: How German Academics Embraced Nazism* (London: Oneworld Books, 2007), 2.

ties began in earnest during the 1934-1935 academic year, when 1,145 professors were dismissed or pensioned off early. This state policy, which offered rapid advancement for young scholars, was welcomed by most younger, Aryan members of faculty—there were literally jobs for the boys. Thus, after 1933, they were inclined to carry out their academic functions in the spirit of National Socialism.

Widespread support for the reduction in the number of Jewish students and teachers had not only made the Nazis popular on campuses before 1933. As a sign of student radicalism, however, many students remained dissatisfied with the 1933 law. They continued to boycott the lectures of Jewish professors, even if they enjoyed exemption under the Aryan paragraph in the Civil Service Law because they were war veterans. This ruthless campaign, which lasted almost two years, finally achieved its goal: almost all Jewish professors who were legally still allowed to teach had resigned from their positions by 1935.

What of Jewish students? They were hit by the euphemistic "Law against the Overcrowding of German Schools and Universities" promulgated on April 25, 1933. This law was complemented by orders of the Prussian Ministry of Education stipulating that the share of non-Aryans could not exceed 5 percent of the already enrolled students. According to the *Niederelbisches Tageblatt*, there were about 4,000 non-Aryans at German universities in 1932. By the summer of 1933, their number had declined to 1,900 nationwide. In the summer semester of 1934, there were only twenty-four Jewish freshmen at German universities, who made up just 0.4 percent of the 6,189 first-year university students. By the winter semester of 1934-1935, there remained only 800 Jewish university students in all of Germany.

Revolutions and purges proceed rapidly once the levers of state power have been seized, since fanatics tend to be very energetic. Hence the aphorism that the price of freedom is eternal vigilance. Totalitarian movements demand and obtain what the Irish poet W.B. Yeats described as a "passionate intensity" capable of overwhelming all other considerations.[19]

In March 1938, the Nazis took over Austria and incorporated it into the Third Reich. Within three weeks, 150 Jewish professors were dismissed from the University of Vienna Medical School alone. As in Germany in 1933, there were no student protests or faculty strikes against Nazi "race policy." And there were no boycotts of German universities by universities in Scandinavia, Britain, or the United States. Refugee scholars from Europe, including Albert Einstein, found themselves excluded from tenured posts. In fact, Ivy League presidents welcomed Nazi Germany's government officials more than they did Jewish

---

[19] In his poem "The Second Coming," first published in *The Dial*, November 1920. See David Lehrman, "A Poet's Apocalyptic Vision," *Wall Street Journal*, July 24, 2015.

students. Since America's top universities and medical schools operated Jewish quotas, they presumably did not feel confident about criticizing Germany. What this sad saga illustrates is that antisemitism was both fashionable and endemic in Western intellectual circles—only the intensity varied across societies. The history of universities in the first half of the twentieth century debunks the notion of progress and a linear progression in the affairs of mankind. In fact, American Jews' relationship with universities has been checkered, and Jews were more welcome in the halls of academe in the 1880s than in the 1930s.[20]

## III. THE PERSISTENCE OF ANTISEMITISM

How do we account for the persistence of antisemitism, a particular and particularly pernicious form of prejudice and racism, across time and space? We can draw explanations from a number of academic disciplines—politics, sociology, economics, psychology, anthropology, theology, literature, and history.

Many writers, from Karl Marx to Protestant theologian Reinhold Niebuhr, believed that "political opinions are inevitably rooted in economic interests of some kind or other."[21] However, the historical record suggests that class analysis is not completely sufficient, since political opinions can arise from religious and philosophical commitments, cultural origins, social aspirations, or perverse animosities without economic roots. In fact, in 1942, Niebuhr argued that racism was located in "group consciousness … the inveterate tendency among men to generalize about individuals in another group upon the basis of the least favorable evidence in regard to them."[22] This view of intergroup relations is very close to social psychologist Henri Tajfel's social identity theory.[23] The tendency toward in-group/out-group bias, whether based on ethnicity or class, is very evident in Marx's *Zur Judenfrage* and a series of antisemitic tracts by Wagner, Houston Chamberlain, John Hobson, Charles Maurras, and Hitler. Apart from their espousal of hatred and defamation, these works are also notable for their search for human perfectionism and political utopianism. I would contend that utopian idealism, a fondness for monism, and a preference for totalitarianism are covariates of antisemitism and that this explains much of its appeal to many intellectuals and academics rooted in both the Christian West and the Muslim lands.

---

[20] Paul Ritterband and Harold S. Wechsler, *Jewish Learning in American Universities: The First Century* (Bloomington: Indiana University Press, 1994).

[21] Reinhold Niebuhr, *Moral Man and Immoral Society: A Study in Ethics and Politics* (New York: Charles Scribner's Sons, 1932), 5.

[22] Reinhold Niebuhr, "The Race Problem," *Christianity and Society* (Summer 1942).

[23] Henri Tajfel, "Social Identity and Intergroup Behaviour," *Social Science Information* 13, no. 2 (1974): 65-93.

The political Right was attracted by religious and racial antisemitism, while the Left has adopted class-based and political antisemitism. The point that needs emphasis here is that the Soviet-led Third International was an ideological movement based on theoretically argued texts. Anti-Zionism was an official policy, and a great deal of attention was given over decades to arguing the case against Zionism as a "reactionary movement" and against the policies and praxis of the State of Israel. A vast library of books, leaflets, historical and theoretical articles, and speeches denouncing Israel and Zionism spewed out of Moscow and its satellites. Though Soviet policy was not based on racial or biological ideas about Jewish "pollution" of the nation, in practice many communist publications in their enthusiasm to denounce Jewish class and religious traits often fell back on classic Jew-baiting and "unofficial" historic antisemitic arguments that degenerated into screeds that would have taken pride of place in pre-war Nazi publications. They gave increasing prominence to Hobson's theory of imperialism, which identified Wall Street Jewish bankers as the controllers of an exploitive colonialism that was pauperizing the world. This approach emphasized conspiracy theories and echoed themes in the infamous *Protocols of the Elders of Zion.* Even sophisticated communist theorists and intellectuals found it difficult to establish the demarcation lines between what they believed was legitimate and vehement criticism of Israel and real anti-semitism. When attacked by western Jewry they fell back on theology. Lenin defined antisemitism as "spreading hostility toward Jews" and characterized it as a "diversionary tactic of capitalists."[24] Antisemitism was a crime under the 1922 Soviet Criminal Code. Thus, a socialist state could not be antisemitic by definition, and the Soviet Union was inevitably an example of tolerance and fraternal internationalism. One finds echoes of this argument in British Labour Party leader Jeremy Corbyn's denials of antisemitism.

This official position meant it was impossible for the Soviet leadership to embrace an open government policy of classic antisemitism whatever the personal inclinations of Politburo members. Thus, the euphemistic term anti-Zionism became the favored label. Unlike antisemitism, it was not an immuta-ble personal characteristic, so it did not automatically threaten each individual Jew but only Jews who thought incorrectly. In fact, anti-Zionism could be and was embraced by good communists (and other Marxist revolutionaries) of Jewish extraction willing to denounce the sins of other Jews duped by capital-ism, religion, and other falsehoods in publications such as *Sovietische Heimland.* The resulting anti-Zionist propaganda material was disseminated by the agitprop departments of Communist parties, fraternal or front organizations,

---

[24] Lionel Kochan, ed., *The Jews in Soviet Russia Since 1917* (New York: Oxford University Press, 1970), 294.

and fellow travelers across the world for decades until it became a central plank in the litany of grievances and accusations against the evil ways of Western imperialism and colonialism.

While the USSR never officially called for the extinction of the State of Israel, Trotskyist and other revolutionary leftist groups were less inhibited and were even fiercer in their anti-Zionist rhetoric and agitation. During the 1970s, their terrorist offshoots, such as the Baader-Meinhof Gang, the Red Brigades and Carlos the Jackal, went into active partnership in the "armed struggle" alongside Palestinian militants, such as Abu Nidal. They participated in attacks on Jews and Israelis across the world in outrages such as the 1972 Munich Olympics massacre and the 1976 Entebbe plane hijacking.

Utopian idealism appeals particularly to the young. Violent revolutionaries—fascist, Marxist, Islamist—are overwhelmingly young adults, the same age group that populates universities. It is not a chance occurrence that Mussolini's fascist anthem was "Giovinezza" meaning youth. So we can postulate a developmental factor at work. The desire to create a new order by a rising generation. Again, it is important to remember that the cultural and artistic movement known as Futurism was embraced by Italian fascism. So what about the role of Western universities today? British government figures show that 47 percent of convicted terrorists in Britain since 2001 attended university (well above the national average), and six convicted terrorists have been presidents of the Islamic society at their university.[25]

But why are the Jews so often a target of utopian idealists from across the political and religious spectrum? Interestingly, most cultural representations of the Jew in art, literary fiction, and film tend to be of an elderly Jewish man. So is it that the Jew represents and is associated with the past and its failures and disappointments? A resentment of the past seems to motivate hatred of the Jew who often seems to symbolize tradition and history—that which must be destroyed in the pursuit of a new order.

Whereas the intelligentsia of the 1920s, which Julian Benda criticized, were drawn from the nationalist right, the situation is different now. Today's treacherous *clercs* are largely found on the left of the political spectrum among the journalists, pundits, moralists, and pontificators of our fast expanding media, along with their supporting cast of "critical" academics. In the past fifteen years, we have been inundated by a barrage of sophisticated agitprop with apocalyptic insinuations that indicts Israel and Washington neoconservatives as the world's misfortune and claims that they are directly to blame for war, terrorism, and globalization. This narrative, whereby Jews are out there

---

[25] Haras Rafiq, "Islamic State: In and Out of Extremism" (lecture, ISGAP Summer Institute, Oxford, August 3, 2016).

somehow frustrating the international community's best interests and firm commitment to peace, prosperity, and human rights, is not new. It is a modern adaptation of the conspiracy thesis of the *Protocols of the Elders of Zion*. Boiled down to its essence, the idea bears an eerie similarity to Hitler's favorite rhetorical line at his rallies when railing about Germany's economic misery and geopolitical problems: "Wer ist schuldig? Der Jude!" (Who is guilty? The Jew!).

The sociologist Vilfredo Pareto's 1901 theory of revolution, which focuses on social mobility, might be relevant here as a sociological explanation for this paradigm shift between the 1920s and today.[26] The social mobility of the European intellectual elite criticized by Benda was ultimately blocked by the economic downturn and overall sense of pessimism and crisis of his time. In 2015, in the wake of postwar decades of plentiful opportunity and mobility for the New Class are not Western intellectuals once again becoming similarly frustrated? Certainly the intelligentsia—especially the university professor—has forfeited social and economic status in Europe and the United States as the result of the "big bang" in finance and new technologies, which generally favor technology entrepreneurs and commercial activity over public service and teaching.

Michael Curtis, in his book *Verdict on Vichy*, shows that the French left-wing intelligentsia has been down this road of tacit support for bigotry before. During the Vichy regime of 1940-1944, Jews were boycotted, their assets were confiscated, and Jews and Jewish influence were removed by statute from public life and the national economy. Yet for its prominent writers—André Gide, Paul Claudel, François Mauriac, Jules Romains, Roger Martin du Gard, even André Malraux until nearly the end of the war—the rule was silence or inaction. This silence was even more deafening in the case of Jean-Paul Sartre and Simone de Beauvoir, who so strongly influenced the climate of intellectual opinion after the war. The "heroic" Simone de Beauvoir worked for a time on a cultural program for *Radio Nationale* in occupied Paris.[27] Her companion, Jean-Paul Sartre, happily replaced a dismissed Jewish professor of philosophy. Sartre's book on the origins of antisemitism was only written in 1947. The liberal professions were no better. It was only in 1997 that the French doctors' association, representing 180,000 members, acknowledged that the "basic values of their profession had been violated when they acquiesced in legislation that discriminated against and excluded their Jewish colleagues" from practicing.[28]

---

[26] Vilfredo Pereto, *The Rise and Fall of Elites: An Application of Theoretical Sociology* (New Brunswick, NJ: Transaction Publications, 1991).

[27] Michael Curtis, *Verdict on Vichy: Power and Prejudice in the Vichy France Regime* (New York: Arcade Publishing, 2003).

[28] Denis Durand de Bousingen, "French Medical Association Apologises to Jews," *The Lancet*, October 18, 1997.

Yet, we must beware of historicism. What we are seeing today is a mutation in the virus of anti-Jewish ideas and prejudice that marks the morphing of anti-semitism into another form. For this reason and others the phenomenon in evidence may be more accurately termed Judeophobia—a fear of and hostility toward Jews as a collectivity rather than the propagation of the racial ideologies of the old antisemitism. It is a mindset characterized by an obsession with the sins of the State of Israel and Diaspora Jews in general, as a consequence of the majority's well-documented strong sense of attachment to Israel. Today's Judeophobia is an assault on the essence of the Jewish collectivity, both in terms of a Jewish sovereign state in its ancient homeland and in terms of the existence of robust, emancipated, and self-aware Diaspora communities. What the new opponents of the Jews share with the prewar fascists and Stalinists is a similar predilection for utopian idealism, which in turn adopts a simple approach to problem solving—eliminate the cancer permanently from the body politic.

Thus, there are strident calls (BDS) for an academic boycott of Israeli univer-sities and scholars and campaigns for economic divestment from Israel, but not for similar actions or boycotts against other states such as Russia, Syria, Iran, China, or Saudi Arabia. Are the pacifist Tibetans and their admirable leader the Dalai Lama inherently less deserving of support and attention than the Palestin-ians? Could it be that the Tibetans just have the wrong sort of oppressors—the fearsome Chinese? Base motivations are at play here. Collaboration with Chinese universities, of course, also offers lucrative career opportunities for Western university faculty and administrators. Recruitment of Arab interna-tional students is also a lucrative source of income for Western universities, while academic supporters of the class, race, and gender thesis embrace Muslims as non-white victims of imperialism and Zionism.

## CONCLUSION

Given historical precedents, the fact that European elites are once again obsessed with "the sins and crimes of the Jews" is neither unprecedented nor unexpected. As the distinguished historian Robert Wistrich asserted, one of the most intriguing and challenging features about antisemitism is that, at different stages in its development, it has come from all parts of the political spectrum and from different religious groups.[29] There are of course inconsistencies and contradictions built into antisemitic thought. Is antisemitism rational or irrational? Obviously it meets perceived needs. Its attraction may be that it takes different forms at different times. It offers a Chinese restaurant menu of options,

---

[29] Robert Wistrich, *A Lethal Obsession: Anti-Semitism from Antiquity to the Global Jihad* (New York: Random House, 2010).

and it is addictive. It is opportunistic. The antisemite can pick and choose according to the context. The virus evolves over time. The motives can be rational or irrational. The antisemite is not obliged to be logical or coherent, a lacuna that is reinforced by postmodernism.

Another factor is that, for the past century, Jews have been over-represented in Western universities in terms of numbers of students and faculty. They have also enjoyed outstanding success in the academic and intellectual arena, as evidenced by the disproportionate number of Nobel prizes awarded to Jews. This success must have consequences. I began with Nietzsche, who claimed that the root of political psychology is resentment—*ressentiment*—and that it was the distinguishing social emotion of modern societies. Jealousy is a powerful passion. Higher education today in the West, particularly in the humanities and social sciences, is under strain, and its future looks uncertain. History shows—and psychology predicts—that in insecure epochs hatred brings order out of chaos and decision out of uncertainty. A competitive, disorderly, insecure, and fearful social and economic environment will almost inevitably make antisemitism attractive, particularly to utopian idealists, who are over-represented in university and intellectual circles. Their individual careerist ambitions combined with their psychological anxieties and political orientations seem to predispose a large fraction of them to embrace boycotts, divestment, and sanctions against Israel and Jews.

# Gaza = Auschwitz:
## The Logic of Holocaust Inversion*

Martin Kramer**

## INTRODUCTION

Holocaust inversion is the claim that Israel acts toward the Palestinians as the Nazis acted toward the Jews. Just what purpose does the claim serve? That it flourishes on crackpot websites or in the alleyways of Karachi is of scant interest. More interesting are situations where it gains traction among people whom we assume to be sophisticated about history and politics, in Western academe and journalism. After all, it is highly unlikely that anyone in these settings really believes that Israel conducts itself as Nazi Germany did. That goes for intellectuals who make or allude to the analogy, as well as their elite audiences. And yet Holocaust inversion continues to surface in these circles and is even gaining wider dissemination. What actual function do these claims fill?

But before I attempt to answer that question, it is useful to sketch a brief history of Holocaust inversion, which evolved in three stages. In the first stage, it was invented by British sympathizers of the Arabs, even as ashes still filled the crematoria. In the second stage, it was adopted by the Soviet Union, with particular fervor after 1967. Its latest and present iterations are on the Left in the West, including the academy, and in the Muslim world—and wherever they overlap.

Let me illustrate with a few examples. We are indebted to the historian Rory Miller, who has shown that the analogy between Zionism and Nazism even predates the creation of Israel.[1] Amazingly, it was a staple of anti-Zionist rhetoric in Britain as early as the mid-1940s, when Europe teemed with Jewish refugees, and before even one Palestinian Arab took to flight. The disseminators

---

* This paper first appeared as a chapter in Martin Kramer, *The War on Error: Israel. Islam and the Middle East* (New Brunswick, NJ: Transaction Publishers, 2016). It is reproduced here with permission.

** Dr. Martin Kramer is President of Shalem College, Jerusalem.

[1] Rory Miller, *Divided Against Zion: Anti-Zionist Opposition in Britain to a Jewish State in Palestine, 1945-1948* (London: Frank Cass, 2000).

of this notion were some British Arabists and the so-called Arab Office, the pro-Arab propaganda outfit set up to make the Palestinian Arab case in London. Their champion, Sir Edward Spears, wrote as long ago as 1945 that

> political Zionism as it is manifested in Palestine today preaches very much the same doctrines as Hitler. ... Zionist policy in Palestine has many features similar to Nazi philosophy ... the politics of Herrenvolk ... the Nazi idea of Lebensraum, is also very in evidence in the Zionist philosophy ... the training of youth is very similar under both organizations that have designed this one and the Nazi one.[2]

If this claim is even worth mentioning at all, it is to demonstrate that the attempt to assimilate Zionism to Nazism began even as the collaborationist Mufti of Jerusalem was on the run, even before the word "Holocaust" became current, and even before the Israeli army fired its first shot. The approach of anti-Zionists was always to associate Zionism with the most threatening and ominous evil of the day. (Accordingly, at the very moment that British Arabists were warning that a Jewish state would behave in a Nazi manner, anti-Zionist Americans were warning that it would behave in a Communist one.[3])

Perhaps the most famous case of a British supporter of the Arab cause propounding the equivalence of Nazism and Zionism was the big-think historian Arnold Toynbee, a cult figure in the English-speaking world, known for his penchant for far-fetched analogies. In his *Study of History*, Toynbee called the contemporary Israeli "a Janus figure, part American farmer technician, part Nazi *sicarius*." He also accused Israel of "inflicting on an innocent weaker neighbour the very sufferings that the original victim had experienced at his stronger neighbour's hands."[4] Toynbee finally outdid even himself when he wrote this sentence: "On the Day of Judgment the gravest crime standing to the German National Socialists' account might be, not that they had exterminated a majority of the Western Jews, but that they had caused the surviving remnant of Jewry to stumble."[5] That stumble, of course, being Zionism and the creation of Israel, here cast as a more criminal venture even than the Nazi extermination.

---

[2] Ibid., 147-8.

[3] In the May 1948 debate before Harry Truman on whether the United States should recognize Israel, Robert Lovett, then Under Secretary of State, said: "How do we know what kind of Jewish state will be set up? We have many reports from British and American intelligence agents that Soviets are sending Jews and communist agents into Palestine from the Black Sea area." Clark Clifford with Richard Holbrooke, *Counsel to the President: A Memoir* (New York: Random House, 1991), 12.

[4] Arnold Toynbee, *A Study of History*, vol. 8 (London: Oxford University Press, 1954), 291, 311.

[5] Ibid., 291.

## I. Holocaust Inversion on the Left

The tremendous boost to the equation of Zionism with Nazism came from the Soviet Union, beginning in the 1950s. It was Soviet propaganda that first began to equate the Star of David with the swastika in cartoons. It was in the Soviet Union that books were published alleging Zionist-Nazi collaboration. And after 1967, it was the Soviets who turned up the volume to high on the Zionist-equals-Nazi amplifier.

For example, Soviet Premier Alexei Kosygin said this at the United Nations in June 1967, when the Israeli occupation was only days old:

> What is going on the Sinai Peninsula and in the Gaza Strip, in the western part of Jordan and on Syrian soil occupied by the Israeli troops, brings to mind the heinous crimes perpetrated by the Fascists during World War II. … In the same way as Hitler Germany used to appoint Gauleiters in the occupied regions, the Israeli government is establishing an occupation administration in the territories seized and is appointing its military governors there.[6]

(In his reply, Israeli foreign minister Abba Eban called the comparison "a flagrant breach of international morality and human decency," and added: "Our nation never compromised with Hitler Germany. It never signed a pact with it as did the USSR in 1939."[7])

It was the Soviet example that the Arab propagandists would emulate. They did so hesitantly at first, since Nazism did not have the same depth of negative associations in the Arab world as Zionism itself. But the more the Arabs became aware of the Holocaust and the extent of Nazi crimes, the more eager they became to equate Zionism with Nazism. This would spread still further into the Muslim world at large.

A prime example dates from 2001, in the lead-up to the Durban conference, when Shimon Peres was Israel's foreign minister. A cartoon of Peres in a Nazi uniform appeared on the cover of an Egyptian weekly. When this drew criticism, a bevy of Egyptian "intellectuals" wrote to defend it. "Peres committed and commits more ugly acts against the Arabs than the Nazis did against the Jews," wrote one of them. Another wrote that Hitler "is the one who is unjustly treated" in the comparison with Peres.[8]

---

6 Text in *Keesing's Record of World Events* 13 (July 1967): 22153ff. For a comprehensive survey of Holocaust inversion in Soviet propaganda and leftist thought, see Robert S. Wistrich, *From Ambivalence to Betrayal: The Left, the Jews, and Israel* (Lincoln, NE: University of Nebraska Press, 2012), 448-78.

7 Meron Medzini, ed., *Israel's Foreign Relations: Selected Documents, 1947-1974* (Jerusalem: Ministry of Foreign Affairs, 1976).

8 Quoted by Götz Nordbruch, "Reinterpreting History: Perceptions of Nazism in Egyptian Media," in *The Middle East and Palestine: Global Politics and Regional Conflict*, ed. Dietrich Jung (New York: Palgrave, 2004), 91.

The preeminent disseminator of Holocaust inversion in the Muslim world today is Turkish president Recep Tayyip Erdoğan, who returns to the theme repeatedly. Here is a prime example, from the summer of 2014:

> What is the difference between Israeli actions and those of the Nazis and Hitler? How can you explain what the Israeli state has been doing in Gaza, Palestine, if not genocide? This is racism. This is fascism. This is keeping Hitler's spirit alive.[9]

In the Western academy, all of these threads have come together: Arabist tradition, leftist agitprop, and Arab-Muslim nationalism have combined to create hothouse conditions for the spread of Holocaust inversion into the writings and classroom pronouncements of professors. Let me end this short history with few examples drawn from the faculty of Columbia University in New York.

The first one is from Joseph Massad, professor of Arab studies. Massad had once been accused by some students of Holocaust inversion in class, and in his defense he insisted that the "lie … claiming that I would equate Israel with Nazi Germany is abhorrent. I have never made such a reprehensible equation."[10] So Massad was fully aware of the "abhorrent" and "reprehensible" nature of Holocaust inversion.

But only four years later, after a flare-up of conflict in Gaza in 2009, he published an article entitled "The Gaza Ghetto Uprising." Illustrated by the famous image of a surrendering child in the Warsaw ghetto, the article invoked an alleged Israeli plan to "make Israel a purely Jewish state that is *Palästinenserrein*." Massad characterized the Palestinian Authority—or, rather, "the Israeli-created Palestinian Collaborationist Authority"—as "the *judenrat*, the Nazi equivalent."[11]

Another Columbia professor, Hamid Dabashi, also known for his inflammatory rhetoric, wrote this under the influence of the Hamas-Israel war in the summer of 2014:

> After Gaza, not a single living Israeli can utter the word "Auschwitz" without it sounding like "Gaza." Auschwitz as a historical fact is now archival.

---

[9] "Turkey PM Slams Israel for 'Hitler-like Fascism'," *RT.com*, August 1, 2014, archived at http://web.archive.org/web/20140804052300/http://rt.com/news/177164-erdogan-israel-gaza-fascism.

[10] "Joseph Massad Responds to the Intimidation of Columbia University," *Electronic Intifada*, November 3, 2004, archived at http://web.archive.org/web/20110609164358/http://electronicintifada.net/content/joseph-massad-responds-intimidation-columbia-university/5289.

[11] Joseph Massad, "The Gaza Ghetto Uprising," *Electronic Intifada*, January 4, 2009, archived at http://web.archive.org/web/20110608193956/http://electronicintifada.net/content/gaza-ghetto-uprising/7919.

> Auschwitz as a metaphor is now Palestinian. From now on, every time any Israeli, every time any Jew, anywhere in the world, utters the word "Auschwitz," or the word "Holocaust," the world will hear "Gaza."[12]

Notice how this species of academic Holocaust inversion has evolved. It is more elusive and allusive, and also more theoretical. We are in the world of metaphors. But whatever its form, the claim of Holocaust inversion remains steady: Israel acts toward the Palestinians as the Nazis acted toward the Jews, albeit on a different scale.

Now some will argue that Holocaust inversion is somehow legitimate because it has surfaced from time to time on the Israeli Left. An often-cited example is the late philosopher Yeshayahu Leibowitz, who called those Israeli judges who authorized moderate physical pressure on Palestinian detainees "Judeo-Nazis."[13] The N-word in Israel does occasionally figure on the Israeli Left, although usually in a refined version. An example is the author Amos Oz, who once called violent settlers on West Bank hilltops "Hebrew neo-Nazis." (I say "refined" because, as Oz himself clarified, neo-Nazis aren't Nazis.[14]) To this we can now add a former Shin Bet head, the late Avraham Shalom, and his statement about the Israeli army in the documentary *The Gatekeepers*: it has become "a brutal occupying army that's similar to the Germans in World War II. Similar, but not identical."[15]

While these statements sound like Toynbee's echo, Leibowitz, Oz, and Shalom nonetheless come from within a Zionist frame of reference, and their comparisons are laden with caveats. Nevertheless, the effect of such statements outside Israel is often to validate Holocaust inversion. Former Israeli ambassador Michael Oren, alluding to Shalom, described the result: "I appear on a

---

[12] Hamid Dabashi, "Gaza: Poetry after Auschwitz," *Aljazeera* website, August 8, 2014, archived at http://web.archive.org/web/20140809023814/http://www.aljazeera.com/indepth/opinion/2014/08/gaza-poetry-after-auschwitz-201487153418967371.html.

[13] Joel Greenberg, "Yeshayahu Leibowitz, 91, Iconoclastic Israeli Thinker," *New York Times*, August 19, 1994.

[14] "I object to comparisons to the Nazis. The comparison I made on Friday wasn't to the Nazis but to the neo-Nazis. Nazis erect ovens and gas chambers; neo-Nazis desecrate places of worship, desecrate cemeteries, beat up innocent people, and scribble racist slogans. That is what they do in Europe, and that is what they do here." For a critique of Oz's statement, see Liel Leibovitz, "No, Rowdy Settlers Aren't Hebrew Neo-Nazis," *Tablet*, May 12, 2014, archived at http://web.archive.org/web/20140515032355/http://www.tabletmag.com/scroll/172564/rowdy-settlers-arent-hebrew-neo-nazis.

[15] Dror Moreh, *The Gatekeepers: Inside Israel's Internal Security Agency* (New York: Skyhorse, 2015), 386. Shalom qualified this: "I'm not talking about their behavior toward the Jews, which is an unusual thing with its own unique aspects. I'm talking about the way they treated the Poles and the Belgians and the Dutch and the Czech and all of them." This comparison is almost as outlandish, since nearly three million Poles perished during the German occupation, for example.

campus and a student gets up and says to me, 'you are speaking of your desire for peace, but your former FBI head is comparing you to a Nazi state. What are your comments on that?'"[16]

## II. FLAWED TACTIC?

There is no doubt that Holocaust inversion today fulfills some of the same functions it always has, namely as a tactic to delegitimize Israel, while perhaps simultaneously diminishing the Holocaust. Historian Deborah Lipstadt has said of Holocaust inversion that it "elevates by a factor of a zillion any wrongdoings Israel might have done, and lessens by a factor of a zillion what the Germans did."[17] The fact that Israel sometimes invokes the Holocaust to justify its existence, as well as its actions, creates a powerful incentive among its enemies or critics either to diminish the Holocaust or, when that seems either impossible or immoral, to claim that Israel is replicating it on some scale in its treatment of the Palestinians.

But does this tactic actually work? On the face of it, Holocaust inversion is a trap. It is, as even Joseph Massad once allowed, so "abhorrent" and "reprehensible" that its effect would seem to be to discredit whoever deploys it. And there are supporters of the Palestinian cause, especially Jewish ones, who from time to time urge that it not be used, because it is so patently preposterous.

For example, Norman Finkelstein, whose project has been to delink the Holocaust from Israel, has been known to discourage such comparisons. Finkelstein said that an Arab once told him that even if the Holocaust did happen, "what about the Palestinian holocaust? I said, you know, why do you have to drag in the Palestinian holocaust? What's happening to Palestinians is awful enough, that you don't have to compare it to the Nazi holocaust."[18]

In 2009, Mark LeVine, a historian and vituperative critic of Israel, published a piece entitled "Gaza is no Warsaw Ghetto." After enumerating Israel's crimes, but also describing the scale of what happened in Warsaw, LeVine warned that

---

[16] Yitzhak Benhorin, "Israel's US Envoy: 'Gatekeepers' Hindering PR Efforts," *Ynet*, March 17, 2013, archived at http://web.archive.org/web/20130317214520/http://www.ynetnews.com/articles/0,7340,L-4357190,00.html. For the history of the Israeli Left's penchant for Holocaust inversion, see Edward Alexander, *The Jewish Wars: Reflections by One of the Belligerents* (Carbondale, IL: Southern Illinois University Press, 1996), 33-44.

[17] Deborah Lipstadt interview by Amy Klein, Jewish Telegraphic Agency, April 19, 2009, archived at http://web.archive.org/web/20150110044610/http://www.jta.org/2009/04/19/life-religion/denying-the-deniers-q-a-with-deborah-lipstadt.

[18] Norman Finkelstein interviewed by Lena Meari and Tanzeen Doha, *Chintaa* website, October 13, 2010, archived at http://web.archive.org/web/20130807235323/http://www.chintaa.com/index.php/chinta/showAerticle/72/english.

the use of highly charged historical comparisons that do not hold up to scrutiny unnecessarily weakens the Palestinian case against the occupation. In a propaganda war in which Palestinians have always struggled to compete, handing Israel's supporters the gift of inaccurate or exaggerated comparisons does not help this struggle, particularly not in Israel and the United States, the two most important battlegrounds in this conflict.[19]

So if Holocaust inversion is such a "gift" to Israel's supporters, why do people continue to give it, in particular people who should know better, like professors at Columbia University, who are surrounded by Israel's supporters and live in one of the world's most Jewishly saturated environments? It is one thing when Holocaust inversion is deployed in Turkey or Palestine—there it makes perfect sense as a tactic. But on the Upper West Side of Manhattan?

I propose two explanations for why Holocaust inversion appears in such settings. The first is that Jews are particularly susceptible to it. That may sound paradoxical. After all, how could Jews, especially in America where Holocaust awareness is very high, be susceptible to equating Nazi extermination of the Jews with Israel's treatment of the Palestinians? The vulnerability emerges from the interpretation of the Holocaust as a unique event that burdens the Jews with a unique responsibility. Ironically, it was two Palestinians who identified this as a point of vulnerability, when they wrote the following:

> The Holocaust does not free the Jewish state or the Jews of accountability. On the contrary, the Nazi crime compounds their moral responsibility and exposes them to greater answerability. They are the ones who have escaped the ugliest crime in history, and now they are perpetrating reprehensible deeds against another people.[20]

The idea that the Holocaust compounds the Jews' moral responsibility was not invented by antisemites. It was invented by Jews who concluded that the Holocaust, itself a unique event, uniquely obligates Jews to stand in the first line of defense against injustice anywhere, particularly any injustice that in any way resembles the Holocaust in *any* of its many phases.

It is this concept—one might go so far as to call it a conceit, in presuming that Jews are gifted with some higher moral sensibility—that makes some Jews especially vulnerable to the claims of Holocaust inverters. And it is why Holocaust inversion is often directed precisely at them. (It is also why it can take on the character of Jew-baiting—a tactic directed not at the widest possible audience, but specifically at Jews, in order to provoke a response from Jews.)

---

[19] Mark LeVine, "Gaza is no Warsaw Ghetto," *Aljazeera* website, February 2, 2009, archived at http://web.archive.org/web/20121008112411/http://www.aljazeera.com/focus/crisisingaza/2009/02/20092191518941246.html.

[20] Hazem Saghiyeh and Saleh Bashir, "Universalizing the Holocaust," *Palestine-Israel Journal* 5, nos. 3-4 (1998): 90-97.

Consider two examples of the vulnerability of two fervently Zionist Jews to Holocaust inversion. The first is the case of Jacobo Timerman, the Argentine Jewish dissident in the dark days of the so-called "Dirty War," who was finally extricated and brought to Israel. In 1982, he reported on the Israeli invasion of Lebanon, and wrote a book highly critical of it. Needless to say, Holocaust inverters made much of Ariel Sharon's march to Beirut, and Timerman seems to see through them:

> The Harvard, Princeton, and Columbia professors who went along with [the PLO] for years, were they allies or accomplices? ... To speak of a Palestinian genocide, of a Palestinian Holocaust, to compare Beirut with Stalingrad or with the Warsaw Ghetto, will move no one and will only serve to feed their egos and settle accounts with other academics in whom these images can arouse guilt feelings. Jews know what genocide is, a Holocaust, a Nazi.[21]

That was a straightforward repudiation of the Holocaust inverters in American academe: Jews know genocide and Nazism when they see it, and they won't be fooled or cajoled. Yet elsewhere, Timerman shows his own specific vulnerability to the tactic used by Holocaust inverters when they pinpoint some supposed similarity between Israeli and Nazi conduct, in order to neutralize the Holocaust as a point of Israeli reference:

> From now on our tragedy will be inseparable from that of the Palestinian. Perhaps some of us will try to sidestep the Israeli moral collapse by resorting to statistics and comparing Auschwitz to Beirut. It will be in vain. The victims of Auschwitz would never have bombed Beirut. Our moral collapse cannot be diluted by statistics.[22]

This dismissive reference to "statistics" deeply discounts one of the core characteristics of the Holocaust, which is its scale and scope. Once this is done, the door is wide open to precisely the kind of Holocaust inversion that Timerman so abhors. For then any Palestinian suffering, regardless of its degree, becomes a "similarity" that places Israel in the dock with Nazism.

Another example, perfectly demonstrating the knowledge that Holocaust inversion is perverse yet also opening the door to it, appears in Ari Shavit's book *My Promised Land*—more specifically in a chapter that is a recycled article from 1991, in which Shavit tells of his reserve duty as a guard at a detention camp in Gaza. There he manages to conjure up an analogy between this detention camp—probably no worse than Guantanamo and undoubtedly better than Abu Ghraib—and a Nazi extermination camp:

---

21 Jacobo Timerman, *The Longest War: Israel in Lebanon* (New York: Knopf, 1982), 40.
22 Ibid., 157.

> Although unjust and unfounded, the haunting analogy is pervasive. … And
> I, who have always abhorred the analogy, who have always argued bitterly
> with anyone who so much as hinted at it, can no longer stop myself. The
> associations are too strong. Like a believer whose faith is wavering I go over
> the long list of counterarguments, all the well-known differences. Most obvi-
> ous, there are no crematoria here. And in the Europe of the 1930s there was
> no existential conflict between two peoples. Germany, with its racist doc-
> trine, was organized evil. The Germans were in no real danger whatsoever.
> But then I realize that the problem is not in the similarity—no one can seri-
> ously think there is any real similarity. The problem is that there isn't enough
> lack of similarity. The lack of similarity is not strong enough to silence once
> and for all the evil echoes.[23]

Shavit notes that "there isn't enough lack of similarity." This is precisely the
opening that Holocaust inverters seek to exploit.

## III. Moral categories

This brings me to my key point: the Holocaust inverter in Western academe
does not believe that there is an actual equivalence between Israel and the Nazis.
The Holocaust inverter knows the history and scale of the Holocaust perfectly
well—as well as Ari Shavit does. The Holocaust inverter even knows that the
analogy is, in some sense, "abhorrent" and "reprehensible." But he or she knows
that by making the analogy, the defendant—the supporter of Israel—will be
compelled to enumerate all the dissimilarities, and in so doing leave exposed
some superficial similarities that prompt the Timerman response. That is,
Auschwitz and Beirut, or Auschwitz and Gaza, are obviously not equivalents,
but they belong to the same moral category.

This is precisely the objective of Holocaust inversion, and Jews are the perfect target for it—because who, if not the Jews, has a duty to sound the alarm
when any form of injustice or cruelty has the potential to culminate in a
holocaust? In the same way, Palestinian propagandists who speak of a Palestinian "holocaust" don't claim that the "Nakba" of 1948 approximates the Holocaust in any historical sense. Their project is to find or allege small-scale
similarities—a massacre in Lydda, a forced labor camp at Ijlin, a hidden mass
grave in Jaffa—all with the purpose of establishing the Palestinians as victims on
an equal plane.

The second reason Holocaust inversion persists, despite its supposedly self-
defeating excess, is that it makes lesser but still preposterous analogies sound
more reasonable. So Israel isn't Nazi-like, but it is fascist. So it isn't guilty of

---

23 Ari Shavit, *My Promised Land: The Triumph and Tragedy of Israel* (New York:
Random House, 2013), 231.

genocide, but it commits massacres and mass killings. Gaza isn't a concentration camp or the Warsaw ghetto, but it is the world's largest outdoor prison camp. And Israel isn't Nazi Germany, but it is apartheid South Africa.

Having exhausted your outrage against the Nazi analogy, you will be a tad less vociferous in expressing your outrage against these other analogies, which are also specious but now appear "reasonable" and worthy of debate. In other words, Holocaust inversion is a rhetorical softening up. Those who use it don't seek to make the Israel-Nazi analogy credible—an impossible task—but to make other analogies seem like debatable propositions. It other words, it is a straw man.

And that is why the urgings of people like Mark LeVine are pointless. Of course Gaza isn't Auschwitz; LeVine isn't telling the Holocaust inverters something they don't know. But if his argument is that it is a flawed tactic, Holocaust inverters think otherwise, believing that it works on the two planes I have outlined.

The counter to LeVine is provided by Jerome Slater, a Jewish academic critic of Israel. He acknowledges that the Nazi analogy is "much too strong" but that it has one merit: it "results in a productive shock of recognition in Israel and among its friends." He then adds:

> Even the most severe criticism of Israel can hardly be counterproductive, in light of the fact that nothing else has proven to be productive. That is not to deny that even limited or hypothetical analogies to Nazi Germany are risky. Nonetheless, because Israel has gone so far down the road to fascism (not Nazism), the risks must be run—desperate times require desperate measures.[24]

So even though Slater knows and admits the analogy to be specious, he still thinks deploying it can be productive in "shocking" Jews and that it is a risk worth taking. Nothing more thoroughly demonstrates the instrumental use of Holocaust inversion: those who use it don't believe it, but they use to it bait Jews into a reaction—a reaction that will usually be one of outrage. But, in some small percentage of instances, they will provoke someone to hear "evil echoes," in the words of Ari Shavit. After all, desperate times require desperate measures. This has been the rationale of dissimulation and deception since time immemorial.

I now come to the final question Is Holocaust inversion antisemitic? The (now officially discarded) Working Definition of Anti-Semitism of the European Monitoring Center on Racism and Xenophobia makes this statement:

---

[24] Jerome Slater, "On the Use of Provocative Analogies (Nazism, Fascism)," *Mondoweiss* website, September 13, 2014, archived at http://web.archive.org/web/2014 0915050611/http://mondoweiss.net/2014/09/provocative-analogies-fascism.

> Examples of the ways in which antisemitism manifests itself with regard to the State of Israel taking into account the overall context could include: … Drawing comparisons of contemporary Israeli policy to that of the Nazis.[25]

The crucial caveat here is the "overall context," which I presume means that there must be other less equivocal evidence of antisemitism in the rhetorical package in which the comparisons appear. This is certainly the usual case when Holocaust inversion surfaces in the Arab-Muslim world, in a setting saturated with antisemitic tropes. But Holocaust inversion is usually deployed, sometimes even by Jews and Israelis, as a tactic. It is a despicable tactic, because it plays on the vulnerabilities of the Jews, on their unresolved ambivalence about having power in the world, on their propensity for moral self-flagellation. But that doesn't make Holocaust inversion antisemitic *ipso facto*. It just makes it exploitative.

If Holocaust inversion is a form of exploitation, then how should it be combated? I have been descriptive so far, not prescriptive. If it is true that people of basic intelligence and honesty simply won't believe it, and that it is usually put forward by people who don't believe it, refuting it by demonstrating that Israel isn't Nazi Germany would be unnecessary and self-abasing. In these instances, Holocaust inversion is probably best ignored, since its purpose is precisely to provoke a discussion around an absurd premise.

The other prescription might be to remove Nazi analogies altogether from currency in regard to Israel. Elie Wiesel has called comparisons of Nazi Germany with Iran "unacceptable." "Iran is a danger," he has said, "but to claim that it is creating a second Auschwitz? I compare nothing to the Holocaust."[26] If the Holocaust is indeed a unique event in human history, and if Nazi Germany is unparalleled as a nexus of absolute evil, then promiscuously invoking them to make some political point in the present should be rejected across the board.

What are the prospects for such a rhetorical truce? I leave that to you to calculate.

---

[25] Kenneth L. Marcus, *The Definition of Anti-Semitism* (Oxford: Oxford University Press, 2015), 163.

[26] Elie Wiesel interviewed by Yaniv Magal, *Globes*, April 19, 2012, archived at http://web.archive.org/web/20151219234156/http://www.globes.co.il/en/article-1000742410.

# Anti-Zionism: The Soft Underbelly in Jihad's Cognitive War on the Western World

Richard Landes*

## INTRODUCTION

Future generations, looking back at the first decade of the twenty-first century (the "aughts" or '00s), will note the exceptional behavior of the Western intelligentsia, which identified itself as liberal and progressive and held unusual sway over discourse in the public sphere during that time. From major news media publications (e.g. *The New York Times*, *The Guardian*, *Ha'aretz*, and *Le Monde*), to major human rights NGOs (e.g. Human Rights Watch, Amnesty International, and Oxfam), to most academic departments in the social sciences (e.g. Middle East studies, sociology, anthropology, political science, and many humanities, especially "critical theory"), to the "new media" intelligentsia (e.g. *Huffington Post*, *The Daily Beast*, *Slate*, and *Media Matters*), we find a striking reluctance to even recognize—much less confront—the major enemy of progressive values in the global community.

In the years immediately following the collapse of the Soviet Union, one of the major intellectual figures in the West identified this enemy. Between 1992 and 1996, Samuel Huntington developed his theory that the end of the Cold War would lead not to the "End of History" but to a "Clash of Civilizations," primarily featuring a conflict between the democratic West and Islam.[1] The book was widely criticized as a xenophobic analysis that actively contributed to, if not created, the conflict it predicted.[2] Indeed, the book's hostile reception reflected a wide-ranging consensus in the Western public sphere that war and

---

* Historian and author; Senior Fellow, Center for International Communication, Bar-Ilan University.

[1] Samuel Huntington, *The Clash of Civilizations and the Remaking of World Order* (New York and London: Simon and Schuster, 1997).

[2] Amartya Sen, "Democracy as a Universal Value," *Journal of Democracy* 10, no. 3 (1999): 3-17; Edward Said, "The Clash of Ignorance," October 4, 2001, *The Nation*, October 22, 2001. In 2015, an American professor told me, "a few years ago, I would have dismissed Huntington's thesis as right-wing nonsense."

violent conflict came from inventing an evil enemy.[3] We were not at war, but thinking we were would make it so.

Nor was this peace-oriented discourse pacific: it aggressively marginalized "unprogressive" attitudes toward "post-colonial" peoples as "racism," and, in the case of Islam, as "Islamophobia."[4] The results of this denial (along with some of the factors contributing to that denial) have created a world where this imperial drive, Islamism, and its military wing, jihadism, have gained a great deal of momentum and progressive values, conversely, have abdicated on multiple fronts.[5]

Even after the outbreak of the al-Aqsa Intifada/Oslo Jihad and the 9/11 attacks, the dominant voices in the West continued for well over a decade to play down these problems as solved or minor[6] and mobilized far more aggressively against

---

[3] Sam Keane, *Faces of the Enemy: Reflections of the Hostile Imagination* (New York: Harper and Row, 1994); Roxanne L. Euben, *Enemy in the Mirror: Islamic Fundamentalism and the Limits of Modern Rationalism* (Princeton: Princeton University Press, 1999); Matthew Frye Jacobson, *Barbarian Virtues: The United States Encounters Foreign Peoples at Home and Abroad, 1876-1917* (New York: Hill and Wang, 2001); Greg Felton, *Enemies by Design: Inventing the War on Terrorism* (Marion, IN: Tree of Life Books, 2005); Michel Chossudovsky, *America's "War on Terrorism"* (Montreal: Global Research, 2005); Umberto Eco, *Inventing the Enemy* (New York: First Mariner, 2013). "They [people concerned about global jihad in Europe] share a bipolar world view, according to which Muslims cannot be Europeans. Their rhetoric concentrates on a representation of the other which, if not effectively combated, will spread irretrievably and destroy the self." Louise Cainkar, "American Muslims at the Dawn of the 21st Century," in *Muslims in the West after 9/11: Religion, Politics, and Law*, ed. Jocelyne Cesari (New York: Routledge, 2009), 210.

[4] On the post-colonial paradigm, see the recent collection: *Postcolonial Theory in the Global Age: Interdisciplinary Essays*, ed. Om Prakash Dwivedi and Martin Kich (Jefferson, NC: McFarland, 2013). On Islamophobia, the first programmatic denunciation of the phenomenon came from a report by the Runnymede Trust in 1996: *Islamophobia: A Challenge for Us All* (1997); follow-up report: *Islamophobia: Issues, Challenges and Action* (2004). For a critique of the term as a means of silencing criticism of Islam, see Paul Marshall and Nina Shea, *Silenced: How Blasphemy and Apostasy Codes are Choking Freedom Worldwide* (New York: Oxford University Press, 2011).

[5] On women, see Phyllis Chesler's denunciation of the progressive feminists in *The Death of Feminism: What's Next in the Struggle for Women's Freedom* (New York: Palgrave MacMillan, 2005); and, more recently, the movie *Honor Diaries* (2013). The response of the "progressive faculty" of Brandeis to the awarding of an honorary degree to Ayaan Hirsi Ali embodies the inversion of values whereby Western feminists protect Muslim men from the critique of women who bore the full brunt of their patriarchal violence. On the Muslim assault on Christians in the Middle East and the near-absent response of the West, including Christians, see Raymond Ibrahim, *Crucified Again: Exposing Islam's New War on Christians* (New York: Regnery, 2013).

[6] In 2009, a *New York Times* editorial declared the demise of Huntington's thesis when Obama visited Turkey: "The End of the Clash of Civilizations," *New York Times*,

what they saw as potential fascism in the West than against what they even refused to refer to as "radical Islam."[7] As a German colleague said to me in 2011, "We are more afraid of our own tendencies toward fascism than those of our Muslims."

Now, some two decades later, that enemy, for all the reluctance of its targets to even acknowledge its presence, is relatively easy to identify. It is the drive among some Muslims for the global dominion of *Dar al-Islam* (the Realm of Submission). This drive necessitates the subjection of all the inhabitants of *Dar al-Harb* (the Realm of the Sword or War) to sharia (Muslim law) and, if they refuse to convert, to the either death or the humiliating conditions of the *dhimma*.[8] In short, the modern world is faced with an extremely primitive religious drive for global conquest and yet lives in denial about it.

Few if any observers in the mid-1990s, for example, would have predicted that, within less than a decade, a serious and growing body of analysts would argue that Islamists already have the upper-hand in a generation-long struggle for control of the Western European continent.[9] Bernard Lewis shocked Euro-

---

April 11, 2009, http://www.nytimes.com/2009/04/12/opinion/12sun2.html. Five years later, Erdogan was working against US (as well as Western and Turkish democratic) interests: Sami Zahed, "Turkey and the 'Jihadist Highway,'" *Al Jazeera English*, September 10, 2014, http://english.alarabiya.net/en/views/news/middle-east/2014/09/10/Turkey-and-the-Jihadist-Highway-.html; Lee Smith, "Barack Obama's Turkish Fruitcake," *Tablet*, December 5, 2014, http://tabletmag.com/jewish-news-and-politics/187383/obama-erdogan. On Obama's now infamous remark about ISIS as a junior varsity team, which White House officials subsequently tried to deny, see "Obama Fumbles JV Question," *FactCheck.org*, September 8, 2014, http://www.factcheck.org/2014/09/obama-fumbles-jv-team-question.

[7] On the inability to talk about "radical Islam" lest we insult Muslims, see the testimony of Eric Holder before Congress, available at: http://youtu.be/HOQt_mP6Pgg; Richard Landes, "How PC Talk Paralyzes Us," *Augean Stables*, May 17, 2010, http://www.theaugeanstables.com/2010/05/17/how-pc-talk-paralyzes-us-holder-before-the-house-on-islamic-radicalism-and-home-grown-terrorism; and the even more disturbing (and comic) exchange between Republican Congressman Dan Lungren and Assistant Secretary of Homeland Defense Paul Stockton, available at: https://www.youtube.com/watch?v=WU6n1mrpAGY. On the mobilization against Islamophobia, see Imran Awan, "'The Muslims are coming!' Why Islamophobia Is So Dangerous," *CNN*, December 3, 2014, http://edition.cnn.com/2014/12/03/opinion/islamophobia-opinion/index.html?hpt=hp_c5.

[8] Most people informed by the dominant voices in the Western public sphere do not even know what these terms mean. In 2013, I spoke to hundreds of professionals attending a conference on Homeland Security, and only about 10% of them knew the meaning of *Dar al-Islam* and *Dar al-Harb*.

[9] The years 2005-2006 saw the publication of several books to this effect: Bat-Ye'or, *Eurabia: The Euro-Arab Axis* (Madison, NJ: Farleigh Dickinson University Press, 2005); Tony Blankley, *The West's Last Chance: Will We Win the Clash of Civilizations?* (Washington, DC: Regnery Publishing, 2005); Robert Spencer, ed., *The Myth of Islamic Tolerance* (Amherst, NY: Prometheus Books, 2005); Oriana Fallaci, *The Force of Reason*

peans in 2006 with his prediction: "Current trends show that Europe will have a Muslim majority by the end of the 21st century at the latest…. Europe will be part of the Arab West—the Maghreb."[10] Even the people tracking Islamism's global ambitions in the 1990s would not have imagined making such a claim only five years earlier.

Critics of these pessimists tended to dismiss them as "Islamophobes" and conspiracy theorists, rather than dealing with the substance of their claims.[11] The resulting *dialogue des sourds* created an uncanny effect. Repeatedly, Western European discourse went, imperceptibly, from "unthinkable" in the 1990s to "inevitable" in the twenty-first century, whether in relation to the role of sharia in Western law courts[12] or the cry of "death to the Jews!" in the streets

---

(New York: Rizzoli International, 2006); Bruce Bawer, *While Europe Slept: How Radical Islam Is Destroying the West from Within* (New York: Doubleday, 2006); Melanie Phillips, *Londonistan: How Britain Is Creating a Terror State Within* (San Francisco: Encounter Books, 2006); Mark Steyn, *America Alone: The End of the World as We Know It* (Washington, DC: Regnery Publishing, 2006). See also, Lee Harris, *The Suicide of Reason: Radical Islam's Threat to the West* (New York: Basic Books, 2007); Walter Laqueur, *The Last Days of Europe: Epitaph for an Old Continent* (New York: Thomas Dunne Books, 2007); Bruce Thornton, *Decline and Fall: Europe's Slow Motion Suicide* (New York: Encounter Books, 2008); Christopher Caldwell, *Reflections on the Revolution in Europe: Immigration, Islam, and the West* (London: Allen Lane, 2009); Abigail Esman, *Radical State: How Jihad Is Winning over Democracy in the West* (Oxford: Praeger, 2010). For someone who initially dismissed Steyn's book and has more recently admitted he was wrong, see n. 66.

[10] "Europa wird Islamisch," interview with Bernard Lewis, *Die Welt*, April 19, 2006, http://www.welt.de/print-welt/article211310/Europa_wird_islamisch.html.

[11] On Bat-Ye'or's *Eurabia*: "What began as an outlandish conspiracy theory has become a dangerous Islamophobic fantasy that has moved ever closer toward mainstream respectability," complained Matt Carr in "You Are Now Entering Eurabia," *Race and Class* 48, no. 1 (2006): 1-22. Similar sentiments from the editors of *The Economist*: "Tales from Eurabia," *Economist*, June 22, 2006. For a critique of the latter article, see Richard Landes, "Who's Afraid of Eurabia?," *Augean Stables*, June 25, 2006, http://www.theaugeanstables.com/2006/06/25/whos-afraid-of-eurabia-fisking-the-economist. More recently, Susan Carland, "Islamophobia, Fear of Loss of Freedom, and the Muslim Woman," *Islam and Christian-Muslim Relations* 22, no. 4 (2011): 469-473; Yasemin Shooman and Riem Spielhaus, "The concept of the Muslim enemy in the public discourse," in *Muslims in the West after 9/11: Religion, Politics, and Law*, ed. Jocelyne Cesari (New York: Routledge, 2010), 198-228.

[12] The single best example of such a vast and unspoken shift occurred after the late 1990s, when any public intellectual in Britain confronted with the possibility of British law incorporating sharia would have responded "unthinkable." And yet, a decade later, Archbishop Rowan Williams considered it inevitable. "Sharia Law in UK 'unavoidable,'" *BBC*, February 7, 2008, http://news.bbc.co.uk/2/hi/7232661.stm. As for the fundamental democratic principle—one law for all—Williams notes dryly that it is "a bit of a danger." For an update, see Soeren Kern, "The Islamization of Britain," *Gatestone Insitute*, December 30, 2013, http://www.gatestoneinstitute.org/4112/islamization-britain.

of European capitals and the ensuing exodus of Jews.[13]

This alarming situation comes partly from a deep misapprehension about both the existence and the theater of this war. Many deny that there is a war, while those who acknowledge it consider it a military war on terror. But terror attacks merely constitute the guerilla tactics of an army that cannot win on the open battlefield. At this stage of the wildly asymmetric war between radical Islamists and the democratic West, the main theater of operations for global jihad is the cognitive battlefield: the Western public sphere.[14] And here, our progressive elites have repeatedly failed to defend the values of civil society and constantly ceded important ground on a wide range of issues crucial to our values, such as freedom of speech and reciprocity.[15] This has imperiled whole areas within Western democracies, what the French call *zones urbaines sensibles* and English Muslims call "sharia zones." These zones can cover areas ranging from specific neighborhoods to entire urban districts and suburbs.[16]

In the twenty-first century, this cultural expansionism occurs on a neighbor-to-neighbor, gang-to-gang, community-to-community, and school-to-school process of intimidation and expanding dominion.[17] The problems emerging in

---

[13] Robert Wistrich, "Summer in Paris," *Mosaic*, October 2014, http://mosaicmaga zine.com/essay/2014/10/summer-in-paris; Soeren Kern, "The 'Explosive Growth' of Jihadism in the Netherlands," *Gatestone Institute*, November 2, 2014, http://www.gate stoneinstitute.org/4835/netherlands-jihadism. Bruce Riedel attributes the anger against European Jews to Israel's actions in Gaza in "Global Jihad Benefits from Gaza Crisis," *Al-Monitor*, July 11, 2014, http://www.al-monitor.com/pulse/originals/2014/07/gaza-global-jihad.html#. I attribute it to the media coverage: Richard Landes, "The Big Winner in the Lose-Lose 'Operation Protective Edge,'" *American Interest*, September 4, 2014, http://www.the-american-interest.com/articles/2014/09/04/the-biggest-winner-in-the-lose-lose-operation-protective-edge.

[14] On this issue, see the foundational study by Stuart Greene, "Cognitive Warfare" (MA Thesis, Joint Military Intelligence College, Washington DC, 2007).

[15] On freedom of speech, see Nick Cohen, *You Can't Read This Book: Censorship in an Age of Freedom* (London: Fourth Estate, 2012); Paul Marshall and Nina Shea, *Silenced: How Apostasy and Blasphemy Codes are Choking Freedom Worldwide* (New York: Oxford University Press, 2011). The West may ardently wish for reciprocity (Tim Shipe, "Catholic-Islam Dialogue: Reciprocity the Key," *The American Catholic*, May 8, 2010, http://the-american-catholic.com/2010/05/12/catholic-islam-dialogue-reciprocity-the-key), but dialogue will not take place unless they relinquish that demand as "insensitive" to Muslims. For one spectacular fail, see Daniel Pipes, "Pope Benedict Criticizes Islam," *New York Sun*, September 19, 2006, http://www.danielpipes.org/3968/pope-benedict-criticizes-islam.

[16] On sharia zones, see Majad Jawaz, "Muslim Patrols Are a Sign of Things to Come," *Times* (London), January 30, 2013, http://www.thetimes.co.uk/tto/opinion/columnists/article3672194.ece.

[17] Soeren Kern, "European 'No-Go' Zones for Non-Muslims Proliferating: 'Occupation Without Tanks or Soldiers,'" *Gatestone Institute*, August 22, 2011, http://www.

cities such as Rotterdam (the Netherlands), Malmo (Sweden), and Birmingham (England) illustrate more advanced stages of the phenomenon.[18] Given the demographic trends, the prognosis is hardly encouraging over the next two decades. And all this takes place while the progressive players in the Western public sphere systematically underplay and even deny the problem—from the contemporary news media[19] and human rights NGOs regarding actual assaults[20] to post-colonial academics who forbid criticizing subalterns.[21]

---

gatestoneinstitute.org/2367/european-muslim-no-go-zones. For an example in England concerning schools, see *Wikipedia*, s.v "Operation Trojan Horse," http://en.wikipedia. org/wiki/Operation_Trojan_Horse. In the United States, see the work of Americans for Peace and Tolerance in Massachusetts, available at http://www.peaceandtolerance.org/ category/c40-campus/c43-k-12-mis-education, and the Thomas More Center in Michigan, available at https://www.thomasmore.org/news/chatham-middle-school-students-taught-islam-true-faith-two-mothers-pilloried-making-public-must-see-video.

[18] On Malmo, see Andrew McCarthy, "Losing Malmo," *National Review Online*, August 27, 2011, http://www.nationalreview.com/articles/275686/losing-malmo-andrew-c-mccarthy#. On Rotterdam, see Sandro Magister, "Eurabia Has a Capital and It's Rotterdam," http://chiesa.espresso.repubblica.it/articolo/1338480?eng=y. For further commentary, see Richard Landes, "So What If by 2020 Rotterdam Is Majority Muslim?" *Augean Stables*, May 22, 2009, http://www.theaugeanstables.com/2009/05/22/so-what-if-by-2020-rotterdam-is-a-majority-muslim-we-already-have-an-answer. On Birmingham, see Mark Steyn, "Belated Alarms," *Steyn Online*, October 2, 2014, http://www.steynonline. com/6583/belated-alarums.

[19] Bruce Bawer, *Surrender: Appeasing Islam, Sacrificing Freedom* (New York: Doubleday, 2009), part 2.

[20] The news media which I refer to here also includes "human rights" NGO reports, which often form the basis of news stories. See the extensive critique of their work by NGO Monitor, available at http://www.ngo-monitor.org. For a relevant example, see Amnesty International's report on attacks on Muslim human rights in Europe today and a critique of the report's systematic failure to discuss Muslim attacks on the rights of infidels in Europe: *Choice and Prejudice: Discrimination Against Muslims in Europe* (London: Amnesty International, 2012); Soeren Kern, "Amnesty International and Muslim Discrimination in Europe," *Gatestone Institute*, May 10, 2012, http://www. gatestoneinstitute.org/3056/amnesty-international-muslim-discrimination-europe. On the close and unexamined alliance of NGOs and journalists and the refusal of AP to even interview Gerald Steinberg of NGO Monitor because of his "right-wing" views, see Matti Friedman, "What the Media Gets Wrong about Israel," *Atlantic Monthly*, November 30, 2014, http://www.theatlantic.com/international/archive/2014/11/how-the-media-makes-the-israel-story/383262. On AP's indignant denial, see Lori Marcus, "AP Disses 'Whistleblower' But a New Whistle Blows," *Jewish Press*, December 3, 2014, http://www. jewishpress.com/news/breaking-news/ap-disses-whistleblower-but-a-new-whistle-blows/ 2014/12/03/0.

[21] The tendency of "subaltern" studies has been to privilege or, according to critics, "fetishize" the voice of the oppressed, with little attention to the role of *ressentiment* in shaping their narratives. See Nancy Koppelman, "When You Want to Do Something, Join Us! The Limits of the Social Justice Mandate in Higher Education," in *The Case*

Indeed, if modern democracy survives into the next generation, historians of its later periods might well view the behavior of the current intelligentsia as akin to that of the Xhosa tribe in South Africa, which in 1856-1857 killed over 400,000 head of their own cattle and starved 40,000 of their own people because every time the promised arrival of salvation did not occur they killed more of their cattle.[22] Our current intelligentsia is on a path that could prove suicidal to the very progressive values it champions. Whence this irrational behavior?

There are many angles from which this investigation could begin, such as an analysis of the way in which ideologues respond to the cognitive dissonance that arises when empirical reality contradicts their most deeply held beliefs.[23] Every time that efforts based on those beliefs fail, rather than questioning the assumptions underlying the strategy or critiquing the soteriological anthropology about what can save mankind, intellectual activists insist on repeating the failed salvific formula and kill more of their own capital. One finds this dynamic among progressive Israeli true-believers in the Oslo peace process, who responded to its failure in 2000 by insisting that, "if only we had made greater concessions, it would have worked."[24] As Mark Steyn specifically warns in the context of his long-ignored warnings about the jihad against the West, the response to a realistic warning is not to double your sleeping pills.[25]

Here, I would like to examine a peculiar weakness in Western democratic culture, which is especially notable in Europe and helps explain both Western vulnerability and the deep resistance to addressing this potentially lethal flaw. In the course of this young century (and even younger millennium), perhaps the single most dramatic weakness in the Western public sphere has been its receptiveness to jihadi antisemitism via its contemporary presenting form, that is to say, ferocious hostility toward Israel. The combination of a news media obsessed with

---

*Against Academic Boycotts of Israel*, ed. Cary Nelson and Gabriel Brahm (Chicago: MLA Members for Scholars' Rights, 2014).

[22] Richard Landes, *Heaven on Earth: The Varieties of the Millennial Experience* (New York: Oxford University Press, 2011), chap. 4. Rael Jean Isaac regards the global warming movement as a Xhosa analog: *Roosters of the Apocalypse: How the Junk Science of Global Warming Nearly Bankrupted the Western World* (Chicago: Heartland Institute, 2012). Isaac fits the pattern I observe in the conclusion to *Heaven on Earth*: an owl on global warming, a rooster on global jihad. The same applies to Ralph Dobrin, *How to Avoid Armageddon* (Hampstead, MD: Old Line Publishing, 2011), 36-38.

[23] For the original study that coined the term "cognitive dissonance," see Leon Festinger et al., *When Prophecy Fails: A Social and Psychological Study of a Modern Group That Predicted the Destruction of the World* (Minneapolis: University of Minnesota Press, 1956, 2008); Joel Cooper, *Cognitive Dissonance: Fifty Years of a Classic Theory* (London: Sage publications, 2007).

[24] Golan Lahat, *Messianic Temptation: The Rise and Fall of the Israeli Left, 1993-2001* [in Hebrew] (Tel Aviv: Am Oved, 2006). See below on deconstruction.

[25] Steyn, "Belated Alarms" (see n. 17).

reporting negatively on Israel and cloaking Palestinian jihadi behavior, relayed by a radical Left in search of a post-Soviet revolutionary cause, has activated an aggressive and expansive "Muslim street" in the West (especially in Europe). At the same time, a profound, one might even say millennial, attachment to a range of ideological commitments, most prominently post-colonial anti-imperialism, has made a reconsideration of this fatal attraction almost impossible.[26]

## 1. Anti-Zionism: the soft underbelly of the West in the Islamists' cognitive war

Of all the battlefields in the cognitive war theater of the Western public sphere, none reveals both the weakness of the West and the apocalyptic dimension of the conflict so much as the problem of Israel. For jihadis to win the cognitive war against the West, they need to get their enemy to adopt their apocalyptic narrative and make choices that will strengthen the jihadis and weaken the West. In the jihadi apocalyptic narrative, Israel is the quintessence of evil, the force of the *Dajjal*, the entity that threatens Islam with annihilation and whose elimination opens up the road for Islamism to impose the Caliphate upon all infidels.[27] And what the jihadis want—and have wanted since they first realized they could not accomplish it themselves—is to have the West help them destroy Israel.

In order to get Westerners to comply without realizing that they are also a target, jihadis had to get them to believe that the Muslim anger against Israel, so at variance with the democratic ethos of the West, arose from a *secular* drama— the justifiable result of having been wronged and needing justice (a Palestinian state) for closure. This in turn would blind Westerners to the *religio-cultural* drama—the humiliation at being weak, the need for vengeance, and the necessity for *Dar al-Islam* to dominate.[28]

If the West could be convinced to sacrifice Israel, Muslims could avenge the most painful of the humiliations inflicted by the modern world.[29] Having purged

---

[26] Richard Landes, "Fatal Attraction: The Shared Antichrist of the Global Progressive Left and Jihad," in *The Case Against Academic Boycotts of Israel*, ed. Cary Nelson and Gabriel Brahm (Chicago: MLA Members for Scholars' Rights, 2014).

[27] Both Shi'i and Sunni versions of global jihad target Jerusalem as a central goal. See Gershom Gorenberg, *The End of Days: Fundamentalism and the Struggle for the Temple Mount* (New York: Free Press, 2000); Dore Gold, *The Fight for Jerusalem: Radical Islam, the West and the Future of the Holy City* (Washington, DC: Regnery Publishers, 2007).

[28] For a recent example, see Peter Beinart, "Why Bibi Is Wrong to Subsume the Palestinian Issue under 'Militant Islam,'" *Ha'aretz*, October 1, 2014, http://www.haaretz. com/misc/article-print-page/.premium-1.618618?trailingPath=2.169%2C2.223%2C.

[29] Richard Landes, "Why the Arab World Is Lost in an Emotional Nakba," *Tablet Magazine*, June 24, 2014, http://www.tabletmag.com/jewish-news-and-politics/176673/ emotional-nakba.

the heart of *Dar al-Islam* of a *dhimmi* revolt, jihadis could then advance to the next stage of global sharia. Of course, to get the West to fall into such a trap, one would have to convince its intellectuals that, if only Israel were no longer a problem for the Muslim world, things would quickly get much better rather than worse[30] and that, if things do not work out according to the secular "positive-sum solution" (Oslo peace process), the fault for that failure (the al-Aqsa Intifada/Oslo Jihad) lies with Israel.

This scapegoating narrative—Israel is the cause of the evil and hence the object of sacrifice—has not only an international dimension but also a domestic one. Starting in October 2000, radical Muslim preachers using a violent anti-Zionist discourse that gained approval from radical "leftists" activated disenfranchised Muslim youth and young adults, who went on to commit a series of increasingly violent attacks, first on Jews (and Muslims) and eventually on the French (and Europeans) in general. The Durban Conference of August-September 2001 and the "anti-war" rallies of 2003 represent key moments in this merger of interests.

In early 2003, fueled by the belief that "world public opinion" constituted a global "superpower" to rival the United States,[31] the "anti-war" Left joined with Muslim warmongers carrying pictures of Saddam Hussein and Yasser Arafat and shouting "Allahu Akhbar" to protest Bush's war in Iraq. The grotesque quality of peace and human rights activists allying with such bellicose forces provoked sharp criticism, which largely isolated dissidents such as Nick Cohen rather than leading to a rise in self-awareness on the Left.[32] By the mid-aughts, after multiple joint demonstrations, the now global "Muslim street" was ready to fly on its own in the West. In 2005, the Parisian Ramadan riots spread to the whole of France;[33] soon thereafter, the Danish cartoon protests "shook the

------

30 On the Palestinian campaign, see "PA Depicts a World Without Israel," *Palestinian Media Watch*, n.d., http://www.palwatch.org/main.aspx?fi=449. On a sign at an anti-Israeli demonstration that reads: "For World Peace Israel Must be Destroyed," see Bruce Bawer, "Poll: Israel as Unpopular as Terror States Iran, North Korea," *Frontpage Mag*, May 23, 2012, http://www.frontpagemag.com/2012/bruce-bawer/poll-israel-as-unpopular-as-terror-states-iran-north-korea.

31 Patrick Tyler, "A New Power in the Streets," *New York Times*, February 17, 2003, http://www.nytimes.com/2003/02/17/world/threats-and-responses-news-analysis-a-new-power-in-the-streets.html.

32 Nick Cohen, "The Disgrace of the Anti-War Movement," *What's Left: How Liberals Lost Their Way* (London: Fourth Estate, 2007), 280-311; critique by (among many) John Hari, "Choosing Sides," *Dissent* 54, no. 3 (2007): 79-85, https://muse.jhu.edu/journals/dissent/v054/54.3.hari.pdf.

33 On the outbreak of Jew-hatred across Western Europe in immediate response to the Intifada, see *Wave of Anti-Jewish Activity in the World—October 2000: Summary and Analysis* (Jerusalem: Ministry of Foreign Affairs, 2000); "Une atmosphere d'insécurité," *Observatoire du monde juif* 1, no. 1 (November 2001), 2-9, with graph on page 9 showing

world,"[34] followed by violent Muslim demonstrations protesting the Pope calling Islam violent.

A new paradigm closely resembling that of apocalyptic Islam now animated the Western "street": Israel was the Antichrist, and peace beckoned just the other side of its destruction.[35]

*Anti-war demonstration, San Francisco, February 2003 (Zombietime).*

At the same time, with particular strength in France, radical Muslims and the gangs they nourished drove Jews from the neighborhoods that Muslims and Jews had once shared, as North African immigrants with much in common. This was the first of the *territoires perdus de la République.*[36] Things went from

the October spike, http://obs.monde.juif.free.fr/pdf/omj01.pdf; Pierre-André Taguieff, *La nouvelle judéophobie* (Paris: Mille et une nuits, 2002), translated by Patrick Camiller as *Rising from the Muck: The New Anti-Semitism in Europe* (New York: Ivan R. Dee, 2004), chap. 4. On the Ramadan Riots of 2005, see *Wikipedia*, s.v. "2005 Civil Unrest in France," http://en.wikipedia.org/wiki/2005_civil_unrest_in_France. On the damage to French society, see Andrew Hussey, *The French Intifada: The Long War between France and Its Arabs* (London: Granta, 2014); Wistrich, "Summer in Paris" (see n. 13).

[34] See Jytte Clausen, *The Cartoons That Shook the World* (New Haven: Yale University Press, 2009). In response to (anticipated) Muslim violence, Yale University Press did *not* publish the cartoons: Patricia Cohen, "Yale Press Bans Images of Muhammad in New Book," *New York Times*, August 12, 2009, http://www.nytimes.com/2009/08/13/books/13book.html?_r=0.

[35] Landes, "Fatal Attraction" (see n. 26).

[36] Emmanuel Brenner et al., *Les territoires perdus de la République: antisémitisme, racisme et sexisme en milieu scolaire* (Paris: Mille et une nuits, 2002); Union des étu-

bad to worse: from the murder of Sebastien Sellam by his Muslim "friend" (2003), to the torture-murder of Ilan Halimi (2005), to the massacre of school-children in Toulouse (2012), and the attack by a French-born Muslim on a Jewish museum in Belgium. By 2014, in the wake of extensive outbreaks of anti-semitic violence during and after "Operation Protective Edge," some began to speak of the end of European Jewry,[37] even as Islamists grew still bolder in claiming territory.[38]

A priori, one might think the jihadi narrative would find few takers among progressives in the West. Based, as it is, on a religious zealotry for which Western progressives cannot show enough contempt in its Christian manifestations (e.g., the Inquisition and the Crusades) and whose rejection made democracy possible, Islamism proffers a lethal (and at its extreme genocidal[39]) apocalyptic grand narrative that threatens every aspect of the progressive ethos, everything that the post-modern sensibility explicitly rejects.[40] Indeed, Islamist show scarcely disguised malevolence not only toward Zionism but also towards all other democracies (whose success Islamists consider the principal source of their agonizing humiliation and whose hegemony they strive to bring low). One could be excused for assuming that so shrewd and *méfiant* a culture as the French, for example, would be immune to the charms of so poisonous a narrative aimed right at its own heart.

And yet, from the perspective of jihadi cognitive warriors, anti-Zionism proved to be the astonishingly soft underbelly of the West. Here is not the place to lay out the full panoply of issues but rather to outline both the value of the target and the vulnerabilities of the West.

From the jihadi perspective, the value of the target could not be greater: Israel represents the greatest of modernity's slaps in Islam's face. Not only has a

---

diants juifs de France (UEJF)/SOS-Racisme, *Les anti-feujs: Le livre blanc des violences anti-Sémites en France depuis septembre 2000* (Paris: Calmann-Lévy, 2002). See the psychological reflections on the phenomenon in Daniel Sibony, *L'énigme antisémite* (Paris: Seuil, 2004).

[37] On the most current and worrisome outbreaks of contemporary antisemitism in Europe, see Jim Yardley, "Europe's Anti-Semitism Comes Out of the Shadows," *New York Times*, September 23, 2014, http://www.nytimes.com/2014/09/24/world/europe/europes-anti-semitism-comes-out-of-shadows.html; see also works cited in n. 9.

[38] See n. 17.

[39] Itamar Marcus and Barbara Crook, *Kill a Jew—Go to Heaven*, Palestinian Media Watch Special Report, January 26, 2005, http://www.palwatch.org/STORAGE/special%20reports/Kill_A_Jew.pdf; Robert Wistrich, *A Lethal Obsession: Anti-Semitism from Antiquity to the Global Jihad* (New York: Random House, 2012), 780-829.

[40] David Cook, *Contemporary Muslim Apocalyptic Literature* (Syracuse: Syracuse University Press, 2005); see also Timothy Furnish, *Holiest Wars: Islamic Mahdis, Their Jihads, and Osama bin Laden* (Westport, CT: Praeger, 2005); Jean-Pierre Filiu, *Apocalypse in Islam* (Berkeley: University of California Press, 2011).

weak, *dhimmi* people declared independence in the heart of *Dar al-Islam*, but they did it by dint of their command of modernity, both socially and technologically. A few million Jews repeatedly defeated hundreds of millions of Arabs, a "fact" every Arab political entity—secular or religious—has found unbearable humiliating. Destroying it would vastly strengthen the Muslim resolve to restore their past glories, which have sunk so low in our own day. And from a purely military point of view, destroying Israel undermines the single most reliable outpost the West has in the Muslim world.[41]

From the Western perspective of the historical "grand narrative" about freedom and human dignity, the Jews have played a central role as the benevolent "other" with whom one can profitably take the social contract's wager and successfully launch modern democracies.[42] From the biblical texts to the modern secular prophets embracing the "other," Jews have contributed extensively to this progressive zeitgeist.[43] So, for malevolent agents bent on destroying democracy (such as the Nazis), the Jews are naturally the key target. Historically speaking, one can generalize that those who wish to go to war attack the Jews, those who wish to enslave mankind accuse the Jews of just that desire, and those who (consciously or unconsciously) fear their freedom allow it to be taken from the Jews.[44]

Given the stakes and values at play, one might expect the progressive West to fight for Israel and the Jews against jihadis. Instead, the post-modern Western public sphere has proven remarkably vulnerable to the jihadi cognitive campaign of misinformation targeting Israel.

– Post-colonial thought formed a "native" ally, since it saw Zionism as a late, fascist, colonial, Western, imperialist adventure, thereby obscuring the democratic dimensions of the movement (as the only democracy and only

---

[41] Richard Kemp, "Israel as a Strategic Asset to Britain" (speech at JCPA conference "100 Years Since the Balfour Declaration," Jerusalem, February 28, 2017), available at https://www.youtube.com/watch?v=uVRk7BakrUY.

[42] On the issue of trust as critical to democratic experiments, see Adam Seligman, *The Problem of Trust* (Princeton: Princeton University Press, 1997). For the argument about the Jew as a benign but irreducible "other," see Jonathan Sacks, *The Dignity of Difference: How to Avoid the Clash of Civilizations* (New York: Bloomsbury, 2003).

[43] For the biblical origins, see Joshua Berman, *Created Equal: How the Bible Broke with Ancient Political Thought* (New York: Oxford University Press, 2008). For the medieval dimension, see Richard Landes, "Economic Development and Demotic Religiosity: Reflections on the Eleventh-Century Takeoff," *History in the Comic Mode: The New Medieval Cultural History*, ed. Rachel Fulton and Bruce Holsinger (New York: Columbia University Press, 2007), 101-116. For the early modern contribution to democracy, see Eric Nelson, *The Hebrew Republic: Jewish Sources and the Transformation of European Political Thought* (Cambridge, MA: Harvard University Press, 2011).

[44] Erich Fromm, *Escape from Freedom* (New York: Farrar and Reinhart, 1941).

thriving minority in the Middle East) even as it lionized the "resistance" ("democratic" Hamas).[45]

– The supersessionist needs of Christians (and a surprising number of post-Christians) to feel superior to Jews inclined Europeans to believe stories of Israelis behaving badly. Jihadis were able to exploit this Western appetite for moral schadenfreude at Israel's "loss of the moral high ground."[46]

– Guilt over the role of Europeans in the Holocaust (whether active or passive) had rendered the normal expression of hostility to Jews, so common in Europe beforehand, politically incorrect. Jihadis were thus able to tap a backlog of suppressed hostility toward Jews among Westerners.

– Finally, Jewish pathologies of self-criticism offered a particularly valuable contribution, soothing the possible doubts and hesitations that non-Jews might feel about adopting these lethal narratives so redolent of previous Jew-hatred. Masters of self-abnegation, Jews, especially assimilated or invisible ones, produce an unusually high percentage of hyper-self-critical Jews, ready to advocate for the "Other," even the hostile "other." Thus, often highly accomplished Jews and Israelis—*alter-juifs*—readily adopt the most lethal narratives about their own people.[47]

---

[45] In 2003, Tony Judt produced a widely hailed (and criticized) piece condemning Israel in post-colonial terms. See Tony Judt, "Israel: The Alternative," *New York Review of Books* 50, no. 16 (October 23, 2003), http://www.nybooks.com/articles/archives/2003/oct/23/israel-the-alternative. For a detailed response, see Richard Landes, "Insights into Why Europe Slept: Revisiting Tony Judt's 'Israel: The Alternative,'" *Augean Stables*, March 9, 2009, http://www.theaugeanstables.com/2009/03/09/insights-into-why-europe-slept-revisiting-tony-judts-israel-the-alternative. On Hamas's "democratic" victory and nature, see Mandy Turner, "Building Democracy in Palestine: Liberal Peace: Theory and the Election of Hamas," *Democratization* 13, no. 5 (2006): 739-755, http://homepage.univie.ac.at/herbert.preiss/files/Turner_Building_Democracy_in_Palestine_Liberal_Peace_Theory_Hamas.pdf; and Cata Charrett, "Understanding Hamas," *Mondoweiss*, July 14, 2014, http://mondoweiss.net/2014/07/understanding-hamas#sthash.cLOZZ5T5.dpuf.

[46] For a good example of the supersessionism that affects even an allegedly secular thinker, see the remarkable letter of Jostein Gaarder, "God's Chosen People," *Aftenblat*, August 5, 2006, http://www.informationclearinghouse.info/article14532.htm. For a response, see Richard Landes, "Open Letter to Jostein Gaarder: Fisking Crypto-Supersessionism," *Augean Stables*, August 2006, http://www.theaugeanstables.com/multiple-part-essays/open-letter-to-jostein-gaarder-fisking-crypto-supersessionism. On supersessionism and anti-Zionism more generally, see Richard Landes, "Anti-Zionism, the 21st Century Avatar of the Longest Hatred," *Fathom*, no. 13 (Summer 2016), http://fathomjournal.org/anti-zionism-21st-century-avatar-of-the-longest-hatred.

[47] Alvin Rosenfeld, *"Progressive" Jewish Thought and the New Anti-Semitism* (New York: American Jewish Committee, 2006), http://www.ajc.org/atf/cf/%7B42D75369-D582-4380-8395-D25925B85EAF%7D/progressive_jewish_thought.pdf; Edward Alexander, *Jews against Themselves* (New Brunswick: Transaction Publishers, 2015).

## 2. THE AL-DURAH BLOOD LIBEL AS NUCLEAR BOMB IN THE JIHADI COGNITIVE WAR

All of these elements come together it what may be the most important untold story of the new century. In the early autumn of 2000, the West, especially Europeans, put on an extraordinary display of self-destructiveness, centered specifically around the "Muhammad al-Durah affair."[48] On September 30, 2000, *France 2* Middle East correspondent Charles Enderlin aired 58 seconds of footage he claimed showed Israeli troops targeting and killing an innocent twelve-year-old boy in the arms of his father. Subsequent examination of both the footage itself and the reporting style of the cameraman, Talal abu Rahmeh, indicated that the scene was staged and that in the final sequence, which Enderlin cut from his broadcast, the boy, who had reportedly already died of a stomach wound, lifted up his elbow and looked out from underneath it. And yet, as an accusation against the IDF for targeting and killing innocent children, this footage had an electrifying effect on the global community.

In Muslim circles, this incident became a global wake-up call to genocidal jihad against Israel and Jews, setting in motion Irwin Cotler's paradox of the early twenty-first century, namely that the Jewish state is the only state in the world that is simultaneously accused of having and the object of genocidal intentions.[49] Palestinians rioted at the site, seething with a rage that burst forth twelve days later in Ramallah, when a crowd shouting "Revenge for the Blood of Muhammad al-Durah" beat two Israeli reservists to death and dragged their mutilated bodies through the streets. Osama bin Laden almost immediately placed the incident at the center of his call to global jihad.

But more ominously—if that were even possible—it also found remarkable resonance within Western intelligentsia, which had virtually defined its progressive voice as one that renounced blood libels and the demonization of the "other." As a result, Israel became a stigmatized nation in the world community, that "shitty little nation."[50] What had once been only the fringe

---

[48] All the material cited here, both written and audiovisual, is available from *The Second Draft* investigation: http://www.seconddraft.org/index.php?option=com_content &view=article&id=62&Itemid=80. On the affair and its impact, see Nidra Poller, *Al Dura: Long-Range Ballistic Myth* (Paris: Authorship International, 2014). Poller has also published an exceptional memoir about the opening years of the new century in Paris. See Nidra Poller, *Troubled Dawn of the 21st Century* (Paris: Authorship International, 2017).

[49] The story spread well beyond the normal circles of the Arab-Israeli conflict. Iran, Pakistan, Indonesia, and Mali also embraced this terrible tale. See Richard Landes, "Arab and Muslim World Responses," May 20, 2013, http://aldurah.com/the-al-durah-inci dent/initial-responses/arab-and-muslim-world-responses.

[50] Robin Shepherd, *A State Beyond the Pale: Europe's Problem with Israel* (London: Weidenfeld and Nicolson, 2009). On French diplomat Daniel Bernard's "shitty" comment, see pp. 54-55.

discourse of neo-Nazis and radical revolutionaries, namely that Israel was the new Nazi nation, went mainstream. The accusation of Zionazism now stigmatized Israel, not the moral sadist making the accusation.[51]

And it did so because of the core logic of the incident's appeal. It served as a get-out-of-Holocaust-guilt-free card. As one highly respected news anchor for *Europe 1* intoned, "this picture erases, replaces that of the boy in the Warsaw ghetto." In so speaking, Christine Nay articulated a wide consensus of European belief and discourse that seemed to find great moral pleasure in allowing a dubious image of an child allegedly killed in a cross-fire begun by his own side to outweigh an image that symbolized the deliberate murder of six million civilians, including one million children. Indeed, the main function of this incident and its moral "logic" was to introduce a discourse about Israel as the new Nazi nation, so that it leapt from the fringes of right-wing, neo-Nazi, and radical Left revolutionary discourse into the progressive mainstream.

Nothing symbolizes this process better than the banner unfurled at a demonstration protesting al-Durah's murder at Place de la République in Paris on October 6, 2000, in which, for the first time since the Nazis, the cry of "Kill the Jews" rang out in a European capital.[52] And although Muslim immigrants initiated the genocidal call, Western leftists accompanying them made no protest.

One could not imagine a better symbol of Europe's self-destructive madness than to see it avidly devour this poisoned meat.

Nor were the consequences easily dismissible as excesses of rhetoric. The al-Durah incident unleashed a torrent of aggression against Jews beginning the very next day after its airing on the *France 2* TV channel. While European Muslims attacked Jews,[53] Christian and post-Christian French demanded of their Jewish co-citizens an explanation for what "*your* people have done to the Palestinians."[54] Defenders of Israel were dismissed as Jewish *communautaristes*.[55]

---

[51] Ibid., 55-60; Wistrich, *Lethal Obsession* (see n. 39), 495-514.

[52] Marie Brenner, "France's Scarlet Letter," *Vanity Fair* (July 2003), http://www.vanityfair.com/news/2003/06/france-muslim-jewish-population; Paul Giniewski, "The Jews of France Tormented by the 'Intifada of the Suburbs,'" *Nativ* 5 (August 2004), http://www.acpr.org.il/ENGLISH-NATIV/05-issue/giniewski-5.htm.

[53] See n. 33. On England, see Jon Ronson's discussion of the immediate, Omar Bakri-inspired violence in England following the broadcast: Jon Ronson, *Them: Adventures with Extremists* (New York: Simon and Schuster, 2011), chap. 12.

[54] This has been repeatedly reported to me by French Jews as occurring both in the workplace and in schools.

[55] Pascale Boniface uses the accusation of "communautarisme" to invalidate any effort to defend Israel as rank partisanship. See Pascale Boniface, *Est-il permis de critiquer Israël?* (Paris: Laffont, 2003). The term "Israel-firster" is similarly used in the United States to tar defenders of Israel as "disloyal" to the larger society. See Lee Smith, "The Hitler Test," *Tablet*, January 27, 2012, http://www.tabletmag.com/jewish-news-

*Feuj*, the slang term for *juif*, became a term of derogation, "c'est un stylo *feuj*," a broken pen.[56]

*Place de la République, Paris, October 6, 2000.*

In the meantime, within the Muslim population, whose restiveness was often ignored but already constituted a growing problem in France (and many other parts of Europe), things turned violent. Arab "immigrants," born in France but less assimilated into French culture than even their first-generation parents, unleashed low grade "pogroms" against Jews. The targets were often their very neighbors, who had preceded them in the journey from North Africa and shared many aspects of their community and culture.[57] A serious socio-cultural problem thus took a sharp turn for the worse.

At the same time, all the measures and safeguards adopted in civil society to reject this kind of violence and hateful rhetoric collapsed like a cultural Maginot Line. In every place that such aggression appeared and should have met with rebuke, it met instead with appeasement. When Muslim pupils bullied Jewish

---

and-politics/89334/the-hitler-test. On the other hand, criticism of the extensive *communautarisme* of the Muslim community provokes accusations of racism and Islamophobia from the same circles. See Ali A. Rizvi, "The Phobia of Being Called Islamophobic," *Huffington Post*, April 28, 2014, http://www.huffingtonpost.com/ali-a-rizvi/the-phobia-of-being-calle_b_5215218.html; Daniel Greenfield, "UK Atheists Realize Islam is the Only Religion They Can't Criticize," *Frontpage Mag*, September 5, 2013, http://www.frontpagemag.com/2013/dgreenfield/uk-atheists-realize-islam-is-the-only-religion-they-cant-criticize.

56 Brenner et al., *Territoires perdus*, 27-29 (see n. 36); UEJF/SOS-Racisme, *Les anti-feujs* (see n. 36).

57 Giniewski, "Jews of France Tormented."

children in a public school, the principle advised the parents move the victim to a Jewish school, leaving the rest of the class subject to further bullying. When dinner-table conversations turned to excoriating Israel for its victimization of the Palestinians, anyone who disagreed was met with the response, "Oh, I didn't know you were Jewish"—even when they were not.[58]

Thus, while the cultural Maginot Line collapsed in Europe and antisemitic discourse and violence spread throughout the land, the news media and diplomatic community—two institutions that apparently enjoy a remarkable overlap in France[59]—had nothing to say. Publicly, it was, "nothing is happening, there is no antisemitism." Off the record, it was the brazen *amalgame*, "what do you expect, look at what your brethren in Israel are doing to their cousins." When suicide bombing came, the burden of blame was laid directly at the feet of the victim of the attacks. As Cherie Blair put it, "If you didn't rob them of hope, then they wouldn't do this." This kind of comment, almost axiomatically accepted in all but the most formal European venues (Prime Minister Tony Blair was not pleased), combines incoherent moral reasoning with a lack of any self-awareness, much less self-criticism.

So while the Europeans sipped on the wine of their distaste for Jews (and Americans[60]), they stocked an open bar of the most delirious hatreds for their Muslim neighbors, watching in quiet approval as their Muslim populations vented their media-induced anger on Europe's Jewish population.[61] And when the Jews complained, authorities and public intellectuals questioned their testimony, told them not to exaggerate, and warned them that to criticize *la nation* publicly was disloyal. Meanwhile, when "as-a-Jew" Jews joined the chorus of condemnation, they got lionized.[62]

---

[58] This anecdote was repeated to me independently by several people in the early aughts: "Ah, je ne savais pas que vous étiez juif."

[59] David Pryce-Jones, *Betrayal: France, the Arabs, and the Jews* (New York: Encounter, 2006), 131-136.

[60] Andrei Markowiecz, *Uncouth Nation: Why Europe Dislikes America* (Princeton: Princeton University Press, 2006), chap. 5. On the French reaction to 9/11, see Poller, *Troubled Dawn*, chap. 2.

[61] Much has been written on the return of antisemitism in the twenty-first century West, starting with Taguieff, *Rising from the Muck* (see n. 33); Phyllis Chesler, *The New Anti-Semitism* (New York: Josey Bass, 2003; Jerusalem: Geffen, 2015); Fiamma Nirenstein, *Terror: The New Anti-Semitism and the War against the West* (New York: Simon and Kraus, 2005); Dennis MacShane, *Globalizing Hatred* (London: Weidenfeld and Nicolson, 2008).

[62] On the role of "alter-juifs" (in English "as-a-Jew" Jews), see "Les Alterjuifs," ed. Shmuel Trigano, special issue, *Controverses*, no. 4 (February 2007), http://www.contro verses.fr/Sommaires/sommaire4.htm. On the term "as-a-Jew," see "'As a Jew' Explained," *CiFWatch*, June 23, 2011, http://cifwatch.com/2011/06/23/as-a-jew-explained. On the almost boundless ability of Jews to be self-critical, see Barry Rubin, *Assimilation*

Thus, to save *la nation* from having its face blackened by accusations of Islamophobia in the world community, the French elites actually encouraged the spread of the virus far and wide in their culture.[63] Through their silent encouragement of Muslim antisemitism, the French lost control of whole school districts and communities, no-go zones, and *zones urbaines sensibles*, where even ambulances dare not venture unaccompanied. In the autumn of 2005, these communities displayed a determined vandalism that literally lit up the map of France with firebombs and cries of "Allahu Akhbar". In response, French intellectuals insisted this had *nothing* to do with Islam.[64]

### 3. COGNITIVE DISSONANCE AND DENIAL: WHY EXPECTING RESISTANCE IS FUTILE

In a telling Twitter exchange, Mark Steyn notes a decade-belated admission by Tarek Fatah that he got it wrong about Steyn's warnings on global jihad. In response to Steyn's book *America Alone* (2005), the Pakistani-born, Canadian Muslim Fatah wrote a review in 2007 that dismissed Steyn's early alarmism as, "fears … grounded in ignorance, but quite often it borders on an alarmist fear of the Muslim world."[65] More recently, however, Fatah tweeted:

> When Mark Steyn wrote "Future Belongs to Islam," I scoffed at it, but 10 yrs later I believe him. Facing Islamism are cowardly wimps.[66]

I interpret this as a sentiment that is probably broadly shared by a number of people of good will who found Steyn's aggressive insistence in the mid-aughts on an imminent threat from Islam unpalatable. I went through the same process

---

*and Its Discontents* (New York: Crown Publishing, 1995); on the current crop of alter-juifs, see Rosenfeld, *"Progressive" Jewish Thought* (see n. 47); Anthony Julius, *Trials of the Diaspora: A History of Anti-Semitism in England* (Oxford: Oxford University Press, 2010), 543-560; Wistrich, *Lethal Obsession* (see n. 39), 515-542.

[63] On the silence, see Tagueiff, *Rising from the Muck* (see n. 33), chap. 4. Fifteen years later, this denial in the service of face-saving came to a head when Fox News reported that Paris had some Muslim "no-go" zones and the mayor of Paris threatened to sue the network for "insulting" her city: "The image of Paris has been prejudiced, and the honor of Paris has been prejudiced," she told CNN. See Gregory Wallace and Brian Stelter, "Paris Mayor Anne Hidalgo: We Intend to Sue Fox News," *CNN*, January 21, 2015, http://money.cnn.com/2015/01/20/media/paris-mayor-sue-fox-news.

[64] "Riots in France," Social Science Research Council (SSRC), http://riotsfrance.ssrc.org.

[65] Tarek Fatah and Farzana Hazzan, "Mark Steyn Has a Right to Be Wrong," *McLean's Magazine*, December 13, 2007, available at https://groups.yahoo.com/neo/groups/muktochinta/conversations/messages/18625.

[66] Tarek Fatah, Twitter message, October 2, 2014, https://twitter.com/TarekFatah/status/517461560953155584.

in the late 1990s, when I first learned of global jihad and its goals of conquest. The Queen of England wearing a burkah? The green flag of Islam flying from the White House? Absurd. Alarmist. Only as a millennial scholar, familiar with the power of the mistaken, outrageous hope that now was the time to radically change the world, did I pause in my dismissal. They may be mistaken, but that hardly limits the damage they can do on their way to their eventual failure.

What I—and I suspect Tarek Fatah—did not foresee was that, faced with this astonishingly primitive, hateful, and violent form of the worst kind of religious bigotry, the progressive West would fail to rise up in opposition.[67] And yet, what happened instead of a vigorous resistance to all the kinds of violent zealotry in both word and deed, which had previously led to the Nazis' success, the West responded just as Chamberlain had done, with *systematic* appeasement.[68] Indeed, one might describe the aughts as the onset of a widespread "proleptic dhimmitude" in which Western elites adopted behavior demanded of *dhimmi* before being, in anticipation of being, conquered and forced into such status.

At every turn, Westerners chose to "show Islam respect," even in cases of aggressive Muslim violence. A Moroccan immigrant murdered Muslim critic Theo Van Gogh in the streets of Amsterdam, and Queen Beatrix donned a hijab to visit a Muslim community center to emphasize the warmth of relations between the Dutch and their Muslim community.[69]

*Dhimmi* behavior continued without interruption not just in Holland but on a global scale. In response to the Pope's in-house quotation of a fourteenth century emperor calling Islam inherently violent, Muslims rioted the world over.[70] Rather than registering, as it should have, as a deeply embarrassing joke on Muslims, Western opinion pressured the Pope to apologize for provoking the Muslim violence. Similarly, publishers kept a worried eye on potential Muslim violence in making editorial decisions.[71]

Some of the most striking examples of proleptic dhimmitude in the twenty-first century came from the news media. Historians looking back with even minimal dispassion on the early years of the twenty-first century will note that there were two major professional failures on the part of the international news media: (1) the exceptionally high moral dudgeon, especially in Europe, sur-

---

[67] In 2007, Fatah still believed that "slowly but surely, the progressive narrative within Islam is gaining ground."

[68] Bawer, *Surrender* (see n. 19); Bruce Thornton, *The Wages of Appeasement: Ancient Athens, Munich and Obama's America* (New York: Encounter Books, 2011).

[69] Bawer, *Surrender*, 234; Esman (*Radical State*) does not seem to have noted the Queen's behavior in immediate response to the murder.

[70] Marshall and Shea, *Silenced*, chap. 13.

[71] Oleg Grabar, "Seeing Is Believing. The Image of the Prophet in Islam: The Real Story," *New Republic*, November 4, 2009.

rounding the behavior of the Israel Defense Forces (IDF); and (2) the equally exceptional silence surrounding the misbehavior of radical Muslims and jihadis in the West, especially in Europe. What unites these two breaches of profession-al behavior are the rules of the *Dhimma*. On the one hand, the news media maintain the essential rule—thou shalt not insult Islam or Muslims; on the other, they adopt as their own the jihadis' enemy—Israel.[72]

Westerners who urge this kind of placatory response to the challenge of Islam believe they are showing the kind of goodwill and determined refusal to generalize negatively about Islam necessary for progressive forces of mutual understanding to prevail. In their minds, they are being generous to Muslims in the hope of reciprocity. Westerners who refuse to criticize Islam, who police the boundaries of "acceptable" criticism by banishing transgressors as "right-wing" *Islamophobes* (including anyone who defends Israel), fulfill the exigencies of the *dhimma*: no infidel has the right to criticize, demean, insult, or blaspheme Islam or any Muslim.[73] Thus, even as the French, for example, rejected any attempt to link Islam and "the vast majority" of peaceful Muslims to jihadi doctrines and aspirations—"surtout pas d'amalgame!"—they indulged precisely this kind of lumping together of French Jews and the behavior of the IDF as reported by their media.

This appeasement had the exact opposite effect of the one desired: it af-firmed the jihadis' belief that they are winning—which they are—and inspired further aggressions on many fronts. To jihadis all these acts of generosity registered as voluntary submission to the laws of *dhimma*, as sure signs of weakness and of the weak Western commitment to alleged Western values, especially *freedom of speech*, which is anathema to Islamism. Armed with both *Islamophobia* as a weapon to silence and a phalanx of well-meaning proleptic *dhimmi* Western leaders ready to patrol their own ranks against violations, jihadis can invade schools, religious dialogues, financial institutions, politics, academia, and even military bases.

The question that this millennial scholar wishes to ask here is as follows. What makes it so hard for Western progressives (on the liberal Left) to realize that their behavior is counter-productive? To paraphrase Dylan and Blake, how many times must a man give in before he feels the mind-forged manacles? The answer is difficult to even discuss, since the conceder/appeaser will do anything

---

[72] This involves two other features of news media behavior: silence regarding the ugliest aspects of Palestinian jihadi behavior and loud denunciation of people stigma-tized as "Islamophobes" (i.e. people violating the rules of *dhimma*).

[73] For a good example of a *dhimmi* enforcer attacking someone who—in his mind—has offended Muslims, see Ben Affleck's response to Sam Harris and Bill Maher's criticism of Islam on *Real Time with Bill Maher*, October 3, 2014, available at https://www.youtube.com/watch?v=vln9D81eO60.

to deny the very pattern that forms the basis of the question. Those who recognize the problem might find it tempting to point to acute cognitive dissonance as an explanation for the pervasive denial at work.

## 4. DIAGNOSIS: THE DANGERS OF DENIAL AND MISINFORMATION

One can turn to a number of medical analogies to describe the condition of the West today. On one level, there is an *aggressive form of acquired-immune deficiency* in which the body social not only fails to mobilize the cells that defend it from invasion but actually attacks the messengers that come to warn it of the attack as racist, xenophobic, and Islamophobic. On another level, there is a form of *congenital analgesia*,[74] in which the nerves—here the news media—fail to communicate to the brain that the body feels pain or, if they do so, choose to euphemize the cause of the pain. For example, the media describe jihadi attacks as psychotic episodes or "work-place violence";[75] the press identifies perpetrators neutrally as "youth" or "Asians"; and systematic abuse gets covered up for decades.[76] An unacknowledged *omertà* governing dozens of deeply disturbing public secrets reigns.[77] Jihadis can yell "Allahu Akhbar" as they kill their many

---

[74] Mario Manfredi et al., "Congenital Absence of Pain," *JAMA Neurology* 38, no. 8 (1981): 507-511, http://archneur.jamanetwork.com/article.aspx?articleid=580002.

[75] Most famously in the scandalous case of Major Hassan's attack on Fort Hood, see Richard Landes, "Anatomy of 'Progressive' Double Speak: Fisking Frank Rich on Fort Hood," *Augean Stables*, November 18, 2009, http://www.theaugeanstables.com/2009/11/18/anatomy-of-progressive-double-speak-fisking-frank-rich-on-fort-hood. Or in the case of a Moroccan-born woman butchering a teacher in front of her class of six-year-olds in Albi (France), see Ivan Rioufol, "Retour sur le meurtre de l'institutrice d'Albi," *Le Figaro*, July 7, 2014, http://blog.lefigaro.fr/rioufol/2014/07/lassassinat-vendredi-matin-de.html.

[76] As in the case of the systematic rape by Pakistani Muslim men of English girls as young as ten in Rotherham, which went on for over a decade without being revealed to the public. See Katrin Bennhold, "Years of Rape and 'Utter Contempt' in Britain," *New York Times*, September 1, 2014, http://www.nytimes.com/2014/09/02/world/europe/reckoning-starts-in-britain-on-abuse-of-girls.html. Note that while the *New York Times* identifies the perpetrators as being "of Pakistani origin," there is no mention of the word Muslim and no allusion to the widespread phenomenon of "rape jihad." See Soeren Kern, "Britain: 'Rape Jihad' Against Children," *Gatestone Institute*, July 11, 2013, http://www.gatestoneinstitute.org/3846/britain-child-grooming.

[77] See Eviatar Zerubavel, *The Elephant in the Room: Silence and Denial in Everyday Life* (New York: Oxford University Press, 2010). Despite his brilliant discussion of the issues involved in pervasive denial, and the fact that he was writing at the height of global jihad's cognitive victories in the West, Zerubavel scarcely mentions the issue. For a good introduction to the issues involved in Islamist aggression, see Stephen Emerson's documentary *Jihad in America: The Grand Deception* (2014), http://www.granddeception.com.

enemies, and Western authorities will insist this has nothing to do with Islam. "ISIS," President Obama remarked, "is neither Islamic nor a state."[78]

In the case of both these syndromes, the immense appetite of Europeans—especially their intelligentsia—for lethal narratives about Israel makes things considerably worse.[79] In the case of auto-immune deficiency, lethal journalism empowers both the jihadi invaders and the key "progressive" players within the West who welcome them. Feeding frenzies of lethal journalism concerning the alleged "Jenin massacre" and, more recently, Operation Protective Edge literally light up European capitals with violent demonstrations of hatred.[80] In the case of congenital analgesia, the reluctance to identify jihadis at home derives in part from the way in which acknowledging the jihadi threat lets Israel off the moral hook. If Europeans acknowledge that Israelis are fighting an implacable enemy whose goal is not the Green Line but the shoreline—jihadis with deep sympathies and links to Europe's own (unacknowledged) enemies—it takes Israel off the moral hot seat. And apparently, it means a great deal to Western self-esteem to keep Israel on that hot seat.[81]

---

[78] Igor Volsky and Jack Jenkins, "Why ISIS Is Not, In Fact, Islamic," *ThinkProgress*, September 11, 2014, http://thinkprogress.org/world/2014/09/11/3566181/why-isis-is-in-fact-not-islamic. After the Charlie Hebdo attacks, UK Prime Minister David Cameron, who had previously agreed with Obama, changed his tune. His contrasting remarks in a press conference with Obama were painful to watch. See "Pres. Obama and PM Cameron Joint Press Conference," MSNBC, January 16, 2015, http://www.msnbc.com/shift/watch/obama-and-cameron-joint-conference-385241667776. A week later, Secretary of State John Kerry explained to a global audience that violent extremism was not Islamic. See "Violent Extremism Is Not Islamic," *CBS News*, January 23, 2015, http://www.cbsnews.com/news/violent-extremism-is-not-islamic-john-kerry-tells-leaders-in-davos.

[79] Richard Landes, "The Western Appetite for Lethal Narratives about Israel: Moral Theology and Replacement Theology," *Augean Stables*, November 12, 2012, http://www.theaugeanstables.com/2012/11/12/western-appetite-for-lethal-narratives-about-israel-moral-schadenfreude-and-replacement-theology.

[80] On the rage churned up in the United States by the reporting of a massacre in Jenin, see Paul Berman, "Bigotry in Print. Crowds Chant Murder. Something's Changed," *Forward*, May 24, 2002, available at http://www.freerepublic.com/focus/news/691327/posts. On the same phenomenon in Europe, see Oriana Fallaci, "On Jew-Hatred in Europe" [in Italian], *Panorama*, April 17, 2002, translation available at http://www.imra.org.il/story.php3?id=11611; see also n. 9.

[81] For a recent example of this seemingly irresistible urge to blame Israel, see the remarks of Secretary of State John Kerry to a Muslim audience about how "the absence of peace deal causes 'humiliation' in the region and drives recruitment for the Islamic State group." Kerry repeatedly blames Israel for this failure. See "Kerry: 'Imperative' to Resume Israel-Palestinian Talks," *Times of Israel*, October 17, 2014, http://www.timesofisrael.com/kerry-imperative-to-resume-israel-palestinian-talks. See also nn. 92 and 104.

This brings us to the last medical analogy: *psychogenic dissociative paralysis*.[82] People suffering from this condition view one of their own limbs as "not their own." In some cases, the sense of horror and revulsion actually makes the owner hostile, or even violent, toward his or her own limb. In this analogy, Israel is a fundamental part of Western democratic society, both in its origins and its current manifestations.[83] One might even go so far as to claim that Israeli democracy, under the conditions of constant and genocidal threat from its neighbors, constitutes one of the most heroic episodes in the relatively short history of modern democracies.[84]

> By any objective standard, Israeli democracy is as robust and pluralistic as any in the world. There are no restrictions on any form of protest or advocacy, including very fierce and unpopular criticism of the government and military. No other democracy can claim to have greater freedom of expression, despite more than six decades of war and terrorism; threats of annihilation; and in parallel, the challenges of developing a cohesive society based on numerous divergent communities scattered for generations as Diasporas, many of which do not have traditions of pluralism and democracy.[85]

And yet, as a result of seeing Israel as "not us," Westerners—and especially Europeans—have made a long series of potentially fatal errors in a civilizational battle with one of the greatest enemies of the democratic ethos.

First, this misidentification has systematically blinded Westerners as to the nature of their enemy. By insisting that Israel was the aggressor and the Palestinian fighters were part of a "progressive" resistance to colonial oppression, they misunderstood both the nature of the hostility to Israel and the damage to their own ability to defend themselves. Westerners insisted that the Second Intifada, which jihadis saw as the onset of the global jihad against the

---

[82] In chapter four of his book *The Man Who Mistook his Wife for a Hat and Other Clinical Tales* (New York: Summit Books, 1985), Oliver Sacks describes a patient who viewed his own leg as a disembodied foreign object. He also wrote of his own personal experience in the matter in *A Leg to Stand on* (New York: Harper and Row, 1984), prompting a significant article from which I draw this diagnosis. See Jon Stone, Jo Perthen and Alan J. Carson, "'A Leg to Stand On' by Oliver Sacks: A Unique Autobiographical Account of Functional Paralysis," *Journal of Neurology, Neurosurgery and Psychiatry* 83, no. 9 (2012): 864-867, http://jnnp.bmj.com/content/83/9/864.full. My term combines several of the multiple cognomens the authors suggest.

[83] See n. 45.

[84] Richard Landes, "From Useful Idiot to Useful Infidel: Meditations on the Folly of 21st Century 'Intellectuals,'" in "Intellectuals and Terror: The Fatal Attraction," ed. Anna Geifman and Helena Rimon, special issue, *Terrorism and Political Violence* 25, no. 4 (2013): 633.

[85] Gerald Steinberg, "Israel's Vibrant Democracy," *Times of Israel*, February 19, 2012, http://blogs.timesofisrael.com/israels-vibrant-democracy/#ixzz3GeSDxW4P.

West,[86] was solely a matter of national liberation.[87] On many occasions, Western officials, deeply influenced by the lethal journalists who report on Israeli "massacres," have insisted that (as French Foreign Minister Laurent Fabius recently put it), "Nothing justifies continued [IDF] attacks and massacres which do nothing but only claim more victims and stoke tensions, hatred."[88] He might have put it differently: "nothing justifies the continued lethal journalism, which only supports jihadi forces and does nothing but stoke tensions and hatred." But he did not, and would not.

The determination to see Israel as the aggressor has meant that Westerners have repeatedly excoriated Israel for its efforts to defend itself against jihadi aggression. On the military battlefield, Israel was held to impossible standards where civilian casualties were concerned, amplified by the willingness to believe Palestinian propaganda on how many civilians were killed.[89] Thus many in the

------

[86] On the jihadi perspective, see Safar Ibn 'Abd al-Rahman al-Hawali, "The Day of Wrath: Is the Intifadha of Rajab Only the Beginning?" [in Arabic] (2001), which is discussed in Cook, *Contemporary Muslim Apocalyptic Literature* (see n. 40), 48-49.

[87] With regard to the Western insistence that Palestinian hostility toward Israel is a form of "national resistance," one of many telling examples comes from a scholar's anecdote. Metropolitan Books (a subsidiary of Holt) had bought Benny Morris' book *1948* before it was written. Upon reading the conclusion, editor Sara Bershtel rejected the book, "specifically the assertion that the 1947-48 Arab assault on the Yishuv/Israel was partially driven by anti-Semitic impulses and Jihadism ... as well as the references to the Palestine Arab leadership's corruption, incompetence and disunity in the run-up to 1948," which she deemed "racist." Rejecting the book as "ideologically and politically driven," she herself worked according to an entirely unselfconscious ideological and political(ly correct) agenda that shielded readers from any exposure to views that highlighted religious motivations. Email correspondence with Benny Morris, October 20, 2014.

[88] "France Condemns Gaza 'Massacres,' Calls for Ceasefire," *The Times of Israel*, July 22, 2014, http://www.timesofisrael.com/france-condemns-gaza-massacres-calls-for-ceasefire/#ixzz3GZFj3sdw.

[89] On the tendency of the media to repeat Hamas-based statistics during Operation Protective Edge and report the "vast majority" of deaths as civilian, see Richard Behar, "The Media Intifada: Bad Math, Ugly Truths about *New York Times* in Israel-Hamas War," *Forbes*, August 21, 2014, http://www.forbes.com/sites/richardbehar/2014/08/21/the-media-intifada-bad-math-ugly-truths-about-new-york-times-in-israel-hamas-war. For a self-critical discussion in the *New York Times*, which according to Behar had little long-term impact on subsequent coverage, see Jodi Rudoren, "Civilian or Not? New Fight in Tallying the Dead From the Gaza Conflict," *New York Times*, August 5, 2014. For an extensive and careful study by the Israeli Intelligence and Terrorism Information Center, which argues that approximately half the identifiable deaths were combatants (i.e. an exceptionally low rate of civilian casualties, especially for urban warfare), see "Examination of the Names of Palestinians Killed in Operation Protective Edge—Part Four," August 25, 2014, http://www.terrorism-info.org.il/Data/articles/Art_20708/E_151_14_1970189202.pdf; and Ben Cohen, "Israeli Think-Tank: Majority of Identified

West believe Israel deliberately targets civilians, even though Israel's record of both targeted killings and urban warfare sets a much higher standard than other Western armies, most notably during the Battle of Jenin.[90] On the one hand, this leads to heavy restraints on Western waging of warfare. The resistance to counter-insurgency (COIN) among American troops illustrates what every IDF soldier who has participated in joint exercises with US troops knows: that Israel's restraints are far higher than America's.[91] On the other, it leads to conscious or unconscious hypocrisy, as in President Obama's outrage at Israeli killings of civilians during Operation Protective Edge, even as he loosened the already (comparatively) loose US standards of acceptable "collateral damage" for US airstrikes in Syria.[92] As Colonel Richard Kemp noted in a talk in Jerusalem:

Gaza War Casualties Were Terrorists," *Algemeiner*, December 2, 2014, http://www.alge meiner.com/2014/12/02/israeli-think-tank-52-percent-of-identified-gaza-war-casualties-were-terrorists. See also next note.

[90] Whatever the estimates and whatever the theater of war (e.g. drone attacks, urban warfare, or aerial bombing), Israeli figures for civilian-combatant casualty ratios are exceptional: between 1:10/30 (drones) to approximately 1:1 (urban warfare). US and NATO figures are the reverse: between 10/30:1 (drones) and 3:1 (urban warfare). See *Wikipedia*, s.v. "Civilian Casualty Ratio," http://en.wikipedia.org/wiki/Civilian_casualty_ratio. A recent report by British NGO *Reprieve* claims to document a 28:1 ratio for US drone strikes in Pakistan. See http://www.reprieve.org.uk/media/downloads/2012_02_22_PUB_drones_UN_HRC_complaint.pdf. In Jenin, after three weeks of urban warfare, there were 56 Palestinians casualties, including 40 combatants (3:1). Nevertheless, the press widely reported a "massacre" of 500-900 civilians in Jenin.

[91] On COIN, see Field Manual (FM) 3-24/Marine Corps Warfighting Publication (MCWP) 3-33.5, *Counterinsurgency*, http://www.marines.mil/Portals/59/MCWP%203-33.5_Part1.pdf. Retired Army lieutenant general and former chief of Combined Forces Command Afghanistan Karl Eikenberry complained that the "clear, hold and build" strategy outlined in FM 3-24 "called for individual soldiers and Marines with the qualities of a modern-day Lawrence of Arabia, versed in languages and attuned to the culture and politics of the host nation. The typical 21-year-old Marine is hard-pressed to win the heart and mind of his mother-in-law. Can he really be expected to do the same with an ethnocentric Pashtun tribal elder? Moreover, T.E. Lawrence specialized in inciting revolts, not in state building." See Richard Sisk, "COIN Doctrine under Fire," *DoDBuzz*, November 19, 2013, http://www.dodbuzz.com/2013/11/19/coin-doctrine-under-fire. See also Celeste Gventer, "Why US Soldiers in Afghanistan Are So Frustrated," *Christian Science Monitor*, June 30, 2010, http://www.csmonitor.com/Commentary/Opinion/2010/0630/Why-US-soldiers-in-Afghanistan-are-so-frustrated; and Andrew Bostom, "McChrystal, Tocqueville, and the Koran: The Postmodern 'COINage' of a Failed Policy," *PJMedia*, June 29, 2010, http://pjmedia.com/blog/mcchrystal-tocqueville-and-the-koran-the-postmodern-coinage-of-a-failed-policy.

[92] Seth Mandel, "Obama's Hypocrisy on Civilian Casualties," *Commentary*, October 1, 2014, http://www.commentarymagazine.com/2014/10/01/obamas-hypocrisy-on-civilian-casualties. Note Secretary of State John Kerry's dismissive (and off-the-record) remark about "a hell of a pin-point bombing" based on US military reports (see Mark Perry, "Why Israel's Bombardment of Gaza Neighborhood Left US Officers 'Stunned,'" *Al*

> Within weeks of the European Parliament endorsing the [Goldstone] report [condemning Israel for "war crimes and possible crimes against humanity"], the European Chairman of NATO's Military Committee was visiting Israel, for the third time in four years, to study ethical methods for dealing with terrorist insurgencies without causing undue harm to civilians.[93]

The same problems of disassociation hold for the cognitive war as for kinetic war. In the case of the former, the assault on Israel installs a discourse that systematically works against the ability of democracies to recognize enemies and defend themselves. Thus, in 2002, under the delusion that Israel had massacred hundreds of Palestinian civilians in Jenin, which was produced by a wave of lethal journalism, Europeans demonstrated their support for the "victims" by wearing mock suicide belts in solidarity with the "resistance."[94] Like those who danced on the skyscraper rooftop to greet the spaceship above in the movie *Independence Day* just before the aliens pulverized them, Europeans lionized jihadis who would soon make them their targets.

And when the attacks came, as in the London streets and underground on July 7, 2005, journalists found themselves forbidden from referring to the attackers as "terrorists." Having renounced using the word "terrorist"—for reasons of both intimidation[95] and specious reasoning[96]—in the context of the Arab-Israeli conflict, both US and British journalists found themselves in diffi-

---

*Jazeera America*, August 27, 2014, http://america.aljazeera.com/articles/2014/8/26/israel-bombing-stunsusofficers.html), when the actual number of deaths (65-70 out of 100,000 inhabitants), 75% of whom were combatants, represents an unprecedented example of pin-point operations (see *Wikipedia*, s.v. "Battle of Shuja'iyya," http://en.wikipedia.org/wiki/Battle_of_Shuja'iyya_(2014)#Casualties).

[93] Kemp, "Israel as a Strategic Asset to Britain" (see n. 41).

[94] Oriana Fallaci, "On Jew Hatred in Europe" (see n. 80).

[95] When a Canadian newspaper changed a Reuters report, using "terrorist" instead of "militant," Reuters requested that they remove the Reuters by-line. David Schlesinger, Reuters' global managing editor explained: "Changes like those made at CanWest could lead to 'confusion' about what Reuters is reporting and possibly endanger its reporters in volatile areas or situations. My goal is to protect our reporters and protect our editorial integrity." In other words, we cannot call these groups "terrorists" without endangering our journalists in the field from the very terrorists who do not wish to be so identified. Ironically then, our media refuse to call a terrorist group "terrorist" because they threaten journalists with terror, a position one would hardly describe as one of "editorial integrity."

[96] For a good example of this speciousness, see Christine Chinlund, "Who Should Wear Their Terrorist Label?," *Boston Globe*, September 8, 2003, p. A15, http://www.boston.com/news/globe/editorial_opinion/editorials/articles/2003/09/08/who_should_wear_the_terrorist_label. For a critique, see Richard Landes, "Boston Globe Ombudsman on 'Who Is a Terrorist?,'" *Augean Stables*, October 22, 2011, http://www.the augeanstables.com/2011/11/27/from-the-archives-boston-globe-ombudsman-on-who-is-a-terrorist.

culty when they suffered their own attacks of 9/11 and 7/7.[97] By assuming that Palestinians hated Israel for purely national (and rational) reasons and that suicide bombings were purely the result of frustration that Israel had not granted them autonomy,[98] Europeans profoundly misjudged the animus at play among jihadis.

The fact that years later, after several attacks and extensive examples of jihadi savagery, the Left still embraced Hamas and Hezbollah as part of the "anti-imperialist, global progressive Left" testifies to how tenaciously "progressives" have clung to their self-destructive fantasies.[99] At the 2008 Democratic Convention, some demonstrators carried a sign that read: "Muqtada Al-Sadr: Anti-

---

[97] Within hours of the 7/7 bombings, the BBC's director of news, Helen Broaden, sent out a memo urging her journalists not to use the word "terrorist" because "the word 'terrorist' itself can be a barrier rather than an aid to understanding. We should try to avoid the term, without attribution." While many complied, others felt it was the height of lunacy. See Matt Born, "BBC Backlash at 'Terrorist' Warning," *Daily Mail*, July 13, 2005. This approach had long been used concerning Israel and the Palestinians. See, for example, the BBC Academy's subject guide on Israel and the Palestinians at http://www.bbc.co.uk/academy/journalism/subject-guides/israel-and-the-palestinians/article/art20130702112133696. Somehow, no one seemed to feel that it was "the height of lunacy" to argue "one man's terrorist is another's freedom fighter" when Palestinians blew themselves up on Israeli buses and in Israeli restaurants and shopping malls.

[98] In June of 2002, after the Jenin "massacre," at a charity event that took place only days after another suicide attack on an Israeli bus that killed nineteen people, many of them children, Cherie Blair, wife of UK Prime Minister Tony Blair, remarked: "As long as young people feel they have got no hope but to blow themselves up you are never going to make progress." The implication here is that, if only the frustrating Israelis would stop taking away their hope, Palestinians would be less angry and violent. As one commenter on the BBC website put it: "If Palestinians FEEL that they have hope of change, they will be less likely to want to die for the cause. This is a *simple statement of fact.*" See Peter D, comment on "Cherie Blair's Comments: Did She Overstep the Mark?," *BBC*, June 24, 2002, http://news.bbc.co.uk/1/hi/talking_point/2052507.stm (emphasis added).

[99] On the "anti-imperialism of fools," best embodied by the impenetrably opaque icon of postmodern transgressive scholarship, Judith Butler, who welcomed Hamas and Hezbollah to the ranks of the "global progressive Left," see Michael J. Totten, "The Anti-Imperialism of Fools," *World Affairs Journal*, August 20, 2012, http://www.worldaffairsjournal.org/blog/michael-j-totten/anti-imperialism-fools; Richard Landes and Benjamin Weinthal, "The Post-Self-Destructivism of Judith Butler," *Wall Street Journal*, September 9, 2012, http://online.wsj.com/news/articles/SB10000872396390443921504577641351255227554. See also Noah Gabriel Brahm, "The Philosophy behind 'BDS': A Review of *Deconstructing Zionism: A Critique of Political Metaphysics,*" *Fathom*, no. 6 (Spring 2014), http://www.fathomjournal.org/reviews-culture/the-philosophy-behind-bds; and Cary Nelson, "The Problem with Judith Butler: The Philosophy of the Movement to Boycott Israel," in *The Case Against Academic Boycotts of Israel*, ed. Cary Nelson and Gabriel Brahm (Chicago: MLA Members for Scholars' Rights, 2014). More generally, on the "Marxist-Islamist" alliance, see Robert Wistrich, *From Ambivalence to Betrayal: The Left, the Jews, and Israel* (Lincoln, NE: University of Nebraska Press, 2012), chap. 18.

Imperialist Solidarity," despite the fact that Al-Sadr's mosques had torture chambers.[100] The following year, in response to the IDF's incursion into Gaza, "leftist" Europeans chanted "We are Hamas!" at the demonstrations in solidarity with the Palestinian victims.[101] Repeatedly, from 9/11 to the emergence of ISIS, Israelis have expected the United States and other Western nations to recognize the fact that they all share a common enemy; yet Westerners have repeatedly preferred to believe more politically correct commentators who argue that Israel has earned the hostility of the Palestinians by refusing them statehood and that "ISIS is not Hamas."[102]

Thus when the 9/11 Commission looked into the reasons why the United States did not anticipate the attacks, they cited "above all, a failure of imagination," which included the inability both to imagine suicide hijackers and to understand the depths of the hatred for the United States.[103] Israel had suffered from both the hatred and the suicide attacks for over a decade, but few raised that point, even ex post facto. On the contrary, Westerners, assumed that the

---

[100] Arwa Darmon, "Chain Wrapped around 'Old Man's Body' Found in Mosque," *CNN*, August 19, 2008, http://www.cnn.com/2008/WORLD/meast/08/19/iraq.mosque/?iref=hpmostpop. The Democratic National Convention took place the following week (August 25-28).

[101] The Workers' Revolutionary party remarked: "Another banner on the march proclaimed 'We are Hamas,' demonstrating the mass support for the elected Palestinian government in Gaza by both the Palestinian people and people all over the world." See "100,000 March against Israeli Barbarism," *WRP News Line*, January 5, 2009, http://www.wrp.org.uk/news/3873; see also "George Galloway Contradicting Himself 'We Are All Hamas' Statement," YouTube video, posted by Daily Politics on June 17, 2013, https://www.youtube.com/watch?v=pJccllIxeEU. "At one rally in Hyde Park, speakers on the main stage urged 'Victory to Hamas!' and received tumultuous cheers of approval (with only a few boos)." See Peter Tatchell, "Hamas No, Human Rights Yes," *Guardian*, February 18, 2009, http://www.theguardian.com/commentisfree/2009/feb/18/hamas-palestine-israel-human-rights.

[102] Beinart, "Why Bibi Is Wrong" (see n. 28). The fallacy in Beinart's effort to distinguish Palestinian "resistance" from Islamist or jihadi "resistance" lies in a sleight of hand (from Netanyahu's *Hamas* equals ISIS to Beinart's *Palestinian resistance* equals ISIS) and an assertion/conviction—based on no known poll—that "not all Palestinians desire a Caliphate." While technically true, Beinart's implication is that significant numbers do not. However, according to a 2013 report by the Pew Research Center, 89% of Palestinians want sharia law. See Pew Forum on Religion and Public Life, *The World's Muslims: Religion, Politics and Society* (Washington, DC: Pew Research Center, 2013), http://www.pewforum.org/2013/04/30/the-worlds-muslims-religion-politics-society-beliefs-about-sharia. Once there is a caliphate, a jihad against Israel can be officially sanctioned, and I suspect that a significant number would therefore support this.

[103] *Final Report of the National Commission on Terrorist Attacks Upon the United States*, July 2004, chap. 11, http://govinfo.library.unt.edu/911/report/911Report_Ch11.htm. See Joel Fishman, "The Need for Imagination in International Affairs," *Israel Journal of Foreign Affairs* 3, no. 3 (2009): 95-108.

Palestinians hated Israel for entirely different reasons, and if they also hated us that was due, in significant part, to our support for Israel.[104]

This last point has serious implications. If one views the Palestinian jihadis' hatred as primarily (and somewhat justifiably) directed against Israel, then one can imagine that, by distancing oneself from Israel, one can appease their wrath. This may indeed play some role in the pervasively negative coverage of the Arab-Israeli conflict. If Israel is to blame for the conflict, then Western outsiders are not the object of the same hatred.[105] The implication here coincides precisely with the way jihadis want Western democracies to respond to terror attacks: *change your foreign policy*.[106] If you get out of the Arab world (including support for Israel) then you will be safe.

Perhaps the most interesting and ominous part of psychogenic dissociative paralysis concerns the revulsion the psyche feels for the body part it refuses to

---

[104] The revelations of Wikileaks made it clear that Arab nations did not share the prevailing paradigm of the Obama administration that solving the Palestinian-Israeli conflict was an advisable prelude to uniting the Arab world against Iran. See Richard Landes, "Thank You, Edward Said: Wikileaks, Linkage, and the Appalling State of Western Understanding of the Arab World," *Augean Stables*, May 24, 2011, http://www. theaugeanstables.com/2011/05/24/3028. For the most recent example of such "linkage," see US Secretary of State John Kerry's placing responsibility on Israel for ISIS's recruiting successes (n. 81). The constant in both cases was the centrality of the "Israeli-Palestinian" conflict, even though in Obama's case the Arab leaders told him "off the record" that they were far more concerned about Iran, while in Kerry's case the Arabs all nodded in agreement when he made the conflict the central issue. Kerry's use of this trope in front of Muslims shows a staggering lack of understanding of the dynamics of Arab culture. Arab leaders, themselves largely responsible for the success of ISIS, were only too happy to have the blame displaced. See Lee Smith, "Kerry Links Rise of ISIS with Failed Peace Talks," *Tablet*, October 22, 2014, http://tabletmag.com/scroll/186443/kerry-links-rise-of-isis-with-failed-peace-talks.

[105] Perhaps the most salient exponent of the relentless drumbeat of blaming Israel for everything from the breakdown of negotiations to the outbreak of conflict is the *New York Times*, whose Jewish character and focus would lead one to expect a more favorable attitude toward Israel, especially after its catastrophic failure during the Holocaust. See Laurel Leff, *Buried by the Times: The Holocaust and America's Most Important Newspaper* (New York: Cambridge University Press, 2005). See also the study of the *New York Times'* Middle East coverage by the Committee for Accuracy in Middle East Reporting in America (CAMERA): *Indicting Israel:* New York Times *Coverage of the Palestinian-Israeli Conflict: A July 1-December 31, 2011 Study* (Boston, MA: CAMERA, 2012), http://www.camera.org/images_user/pdf/final%20monograph.pdf.

[106] For a good example of the way in which this Western discourse works against recognizing the jihadi motives behind the attacks, see Jake Lynch's critique of Tony Blair in "Active and Passive Peace Journalism in Reporting on the 'War on Terrorism' in the Philippines," in *Peace Journalism in Times of War*, ed. Susan Dente Ross and Majid Tehranian (New Brunswick, NJ: Transaction Publishers, 2009), 129-130. For Lynch, the terror attacks arise from ideological objections to Western "foreign policy." Jihad appears nowhere in Lynch's article or in the collection in which it appears.

recognize as its own. In this case, the most striking expression of this psycholog-ical abreaction involves the "global progressive Left." For reasons that deserve a great deal of attention, with the advent of 2000, it became a shibboleth of belonging to the Left to side with the Palestinians. Describing the journalistic circles he moved in during the early twenty-first century, Matti Friedman notes:

> In these circles, in my experience, a distaste for Israel has come to be some-thing between an acceptable prejudice and a prerequisite for entry. I don't mean a critical approach to Israeli policies … but a belief that to some extent the Jews of Israel are a symbol of the world's ills, particularly those connect-ed to nationalism, militarism, colonialism, and racism—an idea quickly becoming one of the central elements of the "progressive" Western *zeitgeist*, spreading from the European left to American college campuses and intellec-tuals, including journalists.[107]

Whereas previously there had been a great deal of tension between the radical anti-Zionist Left and the more centrist liberal-progressive Left, after the outbreak of the First Intifada and especially the circulation of the al-Durah blood libel, the center no longer held: comparisons of Israel to the Nazis became widespread, while moderates, faced with ferocious hostility, fell silent. Disgust overpowered reason.

The result was the greatest single cognitive victory for the jihadis. A major element of the Western public sphere, with a powerful voice among journalists, academics, and NGOs, adopted a key element of their apocalyptic narrative: Israel, the jihadi *Dajjal*, became the secular(!) Left's Antichrist, the new Nazis.[108] The Western intelligentsia not only distanced themselves from their only cultural/civilizational ally in the Middle East, a democracy at war with the most developed elements of global jihad, but the Left turned on them with a venge-ance.

Invaded by conspiracy theories that recycled much of the *Protocols of the Elders of Zion*, drawn into the excitement of massive demonstrations fueled by jihadi energy, seduced by the inane notion that jihadis are allies in the anti-imperialist struggle because they hate America (including, especially, its secular homophilic progressives), the "global progressive Left" became ready dupes for a postmodern version of the classic antisemitic complaint: Israel is our misfor-tune. Even worse, they proved receptive to the projected accusation of those who wish to do so themselves that the Jews want to conquer the world and enslave mankind. As the Palestinian "theologian" al-Hawali put it so succinctly in his celebration of the intifada as the dawn of global jihad, it is for the Zionist enemy not only to abandon his side but to fight for the opposing side. And

---

[107] Matti Friedman, "What the Media Gets Wrong" (see n. 20).
[108] Landes, "Fatal Attraction" (see n. 26).

Western liberals and progressives, Jews and gentiles alike, have proved to be a major force in fulfilling that demand.[109]

## Conclusion: Prognosis

In its most lapidary form, the recipe for European (and Western) democratic survival is: "get over your latent, increasingly blatant, antisemitism." Only when you genuinely renounce the schadenfreude you derive from stories about Jews behaving badly will your journalists begin to plug the massive holes in your cultural edifices that allow the black flags of global jihad to march in.[110] Only when you stop resenting the *shame* of the Holocaust and genuinely accept the *guilt* for it, will you be able to strengthen the kind of positive-sum elements in your culture that make so difficult an experiment as the European Union possible. Only when you appreciate what Judaism and Jews have given to Western democratic culture, will you find the strength to resist the demopathic assault on human rights, tolerance, and the dignity of the "other" that jihadis and their misguided "leftist" allies conduct within your public sphere. Only when your media starts reporting fairly and accurately from the Middle East, will you begin to get a handle on your "Muslim street."

This is a tall order. It calls for a level of awareness and commitment that one would have hoped the cataclysmic Holocaust might have effected. But it turns out that humans and cultures are messier than we might think. It turns out that religious supersessionism (and the resentful envy that underpins it) can survive the rejection of religion and reappear among avowedly, determinedly atheist progressives.[111] It turns out that the scapegoating of a disadvantaged population in an authoritarian society can re-emerge when that population has many of the finest advantages that a civil society has to offer. It turns out that paranoid conspiracy theories projected on the least likely candidate in societies riddled with superstition and chronic fear can re-emerge in allegedly rational societies with ample experience of the catastrophic consequences of such episodes of

---

[109] al-Hawali, "Day of Wrath" (see n. 86).

[110] Nidra Poller, *The Black Flag of Jihad Stalks la République* (Paris: Authorship International, 2015).

[111] Dexter Van Zile, "The Wages of Supersessionism," *New English Review*, April, 2014, http://newenglishreview.org/Dexter_Van_Zile/The_Wages_of_Supersessionism. Portuguese writer and Nobel prize winner José Saramago, in an infamous rant inspired by the Israeli operation in Jenin, denounced the Nazi-like Israelis as "contaminated by the monstrous and rooted 'certitude' that in this catastrophic and absurd world there exists a people chosen by God and that, consequently, all the actions of an obsessive, psychological and pathologically exclusivist racism are justified." See José Saramago, "De las piedras de David a los tanques de Goliat," *El País*, April 21, 2002. The Lebanon war inspired a similar rant from Jostein Gaarder, see n. 46.

delirious hatreds. It turns out that the most squalid aspects of honor-shame culture—envy, revenge, *ressentiment*—can dominate the thoughts and actions of cultures that pride themselves on having left such primitive emotions behind.

In medicine, AIDS has proven a difficult disease to treat. Once the immune system malfunctions, getting it back to healthy operation is almost impossible. One might venture that cultural AIDS similarly resists correction. Defenses against realizing the self-destructive folly of current patterns of interpretation and mobilization are immense: any move to counter the current madness is dismissed as "Israel-firsting," as a Zionist plot, as an expression of Jewish primacy, as an attack on free speech. And, ironically, the fear of Europeans and "progressives" of being manipulated by the Jews has them falling right into the malevolent manipulation of the global jihadis. If pride goes before a fall, then foolish pride goes before an ignominious and, in this case, catastrophic fall. May it not happen in our days.

# From Christian Antisemitism to New Antisemitism: The Case of Philoumenos of Jacob's Well*

David Gurevich and Yisca Harani**

## INTRODUCTION

Ritual murder accusations against Jews have spread through Europe since the twelfth and thirteenth centuries. A prominent element in them was the allegation that Jews secretly performed religious rituals involving the torture and murder of innocent Christian victims (sometimes by crucifixion) and the use of their body parts. In the realm of the Orthodox Church—in Russia and the Ottoman Empire—ritual murder accusations were also widespread during the nineteenth century.[1] Nevertheless, in modern times, ritual murder libels were

---

* This article is an extended and updated version of a previous work: David Gurevich and Yisca Harani, "Philoumenos of Jacob's Well: The Birth of a Contemporary Ritual Murder Narrative," *Israel Studies* 22, no. 2 (2017): 26-54. It is published here with permission.

** David Gurevich is a Post-Doctoral Fellow at the Institute of Archaeology of the Hebrew University of Jerusalem. He was a Fulbright Post-Doctoral Fellow at Harvard University in 2014-2015. Gurevich is the Founder of the academic program Ambassadors Online (*shagririm bareshet*) at the University of Haifa. Yisca Harani is an independent scholar, senior lecturer, and a consultant on the History of Christianity and Christians in the Holy Land. She is the author of "Jewish Tour Guide, Christian Group: Interreligious Encounter Without Pretext," in *Coexistence and Reconciliation in Israel*, ed. Ronald Kronish (Mahwah, NJ, 2015). The authors express their gratitude to Elai Rettig, Yohai Goell, Steven Jaffe, David Rosen, and Yaacov Avrahamy for their assistance in this research.

[1] On medieval blood libels, accusations of Jewish involvement in ritualistic violence, and their socioeconomic context, see Joshua Trachtenberg, *The Devil and the Jews: The Medieval Conception of the Jew and Its Relation to Modern Antisemitism* (Philadelphia, 1983 [1943]); Mitchell B. Merback, *Pilgrimage and Pogrom: Violence, Memory, and Visual Culture at the Host-Miracle Shrines of Germany and Austria* (Chicago, 2012). On blood libels in the Orthodox Christian realm, see: Jacob Barnai, "'Blood Libels' in the Ottoman Empire of the Fifteenth to the Nineteenth Centuries," in *Antisemitism through the Ages*, ed. Shmuel Almog (Oxford and New York, 1988), 189-194; Yehuda Slutsky, "Blood Libel in Russia," in *Encyclopaedia Judaica*, 16 vols. (Jerusalem, 1971), 4:1128-31.

regarded mostly as superstitious by both religious and secular authorities.[2] The popular narrative that was developed after the death of Philoumenos Hasapis in 1979 appears to constitute a retreat to medieval ritual murder motifs. The account is widely accredited by the Orthodox Church, political NGOs, and even among the scholarly community today. This article traces the construction of this popular narrative, analyzes its distribution patterns, and aims to offer an explanation for its widespread publicity.

Philoumenos was murdered in the church of Jacob's Well, near the Palestinian city of Nablus. Since 1979, his veneration as a victim of a Jewish ritual murder gained popularity among Orthodox Christians. In 2009, he was canonized by the Greek Orthodox Church. The perception of Philoumenos' death as a ritual murder stands out in the accounts: Philoumenos was tortured, his eyes were gouged out, the fingers that he needed to perform the liturgy were deliberately amputated, and he died after cross-form cuts were made on his body. According to these accounts, a conspiratorial group of local Jews was behind the murder. The body was taken away by the Israeli authorities and only returned after several days. In the popular narrative, the Israeli authorities are portrayed as acting to conceal the identity of the killers or refusing to find them. The victim was said to perform miracles after his martyrdom that testify to his being a saint, similarly to martyrs who were believed to have been victims of Jewish ritual murders in the past.

This article explores the following questions: How does the popular narrative deviate from or match the factual basis of the events? How was the popular narrative of Philoumenos' martyrdom constructed? What factors contributed to the development of the narrative and its proliferation? The article comprises four sections. The first provides biographical information about Philoumenos Hasapis and the timeline of his veneration. The second traces the development of the popular narrative. This section provides an overview of the studied sources of the popular account; the samples analyzed in this paper were selected to provide an adequate representation of backgrounds (official religious sources, informal religious sources, general-orientation sources, and academic publications). The third section elaborates on the factual basis of the murder and the criminal investigation that was conducted by the Israeli police. Our research identified gaps between the events that occurred vis-à-vis how they were presented in the popular narrative. Hence, the fourth section (the discussion) focuses on an analysis of the patterns that are present in the popular narrative. We utilize the *framing theory* to establish the agenda of agents who contributed to the rephrasing of the popular materials.

---

[2] Hillel J. Kieval, "Ritual Murder (Modern)," in *Antisemitism: A Historical Encyclopedia of Prejudice and Persecution*, ed. Richard S. Levy, 2 vols. (Santa Barbara, CA, 2005), 2:605-8.

The conclusion of this study is that the popular narrative was influenced by a perception of Jews that resonates with the medieval ritual murder accusations, as well as by the framing of the Israeli-Palestinian conflict among Western social movements. Additionally, current political interests of the Orthodox Church and the Palestinian National Authority (PNA) might have contributed to the widespread proliferation of the popular narrative.

## I. PHILOUMENOS, THE MARTYR OF JACOB'S WELL

The Greek Orthodox church of Jacob's Well is located on the outskirts of the Balata refugee camp in Nablus, Samaria (West Bank). The church is famous due to a well in its crypt that probably dates from the Roman period.[3] The Samaritans believe that the well was purchased by Jacob the Patriarch, but Judaism does not attribute any religious significance to the site.[4] The site is venerated today by Orthodox Christianity as the meeting place of Jesus with the Samaritan woman (John 4:5-7). The remains of the partially-built medieval church were restored in 1893 by the Greek Orthodox Church, and a small monastery was added to the compound. According to a Palestinian source, recent renovations authorized by the PNA were conducted during the first decade of the present century.[5]

Philoumenos Hasapis (Khassapis) originated from Orounta in Cyprus. At an early age, he moved to the Holy Land. After he was admitted to the Brotherhood of the Holy Sepulchre, he served in various positions in Greek Orthodox religious institutions. His last appointment was as archimandrite of Jacob's Well.[6] In the afternoon of November 29, 1979, he was murdered by an outsider who infiltrated the compound. Philoumenos was buried in Jerusalem in the Orthodox cemetery on Mt. Zion.

His violent death and the fact that the circumstances of the murder remained unsolved for a long period gave Philoumenos, from the very start, the status of a church martyr and hence his titles of "Hiero-Martyr" (priest-martyr) and "Neo-Martyr" (new martyr).[7] His hagiography (the written life of a saint) was composed in Cyprus by nuns of St. Nicholas Monastery.[8] The quoted individu-

---

[3] Yitzhak Magen, *Flavia Neapolis: Shechem in the Roman Period*, vol. 1 (Jerusalem, 2009), 32.

[4] Ibid.

[5] Mariam Shahin and George B. Azar, *Palestine: A Guide* (Northampton, MA, 2006), 220.

[6] "Archimandrite" denotes a member of the monastic clergy in the contemporary Orthodox Church.

[7] The term "Neo-martyr" is primarily ascribed to martyrs of the Greek Orthodox Church who were killed in ethno-religious conflicts the Ottoman era.

[8] Hiera Monē Hagiou Nikolaou, *Ho Hagios Hieromartys Philoumenos ho Kyprios: Bios- Martyrio-Thaumata meta Paraklētikou Kanonos* (Orounta, 2013) [Greek].

als from the Greek Orthodox Church of Jerusalem testified that four years after his burial, Philoumenos' remains were exhumed from the grave and were found by Patriarch Diodoros to be "producing a pleasant fragrance" and "the rest of the body was incorrupt."[9] Thus began the veneration of the relics. Philoumenos has been the object of spontaneous prayers as well as special hymns. The Translation[10] of his relics to Jacob's Well was carried out during the inauguration ceremony of the renovated church on August 30, 2008.[11] The ceremony was performed under the auspices of the Jerusalem Patriarchate, with an additional tribute to the PNA.[12]

In 2009, thirty years after his martyrdom, Philoumenos was sanctified by the Synod of Jerusalem's Greek Orthodox Patriarchate. The synodic decision describes the killer as a "heterodox fanatic visitor" and a "vile man," without referring to any ethnic or political identification.[13] The Synod refers to the perpetrator as a single individual, who "with an axe, opened a deep cut across his forehead, cut off the fingers of his right hand, and upon escaping threw a grenade which ended the Father's life."[14] Canonization added to Philoumenos' fame and led to the establishment of a Church feast that encouraged the veneration. His relics are used liturgically and also receive the honor of being sent to other locations. In May 2014, the Patriarchate of Jerusalem sent a relic to Cyprus, thus enabling more intensive worship in Philoumenos' homeland.[15]

Canonization and veneration enhanced the ties between Jerusalem's Greek Orthodox Patriarchate and the Cypriot Orthodox Church. In May 2014, a new church was inaugurated at the Holy Sepulcher Exarchy in Nicosia, the prior Exarchy having become inactive forty years earlier. The new church was dedicated to Jesus' Ascension and to Saint Philoumenos. According to the official communiqué, "The entire work was completed with the approval of the Holy Archbishopric of Cyprus, in response to a relevant request by the Holy and

---

[9] "μία ευχάριστη ευωδία … το υπόλοιπο σώμα όμως ήταν κατά πάντα άφθορο." Ibid., 124.

[10] The term "Translation" denotes the transference of holy relics from their burial site to a shrine.

[11] In the YouTube recording of the inauguration ceremony, the sign at the entrance to the Jacob's Well compound bears the date August 30, 2008. See at 0:00:50 in "Ο ΑΓΙΟΣ ΦΙΛΟΥΜΕΝΟΣ Ο ΑΓΙΟΤΑΦΙΤΗΣ," YouTube video, 1:23:55, posted by "megasfilippos," March 8, 2011, http://youtu.be/6PIVzBpiY_I.

[12] The image of Yasser Arafat appeared on the sign inviting the public to participate in the inauguration ceremony. See ibid.

[13] Jerusalem Patriarchate, "Synodic Decision: Classification to the Hagiologion of the New Hieromartyr Filoumenos," last modified September 11, 2009, accessed April 25, 2015, http://www.jp-newsgate.net/en/2009/09/11/624.

[14] Ibid.

[15] Archbishop Aristarchos of Constantina, personal communication with the authors, June 8, 2014.

Sacred Synod of the Patriarchate of Jerusalem."[16] It also emphasized that the location of the Exarchy "lies at a short distance from the Holy Archbishopric of Cyprus." The inauguration ceremony was attended by high-ranking officials representing the Republic of Cyprus.[17]

## II. The popular narrative of Philoumenos' murder

For visitors to the church in Nablus today, the figure of the saint occupies a prime position next to the story of the Samaritan woman. Visitors are shown a *locus* where the remains of Saint Philoumenos are laid in a glass coffin (Fig. 1).

*Fig. 1: The reliquary that hosts the remains of Philoumenos' body at Jacob's Well Church, Nablus. Note a pilgrim venerating the relics. Photograph by the authors, November 2016.*

---

[16] Jerusalem Patriarchate, "Inauguration of the Church of the Holy Sepulcher Exarchy in Cyprus," last modified May 10, 2014, accessed April 25, 2015, http://www.jp-newsgate.net/en/2014/05/10/6808.

[17] Jerusalem Patriarchate, "Inauguration Ceremony for the Church of the Exarchy of the Holy Sepulcher in Cyprus," last modified May 3, 2014, accessed April 25, 2015, http://www.jp-newsgate.net/en/2014/05/03/6671; Jerusalem Patriarchate, "His Beatitude the Patriarch of Jerusalem in Cyprus for the Inauguration of Holy Sepulcher Exarchy," last modified May 9, 2014, accessed April 25, 2015, http://www.jp-newsgate.net/en/2014/05/09/6771.

A big fresco depicts him in a standing position, and another one, behind the coffin, shows a bearded man raising an axe above the reclining monk (Fig. 2).

*Fig. 2: Fresco at Jacob's Well Church, Nablus, depicting a bearded man raising an axe above St. Philoumenos. Source: https://commons.wikimedia. org/wiki/File%3A Wall_painting_of_Saint_Philoumenos_of_Jacob's_Well_ Church_in_Palestine.jpg.*

The saint is also depicted in icons elsewhere in the church and in the crypt of the well where he was murdered. A brochure with the image of Philoumenos, along with a description of his biography and martyrdom, is handed to visitors at Jacob's Well (Fig. 3). The murder is attributed to "fanatic Jews who continue their attacks against the present Archimandrite, Fr. Ioustinos, and his Holy Shrine of pilgrimage."[18] Similar icons and textile souvenirs are sold at the site.[19]

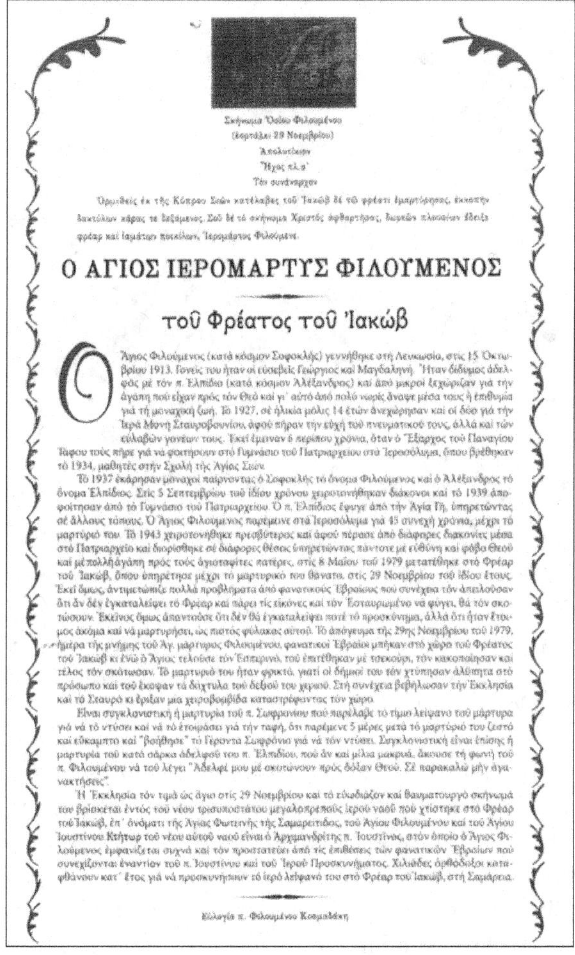

Σκήνωμα Ὁσίου Φιλουμένου
(ἑορτάζει 29 Νοεμβρίου)
Ἀπολυτίκιον
Ἦχος πλ.α'
Τὸν συνάναρχον

Ὁρμηθεὶς ἐκ τῆς Κύπρου Σιῶν κατέλαβες τοῦ Ἰακώβ δὲ τῷ φρέατι ἐμαρτύρησας, ἑκάστην δακτύλων κάρας τε δεξάμενος. Σοῦ δὲ τὸ σκήνωμα Χριστὸς ἀφθαρτήσας, δωρεῶν πλακούντων ἔδειξε φρέαρ καὶ ἰαμάτων ποικίλων, Ἱερομάρτυς Φιλούμενε.

## Ο ΑΓΙΟΣ ΙΕΡΟΜΑΡΤΥΣ ΦΙΛΟΥΜΕΝΟΣ

### τοῦ Φρέατος τοῦ Ἰακώβ

Ὁ Ἅγιος Φιλούμενος (κατά κόσμον Σοφοκλῆς) γεννήθηκε στή Λευκωσία, στίς 15 Ὀκτωβρίου 1913. Γονεῖς του ἦταν οἱ εὐσεβεῖς Γεώργιος καὶ Μαγδαληνή. Ἦταν δίδυμος ἀδελφός μέ τόν π. Ἐλπίδιο (κατά κόσμον Ἀλέξανδρος) καί ἀπό μικροί ἐχώριζαν γιά τήν ἀγάπη πού εἶχαν πρός τόν Θεό καί γι' αὐτό ἀπό πολύ νωρίς ἄναψε μέσα τους ἡ ἐπιθυμία γιά τή μοναχική ζωή. Τό 1927, σέ ἡλικία μόλις 14 ἐτῶν ἀνεχώρησαν καί οἱ δύο γιά τήν Ἱερά Μονή Σταυροβουνίου, ἀφοῦ πῆραν τήν εὐχή τοῦ πνευματικοῦ τους, ἀλλά καί τῶν εὐλαβῶν γονέων τους. Ἐκεῖ ἔμειναν 6 περίπου χρόνια, ὅταν ὁ Ἔξαρχος τοῦ Παναγίου Τάφου τούς πῆρε γιά νά φοιτήσουν στό Γυμνάσιο τοῦ Πατριαρχείου στό Ἱεροσόλυμα, ὅπου βρέθηκαν τό 1934, μαθητές στήν Σχολή τῆς Ἁγίας Σιών.

Τό 1937 ἐκάρησαν μοναχοί παίρνοντας ὁ Σοφοκλῆς τό ὄνομα Φιλούμενος καί ὁ Ἀλέξανδρος τό ὄνομα Ἐλπίδιος. Στίς 5 Σεπτεμβρίου τοῦ ἰδίου χρόνου χειροτονήθηκαν διάκονοι καί τό 1939 ἀποφοίτησαν ἀπό τό Γυμνάσιο τοῦ Πατριαρχείου. Ὁ π. Ἐλπίδιος ἔφυγε ἀπό τήν Ἁγία Γῆ, ὑπηρετώντας σέ ἄλλους τόπους. Ὁ Ἅγιος Φιλούμενος παρέμεινε στά Ἱεροσόλυμα γιά 43 συνεχή χρόνια, μέχρι τό μαρτύριό του. Τό 1943 χειροτονήθηκε πρεσβύτερος καί ἀφού πέρασε ἀπό διάφορες διακονίες μέσα στό Πατριαρχείο καί διορίσθηκε σέ διάφορες θέσεις ὑπηρετώντας πάντοτε μέ εὐθύνη καί φόβο Θεοῦ καί μέ πολλή ἀγάπη πρός τούς ἁγιοταφίτες πατέρες, στίς 8 Μαΐου τοῦ 1979 μετατέθηκε στό Φρέαρ τοῦ Ἰακώβ, ὅπου ὑπηρέτησε μέχρι τό μαρτυρικό του θάνατο, στίς 29 Νοεμβρίου τοῦ ἰδίου ἔτους. Ἐκεῖ ὅμως, ἀντιμετώπιζε πολλά προβλήματα ἀπό φανατικούς Ἑβραίους πού συνέχεια τόν ἀπειλοῦσαν ὅτι ἄν δέν ἐγκαταλείψει τό Φρέαρ καί πάρει τίς εἰκόνες καί τόν Ἐσταυρωμένο νά φύγει, θά τόν σκοτώσουν. Ἐκεῖνος ὅμως ἀπαντοῦσε ὅτι δέν θά ἐγκαταλείψει ποτέ τό προσκύνημα, ἀλλά ὅτι ἦταν ἕτοιμος ἀκόμα καί νά μαρτυρήσει, ὡς πιστός φύλακας αὐτοῦ. Τό ἀπόγευμα τῆς 29ης Νοεμβρίου τοῦ 1979, ἡμέρα τῆς μνήμης τοῦ Ἁγ. μάρτυρος Φιλουμένου, φανατικοί Ἑβραῖοι μπῆκαν στό χῶρο τοῦ Φρέατος τοῦ Ἰακώβ κι ἐνῶ ὁ Ἅγιος τελοῦσε τόν Ἑσπερινό, τοῦ ἐπετέθηκαν μέ τσεκούρι, τόν κακοποίησαν καί τέλος τόν σκότωσαν. Τό μαρτύριό του ἦταν φρικτό, γιατί οἱ δήμιοί του τόν χτύπησαν ἀλύπητα στό πρόσωπο καί τοῦ ἔκοψαν τά δάχτυλα τοῦ δεξιοῦ του χεριοῦ. Στή συνέχεια βεβήλωσαν τήν Ἐκκλησία καί τό Σταυρό κι ἔριξαν μία χειροβομβίδα καταστρέφοντας τόν χῶρο.

Εἶναι συγκλονιστική ἡ μαρτυρία τοῦ π. Σωφρονίου πού παρέλαβε τό τίμιο λείψανο τοῦ μάρτυρα γιά νά τό ντύσει καί νά τό ἑτοιμάσει γιά τήν ταφή, ὅτι παρέμεινε 5 μέρες μετά τό μαρτύριό του ζεστό καί εὔκαμπτο καί "βοήθησε" τό Γέροντα Σωφρόνιο γιά νά τόν ντύσει. Συγκλονιστική εἶναι ἐπίσης ἡ μαρτυρία τοῦ κατά σάρκα ἀδελφού του π. Ἐλπιδίου, πού ἄν καί μίλια μακριά, ἄκουσε τή φωνή τοῦ π. Φιλουμένου νά τοῦ λέγει "Ἀδελφέ μου μέ σκοτώνουν πρός δόξαν Θεοῦ. Σέ παρακαλῶ μήν ἀγανακτήσεις".

Ἡ Ἐκκλησία τόν τιμά ὡς ἅγιο στίς 29 Νοεμβρίου καί τό εὐωδιάζον καί θαυματουργό σκήνωμά του βρίσκεται ἐντός τοῦ νέου τρισυποστάτου μεγαλοπρεπούς ἱερού ναού πού χτίστηκε στό Φρέαρ τοῦ Ἰακώβ, ἐπ' ὀνόματι τῆς Ἁγίας Φωτεινῆς τῆς Σαμαρείτιδος, τοῦ Ἁγίου Φιλουμένου καί τοῦ Ἁγίου Ἰουστίνου. Κτήτωρ τοῦ νέου αὐτοῦ ναού εἶναι ὁ Ἀρχιμανδρίτης π. Ἰουστίνος, στόν ὁποίο ὁ Ἅγιος Φιλούμενος ἐμφανίζεται συχνά καί τόν προστατεύει ἀπό τίς ἐπιθέσεις τῶν φανατικῶν Ἑβραίων πού συνεχίζονται ἐναντίον τοῦ π. Ἰουστίνου καί τοῦ Ἱερού Προσκυνήματος. Χιλιάδες ὀρθόδοξοι καταφθάνουν κατ' ἔτος γιά νά προσκυνήσουν τό ἱερό λείψανό του στό Φρέαρ τοῦ Ἰακώβ, στή Σαμάρεια.

Εὐλογία π. Φιλουμένου Κοσμαδάκη

*Fig. 3: Informative brochure on St. Philoumenos that visitors receive at Jacob's Well Church, Nablus.*

Similar iconography is found in the Machairas Monastery in Cyprus. The painting depicts Philoumenos drawing water from the well while he is assaulted

---

[18] "Τίς ἐπιθέσεις τῶν φανατικῶν Ἑβραίων πού συνεχίζονται ἐναντίον τοῦ π. Ἰουστίνου καί τοῦ Ἱεροῦ Προσκυνῆ" (see Fig. 3).

[19] The information was collected during an on-site visit by the authors in November 2011.

by an Ultra-Orthodox Jew who wears a typical hat, has *payot*, and sports a long beard (Fig. 4). The assaulter raises his axe to slay the monk. The visitor who discovered the painting in 2008, Daniela Schwartz, reported what she perceived to be an antisemitic representation to the Israeli Ministry of Foreign Affairs.[20]

Fig. 4: *Painting of Philoumenos' martyrdom in Machairas Monastery, Cyprus. The text above in Greek reads: "Jacob's Well St. Philoumenos." The text below reads: "The Martyrdom of St. Philoumenos of Cyprus." Photograph by the authors, October 2016.*

The Ministry was assured by Cypriot Church authorities that the painting would be altered and that the attributes of Jewish religious identification would be removed.[21] However, during our visit to the Machairas Monastery in October 2016, we witnessed the painting in its original location without any changes.[22]

Panegyric liturgy dedicated to the new martyr was published in 2003.[23] The forty-five pages of prayers and hymns that glorify the saint are read on the eve and the day of the feast in honor of Philoumenos. The introduction to this

---

[20] Dana Segev, "What Does a Single Antisemitic Painting Reveal?," last modified March 20, 2008, accessed December 3, 2016, http://www.asimon.co.il/ArticlePage.aspx?AID=5412&AcatID=81 [Hebrew].

[21] Ibid.

[22] The painting is located in the vault of the narthex at the monastery's main church. According to a local monk, the paintings of the narthex were made by Russian artists after 2004.

[23] Ch. Mpousias, *Akolouthia tou Hagiou Neou Hieromartyros Philoumenou tou Kypriou* (Orounta, 2003) [Greek].

liturgical booklet repeats the description of a murder committed by "Jewish Zionists."[24]

The first account containing collective accusations can be traced to shortly after the murder. In 1980, *Ma'ariv* reported a wave of hatred in Greece directed against Jews and Israel after the murder became known.[25] The widespread belief was that "radical Jews" tortured the monk and "even cut off the fingers of his hand" before committing the murder. An official in the Jerusalem Greek Orthodox Patriarchate, quoted in Greek newspapers, claimed that "the murder was carried out by radical religious Jews" because of "the way how he [Philoumenos] was murdered, the hatred, the passion, and the cruelty which accompanied the act." The official also added that, a few months before the murder, Philoumenos was involved in an argument with radicals who claimed that "the well does not belong to Christians but to Jews." *Ma'ariv* reported that the Greek press published reports containing similar allegations.

We found the earliest detailed published description of the event as an act of ritual murder in 1989, in *Orthodox America*, a periodical of the Russian Orthodox Church Outside of Russia. The author, Yeghia Yenovkian, presents himself as a monk in the Paradise Monastery (Ellisville, MS) who knew Philoumenos personally from the time they were both serving in monastic institutions in the Holy Land. However, Yenovkian did not witness the murder, as he was already in the United States.[26] According to his account, the murder was committed by "Jewish terrorists" (or "fanatical Zionists"), "satanically-inspired tormentors" who tortured their victim. The following exert describes the martyrdom:

> The week before, a group of fanatical Zionists came to the monastery at Jacob's Well, claiming it as a Jewish holy place and demanding that all crosses and icons be removed. Of course, our father pointed out that the floor upon which they were standing had been built by Emperor Constantine before 331 A.D. and had served as an Orthodox Christian holy place for sixteen centuries before the Israeli State was created, and had been in Samaritan hands eight centuries before that. (The rest of the original church had been destroyed by the invasion of the Shah Khosran Parvis in the seventh century, at which time the Jews had massacred all the Christians of Jerusalem). The group left with threats, insults and obscenities of the kind which local Christians suffer regularly. After a few days, on November 16/29,

---

[24] Ibid., 14.

[25] M. Maor, "Following the Murder of the Priest of Cypriot Origin in Jerusalem," *Ma'ariv*, March 10, 1980, 7 [Hebrew]. Maor relied solely on information from sources in Greece. This explains fundamental inaccuracies (e.g. the site is referred to as "Avraham's Well in Jerusalem").

[26] Our investigation in the archives of the Greek Orthodox Patriarchate and the Armenian Patriarchate in Jerusalem did not produce any results to establish the background of Yeghia Yenovkian.

during a torrential downpour, a group broke into the monastery; the saint had already put on his epitrachelion for Vespers. The piecemeal chopping of the three fingers with which he made the Sign of the Cross showed that he was tortured in an attempt to make him deny his Orthodox Christian Faith. His face was cloven in the form of the Cross. The church and holy things were all defiled. No one was ever arrested.[27]

Yenovkian speculated that the Jerusalem Greek Orthodox Patriarchate had refrained from canonizing Philoumenos on the assumption that such an act would "provoke further violence." He urged the Church of Cyprus "to begin public glorification of its son until such time as pressures are removed from the Patriarchate of Jerusalem."[28]

To all appearances, Yenovkian's account became the basis for later variations of the popular narrative in the Orthodox realm. For instance, *The Church Messenger*, the periodical of the American Carpatho-Russian Orthodox Diocese, reprinted portions of Yenovkian's account in an article by Rev. Fr. Edward Pehanich in 2008.[29] Although this source cites Yenovkian on Philoumenos' early life, the details of his martyrdom are published as Pehanich's own sermon. His narration mentions prior confrontations over custody of the holy site and continues by blaming the murder on "fanatical Zionists," who made the cross-shaped cuts and deliberately amputated the victim's fingers used for making the sign of the cross. The article also states that no one was arrested. Evidently, it is a shortened version of Yenovkian's description.

It seems that the canonization of Philoumenos in 2009 brought his martyrdom into the limelight of the Orthodox Church worldwide. Notes on his martyrdom have been published frequently by sources connected to the Church. We established that the basis for these descriptions is Yenovkian's account, which was enriched by additional details, usually of unidentified origin. For example, a formulation almost identical to Yenovkian's was published by the Orthodox Metropolitanate of Singapore and South Asia, as well as on the website of the Vatopaidi Monastery of Mt. Athos.[30] A new motif appears in these descriptions: the body of the victim was handed back to the Orthodox community six days

---

[27] Yeghia Yenovkian, "Tribute to a New Martyr: Our Holy Father Philoumenos of the Brotherhood of the Holy Sepulchre," *Orthodox America* 10, no. 4 (Issue 94) (1989): 9.

[28] Ibid.

[29] Edward Pehanich, "Lives of the Saints: Father Philoumenos of Jacobs Well 1913-1979," *The Church Messenger* 64, no. 1 (2008): 7, accessed March 30, 2015, http://www. acrod.org/assets/files/PDFS/Messenger/CM%20-%201-08_Web.pdf.

[30] Orthodox Metropolitanate of Singapore and South Asia, "Saint Philoumenos the New Hieromartyr of Jacob's Well," last modified December 12, 2012, accessed March 30, 2015, http://www.omsgsa.org/?p=1143; "Saint Philoumenos the New Hieromartyr of Jacob's Well," *Pemptousia*, last modified December 2, 2012, accessed March 30, 2015, http://pemptousia.com/2012/12/saint-philoumenos-the-new-hieromartyr-of-jacobs-well.

after the murder. No information is provided as to what happened to the body during those six days. On the other hand, the accusation that no suspect was arrested is omitted in this account. The Metropolitanate refers to a Cypriot church magazine from 2012 as its source.[31] Employing a very similar formulation, the Russian Orthodox website "Pravoslavie" states that Philoumenos was murdered by "two Jews."[32]

Further developments of the popular narrative are traced in Orthodox-Wiki—a comprehensive web-based encyclopedia of Orthodox Christianity administrated by individuals affiliated with the Orthodox Church.[33] Orthodox-Wiki collectively accuses "extremist Jewish Zionists" and "fanatical Zionists." This description seems to be an enhanced version of Yenovkian's account, though no reference is provided to Yenovkian in the paragraphs describing the martyrdom. A "dead link" to the former website "All Saints of North America Russian Orthodox Church" is cited as a source for this entry.

> They *burst* into the monastery and with a hatchet *butchered Archimandrite Philoumenos in the form of a cross.* With one vertical stroke they clove his face, with another horizontal stroke they *cut his cheeks as far as his ears. His eyes were plucked out.* The fingers of his right hand were cut into pieces and *its thumb was hacked off.* These were the fingers with which he made the sign of the Cross. The murderers were not content with the butchering of the innocent monk, but proceeded to desecrate the church as well. *A crucifix was destroyed, the sacred vessels were scattered* and defiled, and the church was in general subjected to sacrilege of the most appalling type.[34]

Furthermore, some sources outwardly describe Philoumenos' martyrdom as an example of a continuous custom of Jews to commit ritual murders of Christians. A Belorussian Orthodox website in the Russian language, "Odigitria," provides a narration that fits this context. Its formulation uses the antisemitic derogatory term "Zhids" (Жиды) for the Jews when making the collective accusation. This

---

[31] The source contains a reference to a magazine, *By the Lake* (Παρά την Λίμνην), 11, published by St. Demetrios' Church of Paralimni, Cyprus, November 2012. This publication could not be consulted by the authors.

[32] "The Holy Martyr Philoumenos of the Holy Sepulchre," *Pravoslavie*, last modified November 29, 2012, accessed March 30, 2015, http://www.pravoslavie.ru/orthodox churches/57769.htm [Russian].

[33] While OrthodoxWiki is maintained by administrators affiliated with the Orthodox Church, the website does not aim to be an official voice of the Orthodox Church authorities. See "Frequently Asked Questions," *OrthodoxWiki*, accessed May 17, 2014, http://orthodoxwiki.org/OrthodoxWiki:Frequently_Asked_Questions.

[34] Emphasis added to indicate details that are not present in Yenovkian's account. See "Philoumenos (Hasapis) of Jacob's Well," *OrthodoxWiki*, last modified January 25, 2014, http://orthodoxwiki.org/index.php?title=Philoumenos_(Hasapis)_of_Jacob%27 s_Well&oldid=118113.

description is based on Yenovkian's account with several supplements. Even though this source states that the murderer was found to be insane, the epilogue of the narrative includes a statement of classic anti-Semitic nature:

> We remind that the Russian Orthodox Church has two saints, venerated as "martyred by the Zhids": the monk martyr Evstratiy of Kiev-Pechersk and the infant Gabriel of Belostok. The martyr Evstratiy lived in the eleventh century in Kiev. When in 1096 the Cumans attacked and ravaged Pechersky Monastery in Kiev, exterminating many of the monks, the monk Evstratiy was captured, and with thirty monastic workers and twenty habitants of Kiev was sold into slavery to a Jew, who crucified him on a cross. The holy infant Gabriel was ritually murdered by Jews on 20 April 1690. His body side was pierced to discharge the blood, then the infant martyr was crucified.[35]

Influence of the popular narrative was also found in the official synodic decision of the Russian Orthodox Church.[36] After hearing a report and examining the canonization by the Jerusalem Patriarchate, Moscow's Synod resolved to reiterate the canonization of Philoumenos. However, Moscow's decision has an additional detail that does not appear in the Jerusalem synodic text: a collective accusation of "fanatics of other faith" for the murder. This difference can be explained if Moscow's Synod was influenced by unofficial sources that narrate the popular narrative.

The popular narrative is not confined to religious sources. Descriptions that are consistent with the popular narrative appear in many general-orientation sources. For instance, Wikipedia's entry on "Jacob's Well" contained similar collective accusations until it was altered in January 2012. The event was presented as an outcome of the geopolitical situation in the West Bank:

---

[35] "Напомним, что в Русской Православной Церкви есть два святых, прославленные как «от жидов умученные»: киево-печерский инок преподобномученик Евстратий и младенец Гавриил Белостокский. Преподобномученик Евстратий жил в XI веке в Киеве. Когда в 1096 г. на Киев напали половцы и разорили Печерский монастырь, истребив многих иноков, преподобный Евстратий был взят в плен и вместе с тридцатью монастырскими рабочими и двадцатью киевлянами продан в рабство одному иудею, который распял его на кресте. Святой младенец Гавриил 20 апреля 1690 г. был ритуально убит иудеями. Ему проткнули бок для выпускания крови, затем младенец-мученик был распят на кресте." See: "In Memoriam of Philoumenos of the Holy Sepulchre, Fatally Tortured by Jews in 1979," *Odigitria*, last modified November 29, 2011, accessed March 30, 2015, http://www.odigitria.by/2011/11/29/pamyat-filumena-svyatogrobca-v-1979-godu-iudeyami-umuchennogo [Russian]. Translated by the authors.

[36] Moscow Patriarchate, "Record 18: Records of the Council of the Holy Synod of March 5, 2010," last modified March 5, 2010, accessed March 30 2015, http://www.patriarchia.ru/db/text/1106470.html [Russian].

Since the Israeli occupation of the West Bank, Jacob's Well has been a site of contention between Christians and Jews. In November 1979, a week after a Zionist group came to the monastery claiming it as a Jewish holy place and demanding that all religious iconography be removed, the custodian of the well, Archimandrite Philoumenos, was found hatched to death inside the crypt housing the well. No one was ever arrested for the murder.[37]

Similar accusations were found in Wikipedia's entry on "Philoumenos (Hasapis) of Jacob's Well":

Over a couple of weeks the local Jewish settlers had been coming to pray there and demanded that Christian symbols be removed. Philoumenos complied. Despite this, the settlers threatened him. After his guard left home, Philoumenos was hacked to death with axes by Jewish Zionists, while serving Vespers on November 29, 1979. A grenade was also thrown into the church, which was ransacked. The police confirmed the cause of the death, but declined to seek the perpetrators.[38]

As its source, this Wikipedia entry cites Pehanich's article and a Reuters report dating from 2006.[39] Earlier versions of the entry contained references to Yenovkian's account, while a newer version stated that "according to Rupert Shortt, a religion editor of the Times Literary Supplement, Philoumenos eyes were gouged out, and the fingers of his right hand were hacked off."[40]

The geopolitical situation in the West Bank, as well as accusations against settlers in the popular narrative, contributed to the establishment of a link between the murder and the Israeli-Palestinian conflict. The website of a Christian community in Syria reported that Philoumenos was killed by "a mob of Jewish Israeli extremists."[41] Furthermore, it emphasized that Philoumenos' Saint's Day, November 29, "coincid[es] with UN International Day of Solidarity

---

[37] "Jacob's Well," *Wikipedia*, version of December 23, 2011, accessed March 30, 2015, http://en.wikipedia.org/w/index.php?title=Jacob%27s_Well&oldid=467324402.

[38] "Philoumenos (Hasapis) of Jacob's Well," *Wikipedia*, version of January 26, 2014, accessed March 30, 2015, http://en.wikipedia.org/w/index.php?title=Philoumenos_(Hasapis)_of_Jacob%27s_Well&oldid=592433374.

[39] This report was unavailable on Reuters' website during the composition of the present article.

[40] "Philoumenos (Hasapis) of Jacob's Well," *Wikipedia*, version of August 22, 2014, accessed March 30, 2015, http://en.wikipedia.org/w/index.php?title=Philoumenos_(Hasapis)_of_Jacob%27s_Well&oldid=622393330. For a discussion on Shortt's work, see below.

[41] "Pope Calls for 'a Just and Lasting Solution' to the War in Syria and Respect for Religious Freedom in the Middle East," *Orontes Syria*, last modified November 30, 2013, accessed March 30, 2015, http://orontes.jimdo.com/2013/11/30/pope-calls-for-a-just-and-lasting-solution-to-the-war-in-syria-and-respect-for-religious-freedom-in-the-middle-east.

with the Palestinian People."[42] In an essay criticizing Israeli security restrictions, Maria Khoury, a Christian Orthodox resident of Taibeh in the West Bank, stresses that Philoumenos "was tortured by Israeli settlers."[43]

In a similar context, this popular narrative seems to be utilized in public anti-Israeli campaigns led by groups of foreign activists. For instance, the newsletter of the Irish Congress of Trade Unions published detailed coverage of the solidarity visit of a delegation from the Northern Ireland Public Service Alliance (NIPSA) to the West Bank in 2011. In this newsletter, Philoumenos' murder is presented as an attempt of "Zionist settlers" to "cleanse" the Christian presence from the region:

> The church is spectacular with exquisite iconography. I noticed it had a tomb for a martyr—Archimandrite Philoumenos Hasapis. I asked which century he had been martyred in. "This one" was the short answer. He had been murdered with an axe in a "ritualistic" manner on 16 November 1979 by Zionist settlers who wanted to cleanse the area of any trace of Christianity. Murdered whilst performing vespers, his eyes were plucked out and three of his fingers were cut off—the ones with which he made the sign of the Cross. The attacker was believed to be an American. He was not arrested but merely deported back to America.[44]

The hagiography of Philoumenos, which was composed in his birth village Orounta in Cyprus, places the blame on the Israeli authorities. In that document, the Israelis are said to have attempted to attack the church with "Jewish tanks" in 2005, but the shells landed without exploding thanks to the intervention of the saint.[45]

The events of the geopolitical situation in the West Bank, supplemented by anti-globalization themes, created an ethos that praises Philoumenos as a heroic symbol of struggle by Greek and Cypriot nationalist movements. A website named after him (www.filoumenos.com) advocates various conspiracy theories relating to Israel and the United States and urges the establishment of a "new order." It is also a homepage for diverse antisemitic posts.[46] The website's design

---

42 Ibid. On November 29, 1947, the UN General Assembly adopted Resolution 181(II), also known as the "Partition Plan." In 1977, it adopted Resolution 32/40B establishing "the annual observance of 29 November as the International Day of Solidarity with the Palestinian People."

43 Maria C. Khoury, "Honoring the Mother of God," n.d., accessed March 30, 2015, http://www.saintgeorgetaybeh.org/maria_khourys_page/maria_khourys_archive/mk_article_Aug10.html.

44 Michael Robinson, *Welcome to the Country that Doesn't Exist* (2011), 16-7, accessed March 30, 2015, http://www.sadaka.ie/Articles/OtherReports/OTHER-Global_Solidarity_Palestine.pdf.

45 Hiera Monē, *Ho Hagios*, 148.

46 Notable examples of antisemitic posts on the website include: Dominique, "The Jews and the Financial Disaster in Greece," last modified March 10, 2010, accessed

contains a drawing of the martyr in the upper section of each page and an explanation that Philoumenos was ritually murdered by Zionists.[47] We found a similar ethos in a public speech by the Metropolitan Bishop of Morphou, Neophytos. The birth village of Philoumenos, Orounta, is located in the Metropolitanate's ecclesial district.[48] In his speech, which is published on the Metropolitanate's website, after describing the biography of Philoumenos and his murder by "fanatical Zionists" and "fanatical Jews", the Bishop delivers a polemic against the globalization in which he links the martyrdom to what he believes is its contemporary context:

> All these and even more are contained in the policy of the "New Order of Things"[49] that we described before, which constitutes the global government that is going to control with secret money all the peoples economically, politically, and socially. There are many researchers who, behind all these, see "Zionism", which is slowly and steadily preparing the ground in order to be claimed by the worship of a false God, the Antichrist![50]

We have identified instances of the popular narrative in at least two scholarly publications. The first is the *Encyclopedia of the Israeli-Palestinian Conflict*.[51] Its editorial advisory board consists of academics from the United States and Israel. The entry "Holy Sites in Palestine" includes a collective accusation in relation to

<hr>

March 30, 2015, http://www.filoumenos.com/anthellinismos/ellada-israil/662-oi-ebraioi-kai-i-oikonomiki-katastrofi-tis-elladas.html [Greek]; Philoumenos, "Not One Greek Politician All Are of Jewish Origin," last modified March 12, 2012, accessed May 23, 2014, http://www.filoumenos.com/anthellinismos/ellada-israil/12212-oyte-enas-ellinas-politikos-oloi-toys-einai-evraikis-katagogis.html [Greek].

[47] Translated by the authors: "In Memoriam of the Saint and Neo Martyr Who Was Ritually Slaughtered by Zionists while Celebrating the Office of Vespers in Jacob's Well on 16/29 November 1979."

[48] Since 1974, the city of Morphou is located on the Turkish side in Northern Cyprus, and the Metropolitanate's headquarters were therefore transferred to the village of Evrychou on the Greek-Cypriot side of the border.

[49] In this context, the meaning of this phrase is "New World Order".

[50] "Ὅλα αὐτὰ κι ἄλλα πολλὰ περιέχονται στὴν πολιτικὴ τῆς «Νέας Τάξης Πραγμάτων», ποὺ προαναφέραμε, ἡ ὁποία οἰκοδομεῖ τὴν παγκόσμια κυβέρνηση ποὺ θὰ ἐλέγχει οἰκονομικά, πολιτικὰ καὶ κοινωνικὰ ὅλους τοὺς λαούς, μὲ τὸ μυστικὸ χρῆμα. Πολλοὶ εἶναι οἱ μελετητές, ποὺ πίσω ἀπὸ ὅλα αὐτὰ βλέπουν τὸν «Σιωνισμό», ποὺ ἀργὰ καὶ σταθερὰ προετοιμάζει τὸ ἔδαφος ποὺ θὰ διεκδικήσει ἐν καιρῷ τὴ λατρεία ἑνὸς ψευτοθεοῦ, τοῦ Ἀντιχρίστου!" The speech is undated, but it is positioned on the website between statements dating from 2015. See: Metropolitan of Morphou, "The Saint New Holy Martyr of Christ Philoumenos of Cyprus: The Beginning of Christ's Martyrs of the «New Era»", accessed June 29, 2017, http://www.immorfou.org.cy/speeches-mitropoliti/1187-fil-mirt.html [Greek]. Translated by the authors.

[51] Cheryl Rubenberg, ed., *Encyclopedia of the Israeli-Palestinian Conflict*, 3 vols. (Boulder, CO, 2010).

the murder ("radical rabbi settler and his followers"). The style and content of the passage reveal similarities to Yenovkian's account, including the same chronological storyline, a similar description of a dispute between Philoumenos and the alleged attackers, and the usage of a few identical formulations originating from Yenovkian's article (emphasis added):

> In November 1979 a priest and caretaker of the site, the Archimandrite Father Philoumenos, was murdered in the well chamber. Earlier that month, a radical rabbi settler and his followers came to the monastery and demanded that *the crosses and icons* be taken down, claiming the site belonged to the Jews. They shouted *threats* and blasphemies, but Philoumenos explained that the church had for many years been a sacred Orthodox place. A week later the extremists came back and tortured and killed the priest and desecrated the church. *No one was ever arrested* or tried for the crimes.[52]

The author of the entry clearly failed to approach the issue with the neutrality required of academic research.[53]

Another instance of the uncritical usage of the popular narrative in a scholarly work appears in a monograph on contemporary anti-Christian movements by Rupert Shortt. The author regards it as the authentic description of the 1979 events:

> Settlers are violent towards Christians and others from time to time. … in November 1979, as yet unidentified fanatics murdered Fr Philoumenos Hasapis, an Orthodox monk, at St Photini's Monastery beside Jacob's Well at Nablus. … The killers had already warned Fr Philoumenos to remove Christian symbols from the well, claiming that their presence made it impossible for Jews to pray there. When he refused, they gouged his eyes out and hacked off the fingers of this right hand—the one he used to make the sign of the cross—before ending his life. The current custodian, a veteran of several attacks already, has prepared his tomb for what he senses may be a sudden death.[54]

---

52 Pamela Olson, "Holy Sites in Palestine," in *Encyclopedia of the Israeli-Palestinian Conflict,* ed. Cheryl Rubenberg (Boulder, CO, 2010), 1:563-6.

53 The author of this encyclopedic entry appears to impose her political agenda on the description, as demonstrated in the following quotes [emphasis added]: "Jews from all over the world are given free access to worship at the Western Wall, *but* only a small percentage of the 4 million Palestinians living in the West Bank and Gaza are allowed to pray at the Muslim compound above it," ibid., 564; "The Israeli army rarely curbs the behaviour of the settlers and often aids them in their attempts to take over more Hebron real estate," ibid., 565.

54 Rupert Shortt, *Christianophobia: A Faith under Attack* (Grand Rapids, MI, 2013), 227.

## III. Factual circumstances of Philoumenos' death

We established the factual basis of the events based on classified police files to which we were granted limited access in the course of our research.[55] In addition, we studied Israeli daily newspapers that reported the investigation between 1979 and 1982. The importance of the daily press for our analysis is that these reports constitute a source that was available to the public during the initial stage, when the popular narrative was being developed.

The Israeli authorities launched a serious investigation immediately after the murder. On December 4, 1979, *Ha'aretz* reported that the police had arrested eighteen suspects that and that eight were still being kept in remand.[56] It also noted that an analysis performed by the Abu-Kabir Forensic Institute concluded that the victim had been murdered, that he had been struck with a dark-colored artifact, and that he had been stabbed in different parts of his body. A hand-grenade was also found at the scene.

According to the daily press, a major development in the investigation occurred only in 1982, when an individual who was arrested by the Israeli police confessed to committing the murder.[57] *Ma'ariv* reported that the individual was Asher Raby, aged 37, a resident of Tel-Aviv and not of the West Bank.[58] A biographic profile of Raby, which can be assembled from descriptions in the press, indicates that he was a mentally ill: he wore worn-out clothes, neglected his personal hygiene, and whispered passages from the Scriptures in a weird way.[59] He acted alone, and had never been a member of any religious institution or group. He was arrested on November 17, 1982, when he once again tried to climb over the external fence of the Jacob's Well compound.[60] Raby claimed that he was ordered by Divine decree to expel the evil from a Jewish holy site.[61] The court sent him to a psychiatric clinic for observation.[62]

---

[55] The police file is marked "פא‎ 2253/79 תחנת שכם" Additional files that are expected to be declassified in forthcoming years: 11-ל, 10- ל, 3186/9-ל.

[56] Asher Kayzer, "First Check: The Greek Orthodox Priest Was Murdered," *Ha'aretz*, December 4, 1979, 2 [Hebrew].

[57] Yosef Zalter and Amos Levav, "The Police Reinvestigates Unsolved Murder Cases That Were Conducted Using an Axe," *Ma'ariv*, December 2, 1982, 3; Yitzhak Ben-Horin, "In the Nights He Weeps over Destruction of the Temple," *Ma'ariv*, December 3, 1982, 3; Aya Ornstein, "The Under-Indictment of Monk's Murder to Psychiatric Observation," *Ma'ariv*, December 17, 1982, 5 [all in Hebrew].

[58] Hebrew: אשר רבי. In a few sources his name is given as Asher Rabo (אשר רבו).

[59] According to his neighbors, Raby became religiously observant a few years prior to the murder. He was seen crying at night after reading religious texts. He refused to marry until the restoration of the Temple. In the years before the murder, he quit his job as a truck driver, sold his property, and donated his money. See Ben-Horin, "In the Nights He Weeps."

[60] Zalter and Levav, "The Police Reinvestigates."

[61] Ornstein, "Under-Indictment of Monk's Murder."

[62] Ibid.

According to the press, Raby admitted to committing other murders and murder attempts.[63] As a serial killer, he employed similar techniques to attack his victims. For example, the assaults were carried out with an axe, and he used hand-grenades that he had stolen from the IDF. In March 1979, Raby murdered a Jewish gynecologist in Tel-Aviv. The next month, he murdered the family of a clairvoyant woman in the Israeli town of Lod.[64] He also assaulted a nun at Jacob's Well in April 1982. Raby provided the detectives with accurate data concerning his criminal acts. These details correlated with the findings at the scene of the murder.[65]

The information recorded in the police files confirms the above-mentioned details. The police launched an investigation immediately after the murder. Among those questioned were the Palestinian guard of the church (a resident of Balata refugee camp), officials in the Greek Orthodox Church of the Holy Land, and an Israeli Arab who witnessed an argument between the monk and "an observant Jewish person" a short time before the murder. Police detectives concluded that the destruction in the church was caused by the explosion of a hand-grenade that also devastated the holy artifacts. After throwing a hand-grenade and seeing Philoumenos fleeing the church alive, the perpetrator attacked the monk with an axe, causing his death. A single finger of each of the victim's hands was found detached from the body. The investigation concluded that the monk tried to protect his face with his hands and thus the fingers were cut off. This is confirmed by several photographs taken at the scene of the murder that are included in the files.

Police records confirm that the identity of the murderer was established only in 1982.[66] In both attacks at Jacob's Well (in 1979 and 1982) he used hand-

---

63 Zalter and Levav, "The Police Reinvestigates."

64 The Badre family in Lod was murdered on April 9, 1979. The murderer infiltrated their apartment, threw a grenade, and then opened fire with an automatic rifle. The mother of the family, Abigail, gained a reputation as being clairvoyant and practicing divination, and as a person who, "according to the neighbors, practiced witchcraft." This was the second assault on the family; an earlier attempt was carried out when the parents were not at home. See: Reuven Shapiro, "Blackout Was Imposed on the Murder in Lod," *Davar* April 12, 1979, 10 [Hebrew]; Dalia Mazori, "Anonymous Person with Knives Entered Apartment and Injured Old Women and Teen Girls When They Were Asleep," *Maariv*, February 26, 1979, 12 [Hebrew]. The police immediately suspected that the murderer was mentally unstable. Shortly after, the suspect's profile sketch was released. See: Reuven Shapiro, "Extended Searches for the Murderer of the Family in Lod," *Davar*, April 22, 1979, 4 [Hebrew]. However, despite the high financial reward promised by the authorities for his capture, the murderer was not caught that year. See: "Extended Searches for the Murderer of the Family in Lod," *Davar*, July 5, 1979, 14 [Hebrew].

65 Zalter and Levav, "The Police Reinvestigates."

66 The authors have refrained from publishing the full name of the murderer as recorded in police files due to privacy protection regulations.

grenades, acted alone, and had no contact with any organization or political group. During his questioning, the murderer gave a detailed description of the unnatural experiences he had "seen" and "heard," probably hallucinations that stimulated his actions. A psychiatrist determined that he was suffering from a mental disorder, consistent with family members' testimonies as recorded in the police investigation interviews. He was found mentally incompetent to stand trial and was hospitalized in a psychiatric hospital in late 1982.[67] We obtained an official statement from the Investigation Department of the Israel Police (Fig. 5). A translation of the relevant part of the statement appears below (emphasis in original):

> The deceased monk Philoumenos Hasapis indeed found his death in tragic circumstances and in a cruel way caused by a murderer who broke into the "Jacob's Well" church. Following an extensive and intensive investigation, contrary to [prior] publications, the murderer was captured and the investigation revealed that the murderer acted *solely* [on his own] and did not belong to any ideological group that would stand behind his criminal activity.
>
> The findings at the scene of the murder indicate that the way in which the deceased was murdered was brutal and that his death was caused by the blows of an axe, which resulted in multiple injuries to various body parts. However, it is vital to emphasize that the information of the investigation itself refutes publications regarding anti-Christian characteristics that were attributed to the way in which the murder was performed, such as the plucking out the eyes, axe blows in a cross-shaped form on the face of the deceased, and the amputation of the fingers used to symbolize the Christian blessing motion.
>
> The District Court that discussed the case resolved that the murderer was incapable of standing trial in a criminal case due to the state of his mental health and issued a hospitalization order for the murderer to be admitted to a psychiatric hospital.[68]

## IV. Discussion

The popular narrative that gained publicity differs significantly from the factual basis of the events. In the following paragraphs, we will first explore the gaps between the factual circumstances of Philoumenos' death and their narration in popular sources. Next, we will analyze the major factors that contributed to the existence of such differences and the reasons for them.

---

[67] Tel-Aviv District Court, file 1286182. Information on the fate of the individual after his hospitalization is restricted due to privacy protection regulations.

[68] Translated by the authors.

1

משטרת ישראל
האגף לחקירות ולמודיעין
חטיבת החקירות

27 דצמבר, 2011
סימוכין: פר/104 [מספר בכתב יד]

הגב' יסכה הרני

**הנדון: פנייתך לרח"ט חקירות בעניין סוגיית פרסום מתיק חקירה**

1. בפנייתך לרח"ט חקירות מתבקשת עמדתנו לשאלת אפשרות פרסום של פרטים מתיק החקירה בעניין רצח הנזיר פילומנוס הסאפיס בכנסיית באר יעקב בשכם.

2. לאחר עיון בבקשתך ובאתר וויקיפדיה, מצאנו כי קיים אינטרס ציבורי לאומי בפרסום פרטים מתיק החקירה, על מנת לתקן את המידע המסולף שמופיע באתרים חיצוניים שיש בו כדי לעודד פרסומים אנטי יהודיים ברחבי העולם.

3. עיינתי ברשימת הנושאים שהנך מבקשת להתייחס אליהם בפרסום ומצאתי לנכון להציע לך לעשות שימוש בנוסח כדלקמן, על מנת למצוא את האיזון המתאים שבין האינטרס הלאומי בפרסום לבין האינטרסים המשטרתיים העומדים מנגד:

"הנזיר המנוח פילומנוס הסאפיס אכן מצא את מותו בנסיבות טרגיות ואכזריות בידיו של רוצח אשר פרץ לכנסיית "באר יעקב". בעקבות חקירה מסועפת ומאומצת, בניגוד לפרסומים - נלכד הרוצח והחקירה העלתה כי הרוצח פעל **לבד** ולא השתייך לשום קבוצה אידיולוגית שעמדה מאחורי פעילותו הפלילית.

ממצאי החקירה העלו כי האופן שבו המנוח נרצח היה ברוטאלי, ומותו נגרם ממכות גרזן שגרמו לפגיעות רבות בחלקי גופו השונים. אולם, חשוב להדגיש, כי המידע מתיק החקירה עצמו מפריך את הפרסומים בדבר סממנים אנטי נוצריים שיוחסו לאופן ביצוע הרצח, כגון: עקירת עיניים, מכות גרזן בצורת צלב בפניו של המנוח וקטיעת האצבעות המסמלות את תנועת הברכה הנוצרית.

ביהמ"ש המחוזי שדן בתיק קבע כי הרוצח אינו כשיר לעמוד לדין פלילי עקב מצבו הנפשי ונתן בעניינו של הרוצח צו אישפוז במוסד לחולי נפש. "

4. נשמח לעמוד לרשותך לשאלות ובירורים נוספים.

בברכה,

[חתימה]

רפ"ק יעל אהרונוביץ, עו"ד
קצינת מדור חקירות

העתקים:
רח"ט חקירות
רמ"ד חקירות (3177)
רע"ן מחוז ש"י

*Fig. 5: Israeli police statement to the authors concerning the Philoumenos case, December 27, 2011.*

*1. Patterns of a ritual murder accusation in the popular narratives*

We discovered contradictions when comparing various Orthodox popular narrations, which are found in unofficial[69] and semi-official sources,[70] to the official synodic decision of the Jerusalem Patriarchate[71] that canonized Philoumenos. The Patriarchate's publication is short and is careful not to identify the attacker with a particular ethnic or religious group. The attacker is described as an individual having a malicious nature ("vile man," etc.). In fact, the document does not hint at any group of people. By contrast, the popular material is detailed, elaborates on the methods of torturing the victim, and, moreover, puts the blame on an identified collective—Jews or Zionists—said to be religious fanatics. In the popular narrative, a group planned and executed the murder; collective blaming is its salient motif. Accusing Jews of participating as a group in alleged ritual killings or their cover-up was a primary theme of medieval blood libels.[72]

The brutality of the actual murder was not enough to classify the crime as a ritual murder for some of the popular sources. Therefore, the popular narrative was enhanced in various ways by its narrators in an attempt to emphasize the desired message. One example is the claim that the three fingers of the victim's right hand were deliberately chopped off. The fact that a priest blesses his community with these three fingers is obvious to an Orthodox Christian believer, but is completely foreign to Jews. The photographs of the body taken at the scene of the crime show that "only" a single finger of each hand was missing. The popular narrative assumes that the alleged murderers were so well acquainted with Orthodox Christian practices that their real motive was to put an end to Christian worship in the most physical manner possible. Similarly, the cross-shaped cuts are an embellishment added in the popular narrative to emphasize the torture of the victim and put the blame on alleged Jewish religious customs. The fact that the body was taken away by the police for forensic examination for several days might have encouraged the rumors about the ritual mutilation of the victim's flesh.

---

[69] Yenovkian, "Tribute to a New Martyr"; Pravoslavie, "The Holy Martyr Philoumenos of the Holy Sepulchre"; Odigitria, "In Memoriam of Philoumenos of the Holy Sepulchre"; OrthodoxWiki, "Philoumenos (Hasapis) of Jacob's Well."

[70] Church officials quoted in the information brochure (Fig. 3); Maor, "Following the Murder"; Pehanich, "Lives of the Saints"; Metropolitanate of Singapore, "Saint Philoumenos"; Pemptousia, "Saint Philoumenos the new Hieromartyr"; Hiera Monē, *Ho Hagios*, 148.

[71] Jerusalem Patriarchate, "Synodic Decision."

[72] Emily Rose, "Ritual Murder (Medieval)," in *Antisemitism: A Historical Encyclopedia of Prejudice and Persecution*, ed. Richard S. Levy, 2 vols. (Santa Barbara, CA, 2005), 2:603.

The worldwide proliferation of the popular narrative is partially explained by the fact that Jacob's Well serves as a pilgrimage destination that attracts Christian Orthodox pilgrims from distant countries. It is the many pilgrims that uncritically accept the popular story. Christian Orthodox groups from around the world are able to experience a New Testament site with contemporary added value, as martyrdom is synonymous with saintliness in the Christian tradition. The biblical and contemporary narratives are both explained by the site's current authorities. In addition to the printed material (see Fig. 3), on-site oral interpretations are provided. These may vary depending on the tour guide, but in many cases they describe the death of Philoumenos as a ritual murder performed by a group of settlers (as in the case of the aforementioned NIPSA visit, for instance).

An important element in the Orthodox Christian experience is a belief in miracles and the desire to hear stories about them. It is a deep-rooted belief that a martyr's death makes a man holy.[73] This holiness is further enhanced if he is able to work miracles. The reliability of the popular narrative seems to correspond to the following words in the entry entitled "Martyr" in the *Dictionary of Greek Orthodoxy* by Rev. Patrinacos (emphasis added): "They [the martyrs' stories] were often elaborated by *legends of the invention of their pious biographers*."[74] This observation by an Orthodox clergyman provides a framework to assess the credibility of the various testimonies.

The miracles attributed to Philoumenos as a saint extend from the time he was still alive to right after his death. It was narrated that during his lifetime he had cured Athenian pilgrims in 1978.[75] Among the posthumous miracles are the stigmata left by Philoumenos' blood at the site of martyrdom,[76] the diffusion of a wonderful fragrance from his relics, the incorruption of his body, the movement of his limbs while the body was dressed for burial, his appearance in dreams, his provision of instructions to his believers, healing, and so on.[77] The miracle stories become part and parcel of a worshipper's experience in Jacob's Well. In the past, moreover, a common theme in ritual murder allegations was the appearance of miracles through the body or relics of the Christian victim or near his or her tomb. A frequent miracle of this type was the diffusion of a pleasant fragrance from the sometimes miraculously incorrupt body of the victim.[78] The narratives

---

[73] Donald Weinstein and Rudolph M. Bell, *Saints and Society: The Two Worlds of Western Christendom, 1000-1700* (Chicago, 1982), 160.

[74] Nicon D. Patrinacos, *A Dictionary of Greek Orthodoxy: Lexicon Hellenikes Orthodoxias* (New York, 1984), 245.

[75] Hiera Monē, *Ho Hagios*, 164.

[76] Jerusalem Patriarchate, "Synodic Decision."

[77] Hiera Monē, *Ho Hagios*, 123, 125, 128, 151, 153, 155, 166-83.

[78] Ronnie Po-chia Hsia, *The Myth of Ritual Murder: Jews and Magic in Reformation Germany* (New Haven, 1988), 14-41.

were disseminated through folk tales and songs, explanatory sheets, theological literature, art, and the act of pilgrimage. In medieval times, rumors were the prime factor in the widespread dissemination of the belief that Jews practiced ritual murder.[79] We observed the same patterns in the publicity relating to Philoumenos' martyrdom.

The popular narrative contains apparent antisemitic themes. The inflated number of perpetrators implies that "the Jews" conspire in groups and torture and kill their victims together. The damage inflicted upon the church is perceived as an indication of the war waged by "the Jews" against what Christians consider holy. In this way, Jews are collectively associated with the evil that acts against Christendom. Yenovkian refers to the attackers as "satanically-inspired tormentors." The Metropolitan Bishop of Morphou asserts that Zionism has a secret plan to take over the world and impose the Antichrist. Associating Jews with an evil force was a frequent theme in ritual murder allegations and blood libels.[80]

The claim that religious Jews demanded custody over the site contradicts the fact that the site was never visited by Jews. Even in contemporary politics, no Israeli group has claimed ownership of the site. This accusation aims to emphasize the martyr's role—defending Christianity against the evil of "the Jews."[81] An unequivocal example of this motif in the popular narrative is the saint's intervention to miraculously counter "Jewish tanks," thus preventing harm to the church at Jacob's Well. St. Philoumenos miraculously countered the powerful military of "the Jews" who aimed to harm the Christian shrine. In the Christian Orthodox view, the intervention of a saint changes the unfair balance between the forces in the world—it leads to the victory of the righteous weak over the powers of evil.

By emphasizing the deceased's alleged claim that Jacob's Well was a Christian site "before the Israeli state was created," Yenovkian defines the two antagonists—Christians versus Jewish Israelis. The confrontation is presented as a religious conflict between Jews and non-Jews. Such a view allows Philoumenos' death to be classified as a ritual murder, which was regarded as an established practice in Judaism. The fact that most of the Israeli population in the area is observant may have contributed to the association of various antisemitic libels with the murder.

In the Middle Ages, it was not uncommon for a shrine housing the body of an alleged ritual murder victim to become a pilgrimage destination.[82] The relics

---

[79] Rose, "Ritual Murder (Medieval)," 603.

[80] Trachtenberg, *The Devil and the Jews*, 155; Rose, "Ritual Murder (Medieval)," 603-4.

[81] "Saint Philoumenos encourages Father Ioustinos when often-times the fanatic Jews attack him and the site" (translated by the authors, see Fig. 3).

[82] Rose, "Ritual Murder (Medieval)," 604.

were frequently reported to produce miracles. Local rulers often used such sites to increase their political power or even strengthen their religious authority. In a similar way, the contemporary publicity given to Philoumenos' martyrdom narrative helps increase the influence of the authorities at Jacob's Well. The declaration of a new saint-martyr brought more pilgrims to the site, as the narrative rapidly gained interest among Orthodox Christians worldwide. These pilgrimages resulted in greater financial support and donations. The fact that the incumbent custodian of Jacob's Well, Fr. Ioustinos, has established a splendid burial plot for himself within the Jacob's Well compound, which is decorated with a mosaic of his face, in order to prepare "for what he senses may be a sudden death" at the hands of the same alleged Jewish attackers[83] is another manifestation of the story's widespread publicity.

At Orounta, Philoumenos' birthplace in Cyprus, a new roadside shrine (προσκυνητάρι) with a public prayer area was established at the entrance to the village (Fig. 6). Three large icons are placed on its wall: St. Nikolaus, St. Luke, and in the center—the image of the new St. Philoumenos of Jacob's Well. During our visit to the site in October 2016, we observed a few candles and religious artifacts in the shrine. These signal that the site is frequented by pilgrims.

*Fig. 6: Roadside shrine (προσκυνητάρι) with public prayer area in Orounta, Cyprus. Photograph by the authors, October 2016.*

Moreover, the contemporary geopolitical situation and the Church's desire to ensure its position within it serve as a backdrop to Philoumenos' narrative. In

---

[83] Shortt, *Christianophobia*, 227.

the words of Weinstein and Bell: "Whenever Christianity encountered a frontier, it had a need of martyrs."[84] Therefore, spreading the narrative of Philoumenos' martyrdom was not only a manifestation of its religious significance but was also motivated by the political interests of the ecclesiastical authorities wishing to advance the Church's standing with regional and international players. It is possible that these factors also motivated the decision to canonize Philoumenos in 2009.

### 2. Framing the popular narrative

Another factor underlying the proliferation of the narrative is the environment of the Israeli-Palestinian conflict. The manner in which the conflict is "framed" by the two sides and in the media plays a significant role in the increasing popularity of the narrative.

In relation to ongoing conflicts, *frames* are used to denote how antagonists relate to the unfolding events and construct their perceptions of reality accordingly. In their study on social movements, Robert D. Benford and David A. Snow define *collective action frames* as "action-oriented sets of beliefs and meanings that inspire and legitimate the activities" of activist groups.[85] Such frames are constructed as part of a "shared understanding of some problematic condition or situation they define as in need of change," and "make attributions regarding who or what is to blame." Similar aspects of *framing theory* are applied in communication studies, where frames denote "the process of culling a few elements of perceived reality" by news agents and "assembling a narrative that highlights connections among them to promote a particular interpretation" of the reported events.[86] In relation to the media coverage of conflicts, the process of framing activates "schemas that encourage target audiences to think, feel, and decide in a particular way."[87] In our opinion, analysis of such framing explains some of the motifs that are found in the popular narration of Philoumenos' story.

In his study of the First Intifada, Gadi Wolfsfeld identified two distinct frames in the Israeli-Palestinian conflict through which the antagonists themselves and the global media examined events.[88] The first, the "law and order"

---

84 Weinstein and Bell, *Saints and Society*, 160.

85 Robert D. Benford and David A. Snow, "Framing Processes and Social Movements: An Overview and Assessment," *Annual Review of Sociology* 26, no. 1 (2000): 611-5.

86 Robert M. Entman, "Framing Bias: Media in the Distribution of Power," *Journal of Communication* 57, no. 1 (2007): 164.

87 Ibid.

88 Gadi Wolfsfeld, *Media and Political Conflict: News from the Middle East* (Cambridge, 1997), 141, 144-9.

frame, tends to present the conflict as a matter of civil disorder. Palestinians taking part in riots are mostly presented as outlaws, and the need to prevent violence and to restore the law is emphasized. As such, the "law and order" frame, conceived as supporting Israeli positions, is common among the Israeli public. The second, the "injustice and defiance" frame, which is adopted by Palestinian sources, perceives the Israeli control of the West Bank to be an act of injustice ("occupation"). In this frame, Israel is mostly depicted as a brutal oppressor, while the Palestinians are portrayed as powerless victims fighting to prevent the loss of their land and the denial of their rights.

We suggest that Wolfsfeld's "injustice and defiance" frame has shaped descriptions of the Philoumenos incident in the popular narrative. First, the collective accusations ("radical Zionists," "extremist Jewish Zionists," etc.) point the finger of blame at Israeli citizens in the West Bank (i.e., "settlers"), whose presence in the area is framed as an act of oppression.

The Irish NIPSA report and Khoury's article are both examples of sources that blame settlers in a very direct way. Yenovkian claims that the attacking group left Jacob's Well hurling "insults and obscenities of the kind which local Christians suffer regularly." Thus, he constructs a parallel between the Orthodox Christians and the Palestinian population, hence both are perceived as being powerless victims who suffer under Israeli oppression.

Furthermore, the equation of Orthodox Christians with Palestinians is bolstered by the argument that the Orthodox Church existed long "before the Israeli state was created."[89] The Christians are depicted as an indigenous population, in contrast to the Israelis, who are presented as a new entity in the region. The murder is viewed as part of a much bigger conflict in which Israelis are accused of perpetrating an injustice on the non-Jewish locals. Much as the Palestinians, who are portrayed in the "injustice and defiance" frame as struggling against dispossession, Philoumenos is presented as struggling against the confiscation of Christian holy sites. The popular narrative even employs similar visual language. One of the most well-known visual symbols of the "injustice and defiance" frame is a young Palestinian boy throwing stones at an Israeli tank. Hence, Philoumenos is also described as confronting "Jewish tanks" that were allegedly sent to attack the church.

The fact that Philoumenos' Saint's Day, which is celebrated on November 29, coincides with the International Day of Solidarity with the Palestinian People established by the United Nations General Assembly creates a link between his martyrdom and the Israeli-Palestinian conflict. The murder is not seen solely as a criminal act but is framed as another milestone in what the narrators regard as Israel's oppression of the Palestinians and the continuous injustices caused to

---

[89] For example: Yenovkian, "Tribute to a New Martyr."

the local population as a result of Israeli rule. Moreover, the popular narrative holds the Israeli authorities responsible for the death of the monk or, at the very least, for "covering up" his murder. While Yenovkian's account states that no suspect was ever arrested, NIPSA's rapporteur claims that the attacker was only deported, and Wikipedia contributors have stated that the Israeli authorities refused to search for the attacker.[90] These accusations place the Philoumenos affair in the "injustice and defiance" frame, in which Israelis are perceived as powerful oppressors who abuse their strength to violate the rights of the powerless Palestinians.

The factual basis rules out any links between the criminal act and the Israeli-Palestinian conflict. However, the prominent themes integrated into the popular narrative (such as the identity and motives of the alleged perpetrators) perfectly match the "injustice and defiance" frame of the conflict. This is explained by the narrative being a product of a message. The narrative fits the shared agenda of many social movements, political NGOs, and media agents who relate to the Israeli-Palestinian conflict through the above frame. This contributed to the increased popularity of the story about the Christian saint in non-religious sources.

It is worth noting the differences in the terminology used to describe the alleged attackers in different versions of the popular narrative. Orthodox Christian-oriented sources adopt terms from the religious, ethnic, and political realms, such as "Jews,"[91] "fanatical Jews,"[92] "Jewish terrorists,"[93] "extremist Jewish Zionists,"[94] "Zionist Jews,"[95] "fanatical Zionists,"[96] and "a mob of Jewish Israeli extremists."[97] In contrast, sources of general orientation almost exclusively use terminology from the political realm, such as "settlers,"[98] "Zionist settlers,"[99]

---

90 Wikipedia, "Philoumenos (Hasapis) of Jacob's Well," version of January 26, 2014.

91 Hiera Monē, *Ho Hagios*, 106-7; Odigitria, "In Memoriam of Philoumenos of the Holy Sepulchre"; Pravoslavie, "The Holy Martyr Philoumenos of the Holy Sepulchre."

92 Hiera Monē, *Ho Hagios*, 106, 109; Metropolitan of Morphou, "The Holy New Martyr"; the information brochure on St. Philoumenos that visitors receive at Jacob's Well Church (see Fig. 3).

93 Yenovkian, "Tribute to a New Martyr."

94 OrthodoxWiki, "Philoumenos (Hasapis) of Jacob's Well."

95 Orthodox Metropolitanate, "Saint Philoumenos the New Hieromartyr of Jacob's Well"; Pemptousia, "Saint Philoumenos the New Hieromartyr."

96 Metropolitan of Morphou, "The Holy New Martyr"; Pemptousia, "Saint Philoumenos the New Hieromartyr"; Pehanich, "Lives of the Saints"; Orthodox Metropolitanate, "Saint Philoumenos the New Hieromartyr of Jacob's Well"; OrthodoxWiki, "Philoumenos (Hasapis) of Jacob's Well"; Yenovkian, "Tribute to a New Martyr."

97 Orontes Syria, "Pope Calls for 'a Just and Lasting Solution'."

98 Shortt, *Christianophobia*, 227.

99 Robinson, *Welcome to the Country that Doesn't Exist*, 17.

"Jewish settlers,"[100] "Israeli settlers,"[101] "a radical rabbi settler and his follow-ers,"[102] "Jewish Zionists,"[103] and a "Zionist group."[104] While the religious sources apply language emphasizing racial and religious definitions, the general sources always emphasize contemporary political definitions. This demonstrates an adaptation of the narrative from the Orthodox Christian target audience to the realm of non-Orthodox politically motivated audiences. Despite the change in terminology, the basic points of the account do not differ significantly.

Finally, it appears that the PNA may have utilized the popular narrative in its public relations efforts. Accusations that Zionists allegedly perform ritual murders are common among public figures in the modern Arab world and are frequently found in Palestinian sources.[105] Moreover, Palestinian media and officials have postulated that Israel keeps the bodies of "Palestinian martyrs" for the alleged purpose of harvesting their organs.[106] The leaders of the PLO and the PNA have repeatedly declared that Jesus was a Palestinian who was crucified by Jews.[107] Such discourse creates a link between the Christian medieval perception of Jews as Christ-killers and enemies of Christianity and certain perceptions of the Israeli-Palestinian conflict, which paint the Jews as oppressors of the contemporary Palestinians. While it is questionable whether a planned public relations campaign existed in the PNA prior to 2005,[108] it is plausible that certain enterprises were supported by its authorities with the purpose of emphasizing the desired message. Jacob's Well Church stood in neglect for almost a century but was renovated during the second Intifada. This sudden renovation, which was authorized by the PNA, points to a connection between the increasing publicity of Philoumenos' story and the fact that its message supports the PNA's public relations goals.

On the other hand, the Greek Orthodox Church utilizes the saint's story to advance its own interests within the political system of the PNA. According to Robert S. Wistrich, in the nineteenth-century Ottoman Empire native Chris-

---

100 Wikipedia, "Philoumenos (Hasapis) of Jacob's Well," version of January 26, 2014.

101 Khoury, "Honoring the Mother of God."

102 Olson, "Holy Sites in Palestine," 565-6.

103 Wikipedia, "Philoumenos (Hasapis) of Jacob's Well," version of January 26, 2014.

104 Wikipedia, "Jacob's Well," version of December 23, 2011.

105 See Robert S. Wistrich, "The Old-New Anti-Semitism," *National Interest* 72 (2003): 59-60; Wistrich, *A Lethal Obsession: Anti-Semitism from Antiquity to the Global Jihad* (New York, 2010), 721, 791-2, 806-10.

106 Itamar Marcus and Nan J. Zilberdik, *Deception: Betraying the Peace Process*, 2nd ed. (Jerusalem, 2011), 128-31.

107 Wistrich, *Lethal Obsession*, 709-10.

108 Nashat A. Aqtash, "Palestinian National Authority's Public Relations Policies Relating to Israel: Current Attitudes among Palestinian Officials and Media Experts," *Public Relations Review* 31 (2005): 376-80.

tians also introduced ritual murder accusations as an "attempt at integrating themselves in a Muslim world at times as hostile to Christians as it was to Jews."[109] A similar contemporary motivation could have caused the proliferation of the popular narrative in the case of Philoumenos. Therefore, the PNA and the Greek Orthodox Church have a common interest in promoting the popular version of Philoumenos' murder.

## Conclusions

This article analyzes the popular narrative of the martyrdom of St. Philoumenos of Jacob's Well. After the murder, the Israeli police immediately launched and conducted a thorough investigation. The killer, who had murdered various Jews and non-Jews in a similar manner, was eventually apprehended in 1982. He turned out to be an observant Jew from Tel-Aviv who suffered from hallucinations and acted alone without any connection to a religious or political entity. He was found to be mentally disturbed and was hospitalized in accordance with a decree of the Israeli District Court. It is evident that the Synod of the Jerusalem Greek Orthodox Patriarchate was aware of the murderer's background, and it accordingly refrained from issuing a collective accusation in its official decision on Philoumenos' canonization in 2009. However, antisemitic sentiments inspired rumors of a Jewish ritual murder.

Such rumors initially surfaced in Greece and the Holy Land shortly after the murder. Rumormongering intensified as a product of the geopolitical situation in the West Bank, as well as the growing interest of the global media and political NGOs in the Israeli-Palestinian conflict. To sum up, the medieval-style Christian fear of Jews and international attention in the ongoing conflict together resulted in the emergence of the popular narrative, which differs significantly from the factual basis of what happened in 1979.

According to the popular narrative, Philoumenos met his death in a ritual murder performed by a group of observant Israeli Jews from settlements in the West Bank. The development of the narrative can be traced from an early account published by Yenovkian in 1989 to the publications that appeared after Philoumenos' canonization in 2009, which once again placed his story in the spotlight. This new attention resulted in the addition of details that enhanced the existing narrative. The gaps between the factual basis of the events and the details of the popular narrative seem to be unbridgeable. The development of the popular narrative, as we have observed in this paper, invokes the patterns of ritual murder accusations in the past: the victim was allegedly tortured before the killing, a conspiratorial group of local Jews was involved, the body was taken

---

[109] Wistrich, *Lethal Obsession*, 787.

away, and the martyr revealed his sanctity after his death by performing miracles. The saint is believed to be protecting worshipers at his shrine. Pilgrimage to the church that hosts the martyr's relics has intensified. It is thus clear that the narrative and the patterns of its proliferation have echoes of medieval ritual murder libels.

Furthermore, the application of Wolfsfeld's "injustice and defiance" frame to Philoumenos' story helped establish parallels between the Orthodox Christians in the West Bank and the Palestinians. Both are perceived as weak victims of *injustice* caused by Israeli oppression. Both are framed as struggling against alleged dispossession by Israelis who employ violence. The appearance in Philoumenos' narrative of visual symbols that are usually associated with the Israeli-Palestinian conflict (e.g., unarmed civilians against tanks) emphasizes the link. This helps explain why interest in the story reaches far beyond the Orthodox religious realm.

It is evident that some academic studies failed to recognize the factors that contributed to the popular narrative and instead treated it as an authentic and credible description.[110]

The Jerusalem Orthodox Patriarchate's initiative to venerate Philoumenos has an additional political reasoning, beyond pure religious sentiment. The existence of a new saint encourages pilgrims to visit the site where his relics rest and the site of his birth. The pilgrims bring funds and publicity, which increase the influence of the clergy. The worship, veneration, and canonization contribute to bilateral relations between the Jerusalem Orthodox Patriarchate and the Church of Cyprus, the homeland of the saint. In the local arena, the Patriarchate appears to have mobilized Philoumenos' story to gain influence within the PNA, although the extent of its cooperation with the PNA is unknown.

In his study on contemporary antisemitism as a social phenomenon, David Hirsh suggests that each instance of antisemitism in history left traces in the "cultural reservoir ready to be drawn upon and reinvigorated."[111] One of the two motifs in the cultural reservoir that Hirsh describes is "the blood libel, which charges Jews with ethnically motivated crimes of cruelty, often against children, often involving the consumption or use of blood or body parts." He further notes that "naturally enough, campaigning against Israeli human rights abuses often seeks to engender feelings of compassion for and identification with Israel's Palestinian victims and concomitant feelings of anger toward Israel and Israelis. Sometimes, anti-Semitic themes and images are put to work to help this process."[112] In other words, medieval Christian hatred of the Jews, which is

---

[110] E.g., Olson, "Holy Sites in Palestine"; Shortt, *Christianophobia*.

[111] David Hirsh, "Hostility to Israel and Antisemitism: Toward a Sociological Approach," *Journal for the Study of Antisemitism* 5 (2013): 1415.

[112] Ibid.

residually present in the cultural reservoir of Western society, tends to be invoked in contemporary campaigns against the Jewish state. The present study reveals how such motifs are invoked in the case of Philoumenos. Unlike other known cases in history, where ritual murder allegations were solely an expression of classic antisemitism, religious hatred of the Jews and a desire to delegitimize Israel are both intertwined in the narration of Philoumenos' murder. Therefore, this case is an early and prominent example of contemporary antisemitism (or "new antisemitism").

# The Three Totalitarian Temptations:
# A Different Look at an Essential Aspect
# of the Palestinian-Israeli Conflict

## Col. (res.) Dr. Eran Lerman*

INTRODUCTION

"The Jews are a people that carries out what it says it will," an exiled Palestinian leader, Muhammad 'Izzat Darwazah, told a gathering of Syrian leaders in Damascus in 1938 (a senior Zionist official, an experienced envoy to the Arab world, was listening in from the other room).[1] It was a fine compliment—some would say overstated—but it was not meant as such. It was supposed to serve as a stark wake-up call, not the first of its kind, to the Syrians and other Arab neighbors to provide military aid to the Palestinian armed groups. Darwazah rightly deemed their own strength, much weakened by British repression, to be unequal to the capacities of the dynamic Zionist project.

Similar apprehensions about the scope and momentum of Zionist achievements had already appeared in the writings of thoughtful Arab leaders as early as 1905 and 1913.[2] Still, there was a new sense of urgency in Darwazah's discussion of the threat, as well as a new and promising solution, perhaps a final one. It was to be regretted, he told his colleagues, that a world war had not broken out again (this was a short while after Munich). With German and Italian help, generously given, the Arabs—he believed—would have found it much easier to impose their will on the British Empire and obtain a policy

---

* Lecturer, Program in Middle East and Islamic Studies, Shalem College. Former Deputy Adviser for Foreign Policy and International Affairs on Israel's National Security Council.

[1] E. [Eliyahu] Sasson to M. [Moshe] Shertok, Very Secret [untitled report—code word "Providence"], October 3, 1938. The meeting was held at the home of a Syrian MP who consulted closely with Sasson on these issues and allowed him to listen in from an adjoining room. Darwazah, who found refuge in Damascus, was described as one of the most prominent Palestinian nationalist leaders wanted by the British.

[2] For a discussion of Ruhi al-Khalidi's book, *Zionism or the Zionist Question*, see Amy Dockser Marcus, *Jerusalem 1913: The Origins of the Arab-Israeli Conflict* (New York: Viking, 2007), 99-105.

change that would amount to the abandonment of the Balfour Declaration. Darwazah was not yet aware just how close the British cabinet, under Foreign Office pressure—from Miles Lampson in Cairo and others—had already come to doing just that, in what came to be known as the "White Paper" of 1939.[3]

This was a particular and private discourse, but similar ideas were already being trumpeted by Hajj Amin al-Husseini, the so-called Grand Mufti of Jerusalem. It is also emblematic of a broader but often misunderstood or understated aspect of the Palestinian-Israeli conflict, namely a phenomenon that might properly be referred to as the totalitarian temptation. The Palestinians (or, to be precise, Palestinian leaders) needed an ally that could promise (and deliver) a future without Zionism—perhaps even without Jews.

They felt that they were up against a powerful rival—whether as a result of the reawakening of Jewish national consciousness, as described by Darwazah or a generation earlier by Ruhi al-Khalidi, or in the form of an all-encompassing demonic force, the true determinant of all of modern human history, as described in Nazi propaganda in Arabic[4] and enshrined forty-five years later in the Hamas Covenant of 1988.[5]

To counter it, they therefore needed the help of equally powerful historical forces that were willing to offer them what the West, even when sympathetic to their cause, could not. This was the tempting promise of a revolutionary change in world affairs that among many other aspects could—and indeed must—include the destruction or annihilation of the Zionist project as such. Hence the three totalitarian temptations:

- First came the appeal of the Nazi challenge, due to what prominent Palestinians perceived as the promise to rid them of both the British and the Jews. This was a powerful temptation as long as there was still a prospect that Hitler could deliver on it. The specific details of this bid by Hajj Amin al-Husseini to link the Palestinian people's future to the Nazi project may have faded from our collective memory, giving rise to sadly inaccurate statements,[6] but the scar

---

[3] For an account of the shifts in British policy and the role played by the fears of an impending war, see Netanel Katzburg, *From Partition to the White Paper: Britain's Policy in the Land of Israel: 1936-1940* [in Hebrew] (Jerusalem: Yad Ben Zvi, 1974), 59-81 in particular.

[4] Jeffrey Herf, "Hate Radio: The Long, Toxic Afterlife of Nazi Propaganda in the Arab World," *Chronicle of Higher Education*, November 22, 2009, http://www.chronicle.com/article/Hate-Radio-Nazi-Propaganda-in/49199.

[5] For the Covenant of the Islamic Resistance Movement of August 18, 1988, in particular Article 22, see the translation by the Avalon Project at http://avalon.law.yale.edu/20th_century/hamas.asp.

[6] For an attempt to sort out the confusion caused by Netanyahu's comments, see Eran Lerman, "Setting the Record Straight: Hajj Amin and the Nazis," BESA Center Perspectives Paper no. 318 (BESA Center for Strategic Studies, Bar-Ilan University, Ramat Gan, November 3, 2015).

has not healed and has left its mark on mutual perceptions of what the war of 1948 was all about (given that Husseini reasserted his leadership role among Palestinians even after 1945).

- It took a while for the radical shift from this alliance with the Nazis to a full-fledged Soviet orientation. The Arabs were acutely aware of Stalin's pro-Zionist UN vote in 1947 and the USSR's provision of arms and moral support to Israel in 1948.[7] Still, by 1955 the Soviets were arming Egypt, and by the 1960s they were willing to champion the radical Palestinian vision of destroying "the Imperialists, the Zionists and the Reactionaries," namely the conservative Arab regimes, the British, French, and American presence in the region, and ultimately the State of Israel, scheduled for what Yehoshafat Harkabi once called "politicide."

- By the time this promise also failed—some would say as early as 1967, others at the time of the invasion of Afghanistan or, at the latest, the collapse of the Soviet Union in the late 1980s—there was in place a third, home-grown promise of revolutionary change, through the agency of modern Islamist totalitarianism—*not* Islam as a civilization, as the Huntington thesis would suggest, but a twentieth century political hybrid that owes as much to fascism and Bolshevism as to the concept of *salaf*, a return to the ways of old.[8] Islamist revolutionary totalitarianism took different forms—led earlier in the century by the Muslim Brotherhood; after 1979 by the Iranian regime and its proxies: and in the post-9/11 world by al-Qaeda and its clones. One and all, they explicitly promised the Palestinians a future in which there would be no Israel and no Zionism.

It needs to be said that there are key elements today in the Palestinian leadership—including the president of the Palestinian Authority, Mahmoud Abbas, once a Soviet ally (and agent?) and then a sobered-up pro-Western voice, who left these three temptations behind, despite their past affiliations.[9] Still, the need to latch on to a strong, deterministic current in world affairs that would rid the Palestinians of the need for a painful compromise with a strong adversary at the negotiating table is still there in a different (far more benign but still dangerous)

---

[7] Ya'akov Ro'i, "Soviet Support for the Establishment of the State of Israel" [in Hebrew], in *Hayinu ke-Holmim*, ed. Yehuda Wallach (Ramat Gan: Massada, 1985), 179-199.

[8] One of the most profound interpretations of modern Islamism can be found in Paul Berman, *Terror and Liberalism* (New York: Norton, 2003).

[9] On Abbas's Soviet associations, see, for example, Peter Baker, "Soviet Document Suggests Mahmoud Abbas was a KGB Spy in the 1980's," *New York Times*, September 7, 2016. It could be argued that Abbas's close relations with the Soviets (which included a PhD for an anti-Zionist diatribe that served Soviet interests at the time) were also the reason that he was the first Palestinian leader to realize the depth of the Soviet crisis and the first to advocate a US-oriented strategy (by 1988 at the latest).

form. Specifically, this is the strong preference, particularly within the BDS movement, to work up the false classification of Zionism as a colonialist project and an Apartheid system.[10] It is not the absurdity of these claims about the past and the present that matters—although the argument denying the charge of Apartheid must be heard and has been made quite forcefully by a prominent Israeli peace activist with a solid background in the South African struggle.[11] It is again the promise about the future. Colonialism is essentially a thing of the past; Apartheid has perished. Those who speak the new language about Zionism feed the belief that the Jewish national movement will follow them into the ash heap of history. This belief today is perhaps the most immediate and powerful impediment to peace, side by side with the still active threat of Islamism.

## I. The First Temptation: Hitler's Promise

The story of the infatuation of key Palestinian and Arab leaders with the Nazi vision of a different world future, one that would rid them of their enemies, has been told elsewhere in great detail. Nevertheless, it has faded into the shadows to the point that an Israeli prime minister felt obliged to remind the world of it, albeit in a manner that amounted to a factual misstatement. At the end of the day, one fact stands out: no other people but the Palestinians continued to be lead (however ineffectively and fractiously) by a notorious Nazi collaborator *after* World War II. No account of what befell the Palestinians in 1948 can be truthfully made without cognizance of this basic aspect, which defined for the Jewish side in the war what would be their fate if they lost the struggle or even if they submitted to Arab majority rule in a non-partitioned Palestine, as suggested by the policies outlined in successive British White Papers.[12]

A specific and heroic—if somewhat personal (and at times poorly organized)—effort to give Hebrew readers the full story has been made by a former Yugoslav partisan, Jennie Lebel. After surviving Tito's repression, she revealed the formal evidence that was at the base of Yugoslavia's initial attempt to have Husseini indicted for war crimes committed in its territory. In her book, *Hajj Amin and Berlin*, Lebel offers a broad and documented narrative of the Mufti's role in seeking an alliance with Hitler and delivering Nazi propaganda in Arabic

---

[10] The references to colonialism and Apartheid are central to the BDS concept and take pride of place in the movement's definition of its purpose and aims. See "What is BDS?," BDS movement website, https://bdsmovement.net/what-is-bds.

[11] Benjamin Pogrund, "Israel Has Many Injustices. But It Is Not an Apartheid State," *Guardian*, May 22, 2015.

[12] On this point, and more generally on the perversion of historical memory in this respect, see, for example, David Meir-Levi, *History Upside Down: The Roots of Palestinian Fascism and the Myth of Israeli Aggression* (New York: Brief Encounters, 2007).

through Radio Zeissen.[13] While she also documents in some detail the role of other Arab (and even Indian) pro-Nazi elements who ended up in Berlin, she provides incontrovertible proof of the Mufti's centrality in the Nazis' propaganda and mobilization efforts. True, the *Grossmufti* was not responsible for putting the idea of *fernichtung* in Hitler's mind—it was certainly already there in 1939, in the latter's Reichstag speech in January, well before the war began and almost three years before they met.[14] He was, however, a promoter of the Holocaust, mainly through propaganda and through conversations with Himmler.[15] He was a planner, through the agency of his men working with Walter Rauff's unit in Athens to plan the annihilation of the Jewish population in the *Yishuv* (Palestine). Ultimately he was even a perpetrator (though not in Palestine due to Rommel's defeat at El Alamein), through his role in mobilizing Balkan Muslims to SS divisions, such as the Hanjar (Scimitar) Division, which actively participated in the round-up and extermination of Hungarian Jews in 1944.

More systemic studies have been made in recent years, mainly by German scholars such as Matthias Küntzel, who studied the Nazi roots of Arab anti-semitism,[16] as well as Klaus Mallmann and Martin Cüppers, who focused on the plans for the extermination of the Jewish population of British mandatory Palestine, had Rommel been able to conquer Egypt and advance further east.[17] Useful insights are also offered by two American officer-scholars of Arab origin, the brothers Aboul-Enein, who studied the rivalry of the Nazi and Allied intelligence services in the Arab world during the war.[18] They established the prevalent pattern of Nazi cooperation with Arab elements, in particular with the Mufti and his men (but also, separately, with Fawzi al-Qa'uqji and others in the region), aimed at undermining British hegemony in the Middle East but also at laying the foundations for annihilating the *Yishuv*.

---

[13] Jennie Lebel, *Hajj Amin and Berlin* [in Hebrew] (Tel Aviv: Technosdar, 1996).

[14] "Reichstag Speech, January 30, 1939," Learn about the Holocaust, Timeline of Events, United States Holocaust Memorial Museum, https://www.ushmm.org/learn/timeline-of-events/1939-1941/hitler-speech-to-german-parliament.

[15] A recent item from his correspondence with Himmler was published in 2017 by the National Library of Israel. See Sue Surkes, "In Rediscovered Telegram, Himmler Offers Jerusalem's Mufti Help against 'Jewish Intruders,'" *Times of Israel*, March 30, 2017.

[16] Matthias Küntzel, "National Socialism and Anti-Semitism in the Arab World," *Jewish Political Studies Review* 17, no. 1 (Spring 2005): 99-118.

[17] Klaus-Michael Mallmann and Martin Cüppers, "Elimination of the Jewish National Home in Palestine: The Einsatzkommando of the Panzer Army Africa, 1942," *Yad Vashem Studies* 35, no. 1 (2007).

[18] Youssef Aboul-Enein and Basil Aboul-Enein, *The Secret War for the Middle East: The Influence of Axis and Allied Intelligence Operations during World War II* (Annapolis: Naval Institute Press, 2013), 23-34 in particular.

The Mufti was not alone. King Farouk of Egypt toyed with a Nazi link in the years before the British intervention of February 1942, which forced him to bring the Wafd party to power and secured Egyptian support for the Allied war effort.[19] Based on captured Nazi documents, the British planned to make use of this evidence in the bitter UN Security Council debate on the Egyptian question in the summer of 1947, but ultimately chose to come to an understanding with Prime Minister Mahmoud Fahmi al-Nuqrashi on reducing the level of mutual defamation.[20] Still, the call that rang out among Egyptian youth in the dangerous moments of Axis advances—*ila al-amam ya Rommel!* (Forward, Rommel!)—has left its mark on Egyptian political history.

Even more dramatic was the situation in Iraq, where in April 1941 the "Golden Square," led by the recently deposed Prime Minister Rashid Ali al-Gaylani, took power in a coup with the explicit backing (more verbal than practical, as it turned out) of the Nazis. He was easily defeated by British forces—aided, among others, by Jewish volunteers from the *Yishuv*, including *Irgun* leader David Raziel, who fell in battle during the intervention—which took over Iraq and restored Nuri al-Said to power. This, however, was followed by the infamous *farhud* (pogrom) against the Jews of Baghdad during the first two days of June, in which hundreds were massacred (some estimates put the number at 780), revealing the deep impact of Nazi incitement.[21]

Such sentiments and actions were certainly not universal in the Arabic-speaking lands. Israel Gershoni has written impressively about the strong anti-fascist and later anti-Nazi polemics of Egyptian liberals.[22] The majority party Wafdists in Egypt were largely loyal to the pro-British choices made by their party leadership after 1936, in the face of Italian and then German advances. Robert Satloff had embarked on an extensive journey to document cases of Arabs who risked their lives to help Jews.[23] Among Palestinians, the *mu'aradah* (opposition) to the Mufti was not insignificant, and in 1937 there were leaders among them, such as the Nashashibis, willing to contemplate a partition as offered by the Peel Commission.

---

[19] For a good overview of Egypt during the war—and a reference to the King's pro-Nazi proclivities—see Artemis Cooper, *Cairo in the War 1939-1945* (London: Hamish Hamilton, 1989), 58-60.

[20] Dr. Hasan Husni, *Years With King Farouk: Witness to Truth and History* [in Arabic] (Cairo: Dar al-Shuruq, 2001), 225-230.

[21] Sarah Erlich, "Farhud Memories: Baghdad's 1941 Slaughter of the Jews," *BBC News*, June 1, 2011, http://www.bbc.com/news/world-middle-east-13610702.

[22] Israel Gershoni, *Light in the Shadow: Egypt and Fascism, 1922-1937* [in Hebrew] (Tel Aviv: Am Oved, 1999).

[23] Robert Satloff, *Among the Righteous: Lost Stories from the Holocaust's Long Reach into Arab Lands* (New York: Public Affairs, 2006).

Some modern scholars, such as Gilbert Achcar, have used these and other indicators to decry the so-called "Zionist narrative" regarding the Mufti and the Palestinians.[24] But, at the end of the day, the bare facts remain. The predominant leader of the Palestinian people—in the period leading up to the rejection of the UN Partition Plan, the war, and the *Nakba* that befell them in 1948—was wanted for war crimes in the Balkans, barely escaped justice, and reached shelter in Egypt (with some help from the French) despite British anger and Jewish dismay. With another former Nazi collaborator, Qa'uqji, leading *Jaysh al-Inqadh* (the Arab "Army of Salvation"), it is hardly surprising that for the newly-born State of Israel and the Jewish people the exterminatory threats of contemporary Arab leaders (such as Arab League Secretary-General Abdul Rahman Azzam) carried with them a very real sense that those recently tempted by Hitler were also eager to complete what he had set out to accomplish.

## II. The Second Temptation: The Soviet Proposition

The transition from Nazi sympathies to a Soviet orientation may seem strange, given the ideological abyss separating them, but for some players in the Arab world such as Ahmad Husayn, leader of Misr al-Fatat (Young Egypt Party), it proved to be a relatively short leap. Not long after World War II this former fascist had already redefined himself as a radical socialist. The common theme was a deep and abiding anti-British sentiment. As regards the Zionist project, and then Israel, things were more complicated. Given Stalin's firm support of the Partition Plan and the right of the Jewish people to self-determination, as well as practical support in the form of supplying arms (through Soviet-controlled Czechoslovakia) to the young state fighting for its life, there was little for the Palestinians to latch on to.[25]

Things began to change as early as June 1950, when Israel's first prime minister, David Ben Gurion—to the acute dismay of the Zionist hard Left—made a significant choice. Faced with Truman's request for political support at the United Nations over the Korean crisis, he did not hesitate to cast Israel's lot and stand with the West, abandoning a formal posture of neutrality upheld till then.[26] Stalin was not one to forgive and forget, and Jews soon became the target of a campaign of repression (including the infamous "Doctors' Plot"). As we know now, plans were put in motion to deport, and possibly destroy, the Jewish

---

24 Gilbert Achcar, *The Arabs and the Holocaust: The Arab-Israeli War of Narratives* (New York: Henry Holt, 2010).

25 Ro'i, "Soviet Support."

26 On Israel's decision to support the United States on Korea (and subsequent Israeli efforts to seek a peaceful end to the Korean War), see Young Sam Ma, "Israel's Role in the UN during the Korean War," *Israel Journal of Foreign Affairs* 4, no. 3 (2010): 81-89.

people in the Soviet Union. These designs were ultimately abandoned only because of the dictator's death in March 1953. (There is a chilling passage in Vasily Grossman's *Life and Fate* in which he speaks of how Stalin saved the Jewish people by defeating Hitler at Stalingrad, only to plot a similar annihilation ten years later.)

By the mid-1950s, therefore—even if Stalin's exterminatory urges came to naught—it was no longer absurd to think of the Soviet Union as a potential ally in a long-term strategy to overthrow the existing order, regionally and globally, and, in that context, undo the "Western conspiracy" to impose a Zionist presence in the midst of the awakening Arab world. Once the new Soviet leadership overcame some of Stalin's inhibitions—he was always careful not to risk a confrontation with what he saw as America's superior military capacity— they felt free to court new allies in areas once predominantly under Western control. The huge Czech (read: Soviet) arms deal with Nasser's Egypt was a decisive turning point in this respect.[27]

By January 1957, President Eisenhower—who did so much to help Nasser turn an ignominious military defeat into a glowing diplomatic triumph in 1956—was already treating Egypt and the Arabist radicals, in the implied language of his declared doctrine, as Soviet stooges. It was not the need to protect Israel but a growing fear for the survival of pro-Western regimes in the Arab world that drove his policy, including his decision to intervene in Lebanon in 1958. Indeed, as the Arab "progressive camp" took shape, with Egypt, Syria, post-1958 Iraq, and the FLN in Algeria as its pillars, an "Arab Cold War" was raging, and the Arab-Israeli conflict, too, became increasingly intertwined with the Cold War system.[28] The Soviet Union still had an embassy in Tel Aviv and did not abandon its formal position recognizing Israel's legitimacy, but it was arming forces that actively sought to destroy the Jewish state.

All this did not immediately impact the Palestinian position, because in the decade after the 1948 War of Independence there was—in practical terms—no Palestinian position as such. Most Palestinians, numb and fragmented, were living under Jordanian rule. Those who sought to continue the struggle and resented the incorporation of the West Bank into the Hashemite realm found their place within the Nasserist revolutionary scheme of pan-Arabism as "an eternal truth" (*haqiqah khalidah*). In fact, Palestinian activists played a major part in the front organization, *Harakat al-Qawmiyyin al-Arab* (Arab Nationalist Movement), which served Nasser as his agents of subversion across the

---

[27] Motti Golani, "The Historical Place of the Czech-Egyptian Arms Deal, Fall 1955," *Middle Eastern Studies* 31, no. 4 (October 1955): 803-827.

[28] The best text on this stormy period remains Malcolm H. Kerr, *The Arab Cold War: Gamal 'Abd Al-Nasir and His Rivals, 1958-1970* (London: Oxford University Press, 1971).

region.[29] After the collapse of the union between Egypt and Syria in 1961, however, the Syrians—radical and eager to outbid their former master—gave growing scope to the activities of *Fatah*, a group established in Kuwait in the late 1950s, which used its presence in Syria to launch its "revolution" against Israel on January 1, 1965.

The Palestinians' claim to the mantle of a revolutionary vanguard at that moment in history is the key to understanding how the Soviet proposition linked up with the radical Palestinian and Arab forces. With the Algerian War won, Castro's Cuba and Che Guevara in the background, and Vietnam fast becoming the emblematic story for a generation of young minds in both the West and what was coming to be called the "Third World," Moscow was now making much of the USSR's newly-found willingness to back "movements of national liberation," as long as they promised the violent overthrow of the existing order—usually at the expense of pro-Western regimes and American interests, both economic and strategic.[30]

For some of the Palestinian leaders, particularly Yasser Arafat, this was not necessarily a natural choice. His own affiliation as a young man had been with the *Ikhwan* (Muslim Brotherhood), which may have been one of the reasons why he was obliged to leave Egypt and take refuge in Kuwait. He was certainly not a Marxist, unlike Habash or Nayef Hawatmeh, but he did latch on to the imagery of a global revolution led by forces associated with the Soviet Union—a revolution in which the Palestinian struggle, which was bound to be long and difficult, could play an important part. Indeed, in later years, Arafat wove into his own descriptions of the Palestinian role a dramatic scene in which General Giap, who had been victorious in Vietnam, symbolically gave the Palestinians the task and the honor of becoming the standard bearers of the global revolution. There were certainly regular visits by Palestinian "military" mission to Vietnam, and Giap did extend his best wishes, but Arafat's version is probably embellished.[31]

Unlike the Nazis, the Soviets did not adhere to an exterminatory position when it came to Israel, let alone the Jewish people. And yet they provided the Palestinian organizations not only with arms, training, and political support, culminating in the infamous "Zionism is racism" resolution in the UN General

---

[29] On the origins of the Qawmiyyin—later the PFLP—see, for example, "George Habash: A Profile from the Archives," *Jadaliyya*, September 27, 2012, http://www. jadaliyya.com/pages/index/7547/george-habash_a-profile-from-the-archives.

[30] Roger E. Kanet, "The Superpower Quest for Empire: The Cold War and Soviet Support for 'Wars of National Liberation,'" *Cold War History* 6, no. 3 (2006): 331-352.

[31] See, for example, "Documents and Source Material: Arab Documents on Palestine and the Arab-Israeli Conflict," *Journal of Palestine Studies* 4, no. 4 (Summer 1975): 170-186, which contains several reports on Palestinian-Vietnamese exchanges, indicating the PLO's ardent wish to bask in the glory of the North Vietnamese victory.

Assembly, but also with a sense that they have latched on to the forces of the future, the "progressive camp," whose ultimate success would inevitably undo the existing international order—and with it the conditions that made it possible for Israel to survive and prosper.

After 1967, the humiliation of the defeat of several key Soviet allies was compounded, from Moscow's point of view, by the impetus that this resounding rout of the Arab armies gave to a renascent Jewish national identity within the Soviet Union—not only rejecting the notion of the "New Soviet man" but openly demanding the right to move to Israel.[32] This was an implied threat to the system as a whole—which has been likened (by Natan Sharansky) to a torpedo hitting the Soviet ship of state below the water line. This, in turn, meant that, in addition to their support of Palestinian organizations, the Soviets were now in need of strongly worded anti-Zionist polemics. These polemics, often tinged with old-fashioned antisemitic tropes, became the order of the day. Thus, Mahmoud Abbas's PhD—which was written (for him?) in Moscow during his years as PLO representative there—on the useful theme of alleged "secret Zionist-Nazi relations," which crosses the line into a diminution of the Holocaust, fits in well with the broader pattern of the KGB Tenth Directorate propaganda operations on this front.[33]

The Soviets were thus willing to indulge and support a Palestinian position that essentially denied the legitimacy of Zionism (as in the case of the Soviet-backed UN General Assembly resolution equating Zionism with racism)[34] and sought to put an end not only to the "occupation" of 1967 but also to the results of 1948, namely Israel's existence as a sovereign state. This became even more vital for Arafat—let alone the Marxist-oriented PFLP and DFLP, off-shoots of what had once been the Nasserist Arab Nationalist Movement—in the years after President Anwar Sadat's dramatic set of decisions: to completely abandon the Soviet orientation, to open up Egypt economically (and to a limited degree politically), to turn away from futile pan-Arabism, and in 1977 to visit Jerusalem and make peace with Israel. From a Palestinian point of view, this combination seemed to serve as proof of the importance of the Soviet orientation in resisting such a "betrayal" of the cause.[35]

---

32 This was part of a general Jewish awakening. Seth J. Frantzman, "'Like Dreamers' Author on the Six Day War's True Impact," *Jerusalem Post*, June 2, 2017.

33 Michael Lumish, "The Dissertation of Mahmoud Abbas," *Jews Down Under*, June 28, 2016, https://jewsdownunder.com/2016/06/28/dissertation-mahmoud-abbas.

34 UNGA resolution 3379 (XXX) of November 10, 1975: Elimination of all Forms of Racial Discrimination.

35 For a (Marxist) analysis of the Palestinian predicament in the wake of the Israeli-Egyptian Treaty, see Sameer Abraham, "The PLO at the Crossroads: Moderation, Encirclement, Future Prospects," *MERIP Reports* 9 (September/October 1979) (MER 80), available at http://www.merip.org/mer/mer80/plo-crossroads.

Thus, as the Cold War once again escalated in the early years of the Reagan administration, the PLO was very much on one side of the equation. In this context, the United States was willing to acquiesce, up to a point, in Israel's intervention in Lebanon in 1982, which destroyed the Palestinian "state within a state" and, with it, the network of support for various terror organizations around the globe. This was part of the service the Palestinians were providing to their Soviet allies in return for their support.[36]

Exiled in Tunisia, the PLO leadership was bound to rethink the utility of its historical reliance on a power which, at the end of the day, was unable to prevent this from happening. Soviet influence waned, moreover, as the ability and willingness of the USSR to pursue an aggressive anti-American strategy declined and the war in Afghanistan sapped the its resources and energies, as well as its legitimacy in the Muslim world. Interestingly, it was Abbas, more familiar with the weaknesses of his past masters in Moscow than any other person in Arafat's inner circle, who was among the first—together with Salah Khalaf (Abu Iyad)—to actively pursue a strategy of switching orientations and working within the American rules of the game.[37]

## III. The Third Temptation: First Saddam, Then Islamist Totalitarianism

Thus, as blunt messages from Gorbachev signaled that the "New Thinking" in Moscow left no room for continued support for the global revolutionary agenda, the PLO came to a fork in the road. The locally-initiated Intifada, which began in December 1987, reflected a feeling that the previous modes of action had come to a dead end. Meanwhile, the PLO—still in Tunis—changed course and accepted the need to reorient itself in world affairs. The Palestinians' 1988 Declaration of Independence essentially marked a decision to turn away from a revolutionary identity that had failed to deliver and enter the realm of "international legitimacy" and what would come to be called the two-state solution, albeit on terms that still included the "right of return" (which, if fully implemented, would amount to the dismantling of the Zionist project by other means).[38]

---

[36] For an (embittered and critical) account of the war and the US position, see Joe Stork and James Paul, "The War in Lebanon," *MERIP Reports* 12 (September/October 1982) (MER 108), available at http://www.merip.org/mer/mer108/war-lebanon.

[37] For a detailed description of the dramatic evolution of the Palestinian position in 1988, see Joshua Teitelbaum, "The Palestine Liberation Organization," in *Middle East Contemporary Survey*, vol. 12, ed. Itamar Rabinovich and Haim Shaked (Boulder: Westview Press, 1988), 229-276.

[38] Rashid Khalidi, "The Resolutions of the 19th Palestine National Council," *Journal of Palestine Studies* 19, no. 2 (Winter 1990): 29-42.

By the end of 1988, Arafat was obliged—under American pressure—to pay the verbal price of recognizing Israel's right to exist and, even more uncomfortably, "renouncing" terrorism (merely "denouncing" it—without an implied admission of past practices—turned out to be insufficient for the outgoing Reagan administration). In doing so, he obtained Washington's consent to open a dialogue with the PLO.

The very thin veneer of international legitimacy was soon penetrated, however, by the pull of a new totalitarian promise—albeit a short-lived one. By 1990, Saddam Hussein's ambitious designs for regional hegemony were increasingly drawing Arafat away from his newly-found place in the American-dominated order. Amid a growing rift in the Arab world, the Palestinians firmly associated themselves with Saddam's vision, nurtured by the glow of his military victory over Iran. It was an attempted terror attack in May 1990 by an Iraqi-backed organization—the Palestine Liberation Front—that led to the suspension of the US-PLO dialogue. The incident, involving several speedboats attempting to land on Israeli beaches, may have been of limited significance (four raiders were killed and twelve captured) but could have ended in much larger bloodshed (including an attack on the US embassy).[39] The fact that it took place at all signified a dangerous policy shift toward a return to the armed struggle and a growing reliance on Saddam's alliance. This culminated in Arafat's open support of the Iraqi conquest and annexation of Kuwait in August 1990—a position he adhered to, despite external pressures and internal tensions, until Saddam's disastrous defeat in the war of 1991.[40] This choice was followed by an even briefer infatuation with the short-lived "GKChP" coup against Gorbachev in the summer of 1991, which many Palestinians hoped would put an end to the latter's policy of retreat in Third World conflicts.[41] Arafat's behavior in both cases indicated that, for him at least, the switch away from the totalitarian temptations was not truly a profound act of redefining the Palestinian position in world affairs—abandoning revolutionary legitimacy in favor of the established order—but a temporary setback, to be reversed at the first opportunity.

Having gambled and lost twice (or three times if you count the Soviet coup), Arafat was unable to avoid the conditions set by the United States in response to Israeli demands at the Madrid Peace Conference of 1991: no separate Palestinian delegation, no overt PLO presence, no Jerusalemites, no predetermined

---

[39] "U.S. Embassy Was a Prime Target of Aborted Seaborne Terror Attack," *Jewish Telegraphic Agency (JTA)*, September 14, 1990.

[40] Youssef M. Ibrahim, "Confrontation in the Gulf: Arafat's Support of Iraq Creates Rift in P.L.O.," *New York Times*, August 14, 1990.

[41] Despite Arafat's later denial, there were clear indications that the Palestinian leadership welcomed the coup. See "Arafat Denies Congratulating Soviet Hard-liners over Coup," *JTA*, September 4, 1991.

outcomes, and no coercive international authority. It was a bitter pill to swallow, but Arafat had little choice but to accede to these stipulations.[42] However, the Israelis who happily concluded that this represented a realization by the Palestinians of their own weaknesses and heralded a fundamental strategic reorientation and acceptance of the inevitability of a historic compromise, were to be swiftly and bitterly disappointed. By 1995, faced with mounting evidence that Arafat was playing a double game, many in the Israeli defense establishment no longer believed they had a reliable partner.

For some, disillusionment hit home much earlier. A leaked transcript of a speech Arafat gave in a mosque in Johannesburg implied that he regarded the Oslo Accords as a temporary expedient—and that he had chosen to revert to the Islamic idiom of his youth.[43] His reference to the Prophet's practice over the Treaty of Hudaybiyyah was not only an indication that he saw the present stage as transitory: it was also a sign of a growing shift from a secular nationalist and socialist vocabulary to a more Islamic idiom, culminating in the so-called al-Aqsa Intifada. This, in turn, reflected the changing nature of the conflict itself.

In the meantime, a powerful new temptation appeared on the horizon, once again offering a counter-balance to US power and a future without Israel or Zionism (or even the Jews): Islamist totalitarian politics in its various local, regional, and global manifestations. In the Palestinian arena, the rise of Hamas presented Arafat—a perennial fence-sitter who always sought to maintain his room for maneuver and what he described as the Palestinians' independence to make decisions (*istiqlal al-qarar*)—with both a threat and an opportunity: a challenge to his authority but also an indirect way of increasing the level of pain for Israel and pushing for further concessions. He dodged every effort to force him to deal with the threat of Palestinian terror. In fact, he typically dismissed terror attacks known to have been carried out by Hamas or Palestinian Islamic Jihad from areas under the control of the Palestinian Authority (PA) as alleged provocations by an Israeli-style OAS, modeled after the French paramilitary organization that sought to reverse de Gaulle's withdrawal from Algeria.

By the time he was finally forced to change course, after a series of horrifying attacks in February and March 1996, it was too late to restore the trust of most Israelis in Arafat or his promises of peace. The next few years were marked again and again by this ambivalence (or duplicity). Efforts to reach agreements that would secure further Israeli withdrawals and redeployments were conducted while nurturing a complex relationship with the terror organizations,

---

[42] "The Madrid Framework," Guide to the Mideast Peace Process, Israel Ministry of Foreign Affairs, January 28, 1999, http://mfa.gov.il/MFA/ForeignPolicy/Peace/Guide/Pages/The%20Madrid%20Framework.aspx.

[43] Transcript (in the original English) of Arafat's speech in Johannesburg on May 10, 1994, available at http://www.textfiles.com/politics/arafat.txt.

restraining them while also tolerating their existence and occasionally giving them a wink and a nod when their violence seemed to serve the cause.[44] The situation deteriorated dramatically after the failure of negotiations in 2000 (followed by an equally unsuccessful attempt by Arafat to gain international support for a coercive solution). Although the subsequent eruption of violence is often referred to as the Second Intifada, it was in fact a terror campaign guided from above, not a popular uprising. It became increasingly clear that, under Arafat, the PA had been playing a double game with the Islamist terror groups and was now willing to make common cause with them in an effort to break the spirit of Israeli society.

In regional terms, Arafat's actions translated into an ambivalent position toward Iran. While paying lip service to the concerns of the Palestinians' Arab backers—and the United States—about the Islamic Republic's role as a fountainhead of terrorism, Arafat actively conspired with the Islamic Revolutionary Guard Corps (IRGC) in Tehran to arrange for the supply of significant amounts of Iranian weapons. This famously included a consignment of weapons and ammunition apprehended aboard the "Karine A" by the Israeli navy on the high seas and brought into the port of Eilat in 2002. Despite vigorous and at times absurd denials—at one point Arafat even referred to the vessel as an "alleged ship"[45]—key international players, led by President George W. Bush, saw this as the ultimate proof of Arafat's unreliability—a judgment fed by previous experiences but now confirmed in no uncertain terms.

Not long afterwards, Bush put forward a vision for peace and a Palestinian state that would be achieved in negotiations with a "new and different" Palestinian leadership. This was a sharp departure from past practice (since 1992) and a powerful rejection of all that Arafat stood for. The realization that the present leadership had blatantly lied to him on a matter related to its relationship with the so-called "Axis of Evil" had much to do with this cardinal shift in US policy.[46] Although this strong American reaction was later reversed by President Obama, who took a far more lenient line toward Palestinian misdeeds, it was too late to help Arafat, who died, physically exhausted and diplomatically defeated, in November 2004. In any case, the political and public backlash Arafat reaped in 2002 was all the more acute because the Palestinians' campaign of violence

---

44 For an Israeli practitioner's perspective of this period, see Moshe (Bogie) Ya'alon, A Long Short Road [in Hebrew] (Tel Aviv: Yedioth Ahronoth, 2008).

45 "Statement by IDF Chief-of-Staff Lt.-Gen. Shaul Mofaz regarding interception of ship Karine A," Israel Ministry of Foreign Affairs, January 4, 2002, http://mfa.gov.il/MFA/PressRoom/2002/Pages/Statement%20by%20IDF%20Chief-of-Staff%20Lt-Gen%20Shaul%20Mofaz.aspx.

46 "Full Text of George Bush's Speech on Israel and a Palestinian State," *Guardian*, June 25, 2002.

against Israel was taking place against the backdrop of the Global War on Terrorism launched by the United States and a coalition of willing allies in response to the horrors of the 9/11 attacks on the United States.

Arafat's duplicity was not the only factor that undermined Palestinian relations with the United States and its allies. Images of Palestinians celebrating the 9/11 attacks also helped to expand the traditional gap in opinion polls between Americans who support or sympathize with Israel and those who identify with the Palestinian cause from around 4:1 to roughly 6:1. Beyond that, the lingering question—at least as long as Arafat was alive—was linked to the notion of affiliation and whether, from 1988 onwards, the Palestinians were being sincere when they appeared to accept the legitimate global order and distance themselves (at least temporarily) from the totalitarian forces trying to subvert it.

## IV. A Non-Totalitarian Temptation: International Coercion

It is important to note that, unlike Arafat, Mahmoud Abbas was wise enough not to be swept back into the tempting visions offered by totalitarianism, Islamist or otherwise. His experience with the Soviets was a sad lesson, and his rejection of Arafat's decision to revert to the armed struggle was genuine. In a 2002 essay, entitled "Huzimna" (We have been defeated), Abbas referred to this strategy as *askarat al-intifada* (militarizing the uprising). His break with Hamas was painful and real.

Still, his ability to make the final decisions necessary to achieve a compromise marked by painful concessions on both sides was (and remains) hampered by a different kind of temptation that is much more benign but still highly problematic. This is the delusion (fostered by the likes of Palestinian chief negotiator Saeb Erekat) that there is a better alternative to a negotiated agreement—a so-called BATNA—that would not involve any significant concessions by the Palestinians beyond what they have already conceded in terms of recognizing Israel (though not as a Jewish state nor as the embodiment of the right of the Jewish people to self-determination). This alternative would presumably involve international—particularly European—coercive measures that would force Israel to accept the Palestinian terms of reference. This is not to imply that Abbas is no better than Hamas. His regional allegiance in the post-2011 "game of camps" is with the forces of regional stability, such as Jordan and Abdel Fattah el-Sisi's Egypt, which are also allies of Israel. However, the hope for an imposed solution does derive from the same root as the totalitarian temptations, namely the refusal to accept a negotiated outcome that would reflect the imbalance of power.

# The Political and Intellectual War
# on Israel in Latin America

Luis Fleischman*

## I. INTRODUCTION

In recent years, the situation in the Middle East has become more pertinent in Latin America than ever before. In the past, it was a somewhat exotic, distant region. An issue covered by the news in Latin America, but mainly of concern to the Jewish population in the region. Even for the Left, the situation in the Middle East was not a high priority. It could be said, with a great degree of certainty, that the issue did not raise the same level of passion as it did in Europe and the United States. During this period, Israeli leaders generally regarded Latin America as a friendly region. Despite their far from perfect voting record at the United Nations, Latin American countries did not side unconditionally with the Arab position like many other Third World countries.

In 1947, Latin American countries played a key role in securing the partition of Palestine in the United Nations General Assembly. At a time when they constituted about one-third of the entire membership of the General Assembly, they largely supported Resolution 181.[1] Between 1947 and 1967, Latin American countries held positions that were mostly supportive of Israel. Most of them sympathized with Zionism given the horrors of the Holocaust. In addition, they were aligned with the United States and Western countries, with the exception of Cuba after 1959.[2] This situation continued until 1974. After the Arab oil embargo, Latin American countries, which now constituted no more than 13% of the membership of the General Assembly, started moving closer to the Palestinian and Arab position due to their fear of further sanctions. Brazil, which

---

* Senior Adviser to the Menges Hemispheric Security Project at the Center for Security Policy (CSP); co-editor of the CSP internet publication *The Americas Report*; author of *Latin America in the Post-Chávez Era: The Threat to U.S. Security* (Dulles: Potomac Books Inc., 2013).

[1] Cecilia Baeza, "América Latina y la cuestión palestina," *Araucaria Revista Iberoamericana de Filosofía, Politica y Humanidades* 14, no. 28 (2012): 111-131 at 113.

[2] Ibid., 115.

was the most dependent on Arab oil, began to vote in support of Arab resolutions, particularly concerning the Palestinian cause. Despite his initial anti-Arab posture, Chile's Pinochet followed suit for similar reasons. In November 1975, Brazil and Mexico thus joined Cuba in supporting the infamous UN General Assembly resolution equating Zionism with racism (Resolution 3379), a position later mitigated purely as a result of American pressure.

In the following years, as many Latin American countries began their transition to democracy and focused primarily on their own problems, they once again showed a lack of interest in issues related to the Middle East.[3] However, things began to change in the early 2000s, as the Left triumphed in national elections in a number of countries. As a result, Latin American countries are now looking to pursue a foreign policy that is independent from that of the United States and closer to the interests of the Third World. This has led them to be sympathetic to the Palestinian cause for ideological reasons, such as anti-colonialism and opposition to US influence in the region, rather than for reasons related to Arab oil.

Generally speaking, changes in attitudes toward Israel are taking place in three areas: the political sphere, civil society, and the intellectual environment.


## II. THE POLITICAL SPHERE

In terms of government policy, there are two major political streams within the Left that dramatically affect Israel. The first is the Bolivarian Alliance (ALBA), a group of countries led by Venezuela, including Ecuador, Bolivia, Nicaragua, and several Caribbean countries. The second stream is the so-called moderate Left, which includes countries such as Brazil, Argentina, Uruguay, and Chile. In contrast, countries like Paraguay and Colombia have maintained their classic pro-US and pro-Israel position.


### 1. The radical Left

The leader of the radical-left ALBA group is Venezuela. The country's former president, Hugo Chávez, was a revolutionary leader who sought to unify Latin America under the Bolivarian revolution. Chávez's revolution rejected capitalism and democracy and destroyed private property and the middle classes. It also claimed to speak on behalf of the poor and rejected the previous two-party system that dominated Venezuelan politics for four decades. In addition to all this, it was also fiercely anti-American. Chávez thus gave birth to a regime that continues to head in the direction of totalitarianism, even after his death in early 2013.

---

[3] Ibid., 117-120.

Under Chávez, Venezuela became a revolutionary model for a number of countries, including Bolivia, Ecuador, and Nicaragua. All three countries have adopted a government with strong executive prerogatives and a policy of strong anti-Americanism. This inclination does not limit itself to mere rhetoric but actively seeks to remove US influence from the region by setting up alliances with countries outside the region that share their anti-American feelings.

A clear affinity exists between the regime established by Chávez and Middle Eastern dictatorships. Both abhor "Western colonialism" and "US imperialism." Leaders such as Chávez and Middle Eastern autocrats tend to overstate the culpability of the developed world for their own miseries. Identity based on resentment sets the ideological tone that strengthens the ties of solidarity between these two groups. Likewise, both see democracy as a threat to their rule.

Iran, in particular, seemed to be a natural ally for Chávez and his Latin American partners on the radical Left. As a result of its nuclear program, Iran became a target for international isolation led by the United States. Venezuela came to the country's aid by providing a banking system capable of alleviating its international isolation. Iran is also involved at a regional level in Latin America. For example, it helped build and design an ALBA-owned military school that is headquartered in eastern Bolivia. The former Iranian Secretary of Defense, who is also accused of being part of the plan to bomb the AMIA headquarters in Buenos Aires, attended and presided over the inauguration of the school. Iran is reportedly providing training at the facility.[4]

Chávez also promoted the presence of Hamas and Hezbollah in Venezuela and developed relations with both groups. Pentagon officials reported the presence of Iranian Revolutionary Guards in Venezuela in early 2010.[5] It has also been reported that Chávez organized a summit in Caracas in August 2010 that was attended by the top leadership of Hamas, Hezbollah, and Islamic Jihad, including Khaled Meshaal (Hamas), Ramadan Abdullah Mohammad Shallah (Islamic Jihad), and Hezbollah's chief operating officer, whose identity has not been made public.[6] There have also been reports of cooperation with Hezbollah, including training of Venezuelans in Hezbollah camps in Lebanon.[7] Most recently, Rafael Isea, a former deputy minister of finance and president of the

---

4 Ilan Berman, "Threat to the Homeland: Iran's Extending Influence in the Western Hemisphere," Testimony in Congress, July 10, 2013, http://interamericansecuritywatch. com/ilan-berman-testimony-threat-to-the-homeland-irans-extending-influence-in-the-western-hemisphere.

5 Bill Gertz, "Iran boosts Qods shock troops in Venezuela," *Washington Times*, April 21, 2010.

6 "Chávez Hosts Terrorism Summit in Venezuela," *Americas Forum*, March 29, 2010, http://www.americas-forum.com/content/chavez-hosts-terrorist-summit-venezuela.

7 Douglas Schoen and Michael Rowan, *Hugo Chávez and the War against America: The Threat Closer to Home* (New York: Free Press, 2009), 126-127.

Venezuelan Bank of Economic and Social Development now living in the United States, told a Spanish journalist that current President Nicolás Maduro travelled to Damascus in 2007 to meet with Hezbollah leader Hassan Nasrallah while serving as minister of foreign affairs under Chávez. The purpose of that meeting was to negotiate the installation of Hezbollah cells in Venezuela. This agreement protected Hezbollah's drug trafficking and money laundering activities, as well as arms supplies and the provision of passports. These passports and visas were prepared by Ghazi Nassereddine, a counselor in the Venezuelan embassy in Syria. Nassereddine, who was born in Lebanon and became a Venezuelan citizen, was later blacklisted by the FBI.[8]

Isea himself attended the Maduro-Nasrallah meeting in 2007. That was the year when mysterious direct flights between Caracas and Teheran were first noticed. Isea has confirmed that more than 300 Hezbollah members, including roughly a dozen known terrorists, were included on those flights. Their role, according to Isea, was to participate in drug trafficking and money laundering in order to secure funding for Hezbollah.[9]

Thanks to Venezuela, Iran's influence has expanded in the region. Its relations with Bolivia, Ecuador, and Nicaragua have likewise been enhanced through commercial agreements worth billions of dollars, mutual visits, and other types of cooperation. Iranian state television made a commitment to provide Bolivian television with Spanish-speaking programming that is likely to take the form of direct or indirect pro-Iranian propaganda. Iran will also help Nicaragua construct a strategic deep-water port on the country's eastern shore at a cost of $350 million. In December 2008, Ecuadorian president Rafael Correa declared Iran a strategic partner and expressed his support for the expansion of military ties between the two countries.[10]

Hostility toward Israel is part of this equation. Venezuela and Bolivia severed relations with Israel in the aftermath of Operation Cast Lead in Gaza in 2009. Chávez blasted the state of Israel and intimidated its Jewish population in an effort to impose his government's view on the Gaza conflict. Likewise, during Operation Protective Edge in the summer of 2014, the government of Venezuela, whose official and semi-official bodies have openly engaged in antisemitism, urged the local Jewish community to speak out against Israel. This led to the

---

8 Luis Fleischman, "New Evidence of Iran's Presence in Latin America," Center for Security Policy, May 11, 2015, https://www.centerforsecuritypolicy.org/2015/05/11/new-evidence-of-irans-presence-in-latin-america.

9 Emili J. Blasco, *Bumerán Chávez: Los fraudes que llevaron al colapso de Venezuela* (Washington, DC: Center for Investigative Journalism in the Americas, 2015).

10 Ely Karmon, "Iran's Strategic Penetration in Latin America," *Right Side News*, April 25, 2009, http://www.rightsidenews.com/world/islamic-terrorism/irans-strategic-penetration-in-latin-america.

Wiesenthal Center to appeal to the Organization of American States (OAS) to defend the rights of Jewish citizens.

The actions of the Venezuelan government contain a strong element of anti-semitism. At one point, Chávez ordered a raid on a Jewish school on the pretext that the Mossad was involved in the assassination of a corrupt Venezuelan prosecutor associated with Chávez. On another occasion, Chávez stated that "descendants of the same ones that crucified Christ" had looted the world's riches.

Antisemitism is apparent throughout the region. A former president of Honduras, Manuel Zelaya, who joined the Bolivarian Alliance and attempted to carry out a Chávez-style revolution in Honduras during his tenure, has accused Israeli mercenaries of torturing him with high-frequency radiation while he was hiding in the Brazilian embassy in Tegucigalpa.[11] The source of this accusation is unclear, but it is worth noting that Chávez served as Zelaya's mentor and ally. Bolivia also severed diplomatic relations with Israel during the first Gaza war. In addition, during Operation Protective Edge, it defined Israel as a terrorist state and changed visa procedures for Israelis seeking to visit the country. Finally, Nicaraguan president Daniel Ortega, who served as leader of the Sandinista rebels in late 1970s, has stated that Israeli Prime Minister Benjamin Netanyahu is possessed by the devil and urged Pope Francis "to remove the demons from the Prime Minister's head."[12]

It would thus appear that anti-Zionism and antisemitism have become part of the Bolivarian Alliance's ideology, both tacitly and explicitly. The ALBA countries are following in the footsteps of Iran's delegitimization of Israel. As a result, the Jewish population in countries such as Venezuela has dramatically declined.


## 2. The moderate Left

Under the leadership of President Jose Inácio Lula da Silva (2003-2011), Brazil became more and more involved in international affairs. Motivated by a desire for economic growth and global influence, it developed an active foreign policy aimed at achieving regional integration and turning South America into an autonomous and powerful regional actor with a key role in world affairs. Officially, this regional integration was meant to lead to the convergence of the region's two main commercial blocks—South America's Mercosur and the

---

11 "Jews Scapegoat in Honduras Political Stalemate," Anti-Defamation League, October 1, 2009, http://www.adl.org/PresRele/ASInt_13/5615_13.htm.

12 Luis Fleischman, "Hostility Against Israel In Latin America: What Does It Really Mean?," Center for Security Policy, August 22, 2014, https://www.centerforsecuritypolicy.org/2014/08/22/hostility-against-israel-in-latin-america-what-does-it-really-mean.

Andean Community (CAN)—extending beyond Chile, Suriname and Guyana. However, regional integration goes beyond economics, and Brazil's efforts resulted in a political block that marks the beginning of a new era.

The resulting organizations, such as the Union of South American Nations (UNASUR) and the Community of Latin American and Caribbean States (CELAC), as well as the Bolivarian Alliance (ALBA), are not just economic entities but institutions that reinforce this sense of purpose and counter-hegemony. Although, the ALBA countries tend to express this sense of counter-hegemony more aggressively, it is the more moderate Workers' Party of Brazil that most effectively embodies and leads this counter-hegemonic change.

Former Brazilian foreign minister Celso Amorim has outlined the basics of Brazil's foreign policy.[13] First, Brazil supports the idea of a multi-polar world order, as opposed to the unipolar order of the post-Cold War era. Brazil sees itself as a leader, given its economic success and status as an emerging world power.[14] It views itself as one of the new emerging economies and world powers alongside Russia, India, China, and South Africa (the so-called BRICS). Brazil is seeking a seat on the UN Security Council and tried to assume responsibility for resolving the Iranian nuclear crisis. In late 2010, it joined forces with Turkey to cut a deal with Iran. This deal was rejected immediately by the Western powers, since it demanded very little from Iran and would not have prevented it from developing nuclear weapons.[15]

In addition, Brazil has promoted the development of South-South cooperation—a sort of economic, political, and spiritual alliance between developing countries. As part of this philosophy, it has organized several Latin American-Arab summits. These summits adopted a number of resolutions that reflect the Arab position on a variety of issues. For example, Latin American and Arab leaders called for the elimination of the Syria Accountability and Lebanese Sovereignty Restoration Act (SALSRA), a law passed by the US Congress to impose sanctions on Syria in response to its support for terrorism. They also supported the territorial integrity of Sudan and praised its government for its assistance in trying to solve the problem in the Darfur region, without mentioning its responsibility for the genocide that took place there. Another notorious resolution called for an international conference to study and define terrorism in such a way as to avoid a clear and unequivocal condemnation of terrorism.

---

[13] Celso Amorim, "Brazilian Foreign Policy under President Lula (2003-2010): An Overview," *Revista Brasileira de Politica Internacional* 53 (2010).

[14] Ibid.

[15] Luis Fleischman, "Turkey and Brazil, Iran Supporters for Different Reasons," *Cutting Edge News*, May 24, 2010, http://www.thecuttingedgenews.com/index.php?article=12211&pageid=&pagename=.

Against this background, we can also make sense of Brazil's position on the Middle-East conflict, namely the unilateral creation of a Palestinian state based on the pre-1967 borders. Brazil argued that its statement in this regard in December 2010 was intended to force the peace process out of its stagnation. About a week later, Brazil openly declared that peace in the Middle East would not be achieved as long as the United States continued to serve as mediator.[16] Other South American countries followed suit, with the exception of Colombia and Mexico. Among those that followed Brazil's lead, no other country, with the exception of Chile, has called on the Palestinians to secure the establishment of their future state through negotiations with Israel.

What is especially worrisome about Brazil's position on the Middle East is that it appears to be largely influenced by the Arab approach to the conflict. When President Lula visited Jerusalem in early 2010, he called on Israel to tear down the fence it had built between the country and the West Bank, without any consideration for the fact that it effectively helped prevent deadly terrorist attacks on Israeli citizens. Lula was also influenced by the Arab delegitimization of Israel, as reflected by his refusal to visit the grave of Theodor Herzl, the founder of the Zionist movement. This event was very serious because it showed that Brazil had fallen under the spell of hostile anti-Israel Arab forces.[17]

As Giselle Datz and Joel Peters point out:

> Along with the goal of attaining greater geopolitical relevance, Brazilian foreign policy has also been fueled by idealism. This is nowhere clearer than in the country's position toward the Israeli-Palestine cause, which has offered Brazil an opportunity to display its newfound global assertiveness at relatively low costs. … The Israeli-Palestinian conflict sets up a marker of a "post-American" position, confirming Brazil's new role in the lead-pack group [of new actors that challenge the unipolar US-dominated model].[18]

Brazil is no longer dependent on Arab oil thanks to its production of ethanol and the discovery of a large oil deposit. Instead, the country's anti-Israel bias is part of a deliberate strategy aimed at reinforcing new alliances and downgrading America's position in the world. This attitude also has continental implications as it spreads to other leftist governments in the region.

---

16 "Mideast Peace Process Futile while U.S. in Charge, Lula Says," *Fox News Latino*, December 20, 2010, http://latino.foxnews.com/latino/politics/2010/12/20/mideast-peace-process-futile-charge-lula-says.

17 Luis Fleischman, "The Logic Behind South American Countries' Support for a Palestinian State," *Cutting Edge News*, December 27, 2010, http://www.thecuttingedge news.com/index.php?article=12211&pageid=&pagename=.

18 Giselle Datz and Joel Peters, "Brazil and the Israeli-Palestinian Conflict in the New Century: Between Ambition, Idealism, and Pragmatism," *Israel Journal of Foreign Affairs* 7, no. 2 (2013): 45.

For example, countries belonging to the moderate Left adopted a biased attitude toward the state of Israel during Operation Protective Edge. Indeed, before any hard evidence regarding the circumstances under which this war was fought were available, several Latin American countries, including Brazil, Chile, El Salvador, Ecuador and Peru, temporarily withdrew their ambassadors from Tel-Aviv in protest.[19] At a meeting of the Mercosur trade bloc, the presidents of Uruguay, Brazil, Argentina and Venezuela and issued a joint statement condemning "the disproportionate use of force on the part of the Israeli armed forces in the Gaza Strip, force which has almost exclusively affected civilians, including many women and children."[20]

In Argentina, President Cristina Kirchner's supporters in Congress rushed to condemn the killing of innocent civilians in Gaza, expressing solidarity with Palestinian victims without condemning Hamas or expressing any solidarity with the Israeli victims of terror.[21] Mercosur called on the United Nations to probe Israeli war crimes, echoing the discourse in the famously biased UN Human Rights Council. Marco Aurélio Garcia, a left-wing ideologue and architect of Brazil's foreign policy, described Israel's actions as "genocide." The government of Uruguay, which did not recall its ambassador, also described the Israeli actions as "genocide." According to one of the leaders of the Uruguayan Jewish community, the foreign minister of Uruguay later admitted that the government's declaration was issued under pressure from Brazil and Venezuela. In all this, not a word was said about Hamas's aggression.

In this context, it is important to clarify that Brazil and the rest of the moderate left-wing countries believe in a two-state solution and do not have a policy of delegitimizing Israel.[22] Furthermore, all the governments and legislative bodies of the Mercosur countries, including Brazil, Argentina, Paraguay and Uruguay, have approved a free trade agreement between the organization and Israel.[23] The

---

[19] Barak Ravid, "El Salvador Becomes Fifth Latin American Country to Recall Israel Envoy," *Haaretz*, July 29, 2014, https://www.haaretz.com/el-salvador-recalls-israel-envoy-1.5257361.

[20] Ishaan Tharoor, "Latin America's support for Palestinians and the echoes of the Cold War," *Washington Post*, July 31, 2014, https://www.washingtonpost.com/news/worldviews/wp/2014/07/31/latin-americas-support-for-palestinians-and-the-echoes-of-the-cold-war.

[21] "El Frente para la Victoria repudió a Israel por defenderse de los ataques de Hamás," *Cadena Judía de Información—Visàvis*, July 19, 2014, http://visavis.com.ar/?p=15745.

[22] "Brasil reconhece Estado Palestino com as fronteiras de 1967," *Globo*, December 3, 2010, http://g1.globo.com/mundo/noticia/2010/12/brasil-reconhece-estado-palestino-com-fronteiras-de-1967.html.

[23] "Mercosur/Israel Free Trade Agreement Becomes Effective April," MercoPress South Atlantic News Agency, March 16, 2011, http://en.mercopress.com/2010/03/16/mercosur-israel-free-trade-agreement-becomes-effective-april; "Declaración Final de la

Palestinian cause thus appears to provide these countries with another ideological tool to ingratiate themselves with Third World countries and send a clear message that the United States is no longer the only key player in the region.

## III. CIVIL SOCIETY

Anti-Israel feelings have also penetrated at grassroots level. The past two decades have seen the rise of new social movements defending the rights of previously marginalized groups, including indigenous groups and inhabitants of shantytowns who never had a political voice. Many of these movements support a radical social and political agenda, although they vary from country to country. Likewise, many of them were connected to and/or were funded by Venezuela during the Chávez presidency.

In Brazil, the ruling Workers' Party (Partido dos Trabalhadores or PT) grew out of the grassroots. It was founded in 1980 by trade unions that emerged as a result of increasing urbanization in Brazil. In contrast to many party elites in Latin America, the PT has established permanent structures to include grassroots organizations in decision making at every level. It encompasses a whole range of Socialist and popular movements, such as unions, human rights groups, Liberation Theology groups within the Catholic Church (which try to reconcile between Christian theology and Marxism), environmentalists, women's groups, indigenous groups, Afro-Brazilians, and the powerful Landless Workers' Movement (Movimento dos Trabalhadores Sem Terra or MST).

Some of these groups have connections to Palestinian non-governmental solidarity organizations. For example, the MST, which is the largest grassroots movement in Brazil, planted its flag in the city of Ramallah in the West Bank. It supports a one-state solution, a formula supported by Hamas and others wishing to destroy the Jewish character of Israel. The MST has a one-sided, dualistic view of the Palestinian conflict, in which Israel is the villain and the Palestinians are the victims. It has also asked Mercosur to terminate its free trade agreement with Israel. The largest Brazilian trade union, the Unified Workers' Central (Central Única dos Trabalhadores or CUT), has also adopted an anti-Israel position. The CUT considers Israel an apartheid state that practices terrorism against the Palestinians.

In fact, almost all the social movements that support the current government view Israel as a terrorist and apartheid state. The MST believes that Israeli leaders have ignored UN resolutions and prevented the freedom of Palestinians

---

Cumbre de Comunicación Indígena del Abya Yala," Confederación de Nacionalidades Indígenas del Ecuador, November 26, 2010, http://www.conaie.org/component/content/article/4-noits4/312-declaracion-final-de-la-cumbre-de-comunicacion-indigena-del-abya-yala.

since 1947, while totally disregarding the fact that the Palestinians and Arab countries have rejected Israel's legal and legitimate existence, as sanctioned by the United Nations, while repeatedly attacking it.[24] The fact that these groups are not marginal groups but part of the ruling coalition could have serious political, cultural, and even economic implications. As grassroots movements become more vocal on the issue, they insert into government policy more of what Antonio Gramsci calls the "prejudices and notions that constitute hegemony"—a set of ideas accepted as truths. The hegemonic advance of these ideas could make it very difficult to reverse them.

In late 2014, for example, the Brazilian state of Rio Grande do Sul cancelled an important cooperation agreement with ELBIT, an Israeli company that specializes in military products. Various Brazilian social movements and trade unions demanded that the authorities cancel the agreement on account of ELBIT's involvement in the construction of the so-called "Apartheid Wall" (the security fence separating Israel from the West Bank) and its connection to the Israel Defense Forces. Among those demanding such action was the CUT.[25] Likewise, an administrator at Brazil's Federal University of Santa Maria sent a memo to other officials requesting information on Israeli students or faculty members at the institution. This was clearly an act of racism encouraged by Palestinians seeking to delegitimize Israel. Although apologies and explanations were subsequently offered, it is clear that the idea of applying such discriminatory measures against Israel and its citizens is considered acceptable.[26]

In Argentina, the Piqueteros movement organized demonstrations in Buenos Aires during the Gaza operation. The Piqueteros were born out of the social protests that took place across the country during the 1990s. The movement was consolidated in the 2000s, as a result of a demonstration that successfully toppled the government of President Fernando de la Rua (1999-2001) during the country's deep economic crisis.[27] The Piqueteros have developed a strong anti-establishment ideology based on the rejection of economic neo-liberalism and US hegemony in the region. Most of the movement's leadership identifies with the Venezuelan regime. Similarly, it has developed an obsessive fondness

---

[24] Leonardo Severo, "Centrais e movimentos sociais promovem ato pela Palestina livre e soberana," September 22, 2011, http://www.mst.org.br/Centrais-e-movimentos-sociais-promovem-ato-pela-Palestina-livre-e-soberana.

[25] "Elbit Systems pierde un contrato clave debido a protestas propalestinas," Campaña BDS, December 9, 2014, http://boicotisrael.net/bds/elbit-systems-pierde-un-contrato-clave-en-brasil-debido-protestas-propalestinas.

[26] Scott Jaschick, "Tracking Israeli Students," *Inside Higher Ed*, June 8, 2015, https://www.insidehighered.com/news/2015/06/08/controversy-over-brazilian-universitys-request-identify-israeli-students.

[27] Andrés Benavente Urbina and Julio Alberto Cirino, *La Democracia Defraudada: Populismo Revolucionario en America Latina* (Buenos Aires: Grito Sagrado, 2005), 299.

for Iran and a vicious hatred of Israel and Zionism. Piquetero leader Luis D'Elía, who has strong ties to former Argentinean president Cristina Kirchner, expressed open support for the Iranian regime and attended seminars in Iran. On one of his trips to Iran, he met with Mohsen Rabbani, one of the main suspects in the AMIA bombing.[28]

According to the late Argentinean prosecutor Alberto Nisman, who was in charge of investigating the AMIA bombing, the Argentinean government was involved in a conspiracy with D'Elía and the leader of a militant Quebracho group, which maintains direct communications with Iran via its embassy in Argentina.[29] The alleged purpose of this conspiracy was to absolve Iran from the responsibility for the AMIA bombing in order to normalize economic and political relations between the two countries. This scheme resulted in a memorandum of understanding between Argentina and Iran stating that Iran would become part of the investigation in which it was the suspect.

However, it could be argued that the normalization of Argentina's relations with Iran was also part of an ideological stand, as the Argentinean government is actually sympathetic to Iran and supports its anti-American stance. Furthermore, journalist Emili Blasco appears to confirm that it was Hugo Chávez who prepared the ground for strengthening cooperation between Iran and Argentina while the Venezuelan leader and President Kirchner were busy strengthening their own cooperation. According to Blasco, Argentinean nuclear scientists have even visited Iran.[30] Another factor that influenced Argentina's position on Iran is the mobilization of Arab communities in Latin America. These communities, which have lived in the country for three generations, have only recently become more active politically.

Islamic websites are flourishing in Latin America. They include a substantial amount of content that seeks to delegitimize Israel. Many of these websites have been promoted by Iran. It is not yet clear just how much influence they exert on the Latin American population. The concern is not so much that regular people may read these websites but that the local population of Arab origin, which has lived in peace with the Jewish community for well over a century, may be radicalized.

Historically, relations between the Arab and Jewish communities in Argentina were cordial, although they were mainly based on personal relations between individuals. After the terrorist attack on the Jewish community headquarters in Buenos Aires in 1994, the organized Jewish community initiated a dialogue that

---

[28] "D'Elía Admits He Met AMIA Attack Suspect," *Buenos Aires Herald*, March 8, 2010.

[29] Ely Karmon, "Hezbollah Latin America: Strange Group or Real Threat," Institute for Counterterrorism, November 14, 2006.

[30] Blasco, *Bumerán Chávez*, ch. 11.

was welcomed by the Argentinean Arab Federation (FEARAB), which is regarded as a moderate umbrella organization for local Arab communities.[31] Over the past several years, however, FEARAB has issued hostile and even antisemitic statements against the Jewish community.[32] It even went so far as to declare that the Jewish community was not loyal to Argentina but to Israel. In addition, it implied that Israel was an illegitimate state by stating that the occupation of Palestine began in 1948.[33]

A similar situation has arisen in Chile. In November 2013, a Chilean senator of Palestinian-Christian origin pointed out that young Israeli tourists visiting Chilean Patagonia represented a danger to Chile's territorial continuity. These remarks by Senator Eugenio Tuma, who was also the coordinator of President Michelle Bachelet's election campaign, alluded to an infamous antisemitic myth that the Jews want to take possession of Patagonia. Fuad Chain, another Chilean-Arab congressional representative and vice-president of the Democratic-Christian party, echoed this calumny. Following an accidental fire in a national park in Chilean Patagonia, which was apparently started by an Israeli backpacker, Chain claimed that the culprit was a young man sent by his country to Chile after killing Palestinian children. Senator Tuma, who is also the chair of the Senate Foreign Relations Committee, pointed out that "thousands of Israelis enter Chile as if it were their home" and that "the state of Israel should take responsibility for the damage since [these tourists] are funded by Israel."[34]

The Palestinian community in Chile is mostly Christian and emigrated to Chile at the turn of the twentieth century, well before the publication of the Balfour Declaration. In interviews, leaders of the Jewish and Palestinian communities have acknowledged that the Palestinian community has never been as active in its support of the Palestinian cause as it is today.[35] A process of radicalization is taking place in local Arab communities, which suggests that

---

[31] Isaac Caro, "Conflicto y Pacificación entre las comunidades judías, árabes y musulmanas en Argentina y Chile," *Revista Encrucijada Americana* 2, no. 1 (2008): 42-46.

[32] FEARAB's secretary-general denounced connections between the Buenos Aires city police and the State of Israel, pointing his finger toward the spokesperson of the force who happens to be Jewish and accusing him of being a spokesperson for the Israel Defense Forces. "Cruces entre el secretario de la FEARAB y el PRO," *El Mesnajero Diario*, October 6, 2010, http://www.elmensajerodiario.com.ar/contenidos/cruces-secretario-fearab-pro_1327.

[33] "Amia: Su verdadera cara—Comunicado de FEARAB Argentina," *Prensa Islámica*, December 21, 2010, http://www.prensaislamica.com/nota5985.html.

[34] Monica Cooper, "Sin lugar a duda: El odio a Israel es antisemitismo. La historia de Chile," *Revista de Medio Oriente*, February 28, 2012.

[35] Gil Shefler, "In Chile, Jews Face New Dangers and Old Fears," *Jerusalem Post*, August 23, 2012, http://www.jpost.com/Jewish-World/Jewish-News/In-Chile-Jews-face-new-dangers-and-old-fears.

elements in the Middle East have worked hard to exacerbate Arab feelings of resentment. This is a very serious development, since it represents a major victory for the narrative of Arab and Muslim rejectionists and the movement that seeks to delegitimize Israel.

## IV. The Intellectual Environment

Frei Betto is a leading Brazilian intellectual. He is closely associated with Liberation Theology and the Christian Base communities, as well as with the Landless Workers' Movement (MST). Also, although he has been critical of the Workers' Party over its inclusion of conservative elements, he has remained supportive of the party, particularly during elections. Frei Betto harshly criticizes globalization and neo-liberal polices and supports the Cuban and Bolivarian revolutions, despite their failure and the oppression to which they gave rise. He remains a key figure in the Brazilian social movement, both as a fighter for social justice and as a fugitive of the Brazilian dictatorship of the 1970s. In contemporary Brazil he is not a marginal intellectual, but a very influential one. In an article co-authored with João Pedro Stedile, the head of the MST, Frei Betto points out:

> It is in this context that there emerged in Iran a government that refuses to submit itself to the interests of the United States. It has built nuclear plants within the framework of its policy of national development, and *that* is what the empire finds intolerable. … The United States transferred nuclear technology to Pakistan and Israel, which today have nuclear bombs. But it doesn't tolerate Iran's access to nuclear technology, even for peaceful purposes. Why? What justifies such imperial exercises of power? Some international convention? No, just its military supremacy. … The government of Iran dares to defend its sovereignty.[36]

According to Frei Betto, Iran is thus a heroic state struggling against US imperialism. Since the struggle against imperialism is the real struggle that he is concerned about, he believes that Iran is another victim of such imperialism trying to defend itself from such aggression. In other writings, Frei Betto points out that the events of 9/11 were indeed horrendous, but that they should at least motivate the United States to review its policies. He believes that the misery experienced by Africa, including epidemics and diseases, is the result of decades of Western colonialism.[37] During Operation Protective Edge, Frei Betto signed a

---

36 Frei Betto and João Pedro Stedile, "Empire against Democracy," *Monthly Review*, May 28, 2010, http://mrzine.monthlyreview.org/2010/bs280510.html.

37 Frei Betto, "La Paz de Mis Suenos," *Rebelion*, December 28, 2005, http://www.rebelion.org/noticia.php?id=24765.

letter drafted by a group of intellectuals accusing Israel of war crimes and crimes against humanity and calling on world nations to impose an embargo on Israel similar to the one imposed on South Africa.[38]

Another case is Eduardo Galeano, a Uruguayan writer and intellectual who is close to the ruling Broad Front party. In reaction to events in Gaza in 2012, Galeano not only attacked Israel's specific actions but also claimed "that Israel was built at the expense of the Palestinians and continues to expand."[39] He uses elements drawn directly from Arab propaganda and distortion. For example, he claims that "the persecution of the Jews has been an old European habit, but in the last half century this historical debt has been charged to the Palestinians, who have never been antisemitic. Furthermore, they are Semitic themselves."[40] Galeano also argues that the threat of a nuclear Iran is an invention of the pro-American media and that the real nuclear threat comes from the United States, which destroyed Hiroshima and Nagasaki.

Another high-profile intellectual who engages in these distortions is the Argentinean Nobel laureate Adolfo Pérez Esquivel, who received the prestigious prize for his activism on behalf of human rights. Like the aforementioned intellectuals, he blames Israel for the conflict in Gaza, calling it a "terrorist state," and launched a petition calling for a boycott of Israel. In one of his articles criticizing Israel, Pérez Esquivel writes:

> When will the international community stop allowing Israel to act with impunity, without attempting to limit its aggression against the Palestinian people? When will the United States and the European Union stop being part of the aggression against the people of the Middle East, Palestine, Syria, Libya, Afghanistan and Iraq? When will they stop threatening Iran?[41]

Pérez Esquivel denounced the European countries' intervention in the conflict in Libya and warned them against intervening in Syria. Despite his status as an internationally recognized human rights activist. he declines to mention that in both Syria and Libya murderous dictators launched a merciless war against their own people.

However, Pérez Esquivel can be even more outrageous. In an open letter to President Obama following the killing of Osama bin Laden in 2012, he asks why

---

[38] "Nobel Peace Laureates and Celebrities Call for Military Embargo on Israel," BDS Movement, July 19, 2014, http://www.bdsmovement.net/2014/nobel-celebrities-call-for-military-embargo-12316#sthash.I3GBBewd.kjpcv3Gp.dpuf.

[39] Luis Fleischman, "The Gaza Crisis and the Intellectual Left in Latin America," Center for Security Policy, December 7, 2012, https://www.centerforsecuritypolicy.org/2012/12/07/the-gaza-crisis-and-the-intellectual-left-in-latin-america.

[40] Ibid.

[41] Adolfo Pérez Esquivel, "Israel, Basta de Terrorismo de Estado," November 20, 2012, http://www.adolfoperezesquivel.org/?p=2783.

the United States did not capture bin Laden and try him in a court of law. He then answers his own question by suggesting that bin Laden probably knew information that the United States did not want him to disclose, suggesting that the tragic events of September 11, 2001 might have been the result of a self-inflicted attack whose only purpose was to launch a war against Afghanistan and Iraq and subsequently against Libya.[42]

Another example of intellectual deceitfulness comes in the form of the Argentinean "Open Letter" ("Carta Abierta") group, a collection of journalists, artist, and academics identified with the governments of Nestor Kirchner (2003-2007) and Cristina Kirchner (2007-2015). The group, which promotes a nationalist and populist ideology, opposes neo-liberalism and the "subordinate role" of Argentina in the globalized economy. The group is critical of the United States and supported former Venezuelan president Hugo Chávez, whom they regard as a champion of social justice.

During Operation Cast Lead in Gaza, "Open Letter" issued a statement blaming Israel for war crimes against the Palestinian people, pointing out that the operation took place after an eighteen-month blockade on Gaza. The statement talks about the need to reach a just solution and peace between the Israelis and the Palestinians. However, it ignores the fact that Hamas took over Gaza by force and perpetrated terrorist attacks against Israeli civilians and Israeli towns. It goes so far as to describe Israel's actions as a "ruthless and brutal Israeli invasion against a defenseless civilian population in Gaza," carried out with "the complicity of the United States." At the same time, the Palestinians are portrayed as entirely innocent and the words "terrorism" or "Hamas" are not even mentioned.[43]

The founder of "Open Letter', Ricardo Forster, has discussed the Israeli-Palestinian conflict in depth. For example, he points out that Theodor Herzl's Zionism was inspired by Otto von Bismarck's nationalism. To Forster, Israel is more similar to Sparta, chauvinistic and militaristic, than to Athens, which practiced humanism and philosophy. He claims that the Jews, traditionally a nation of writers and philosophers, have become a military nation that has "wounded" Israeli society and uses Auschwitz as a justification for anti-Palestinian aggression. He also believes that Israelis do not want peace or coexistence with the Palestinians.[44]

---

42 Adolfo Pérez Esquivel, "Carta a Obama, de Perez Esquivel," *Cuba Debate*, May 9, 2011, http://www.cubadebate.cu/opinion/2011/05/09/carta-a-obama-de-perez-esquivel/#.VJi3SO2AA.

43 "Gaza: Una Reflexión y una Postura Ineludibles," Espacio Carta Abierta, June 3, 2009, http://www.cartaabierta.org.ar/index.php?option=com_content&view=article&id=333:declaracion-sobre-gaza&catid=130:comunicados&Itemid=823.

44 Ricardo Forster, "Israel, lo judío, los palestinos y los dilemas de la historia," *Página 12*, November 23, 2012, https://www.pagina12.com.ar/diario/elmundo/4-208389-2012-11-23.html.

Forster deliberately ignores the history of Israeli-Palestinian peace negotiations and disregards Israel's accomplishments as a democratic and humanistic society, such as the emergence of "Peace Now" and the rise in the 1970s and 1980s of political parties that supported dialogue with the PLO and subsequently the establishment of a Palestinian state. Years later, these ideas were adopted by mainstream political parties, leading to the launch of the 1993 Oslo Peace Process. In contrast, Forster defines Palestinian society as humanistic and democratic without providing any evidence to support this claim. The simplistic and opinionated character of his views also allows him to ignore the fact that Palestinian society is constantly exposed to incitement organized not just by radical groups such as Hamas but also by the Palestinian Authority.

The aforementioned intellectuals do not necessarily delegitimize Israel in an official sense. In its articles on the Israeli-Palestinian conflict, for example, "Open Letter" supports the two-state solution. However, by distorting the facts surrounding the Gaza operation and the Israeli-Palestinian conflict as a whole, "Open Letter" and other leading intellectuals actually contribute a great deal to the delegitimization of Israel.


## V. CONCLUSIONS

In Latin America, attacks against Israel take place at the level of government, civil society, and the intellectual environment. The scope of these attacks is unprecedented in the region's history.

Although the Left in Latin America is not homogenous, the moderate and extreme camps are making common cause to ensure that their rule does not remain temporary. They believe that the Left in Latin America must be unified in order to establish what Gramsci has referred to as "hegemony." This encompasses the spread of a new culture and new public beliefs, in addition to new domestic and foreign policies. As pointed out earlier, in the quote from Riggirozzi and Tussie, the rise of the Left in Latin America has given rise to a re-politization (and re-education) of the region. This trend has a strong impact on Israel. As a journalist associated with the Kirchner government has noted: "What matters about Gaza is what it represents. In the 1960s it was Vietnam and Cuba. It is about the struggle between the oppressors and the oppressed."[45]

Despite the fact that Israel has made several concessions, such as withdrawing from Gaza and dismantling settlements, the Palestinian cause continues to nourish the Left's hegemonic moment. The Palestinians have come to symbolize and even justify the existence of the Left in Latin America. In their eyes, they are

---

45 Pedro Brieger, "Franja de Gaza: Ni reir, ni llorar, solo comprender," La Cámpora Derechos Humanos, July 24, 2014, http://lacamporaddhh.org/franja-de-gaza-no-reir-ni-llorar-sino-comprender.

both freedom fighters opposing a powerful Western enemy. In addition, while the liberal parties and media traditionally adopt pro-Israel positions, anti-Israel prejudice is now so deeply embedded in the system that counteracting it will require hard work. Finally, Iran's growing influence and the widespread dissemination of Palestinian propaganda are having a negative influence on the Arab and Muslim diaspora in Latin America, undermining the harmony of the past.

The most disturbing aspect of these developments is that the rise of the Left may have a lasting impact on Latin American politics and civil society, even if it is eventually removed from power. This is because the "hegemony" imposed by the agents of the Left is likely to leave an indelible mark on the political, social, and cultural landscape. Knowledgeable and courageous individuals must therefore be willing confront hostile actors in order to provide a counterweight to the forces that are flooding politics, civil society, the media, academia, and the intellectual environment with irrational prejudice and false narratives.

## REFERENCES


Amorim, Celso. "Brazilian Foreign Policy under President Lula (2003-2010): An Overview." *Revista Brasileira de Politica Internacional* 53 (2010): 214-240.

Baeza, Cecilia. "América Latina y la cuestión palestina." *Araucaria Revista Ibero-americana de Filosofía, Politica y Humanidades* 14, no. 28 (2012): 111-131.

Benavente Urbina, Andrés and Julio Alberto Cirino. *La Democracia Defraudada: Populismo Revolucionario en America Latina* (Buenos Aires: Grito Sagrado, 2005).

Berman, Ilan. "Threat to the Homeland: Iran's Extending Influence in the Western Hemisphere." Testimony in Congress, July 10, 2013. http://inter americansecuritywatch.com/ilan-berman-testimony-threat-to-the-homeland-irans-extending-influence-in-the-western-hemisphere.

Betto, Frei. "La Paz de Mis Suenos." *Rebelion*, December 28, 2005. http://www. rebelion.org/noticia.php?id=24765.

Betto, Frei and João Pedro Stedile. "Empire against Democracy." *Monthly Review*, May 28, 2010. http://mrzine.monthlyreview.org/2010/bs280510.html.

Blasco Emili J., *Bumerán Chávez: Los fraudes que llevaron al colapso de Vene-zuela* (Washington, DC: Center for Investigative Journalism in the Americas, 2015).

Brieger, Pedro. "Franja de Gaza: Ni reir, ni llorar, solo comprender." *La Campora Derechos Humanos*, July 24, 2014. http://lacamporaddhh.org/franja-de-gaza-no-reir-ni-llorar-sino-comprender.

Caro, Isaac. "Conflicto y Pacificación entre las comunidades judías, árabes y musulmanas en Argentina y Chile." *Revista Encrucijada Americana* 2, no. 1 (2008): 37-70.

Cooper, Monica. "Sin lugar a duda: El odio a Israel es antisemitismo. La historia de Chile." *Revista de Medio Oriente*, February 28, 2012.

Datz, Giselle and Joel Peters. "Brazil and the Israeli-Palestinian Conflict in the New Century: Between Ambition, Idealism, and Pragmatism." *Israel Journal of Foreign Affairs* 7, no. 2 (2013): 43-57.

Fleischman, Luis. "The Logic Behind South American Countries' Support for a Palestinian State." *Cutting Edge News*, December 27, 2010. http://www.thecuttingedgenews.com/index.php?article=12211&pageid=&pagename=.

Fleischman, Luis. "Turkey and Brazil, Iran Supporters for Different Reasons." *Cutting Edge News*, May 24, 2010. http://www.thecuttingedgenews.com/index.php?article=12211&pageid=&pagename=.

Forster, Ricardo. "Israel, lo judío, los palestinos y los dilemmas de la historia." *Página 12*, November 23, 2012. https://www.pagina12.com.ar/diario/elmundo/4-208389-2012-11-23.html.

"Gaza: Una Reflexión y una Postura Ineludibles." Espacio Carta Abierta, June 3, 2009. http://www.cartaabierta.org.ar/index.php?option=com_content&view=article&id=333:declaracion-sobre-gaza&catid=130:comunicados&Itemid=823.

Jaschick, Scott. "Tracking Israeli Students." *Inside Higher Ed*, June 8, 2015. https://www.insidehighered.com/news/2015/06/08/controversy-over-brazilian-universitys-request-identify-israeli-students.

Karmon, Ely. "Iran's Strategic Penetration in Latin America." *Right Side News*, April 25, 2009. http://www.rightsidenews.com/world/islamic-terrorism/irans-strategic-penetration-in-latin-america.

Karmon, Ely. "Hezbollah Latin America: Strange Group or Real Threat." Institute for Counterterrorism, November 14, 2006.

Pérez Esquivel, Adolfo. "Israel, Basta de Terrorismo de Estado." November 20, 2012. http://www.adolfoperezesquivel.org/?p=2783.

Pérez Esquivel, Adolfo. "Carta a Obama, de Perez Esquivel." *Cuba Debate*, May 9, 2011, http://www.cubadebate.cu/opinion/2011/05/09/carta-a-obama-de-perez-esquivel/#.VJi3SO2AA.

Riggirozzi, Pía and Diana Tussie. "The Rise of Post-Hegemonic Regionalism in Latin America." In *The Rise of Post-Hegemonic Regionalism: The Case of Latin America*, edited by Pía Riggirozzi and Diana Tussie, 1-16. United Nations Series on Regionalism. New York: Springer, 2012.

Schoen, Douglas and Michael Rowan. *Hugo Chávez and the War against America: The Threat Closer to Home.* New York: Free Press, 2009.

Severo, Leonardo. "Centrais e movimentos sociais promovem ato pela Palestina livre e soberana." September 22, 2011. http://www.mst.org.br/Centrais-e-movimentos-sociais-promovem-ato-pela-Palestina-livre-e-soberana.

Shefler, Gil. "In Chile, Jews Face New Dangers and Old Fears." *Jerusalem Post,* August 23, 2012. http://www.jpost.com/Jewish-World/Jewish-News/In-Chile-Jews-face-new-dangers-and-old-fears.

## Newspapers and documents

"Amia: Su verdadera cara—Comunicado de FEARAB Argentina." *Prensa Islámica,* December 21, 2010. http://www.prensaislamica.com/nota5985.html.

"Cruces entre el secretario de la FEARAB y el PRO." *El Mesnajero Diario,* October 6, 2010. http://www.elmensajerodiario.com.ar/contenidos/cruces-secretario-fearab-pro_1327.

"Declaración Final de la Cumbre de Comunicación Indígena del Abya Yala." Confederación de Nacionalidades Indígenas del Ecuador, November 26, 2010. http://www.conaie.org/component/content/article/4-noits4/312-decla racion-final-de-la-cumbre-de-comunicacion-indigena-del-abya-yala.

"D'Elía Admits He Met AMIA Attack Suspect." *Buenos Aires Herald,* March 8, 2010.

"Elbit Systems pierde un contrato clave debido a protestas propalestinas." Campaña BDS, December 9, 2014. http://boicotisrael.net/bds/elbit-systems-pierde-un-contrato-clave-en-brasil-debido-protestas-propalestinas.

"Mercosur/Israel Free Trade Agreement Becomes Effective April." MercoPress South Atlantic News Agency, March 16, 2011. http://en.mercopress.com/2010/03/16/mercosur-israel-free-trade-agreement-becomes-effective-april.

"Nobel Peace Laureates and Celebrities Call for Military Embargo on Israel." BDS Movement, July 19, 2014. http://www.bdsmovement.net/2014/nobel-celebrities-call-for-military-embargo-12316#sthash.I3GBBewd.kjpcv3Gp.dpuf.

# Primary Holocaust Inversion and Eastern European Antisemitism

Dovid Katz*

## INTRODUCTION

As a strategy for arguing about almost anything adversarial, be it interpersonal or intergroup, inversion is as old as language and as human-grade thought itself. Its prime location in the psyche is in the realm of defense against a complaint or accusation. From the kindergarten child admonished for wronging a peer to the adult before a court of law defending him or herself against some accusation or other, a prime human rejoinder is to bring up how the wrongdoer was wronged or how the wronged is not wholly blameless, is equally at fault, or is perhaps even the real wrongdoer, who initiated an unfortunate chain of events that got out of hand, to cite just a few common examples.

Little wonder that inversion strategies are paramount in intergroup relations, including interpersonal, societal, political and prejudicial relations. While academics and scholars are just as human as anyone else, it does behoove them to at least attempt to compensate for this pan-human defense mechanism in their professional work by examining the facts of a situation with enhanced sensitivity for the perpetration of false equivalence and bogus symmetry by the perpetrator. In the legal and judicial sphere, there is scrutiny and oversight and an automatic two-sided dispute that helps expose fallacious or mendacious presentations on either side. By contrast, the academic world has no such built-in protections, least of all in the sphere of history, where there is no a priori practical point of law or punishment to be decided. That lack of protection can be amplified exponentially when governments or other wealthy forces invest in promoting a particular version of history or a particularly desired revision of history. If a government believes that a certain historical narrative is beneficial to its current and future security, the temptation to influence this narrative grows, and academics' all-too-human appetite for funding, support, recognition, honors and other favors can come into play.

---

* Vilnius Gediminas Technical University, Lithuania.

Translated into the realm of Holocaust studies and the closely allied field of antisemitism studies, scholars have for years discerned, first, that attempts to obfuscate, distort, minimize, or explain away the Holocaust are inextricably linked to antisemitism (see Vidal-Naquet 1992; Gerstenfeld 2009; Lipstadt 1993; Wistrich 2010; Heni 2012). In the case of the "nationalist" parts of Eastern Europe, particularly the Baltics, researchers have found, second, that issues relating to the Holocaust narrative can even be at the heart of contemporary antisemitism (see Donskis 2004, 2006; Zuroff 2005; Katz 2009; Heni 2012). The reader is invited to peruse the works cited below for further sources, as these two cardinal points cannot be relitigated here.

It is quite natural that this second phenomenon, the Far Right's nationalist revision of Holocaust-era history in a tilt away from the classic Western (and Jewish) narrative, has generally been studied by a very small group of specialists on those parts of Eastern Europe, without attracting more widespread attention. At international level, the main issues relating to antisemitism are obviously those that have shown a capacity to lead to violence, have manifestations in many parts of the world, and pose a threat to the security of the State of Israel. Turning to Europe, one discerns a clear divide between east and west.

Antisemitism in Western Europe is nowadays overwhelmingly a product of the (Far) Left. Its practitioners are socially, educationally, and demographically diverse. It focuses above all on Middle Eastern affairs and the Israeli-Palestinian conflict, distinguishing—or not distinguishing, as the case may be—between Jews and Israeli policies and between different types of Jews on a scale of presumed "Zionicity," in order to determine which individuals and groups are to be designated as villains. Both before and after the insertion of Western European jihadism and Islamic radicalism into the mix, there have been tragic acts of violence. There have also been curious cases of staunch anti-Zionists going to extraordinary lengths to prove they are not antisemites, including a young taxi driver in the United Kingdom who had his name tattooed on his wrist in Hebrew letters to make the point with panache (and permanence).

By contrast, antisemitism in the "nationalist" parts of Eastern Europe, comprising the new EU/NATO member states as well as (western) Ukraine, has thus far thankfully been mostly nonviolent. It is overwhelmingly a product of the nationalist (Far) Right. Its practitioners tend to be suave, educated elites and often include members of the country's political, academic, and media establishment. The vast majority of these people are generally positive toward Israel, have no interest in Palestinian or other Arab causes, and have little or nothing against Jews abroad. I have heard hundreds of versions of the following during my eighteen years in Vilnius, the beautiful Lithuanian capital, where, I hasten to add, I have been treated splendidly by everyday people: "We love American, British, and Israeli Jews! It's just the local Jews here that are awful. They think that our national heroes helped murder their families during the war and that the Russians saved their families!"

So there you have it, in a colloquial nutshell. To translate this sentiment into scholarly terms, Eastern European antisemitism is a (Far) Right movement that is laser-focused on World War II, the Holocaust, and local Jews' (historically accurate) collective memory of these events. Their antisemitism is directed at fellow citizens who do not share the state's official historical narrative concerning the war years. For Westerners accustomed to even educated younger people caring little—and knowing even less—about history, it can come as a surprise that state versions of history can (and are) being turned into components of contemporary national identity. Moreover, there is more than a little irony in the fact that, while many young Jews around the world spend very little time thinking about the Holocaust, right-wing antisemites in Eastern Europe are haunted by it and are determined to "fix" history. They want to fix it because, like many ultra-nationalists, they covet a history devoid of stains and errors (although such countries do not exist). Deep in the Freudian core of today's Eastern European antisemitism lurks a serious case of Holocaust envy, a phenomenon that merits further study (see Katz 2015). They continue to suffer from Aryanist models of imagined, nationwide racial, ethnic, and linguistic purity (with its concomitant disdain for local Jews, leftists, Russians, Roma, homosexuals and the other "Others" targeted by the Nazis). Their ranks overflow with members of the elite, historians, sundry academics, and PR specialists. They have hit on a big-time project.

This is a form of antisemitism whose only direct living victims are local Jews, who are disliked by parts of elite society because they adhere to a different Holocaust narrative. In many cases, their lives are not impacted negatively, because they are able to live full and rich lives far removed from these elite governmental, media, academic, arts and other circles. The much more profound victims are the dead Jews whose fate is being obfuscated and distorted. Beyond that, the Holocaust itself is being reduced, without a single death necessarily being denied, to one of two "equal genocides." This revisionist paradigm, which has come to be known as "double genocide" (see, e.g., Katz 2011; Ben-Moshe 2012), has been debunked by leading Holocaust scholars, including Yehuda Bauer (2010).

The "double genocide" project is a form of historical revisionism that inverts the Holocaust through an array of sleight-of-hand tricks and ruses. It is not a conspiracy but a public program of revisionism supported by substantial financial investment from governments. Its components include: the redefinition (or downgrading via conceptual inflation) of "genocide" to include such Soviet crimes as deportation, wrongful imprisonment, and deprivation of rights (as well as noting the chronological firstness of Soviet crimes in the areas first invaded by the Nazis during Operation Barbarossa in June 1941 in order to recast the Nazi genocide as a "reaction"); the glorification of local Holocaust collaborators as "anti-Soviet heroes" (since virtually all Eastern European Holocaust perpetrators were reliably "anti-Soviet"); and the vilification of Jewish ghetto residents who fled to join the anti-Nazi (Soviet-sponsored) partisans in the forests and are rightfully regarded in the West as heroes of the free world. In various Eastern European states, laws have actually been passed to criminalize the opinion that only the Nazis were guilty of genocide and the Soviets of other crimes. Large amounts of money and political and diplomatic capital have been invested in exporting these ideas, in various forms and guises, to the West, Israel, and the world at large, most famously through the project's "constitution," the 2008 Prague Declaration on European Conscience and Communism, which is discussed below.

## I. Secondary Holocaust inversion

The term "Holocaust inversion" is widely used in the sense described by Melanie Phillips:

> The key motif [in contemporary antisemitism] is a kind of Holocaust inversion, with the Israelis being demonized as Nazis and the Palestinians being regarded as the new Jews. Israel and the Jews are being systematically delegitimised and dehumanised – a necessary prelude to their destruction – with both Islamists and the Western media using anti-Zionism as a fig-leaf for prejudices rooted in both mediaeval Christian and Nazi demonology. (Phillips 2003)

It was further popularized by others, including Manfred Gerstenfeld in a 2008 *Wall Street Journal* op-ed (Gerstenfeld 2008). Academically, the term reached its apex in Robert Wistrich's *From Ambivalence to Betrayal: The Left, the Jews, and Israel* (Wistrich 2012). In a chapter entitled "The Holocaust Inversion of the Left," Wistrich traces this type of Holocaust Inversion to Soviet anti-Zionist (anti-Israel) usage that made its way into the parlance and culture of the anti-Israel Left in the West:

> The Soviet specter of "Zionist Nazism" was an almost perfect mirror-image of the Nazi propaganda myth of "Jewish Bolshevism." In the Nazi worldview, Bolshevism was a central part of the international Jewish conspiracy, linking Moscow with Wall Street and the City of London. For the neo-Stalinists, "Zionist Nazism" was the sinister agent of imperialism and a clique of international financiers seeking to subvert the socialist camp led by the U.S.S.R. The great difference is that the Holocaust inversion of the Left, which execrates Zionism as a form of Nazism is still very much with us today. Indeed its rapid spread into the Western world during recent decades suggests that it still has a future before it. The twinning of the Nazi Swastika and the Star

of David as symbols of genocidal fascism (today a commonplace) was, however, at one time an exclusive Soviet preserve. (Wistrich 2012: 448)

Phillips in the media and Wistrich in academia are among those who have brought the concept of Holocaust inversion into the contemporary discourse on antisemitism. They were both right to do so for the simple reason that it was not an a priori construct or comparison. It came about as an analysis of and a response to the practice of using Nazi symbols and terminology to characterize twenty-first century Israel. This practice has been observed in the highest circles of society, particularly in Europe, and not just among left-wing extremists and Islamists (see Klaff 2014). Wistrich's posthumously published essay is the last word to date on this issue (Wistrich 2017).

Secondary Holocaust inversion is a strategy that aims to turn the Holocaust into a propaganda tool against the Jewish people, Jewish causes, and the Jewish state. It is a malignant and spiteful strategy that is disconnected from the Holocaust both temporally and geographically. It is encouraging that various journalists, activists and scholars have taken on these abusers of history and language by entering the fray, especially at a time when the prevailing intellectual mood is not necessarily in their favor.


## II. Primary Holocaust inversion

By contrast, primary Holocaust inversion—or, to put it more colloquially, "real Holocaust Inversion"—entails the conceptually much more audacious effort to falsify Holocaust history per se and to pull off this impossible-sounding feat not—or at least not openly—as part of an "anti-Jewish" campaign but as part of "ongoing research" and so-called "progress." That "progress" is of course the "double genocide" theory, which seeks to equate Nazi crimes with Soviet crimes through extensive recourse to terminology emphasizing the equality of all suffering and evil. In fact, the 2008 Prague Declaration uses the word "same" five times:

1. "consciousness of the crimes against humanity committed by the Communist regimes throughout the continent must inform all European minds to the *same* extent as the Nazi regimes crimes did";
2. "believing that millions of victims of Communism and their families are entitled to enjoy justice, sympathy, understanding and recognition for their sufferings in the *same* way as the victims of Nazism have been morally and politically recognized";
3. "recognition that many crimes committed in the name of Communism should be assessed as crimes against humanity serving as a warning for future generations, in the *same* way Nazi crimes were assessed by the Nuremberg Tribunal";

4. "establishment of 23rd August, the day of signing of the Hitler-Stalin Pact, known as the Molotov-Ribbentrop Pact, as a day of remembrance of the victims of both Nazi and Communist totalitarian regimes, in the *same* way Europe remembers the victims of the Holocaust on January 27th";
5. "adjustment and overhaul of European history textbooks so that children could learn and be warned about Communism and its crimes in the *same* way as they have been taught to assess the Nazi crimes."[1]

Critics of the Prague Declaration have pointed out that it contains several false analogies (e.g. comparing the ordeal of people sent to Siberia to the genocide of an entire ethnic minority) and Orwellian attempts at mind control (e.g. demanding that all "European minds" must think alike and—in a case of supreme irony—that all history textbooks across the continent must adhere Soviet-style to the same holy narrative). For a partial bibliography of critiques to date, see Katz (2017b). The main academic rejoinder is from Heni (2009), while the main political response comes from UK MP John Mann, who referred to it as a "sinister" document (Mann 2009). The present author is proud to have partnered with Professor Danny Ben Moshe in drafting a response, the Seventy Years Declaration (SYD), in 2012. This "battle of declarations" has been discussed in recent history books (see, e.g., Stone 2014: 281). These issues therefore need not be relitigated here.

Instead, we intend to take the debate a step further. The false "equality" of Soviet and Nazi crimes is not only the official stance of the "double genocide" movement and a viewpoint that is attractive to Western ears and sensibilities. It has also enabled the newest strain of mainstream Holocaust revisionism to latch on to a range of external circumstances, including attempts to tie Holocaust obfuscation to the new Cold War and anti-Putin efforts (on the basis that the accurate narrative "helps Russian propaganda"), the hunger of many Jews of Eastern European origin to enjoy trips to the ancestral homeland unfettered by current events, and the even greater hunger of some dignitaries and organizations for Eastern European medals, honors, grants, and junkets. In practice, however, it is hard to find a single person in Eastern Europe, or beyond, who genuinely believes that Nazi and Soviet crimes were "equal." Behind this alleged equality lurks something else.

That something else is primary Holocaust inversion. The genesis of this idea took root in the minds of the planners, perpetrators, and collaborators of the Holocaust before, during, and after the actual murders. At first, it was not formulated so clearly. Later, it was (and sometimes still is) repeated as part of

---

[1] Prague Declaration on European Conscience and Communism, adopted on June 3, 2008 at an international conference hosted by the Senate of the Parliament of the Czech Republic, http://www.praguedeclaration.eu.

Eastern European antisemitic discourse: "The Jews were all Communists and supported the Soviet takeover of our county. They therefore got what they deserved." Given that virtually all the local murderers and accomplices in the Baltics were reliably "anti-Soviet" and that this motivation was universally regarded as "good," the scene was set for the first seeds of primary Holocaust inversion.

In the time between the collapse of the Soviet Union and the rise of independent democratic states on its former western frontier, including the successful Baltic states, the intellectual manifestations of those earlier antisemitic and ultranationalist sentiments contributed to the emergence of a two-track "double genocide" paradigm. On the one hand, in European Parliament resolutions and conferences for foreign—especially Jewish—audiences, the emphasis has been on moving the narrative in the direction of "double genocide." See, for example, Zuroff (2011) on a University College London conference sponsored by the Lithuanian Foreign Ministry. On the other hand, the emphasis has been on creating a "united history" under the banner of European unity—the rather absurd notion that European unity depends on all of Europe (or even the world) adopting the Eastern European narrative concerning World War II, which equates Nazi and Soviet crimes. See, for example, Fridberg (2013) on a conference in Vilnius promoting these ideas.

For local consumption, however, the accepted historical narrative has slipped even further, from equalization to inversion. It is perhaps psychologically and sociologically inevitable that this would happen, given that equalization is itself a ruse (a) to cover up the massive local voluntary participation in the murder of the Jewish minority in the three Baltic states, western Ukraine, and elsewhere; and (b) to diminish the Holocaust altogether as part of historic anti-Jewish prejudice and as a strategy aimed at depriving modern Russia, the successor state of the Soviet Union, of its one grand achievement, namely the defeat of Hitler in alliance with Great Britain, the United States, and the other allies.

Twenty-first century examples of Holocaust inversion, which blame the Soviet Union, the Jews, or both, for Eastern European suffering can be found in state-sponsored events and projects throughout the Baltic states and Ukraine. Museums and exhibits often dip into the history of other states. In 2008, for example, an exhibit on the Ukrainian famine of the 1930s at Vilnius's Museum of Genocide Victims, which did not even mention the Holocaust until 2011, featured a poster on which an elderly woman states: "[In Auschwitz] we were given some spinach and a little bread. War is terrible, but famine is even worse" (see Katz 2016: 17). In 2011, the elitist Estonian National Movement declared that "the Holocaust pales before the crimes of Communism" (BNS 2011). Latvia and Estonia continue to honor their *Waffen SS* units (see Rudling 2012). In

2012, in a rare slip before a Western audience, a former foreign minister of Lithuania wrote in the *Wall Street Journal* that "we had a few years' respite from the Communists while the Nazis were in control during World War II" (Ušackas 2012).

In terms of actual policy and actions, rather than just exhibits, events, and quotations, the Lithuanian authorities have gone beyond other states in the region by taking inversion to the point of absurdity. While having done everything to avoid prosecuting alleged Nazi war criminals while they were alive and well enough to stand trial, the nation's prosecutors and affiliated elites have since 2006 been defaming Jewish survivors of the Holocaust who joined the anti-Nazi resistance—the partisan groups sponsored by the Soviet Union that formed the only serious resistance to the Nazis during the country's occupation—as suspects of "war crimes," in effect for having survived. Other survivors have "merely" been accused of libeling Lithuanian heroes by naming alleged local collaborators. Charges were never brought, because there was never anything to charge anyone with. Instead, this was a massive state-sponsored campaign of historical distortion designed to complete the inversion paradigm. While local collaborators have streets named after them for their "anti-Soviet heroism," survivors who joined the resistance are defamed in history books and on the internet as alleged suspects of war crimes. See the timeline in Defending History (2017).

Most recently, primary Holocaust inversion reached a crescendo in Ukraine. For the second time, a boulevard in Kiev, the nation's capital, was named after a Holocaust perpetrator (Eichner 2017b). At roughly the same time, the country's prosecutors began taking action against a 94-year-old Jewish veteran of the Red Army's war against Hitler (see Eichner 2017a). For a long time, the mainstream Western media, led by *The New York Times*, has systematically covered up Holocaust revisionism and inversion in Ukraine (see Katz 2014). It is heartening to see, at long last, some impressive breaches of the embargo on critiquing US and Western allies on Holocaust issues, including inversion, which by virtue of inverting perpetrators and victims is an affront to the most elementary values of Western democracy. Among those breaches are two recent op-eds that will go down in the history for having broken a long and shameful taboo in our supposedly free Western media: Eduard Dolinsky's "What Ukraine's Jews Fear" in *The New York Times* (Dolinsky 2017) and Josh Cohen's "How Trump Can Show He's Tough on Antisemitism" on *Reuters* (Cohen 2017), which refers to a meeting with Ukraine's president.

A final and telling example of Holocaust inversion, which starts from the premise that perpetrators and victims are interchangeable in certain circumstances, involves an "explanation" provided by the executive director of the Orwellian-sounding Commission for the Evaluation of the Crimes of the Nazi and Soviet Occupation Regimes of Lithuania, in which he offers his justification for the Lithuanian prosecutors' harassment of a Holocaust survivor who joined the resistance.[2]

## CONCLUSION

If the Eastern European Far Right, supported by generous government financing and taking ample advantage of the current crisis in East-West relations emanating from the corrupt, authoritarian, and revanchist regime of Vladimir Putin, succeeds in further chipping away at the truth of the Holocaust, this will represent a major setback for human rights, the struggle against antisemitism, and key values of democratic societies. In a worrying development, the trend in "acceptable" Holocaust revisionism is drifting, slowly but surely, from the equalization of Nazi and Soviet crimes in the framework of the "double genocide" paradigm to the even more dismaying inversion paradigm, which uses various ruses to praise the perpetrators and defame the victims of the Holocaust in a pseudo-postmodernist reversal of the narrative. It is imperative that the Western timidity in responding meaningfully to such deliberate distortions of history is overcome. It is equally imperative that scholars of antisemitism devote attention to the old, new, and recombined strains of this pernicious malady that are emerging from the nationalist (Far) Right, which stands at the helm of a number of Eastern European states currently allied with the United States and the West.

*References*

Bauer, Yehuda. 2010. "Remembering Accurately on International Holocaust Remembrance Day." *Jerusalem Post*, January 25. http://www.jpost.com/ Features/InThespotlight/Rememberingaccurately-on-Intl-Holocaust-Rem embrance-Day.

Ben-Moshe, Danny. 2012. "Saying No to 'Double Genocide.'" *Jerusalem Post*, March 12. http://www.jpost.com/Opinion/Op-Ed-Contributors/Saying-no- to-double-genocide.

---

2 "Ronaldas Račinskas on Fania Brancovskaya," excerpt from the documentary film *Liza ruft!* (2015), Youtube video, uploaded April 22, 2015, https://www.youtube.com/ watch?v=pxjJ0DvqJP8&t=1s.

BNS. 2011. "Estijos nacionalinis judėjimas: Holokaustas nublanksta prieš komunizmo nusikaltimus." DELFI, May 9. http://www.delfi.lt/news/daily/world/estijos-nacionalinis-judejimas-holokaustas-nublanksta-pries-komunizmo-nusikaltimus.d?id=45264429. Available in English ["Estonian Nationalist Movement: The Holocaust Pales Before the Crimes of Communism"] at http://holocaustinthebaltics.com/wp-content/uploads/2011/05/Estonian-Nationalists-say-Holocaust-Pales-by-Comparison-9-May-2011.pdf.

Cohen, Josh. 2017. "Commentary: How Trump Can Show He's Tough on Anti-Semitism," *Reuters*, June 21. http://www.reuters.com/article/us-cohen-anti-semitism-idUSKBN19B2SS.

Defending History. 2017. "Blaming the Victims? State Agencies and Other Elites Defame Holocaust Survivors." http://defendinghistory.com/blaming-the-victims.

Dolinsky, Eduard. 2017. "What Ukraine's Jews Fear." *New York Times*, April 11. https://www.nytimes.com/2017/04/11/opinion/what-ukraines-jews-fear.html?_r=0.

Donskis, Leonidas. 2004. Preface to *The Vanished World of Lithuanian Jews*, edited by Alvydas Nikžentaitis, Stefan Schreiner, and Darius Staliūnas, ix-xv. Amsterdam/New York: Rodopi.

Donskis, Leonidas. 2006. "Another Word for Uncertainty: Antisemitism in Modern Lithuania." *NORDEUROPAForum* 1: 7-26. http://edoc.hu-berlin.de/nordeuropaforum/2006-1/donskis-leonidas-7/PDF/donskis.pdf.

Eichner, Itamar. 2017a. "Ukraine Opens Criminal Probe Against 94-Year-Old Jewish World War II Hero." *Ynet*, April 30. http://www.ynetnews.com/articles/0,7340,L-4955865,00.html.

Eichner, Itamar. 2017b. "Protests Erupt in Kiev against Renaming Main Street after SS Officer." *Ynet*, June 19. https://www.ynetnews.com/articles/0,7340,L-4978080,00.html.

Fridberg, Pinchos. 2013. "Instead of Truth about the Holocaust—Myths about Saving Jews." *Defending History*, January 1. http://defendinghistory.com/more-mythology-instead-of-the-truth-about-the-holocaust/47587.

Gerstenfeld, Manfred. 2008. "Holocaust Inversion." *Wall Street Journal*, January 28. https://www.wsj.com/articles/SB120147388696520647.

Gerstenfeld, Manfred. 2009. *The Abuse of Holocaust Memory: Distortions and Responses*. Jerusalem: Jerusalem Center for Public Affairs and Anti-Defamation League.

Heni, Clemens. 2009. "The Prague Declaration, Holocaust Trivialization and Antisemitism." October 26. Available at http://www.clemensheni.net/allgemein/the-prague-declaration-holocaust-obfuscation-and-antisemitism.

Heni, Clemens. 2012. *Antisemitism: A Unique Phenomenon*. Berlin: Edition Critic.

Katz, Dovid. 2009. "On Three Definitions: Genocide; Holocaust Denial; Holocaust Obfuscation." In *A Litmus Test Case of Modernity: Examining Modern Sensibilities and the Public Domain in the Baltic States at the Turn of the Century*, edited by Leonidas Donskis, 259-277. Bern: Peter Lang. Available at http://www.holocaustinthebaltics.com/2009SeptDovidKatz3Definitions.pdf.

Katz, Dovid. 2011. "Understanding 'Double Genocide': A Lethal New Threat to Holocaust Memory and Honesty." *JHC Centre News* 33(2): 6-8. Available at http://defendinghistory.com/wp-content/uploads/2011/10/Dovid-Katz-in-JHC.pdf.

Katz, Dovid. 2014. "Getting it Wrong on Ukraine." *Times of Israel*, June 11. http://blogs.timesofisrael.com/the-tarnished-hukraine.

Katz, Dovid. 2015. "From Holocaust Envy to Holocaust Theft." *Times of Israel*, May 11. http://blogs.timesofisrael.com/from-holocaust-envy-to-holocaust-theft.

Katz, Dovid. 2016. "Is Eastern European 'Double Genocide' Revisionism Reaching Museums?" *Dapim: Studies on the Holocaust* 30(3): 1-30. Available at http://defendinghistory.com/wp-content/uploads/2017/01/Dovid-Katz-2016-Dapim-paper-PROOF-ONLY.pdf.

Katz, Dovid. 2017a. "Free Trade Awry? The Westward Export of Double Genocide." In *Mélanges offerts à Jeff Richards par ses amis à l'occasion de son 65ᵉ anniversaire*, edited by Danielle Buschinger et al. Amiens: Centre d'Études Médiévales de la Picardie. Available at http://defendinghistory.com/wp-content/uploads/2017/04/Dovid-Katzs-paper-in-Earl-Jeffrey-Richards-festschrift-2017.pdf.

Katz, Dovid. 2017b. "Critiques of the 2008 Prague Declaration (Select Bibliography)." *Defending History*. http://defendinghistory.com/prague-declaration/opposition.

Katz, Dovid. Forthcoming. "The Baltic Movement to Obfuscate the Holocaust." In *Reconceiving Nazi Criminality: New Debates and Perspectives*, edited by Alex J. Kay and David Stahel. Bloomington: Indiana University Press.

Klaff, Lesley. 2014. "Holocaust Inversion and Contemporary Antisemitism." *Fathom* 5. http://fathomjournal.org/holocaust-inversion-and-contemporary-antisemitism.

Lipstadt, Deborah. 1993. *Denying the Holocaust*. New York: Free Press.

Mann, John. 2009. "Europe Must Focus on Baltic Hate." *Jewish Chronicle*, October 29. http://www.thejc.com/comment/comment/21392/europe-must-focus-baltic-hate.

Phillips, Melanie. 2003. "The New Anti-Semitism." *Spectator*, March 22. http://archive.spectator.co.uk/article/22nd-march-2003/21/the-new-anti-semitism.

Rudling, Per Anders. 2012. "The Waffen-SS as Freedom Fighters." *Defending History*, January 24. http://defendinghistory.com/the-waffen-ss-as-freedom-fighters-by-per-anders-rudling/29648.

Stone, Dan. 2014. *Goodbye to All That? A History of Europe Since 1945*. Oxford: Oxford University Press.

Ušackas, Vygaudas. 2012. "My Long, Strange Journey to Afghanistan." *Wall Street Journal*, December 6. https://www.wsj.com/articles/SB10001424052 9702049038045770802723908030082.

Vidal-Naquet, Pierre. 1992. *Assassins of Memory: Essays on the Denial of the Holocaust*. Translated and with a foreword by Jeffrey Mehlman. New York: Columbia University Press.

Wistrich, Robert. 2010. "Lying about the Holocaust." *A Lethal Obsession: Antisemitism from Antiquity to the Global Jihad*, 631-661 and 1065-1070. New York: Random House.

Wistrich, Robert. 2012. "The Holocaust Inversion of the Left." *From Ambivalence to Betrayal: The Left, the Jews, and Israel*, 448-478. Lincoln: University of Nebraska Press.

Wistrich, Robert. 2017. "Antisemitism and Holocaust Inversion." In *Antisemitism before and since the Holocaust*, edited by Anthony McElligott and Jeffrey Herf, 37-49. Palgrave Macmillan.

Zuroff, Efraim. 2005 "Eastern Europe: Antisemitism in the Wake of Holocaust Related Issues." *Jewish Political Studies Review* 17(1-2): 63-79. Available at: http://www.jcpa.org/phas/phas-zuroff-s05.htm.

Zuroff, Efraim. 2011. "A Shameful Shoah Whitewash." *Jewish Chronicle*, February 4. Available at https://www.pressreader.com/uk/the-jewish-chronicle/20110204/283450662873281.

# Post-Communist Russia and Ukraine:
# Countries with Philosemitic Pretensions and
# Societies with Antisemitic Sentiments?

Vladimir (Ze'ev) Khanin*

In an effort to understand antisemitism in the contemporary context, attention must not only be allocated to antisemitic events in Western Europe, the United States, and the Muslim world, but also to former communist countries. In April 2018, fifty-seven Members of Congress signed a letter to the US Department of State expressing their concern over the increasing rates of antisemitism and Nazism in Poland and Ukraine.[1] Moreover, a 2017 report released by the Israeli Ministry of Jewish Diaspora Affairs, which analyzed global trends of antisemitism, also paid much attention to post-Soviet countries, notably Russia and Ukraine. According to the report, "the number of antisemitic incidents doubled [in Ukraine], exceeding the number of incidents reported in the whole region."[2]

Additionally, a report released by Tel Aviv University's Kantor Center for the Study of Contemporary European Jewry also placed Ukraine among a few select countries where antisemitic incidents of all types increased substantially over the last two years, adding that "the actual number of cases is higher, because Jews refrain from reporting." According to the report, in other post-Soviet areas, "the situation is equal to that of last year: a low average of cases, yet the attempts to exonerate and glorify nationalist leaders who actively cooperated with the German anti-Jewish policies of persecutions and murder during WWII, intensify due to the renewed nationalist aspirations in Eastern Europe."[3]

---

* Chief Scientist (Senior Adviser to Minister on Research and Strategic Planning) of the Israeli Ministry of Immigrant Absorption; Associate Professor, Department of Political and Middle Eastern Studies, Ariel University of Samaria.

[1] Letter to Deputy Secretary John Sullivan, Congress of the United States, April 23, 2018, https://khanna.house.gov/sites/khanna.house.gov/files/Combat%20Anti-Semitism%20Letter.pdf.

[2] *Antisemitism in 2017: Overview, Trends and Events* (Ministry of Jewish Diaspora Affairs, 2017), 11.

[3] Dina Porat, ed., *Antisemitism Worldwide 2017: General Analysis: Draft* (Tel-Aviv University: Kantor Center for Study of Contemporary Jewry, 2017), 10, http://kantorcenter.tau.ac.il/sites/default/files/Doch_full_2018_220418.pdf.

These facts have received harsh criticism in both countries, where elites—for diplomatic, political, and economic reasons—are working diligently to remove their reputations as antisemitic nations. While Russian commentators lightly criticized the report, they were largely pleased with the information provided by the aforementioned Israeli monitoring institutions.[4] Ukrainian journalists and officials, however, rejected this conclusion[5] and quoted a 2017 study conducted by the Washington-based Pew Research Center,[6] which found Ukrainians to be far more accepting of Jewish fellow citizens than other countries throughout the former Eastern Bloc.[7]

Rival local Jewish leaders joined these efforts. Among those who attacked the reports included Alexander Levin,[8] Vice-President of the Euro-Asian Jewish Congress and Chairman of the Jewish community of Kyiv, and Josef Zisels, Chairman of the Association of Jewish Organizations and Communities of Ukraine, who called the report released by the Israeli Ministry of the Diaspora Affairs "ungrounded."[9]

This paper aims to analyze these issues by focusing on the following questions:

- First, what is the real picture and structure of antisemitic incidents and aspirations in the post-Soviet space? This question will use Russia and Ukraine, with their large Jewish populations, as indicative cases.
- Second, is this phenomenon a manifestation of traditional (classic) antisemitism or a new form of antisemitism?
- Third, in more general terms, what are the implications for the Jewish population with regard to contemporary Russian and Ukrainian society? Should we regard antisemitic sentiments as an "echo" of the past or are they indicative of what we may face in the foreseeable future?

---

[4] Anton Skripunov, "Level of antisemitism in Ukraine is growing, while they are talking about the 'failure of the Kremlin,'" Russian Information Agency, April 12, 2018, https://ria.ru/religion/20180412/1518427534.html (in Russian).

[5] "Does the government finance antisemitism? Reaction to the statement of 57 US Congressmen," Jews of Eurasia, April 24, 2018, http://jewseurasia.org/page18/news 60327.html (in Russian).

[6] "Religious Belief and National Belonging in Central and Eastern Europe," Pew Research Center, May 10, 2017, http://www.pewforum.org/2017/05/10/religious-belief-and-national-belonging-in-central-and-eastern-europe.

[7] "Survey: Anti-Semitism rate in Ukraine overestimated," UNIAN Information Agency, March 29, 2018, https://www.unian.info/society/10061345-survey-anti-semitism-rate-in-ukraine-overestimated.html.

[8] "Alexander Levin: Are Jews of Ukraine Afraid to Report Antisemitism?," *Forum Daily*, April 16, 2018 (in Russian).

[9] Quoted in Veronika Melkozerova, "Ukrainian Jewish leaders challenge report on rising anti-Semitism," *Kyiv Post*, January 29, 2018.

–   Finally, can we define Ukrainian and Russian societies as inherently antisemitic or, as some scholars insist, asemitic?[10]

In this paper, I will attempt to answer at least part of these questions, based on
various data sources. These sources include, but are not limited to, interviews
and internal observations of events in Russia and Ukraine related to antisemitism and xenophobia in 2014-2018; the ongoing study by the Moscow-
based Yuri Levada Analytical Center regarding public attitudes toward various
ethnic/religious groups in the Russian Federation, 1992-2015; the ongoing
monitoring of antisemitic incidents by the Eurasian Jewish Congress (EAJC) in
the Former Soviet Union (FSU), 2010-2017; selected data from public opinion
polls in Ukraine, 2013-2017; and the Levada Center/Russian Jewish Congress
(RJC) research on antisemitism and attitudes toward Jews in Russia, 2016
(where this author served as a member of the academic advisory committee).

ANTISEMITISM IN RUSSIA AND THE FSU: GENERAL PICTURE OF PUBLIC
ATTITUDES

Since the abolition of the USSR's state-sponsored discrimination of Jews, the
post-Soviet space, including Russia and Ukraine, is believed to be a "secure
island" in terms of hard-core antisemitic manifestations compared to Europe
and the Middle East. A comprehensive study of public attitudes toward Jews
conducted by the Russian Jewish Congress and the Levada Center states that the
"Jewish question" has lost its previous importance to society. According to the
researchers:

> In public opinion, Jews have ceased being a specific, ethnically, and socially
> marked group that was previously a convenient source for channeling politi-
> cal and national aggressiveness and hatred … as well as the source for "col-
> lective punishment and responsibility" for various events, including the
> failures of State policies.[11]

The ongoing monitoring of attitudes toward Jews and other ethnic, national,
and religious groups since 1992 by the Levada Center indicates that mass public
opinion regarding Jews has been improving during the course of the last quarter
century: about 10% of the Russian population views Jews with sympathy, while
more than 80% demonstrate a "positively-neutral" approach toward them. An

---

[10] Cf. Diana Pinto, "Negotiating Jewish identity in an asemitic age," *Jewish Culture
and History* 14 (2013): 68-77, observing that "European societies are becoming asemitic.
They no longer consider Jewish life as a Holocaust-related responsibility, but simply as
one piece of an ever more pluralistic kaleidoscope."

[11] Lev Gudkov, *Anti-Semitism in Contemporary Russia: Research Report* (Moscow:
Yuri Levada Analytical Center and Russian Jewish Congress, 2016), 60.

openly negative opinion was demonstrated by 13%, 16%, and 8% of respondents in the countrywide representative samples in 1992, 1997, and 2015, respectively.[12]

The same is true for many other FSU states, where Jewish communities decreased dramatically in demographic terms and Jews became an "invisible object" for attacks. In the public consciousness, the Jews, who for centuries held the position of "major enemy," have been replaced by other ethnic and religious groups. For the Russians, the Jews have been replaced by Muslim migrants from the Caucasus and post-Soviet Central Asian areas, as well as "new-old" enemies (the West) and new enemies (Georgia, Ukraine, and the Baltic states). For Ukraine, the leading enemy has been replaced by "imperialist Russia," while the conflict between the neighboring enemies of Azerbaijan and Armenia does not leave much time or resources for negative treatment of the diminishing Jewish communities in both countries, as many local observers believe.[13]

One of the reasons for this is that there are almost no leftist-oriented intellectuals in the FSU who are burdened by guilt regarding Third World peoples, as there are in Europe. The Russian *intelligentsia* is currently not inclined to see Israel as the "last colonial power" and accordingly does not blame local Jews for "Israeli crimes against the Palestinian people." Additionally, in most of the FSU, traditional Muslims view their identities as ethnic-national rather than religious. As a result, anti-Israel sentiment, as part of pan-Muslim solidarity, is now an abstract concept. Finally, post-Soviet authoritarian regimes see "non-authorized violence" as a threat and attempt to stop it. As a result, potential "troublemakers" (such as radical nationalists) either remain underground or direct their energy outside the country (Caucasus, the Middle East, or Eastern Ukraine).

As a result, the number of respondents in the Russian Federation who estimated that few of their fellow citizens held anti-Jewish sentiments over the course of twenty-five years (1990-2015) doubled (from 21% to 45%), while only about one-fifth or less of the respondents believed that this social phenomenon was still widespread in Russia.

In general terms, among those who declared that "there are ethnic and religious groups that cause their antipathy," 10% mentioned the Jews, thus placing them in ninth position (after Gypsies/Roma, Azerbaijanis, Tajikistanis, Americans, Ukrainians, Uzbeks, Chechens, and Armenians) in the rating of groups that are least appreciated by the Russians.

As indicated in the table below, Gypsies (Roma) and Chechens provoke the greatest negativism and antipathy among respondents, followed by Americans,

---

[12] See the Yuri Levada Analytical Center's ongoing study of public attitudes toward various ethnic/religious groups in the Russian Federation, 1992-2015, at http://www.levada.ru.

[13] Author's interviews with Azerbaijani Jewish community leaders in 2012 and 2013 and personal observations.

*Table 1: Estimations regarding the amount of citizens in the Russian Federation with anti-Jewish sentiments*

| Opinion regarding amount of antisemites in Russian society | Year of research | | | |
|---|---|---|---|---|
| | 1990 | 1992 | 1997 | 2015 |
| Almost everybody | 4% | 4% | 2% | 2% |
| More than a half | 15% | 16% | 20% | 14% |
| Less than a half | 15% | 13% | 25% | 24% |
| Quite few | 21% | 16% | 30% | 45% |
| Hard to estimate | 45% | 52% | 24% | 16% |

*Source: Levada Center studies (1990-2015)*

*Table 2: Attitudes toward various races and ethnic groups—negative estimations summary*

| Ethnic Groups | Year of research | | | | | | | | | |
|---|---|---|---|---|---|---|---|---|---|---|
| | 1996 | 1998 | 2000 | 2002 | 2003 | 2004 | 2005 | 2006 | 2007 | 2015 |
| Chechens | 47 | 50 | 53 | 66 | 53 | 53 | 52 | 44 | 41 | 33 |
| Americans | 9 | 13 | 9 | 17 | 16 | 16 | 20 | 17 | 20 | 31 |
| Arabs | – | – | 15 | 28 | 22 | 24 | 22 | 18 | 18 | 25 |
| Azerbaijanis | 29 | 35 | 30 | 39 | 33 | 30 | 33 | 26 | 25 | 24 |
| Gypsies (Roma) | 40 | 48 | 43 | 52 | 50 | 53 | 52 | 49 | 43 | 47 |
| Georgians | – | – | – | – | – | – | – | 29 | 27 | 20 |
| Africans ("Blacks") | | | 9 | 14 | 10 | 10 | 16 | 10 | 12 | 18 |
| Estonians | 12 | 13 | 14 | 16 | 14 | 10 | 14 | 11 | 18 | 13 |
| Germans | | | 6 | 12 | 9 | 7 | 9 | 6 | 8 | 10 |
| Jews | 12 | 16 | 15 | 21 | 14 | 14 | 16 | 15 | 5 | 8 |

*Source: Levada Center studies (1996-2015)*

the current "political enemy" of the Russian Federation. These groups were then followed by cultural and religious "strangers," including Arabs and Azerbaijanis. The Islamic factor is stronger than racial phobias, due to the propagandistic effect of international terrorism. Additionally, there is a routine dislike of Azerbaijanis as "market speculators" and "unfair traders."

If this is the case, the potential of Jews as a negative identity factor is coming to an end, which proves the popular hypotheses that antisemitism, as opposed to other phobias in Russian public consciousness, is lower than ever before. However, remnants of historical enmity, both traditional antisemitism (rooted in the pre-revolutionary ideology of rural and anti-modernist populations, as the authors of the Levada Center/RJC report suggest) and Soviet state antisemitism are still highly visible. This can be seen in the Russian authorities' support for ethnic discrimination policies and the limitation of access to positions of power for all non-ethnic Russians, including Jews.

In the meantime, however, the clear-cut antisemitism by the authorities vis-à-vis society and by the public vis-à-vis the ruling elites is believed to be almost non-existent. Still, "the most alive" form of antisemitism in Russia, as Alexey Levinson of the Levada Center explains, is spreading among elite population groups,[14] including the young and successful urban population. This group (quite often in political opposition to the current ruling class in the Russian Federation) became a new purveyor of antisemitism due to the intensifying competition for middle and upper class positions as a result of the country's general economic crises. Yet, at the lower professional levels, Jews rarely compete with Russians, and therefore do not provoke negative reactions.[15]

Levinson and Gudkov,[16] the authors of a 2016 report on antisemitism in Russia, define a number of levels of intensity regarding antisemitic feelings among the Russian population:

1. Eight to sixteen percent of respondents compose the strong core of antisemites and "general" xenophobes (three-quarters of them normally overlap).
2. Eighteen to thirty-five percent compose a more blurred stratum of less stable anti-Jewish attitudes, a function of a more general antipathy and prejudice (e.g., those who believe that "some ethnicities are better than others" or that "a person, who is not an ethnic Russian, cannot be a Russian patriot").
3. Forty to sixty-five percent of respondents' negative reactions were not addressed specifically toward Jews but rather serve the purpose of psychological self-defense on a personal level and preservation by the ethnic majority of collective values, guaranteed by such institutions as power and family. Generally, these needs are reflected through the demand to reserve a number of privileges for the "titular" nation, such as the notion that "ethnic Russians must enjoy priorities before other groups," expressed by 41% of respondents in general and 59% in Moscow, or the belief that "it is undesirable for a Jew to become president of the Russian Federation," expressed by 67% of respondents.

Thus, according to this study, antisemitism, in the structure of the xenophobic attitudes of the Russian population, captures a relatively "modest" place. Antisemitic beliefs among the population of the Russian Federation may be cautiously defined as "passive," meaning that there is limited potential for aggressive mobilization of this population against the Jews compared to other types of

---

[14] Alexey Levinson and Yuri Kanner, "Russians believe that they must be ruled by [ethnic] Russians," *Meduza*, April 21, 2016 (in Russian).

[15] "Levada Center Director reported on 'sleeping phase' of antisemitism in Russia," TASS Information Agency, November 1, 2016, http://tass.ru/obschestvo/3752043.

[16] Lev Gudkov and Alexey Levinson, "Attitudes towards Jews in the Commonwealth of Independent States," in *Working Papers on Contemporary Antisemitism*, ed. D. Singer (New York: American Jewish Committee/Institute of Human Relations, 1994); Lev Gudkov, "Parameters of Antisemitism: Attitudes Towards Jews in Russia 1990-1997," *Sociological Research*, July/August 1999.

xenophobia, including racial exclusion, hatred of migrants from Central Asia and the Caucasus, and distrust of Westerners.

## The case of Ukraine

As opposed to Russia, there is currently no comprehensive study of attitudes toward Jews in Ukraine within the last decade, aside from the aforementioned Pew Research Center report.[17] It is clear, however, that like other FSU countries and elsewhere, there is an essential overlap among the Ukrainian public with regard to those who hold general xenophobic sentiments and those who hold specifically antisemitic sentiments.

*Table 3: Average index of xenophobia among Ukrainian respondents with favorable and unfavorable attitudes toward Jews (where 1 indicates the lowest and 7 the highest level of hatred)*[18]

| Year of research | Antisemites | Favorable attitudes toward Jews | All respondents |
| --- | --- | --- | --- |
| 1994 | 5.10 | 2.17 | 3.97 |
| 1999 | 5.52 | 2.40 | 4.37 |
| 2004 | 6.40 | 2.85 | 4.94 |
| 2009 | 5.67 | 2.70 | 4.86 |
| 2013 | 5.52 | 2.07 | 4.56 |
| 2016 | 5.16 | 2.12 | 4.31 |

Thus, in 1994-2007, the Kyiv International Institute of Sociology monitored xenophobic attitudes among the Ukrainian population and showed that the level of antisemitism was consistent with gradual and substantial growth of the general level of xenophobia in society, reaching its height in 2007.[19] Using this method, other researchers estimated that since 2009 there has been a gradual decline in antisemitic attitudes, until a spike in such attitudes in 2015. The decline continued shortly thereafter.[20] This, of course, needs to be proved or dismissed by a comprehensive quantitative sample.

---

[17] "Religious Belief and National Belonging"; David Masci, "Most Poles accept Jews as fellow citizens and neighbors, but a minority do not," Pew Research Center, March 28, 2018, http://www.pewresearch.org/fact-tank/2018/03/28/most-poles-accept-jews-as-fel low-citizens-and-neighbors-but-a-minority-do-not.

[18] Data from the Kiev International Institute of Sociology, quoted in Vitaly Nakhmanovych, *The Jewish Question in Ukraine* (Kyiv: National Academy of Sciences of Ukraine/Institute of Political and Ethnic Studies, 2017), 399 (in Ukrainian).

[19] Viktor Paniotto, "Dynamics of Xenophobia and Antisemitism in Ukraine, 1994-2007," *Sociology: Theory, Methods and Marketing* (2008), 197-214 (in Russian).

[20] Anastasya Mazurok, Volodymyr Paniotto and Natalia Kharchenko, "Factors of Electoral Popularity of All-Ukrainian Union 'Svoboda,'" Kiev International Institute of

A pilot study of public opinion concerning Jews conducted in May 2018 by the Tkuma Ukrainian Institute for Holocaust Studies, at the request of this author, showed that in the city of Dnipro (formerly Dnipropetrovsk), an industrial and culture center in eastern Ukraine and the country's informal "Jewish capital," with a population of one million citizens, a fifth of respondents refer to Jews "with annoyance, distrust, or fear," while slightly more that 12% expressed "interest and sympathy" toward them (Jews captured fifth place, following Americans, Crimean Tatars, Georgians, and Poles on the list of nine favorable nations for Ukrainian citizens).

At the same time, about 70% expressed a neutral approach toward Jews (i.e., "like any other" or "without special feelings"), and half of eastern Ukrainian urban respondents estimated that more than half of the citizens of their country did not hold negative views of Jews. However, the same study also found that almost a third of Dnipro residents were sure that more than half or more of their fellow citizens held anti-Jewish sentiments (1.5 times more than in Moscow and 2.5 more than respondents from other large cities in Russia, according to an RJC-sponsored Levada Center study of 2015). A fifth of Ukrainian respondents (as opposed to half in Moscow and more than a third in large Russian urban areas) believed this phenomenon to be almost non-existent.

*Table 4: Estimations of amounts of citizens from large urban areas in Ukraine and Russian Federation with anti-Jewish sentiments*

| Opinion | Dnipro (Ukraine)* | Big cities in Russia** | |
| --- | --- | --- | --- |
| | | Cities with a population > 500,000 | Moscow |
| Almost everybody | 1.5% | 2% | 3% |
| More than a half | 27% | 11% | 20% |
| Less than a half | 50.5% | 25% | 28% |
| Quite few | 21% | 52% | 36% |
| Hard to estimate | – | 11% | 14% |

** Source: Tkuma Institute (2018)    ** Source: Levada Center (2016)*

Nevertheless, respondents who exhibited a positive approach toward Jews often did not want to see them in power or have a Jew as president of their country. Researchers also identified a statistically significant number of negative stereotypes among the older population, including a number who supported the conspiracy theory that, in the last days of the USSR, Michael Gorbachev formed an alliance with Jews and Americans to ruin the country.

---

Sociology, September 8, 2014 (in Ukrainian); Nakhmanovych, *Jewish Question in Ukraine*, 397. See also Peter Burkovsky, Tatyana Chernenko, Victoria Zorko and Galina Kokhan, *Evaluation of Tolerance in Ukrainian Society: Risks and Ways for National Unity* (Kyiv: National Institute for Strategic Studies, 2011), http://www.niss.gov.ua/articles/500 (in Ukrainian).

In general, the level of intolerance among people over the age of thirty was higher than among younger generations. However, younger respondents more often believed that "ethnic Ukrainians should have priority over all others," which coincides with the results of the 2014 study by the Kyiv International Institute of Sociology, which also investigated the views of respondents on granting priority to ethnic Ukrainians and including "ethnicity" in identity documents. It was discovered that more than a quarter of all respondents supported both ideas, while another third supported one of them.

Currently, there is no answer regarding how this data could be applied to the current trends in Ukraine. Two Ukrainian institutions—the Ethnic Minorities' Rights Monitoring Group, headed by Vyacheslav Likhachev, and the Ukrainian Jewish Committee, headed by Eduard Dolinsky—simply register the number of antisemitic cases in the country. According to Ukrainian investigative journalist Igor Levinshtein, this data is more political than practical.[21]

Indeed, while the Ethnic Minorities' Rights Monitoring Group stressed the data reported by the Pew Research Center, which found that the intolerance rate stood at a mere 5% in Ukraine against higher figures in other countries, the Ukrainian Jewish Committee agued that "the full picture is substantially different from what was shown in Ukrainian media."[22] According to Dolinsky, one should pay more attention to the attitudes of those who feel that their culture is superior (within this group, 13% of followers of the Ukrainian Orthodox Church and 21% of Ukrainian Catholics were not ready to accept Jews as their neighbors; 29% and 48%, respectively, were not ready to accept Jews as their family members).

## ANTISEMITISM IN ACTION

Where is the truth? If we look at the number of incidents of antisemitic vandalism in 2010-2015, as recorded by the Eurasian Jewish Congress, we may conclude that the picture is not so dramatic. Such vandalism includes damage to synagogues, community centers, tombs in Jewish cemeteries, and memorials, as well as antisemitic or neo-Nazi graffiti on such targets. The relevant numbers ranged from 9 to 24-28 cases in Ukraine and from 6 to 17 cases in Russia, with the trend set to increase by the middle of the decade.

However, as the Kantor Center report stated, 2017 was a very difficult time for antisemitism monitoring in the post-Soviet region compared to previous years. Different trends were observed, including more verbal antisemitism in Russia and more violence in Ukraine. In general, we can state that the same

---

[21] Personal interview with the author, April 2018.

[22] Facebook post by Eduard Dolinsky, March 29, 2018, https://www.facebook.com/eduard.dolinsky/posts/1869021166463276.

types of incidents also continued during this year: vandalism, antisemitic propaganda (blaming Jews for all of the world's problems), and the use of anti-semitic content for political purposes.[23] The 2018 report of the Israeli Ministry for Diaspora Affairs also noted that in 2017 the number of antisemitic incidents in Ukraine doubled compared to the previous year. Moreover, a report commissioned by the Russian Jewish Congress and produced by the SOVA Centre for Information and Analysis registered a growing number of hate declarations by politicians and public figures, which in its opinion had led to the legitimization of antisemitism in the public domain.[24]

*Table 5: Incidents of antisemitic vandalism and violence*

| Years | Ukraine | | Russia | |
|---|---|---|---|---|
| | EAJC | Kantor Center | EAJC | Kantor Center |
| 2010 | 16 | 16 | 10 | 17 |
| 2011 | 9 | 16 | 6 | 15 |
| 2012 | 9 | 15 | 9 | 11 |
| 2013 | 9 | 23 | 10 | 15 |
| 2014 | 23 | 28 | 12 | 12 |
| 2015 | 22 | 23 | 12 | 8 |
| 2016 | 19 | 20 | n/d | 7 |
| 2017 | 24 | 22 | n/d | 3 |

The experts of the Eurasian Jewish Congress argue that, at least for Ukraine, these conclusions are exaggerated. According to their data, since the beginning of systematic monitoring in 2004, antisemitic incidents peaked in 2005, while 2005-2007 was marked by a wave of violent street attacks. However, following 2007, "a noticeable decline is seen, and in the past ten years, the number of such incidents remains at a stable low level," aside from certain increases in 2012-2014 and another decline in 2015-2016.[25] According to Eurasian Jewish Congress monitoring, no cases of antisemitic violence were registered in 2017.

Antisemitism in the FSU is not limited to vandalism and physical violence and should also be seen—as Israeli and FSU observers argue—together with other forms of hate crimes against Jews, including antisemitic incitement, xenophobic provocation, defamation, Holocaust denial, and antisemitism that

---

[23] See Irena Cantorovich, "The Post-Soviet Region," in *Antisemitism Worldwide 2017*, 19-20.

[24] Quoted in Yelena Mukhametshina, "Russian politicians begin to allow themselves to use antisemitism," *Vedomosti*, February 28, 2018, https://www.vedomosti.ru/politics/articles/2018/02/28/752211-politiki-antisemitizm (in Russian).

[25] Vyacheslav Lykhachev, *Antisemitism in Ukraine, 2017: Monitoring Report* (Kyiv: Ethnic Minorities' Rights Monitoring Group, 2018), 2, http://vaadua.org/sites/default/files/files/Antisemitism_in_Ukraine2017Eng.pdf.

emerges from anti-Zionism. Experts have identified the following categories of antisemitic incidents in FSU states: crimes inspired by Judeophobia, incitement to hostility against Jews, media-sponsored public antisemitism, and antisemitic stereotypes.

*Figure 1: Dynamics of registered acts of antisemitic vandalism and numbers of victims of antisemitic incidents*[26]

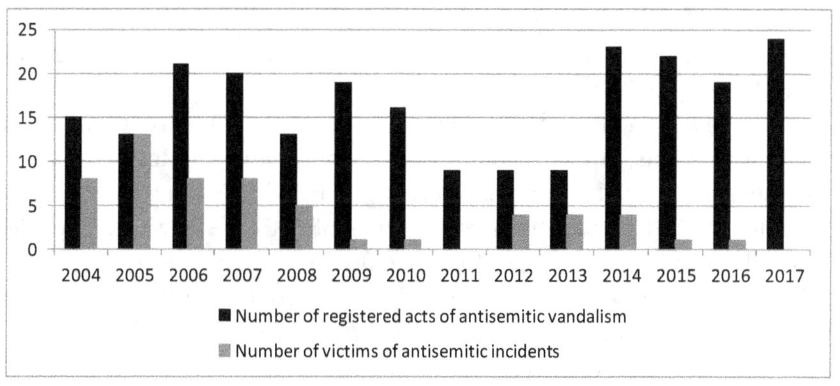


## Crimes inspired by Judeophobia

This category includes antisemitic graffiti and swastikas at military and Holocaust memorials, as well as vandalism at synagogues and Jewish educational institutions. The following two cases are examples of this trend that received much publicity. In the Siberian city of Novokuznetsk, vandals damaged a monument symbolizing Russian-Armenian friendship. The monument is in the form of an open book, with the Armenian and Russian alphabets inscribed on opposing pages. Criminals drew a swastika on the pedestal of the monument, along with a message addressed to the Jews.[27] According to RJC President Yuri Kanner, antisemitism is always a result of ignorance: the vandals presumably confused the Armenian alphabet with the Hebrew alphabet. Without being aware of it, the unknown perpetrator expressed the universal essence of antisemitism, which is based on a hatred of strangers in which the Jews are the personification of strangers.[28] Another recent case took place near the town of

---



[26] Ibid.

[27] "Vandals confuse Armenians with Jews and damage the wrong monument," European Jewish Congress, February 28, 2018, https://eurojewcong.org/news/commu nities-news/russian-federation/vandals-confuse-armenians-jews-damage-wrong-monu ment.

[28] Facebook post by Yuri Kanner, February 27, 2018, https://www.facebook.com/ yurykanner/posts/1604009729686945.

Nemyrov in western Ukraine, which had a large Jewish population before WWII. On April 27, 2018, vandals desecrated a monument in Ternopil that had been erected to honor thousands of local Jews who perished during the Holocaust.[29]

## Incitement to hostility against Jews

This category includes incitement to hostility against Jews through various information channels, including hundreds of antisemitic or semi-antisemitic publications a year in the field of printed and electronic media. According to the Chairman of Russia's Presidential Council for the Development of Civil Society and Human Rights, Mikhail Fedotov, "today antisemitism in Russia and other FSU states moves to the Internet where it gets new life."[30] This point may be illustrated by the fact that, during the first half of 2015, the Russian authorities removed extremist information from 4,500 websites and blocked 800 more, including 160 opened to raise funds and recruit activists for terrorist groups. Furthermore, over a third (231 out of 688) of the items on the federal list of extremist materials show clear signs of antisemitism.[31]

## Media-sponsored public antisemitism

This category includes the promotion of negative public stereotypes regarding the "inherent behavioral patterns" of the Jewish people and the attribution to Jews of hostile actions and dangerous attitudes toward other national, racial, and religious communities. According to a review of antisemitism in Russia prepared by the SOVA Centre for Information and Analysis on behalf of the Russian Jewish Congress, while the level of antisemitic crime in the Russian Federation decreased in 2017 compared to 2016, antisemitism in the media increased substantially.[32]

On January 23, 2017 while criticizing protesters speaking out against the transfer of St. Isaac's Cathedral in St. Petersburg to the Russian Orthodox Church, Pyotr Tolstoy, the deputy chairman of Russia's State Duma, called them

---

[29] "Another act of vandalism in Ternopil," *Vaadua*, April 27, 2018, http://www.vaadua.org/news/ocherednoy-akt-vandalizma-v-ternopole (in Ukrainian).

[30] This opinion was presented at the Moscow International Conference on Combating Antisemitism, Racism and Xenophobia, *November 1, 2016*.

[31] Rodion Rudnev, "Who benefits from stirring up antisemitic sentiments: a RAPSI investigation," Russian Legal Information Agency (RAPSI), February 21, 2017, http://rapsinews.ru/incident_publication/20170221/277831139.html.

[32] "Report 2017: The Situation of Antisemitism in Russia," Moscow International Conference on Combating Antisemitism, Racism and Xenophobia, March 27, 2018, http://mcca.ru/ru/news/27.

"the grandchildren and great-grandchildren of those who destroyed our churches, [of those] who jumped out of the Pale of Settlement with revolvers in 1917, now their grandchildren, working in various very respectable places—on radio stations, in legislative assemblies—continue the work of their grandfathers and great-grandfathers."[33] State Duma deputy Vitaly Milonov noted the ethnic Jewish origin of the protest organizers, such as members of the St. Petersburg City Council Boris Vishnevsky and Maxim Reznik, claiming that "their ancestors boiled Christians in cauldrons and gave them to beasts [to be] mauled."[34] Neither Tolstoy nor Milonov received disciplinary punishment. A majority of other deputies, party officials, and local and national journalists who made antisemitic declarations also did not receive disciplinary punishment.

Another case was the controversial discussion surrounding the film *Matilda*, directed by Alexander Uchitel, who is Jewish. The antisemitic attacks made in connection with the film, which describes the love affair between Tsar Nicholas II and ballerina Matilda Kschessinska, reflect the fact that some in Russia have recently started referring to the execution of the Tsar and royal family in 1918 following the Bolshevik Revolution of October 1917 as a "ritual murder." According to Natalia Poklonskaya, a deputy of the Russian State Duma, "They murdered the entire royal family… This is a crime, a frightening ritual murder. Many people are afraid to talk about it—but everyone understands that it happened. It is evil."[35]

According to sociologist Denis Volkov, "The Duma has a low level of approval, but deputies are those people who have access to television screens and speak from positions of power." Moreover, Alexander Verkhovsky, Director of the Moscow-based SOVA Centre for Information and Analysis, states that, "For many years it was a particularly taboo phobia, and antisemitism was a sign of marginalization. The fact that it has now left the marginal field can lead to the fact that antisemitism will be greater and it will become more normalized."[36]

---

[33] Adam Taylor, "A dispute over St. Petersburg's grand Orthodox cathedral stirs up Russia's anti-Semitic conspiracies," *Washington Post*, January 24, 2017, https://www.washingtonpost.com/news/worldviews/wp/2017/01/24/a-dispute-over-st-petersburgs-grand-orthodox-cathedral-stirs-up-russias-anti-semitic-conspiracies/?noredirect=on&utm_term=.fa89ccc1cc28.

[34] Both quoted in Moy Rayon, "Duma deputy says ancestors of Jews cooked Christians in cauldrons," *Meduza*, February 13, 2017, https://meduza.io/en/news/2017/02/13/milonov-the-ancestors-of-deputies-reznik-and-vishnevsky-cooked-christians-in-cauldrons.

[35] Natalia Poklonskaya's statement on the *Nasha strana* (Our country) program on Russian-Orthodox Tsargrad TV, March 4, 2017.

[36] Both quoted in Mukhametshina, "Russian politicians allow themselves."

*Antisemitic stereotypes*

This category includes antisemitic stereotypes that circulate on FSU media, including allegations that "the Jews rule Russia and the world," "the Jews are responsible for antisemitism themselves," and "the Jews believe they are the Chosen People." Other stereotypes include referring to Jews as "greedy and tricky" and the belief that they have "captured power and all good (convenient and profitable) positions in the country." False stereotypes, for example that "the Jews lack patriotism and are always looking for better conditions just for themselves," are still rooted in substantial parts of the FSU population. Indeed, the Levada Center's research shows that the number of Russian citizens who agree with the assumption that "the Jews are mostly loyal to their own interests, rather than interests of the country they live in," grew from just over 40% in 1997 to almost 50% in 2015.

*Table 6: "Do you agree that the Jews are mostly loyal to their own interests, rather than the interests of the country in which they live?"*

| | 1997 | 2015 | 2015 | | | | 1997/2015 |
|---|---|---|---|---|---|---|---|
| Opinions | General | General | Age | | | | |
| | | | 18-24 | 25-39 | 40-54 | 55+ | |
| Agree | 43% | 49% | 36% | 47% | 52% | 55% | +6% |
| Disagree | 31% | 32% | 32% | 39% | 29% | 29% | +1% |
| Hard to say | 26% | 19% | 32% | 14% | 19% | 16% | -7% |

| | 1997 | 2015 | 2015 | | | |
|---|---|---|---|---|---|---|
| Opinions | General | General | Education | | | |
| | | | Higher | Post-secondary vocational | High school | Less than high school |
| Agree | 43% | 49% | 45% | 52% | 52% | 51% |
| Disagree | 31% | 32% | 35% | 31% | 34% | 26% |
| Hard to say | 26% | 19% | 20% | 17% | 15% | 23% |

*Source: Levada Center (2016)*

It is logical that all this leads to *diverse models of political antisemitism,* including accusations of playing the "Jewish card" in politics, antisemitism within the radical Right and radical Left movements, blackmailing of political enemies, "bureaucratic antisemitism," references to the "Jewish aspect" of the Russian-Ukrainian crisis, Holocaust revisionism, denial of the right of the State of Israel to exist and defend itself, and attempts to justify anti-Jewish and anti-Israeli terrorism.

## Conclusion

In conclusion, the observed decline in antisemitism and antisemitic violence in Russia and Ukraine does not mean that antisemitism has disappeared. Sociological assessments of Russian and Ukrainian society reveal a refusal to accept open declarations of ethnic inequality and hatred or disapproval of discriminatory measures directed against "other" ethnic groups. However, this does not necessarily imply the weakening or disappearance of ethnic prejudices or phobias and does not exclude potential feelings of xenophobia and ethnic or racial superiority on the part of a substantial part of society. This, as observers note, opens the way to relatively easy violations of the public ban on antisemitism and ethnic discrimination by various institutions in the public sphere.[37]

Long-term political and ideological campaigns launched by the Russian government in 2004-2007 have led to an increase in Russian chauvinistic nationalism and a decrease in ethnic, national and religious tolerance, especially since 2012. Russian society still enjoys a "hard core" of antisemites that amount to approximately 8-10% of the population and have not disappeared despite the general decline in levels of xenophobia. In Ukraine, the number of "hard-core" antisemites might be smaller, but it is still visible. In addition, the majority of xenophobic groups in FSU society feature "latent" or "sleeping" antisemitism. Thus, the general trend toward a decline in classic antisemitic attitudes in Russia will not necessarily prevent their resurgence in the future.

Today, however, the operative level of threats and risks to the Jewish population of Russia is relatively low. The most dangerous phenomenon may be the return of "state antisemitism," for example in the form of antisemitic statements and actions carried out by the media, bureaucratic institutions, and other actors controlled by the government. Such a development is currently unlikely in the Russian Federation, and even more so in Ukraine, but if such a scenario does occur it will find an echo in public consciousness.

---

[37] Levinson and Kanner, "Russians believe that they must be ruled"; Vyacheslav Likhachev, "Antisemitism as a PR-Strategy," *Khadashot*, June 2010 (in Russian).

# Butchering History But Not the Jews:
# The Case of Post-Revolutionary Ukraine

Samuel Sokol*

## Introduction

Two of the lesser reported aspects of the Ukrainian conflict are the propaganda war that has been waged over the country's Jews and the conflict that erupted in early 2014 between Jewish communal leaders in Moscow and Kiev. Much has been reported regarding hybrid warfare, the distortion of history for political ends, and the rise and fall of the Far Right in Ukraine, but there has been little work thus far integrating such research and reporting into a unified history of the Jewish experience in post-revolutionary Ukraine. Much of my work over the past several years at the *Jerusalem Post* centered around this topic, along with chronicling the destruction of the Jewish communities of Donetsk and Luhansk and their leaders' subsequent efforts to rebuild their shattered congregations in internal exile. The following paper details the Ukrainian conflict as perceived by Jewish observers, hopefully offering a fresh perspective. The flight of the Jewish communities of the Donbas and the subsequent migration of thousands of Ukrainian Jews to Israel I leave for another time.

## I. "Glory to the nation! Death to the enemies!"

This chant was heard across Kiev's central Maidan Square in late 2013 as thousands of Ukrainians massed in protest against the corruption and brutality of Viktor Yanukovych, their pro-Russian president. It was a chilling slogan, bearing harsh connotations for those who understood its identification with the Ukrainian nationalist movement of the early to mid-twentieth century, especially the descendants of their Jewish victims. Carrying the red and black flags of the

---

* Samuel Sokol was until recently the Jewish World correspondent for the *Jerusalem Post*. His reporting on the Jewish refugees of revolutionary Ukraine garnered the 2015 B'nai B'rith World Center Award for Journalism Recognizing Excellence in Diaspora Reportage. He is currently writing a book on Ukrainian antisemitism and Russian propaganda.

Ukrainian Insurgent Army (UPA), which murdered thousands of Jews in western Ukraine during the Holocaust,[1] as well as those of the Svoboda party (the UPA's self-proclaimed spiritual heir), those screaming ultra-nationalist protesters represented a minority of those who had come out to vent their rage, albeit a disproportionately vocal and violent one.

During the years immediately prior to the conflagration, which would engulf the Ukrainian capital and split the country in two, Ukrainian Jews had become increasingly worried about the rise of Svoboda. Proudly antisemitic, the party had a history of harassing Jews and had been declared a neo-Nazi faction by both local community leaders and the World Jewish Congress. Initially known as the Social-National Party of Ukraine, the party that would become Svoboda was a fringe movement for much of its history, only coming to prominence following elections in 2012, when it won 36 out of 450 seats in the Verkhovna Rada, Ukraine's parliament. Party cadres, alongside members of the newly formed ultra-nationalist Pravy Sektor (Right Sector) coalition, provided most of the fighters who took part in violent clashes with the Berkut (riot police) and the Titushky[2] (hired thugs used by the government against the Maidan activists).

During the early stages of the protests, several signs pointed to the possibility of an upswing in nationalist sentiment that could prove dangerous to Kiev's Jewish population. Prior to the outbreak of protests in late 2013, physical violence against Jews was not a major concern for most community members, although antisemitic propaganda and vandalism were distressingly common.[3]

On December 1, 2013, oligarch Petro Poroshenko, who would later be elected as Ukraine's first post-maiden president, was booed in the square by protesters screaming "piss off you Jewish garbage."[4] While not Jewish himself, conspiracy theories claiming that Poroshenko is really the son of a Jew named Valtzman have dogged the Ukrainian leader for years.[5] Scattered graffiti against Jews,[6] such as a

---

[1] John-Paul Himka, "The Ukrainian Insurgent Army and the Holocaust" (paper prepared for the 41st National Convention of the American Association for the Advancement of Slavic Studies, Boston, November 12-15, 2009).

[2] For a detailed explanation of the origins of the term, see Andreï Kurkov, *Ukraine Diaries: Dispatches from Kiev* (London: Random House, 2014).

[3] Dina Porat, ed., *Antisemitism Worldwide 2013: General Analysis* (Tel Aviv: Kantor Center for the Study of Contemporary Antisemitism and Racism, 2014).

[4] "The Chocolate King Rises; Part 2: 'Piss Off, You Jewish Garbage,'" *Der Spiegel*, May 22, 2014, http://www.spiegel.de/international/europe/profile-of-petro-poroshenko-in-the-run-up-to-the-ukraine-elections-a-970325-2.html.

[5] Cnaan Lipshiz, "Ukraine Presidential Frontrunner Petro Poroshenko and His Secret Jewish Roots," *Forward*, May 23, 2014, http://forward.com/news/world/198758/ukraine-presidential-frontrunner-petro-poroshenko.

[6] "Yid on the Maidan: Jews and Antisemites in the Epicenter of the Ukrainian Protest," *Forum Daily*, January 1, 2014 (in Russian), http://www.forumdaily.com/zhid-na-majdane-evrei-i-antisemity-v-epicentre-ukrainskogo-protesta.

swastika down the block from the offices of the Ukrainian Jewish Committee (UJC),[7] contributed further to an atmosphere of worry. "It's not a surprise. You can see a lot of them here," Eduard Dolinsky of the UJC said when asked about the scrawls. And while one ultra-orthodox cleric was invited to address the Maidan[8] from the main stage in late December, only two days later a Svoboda MP would use the same platform to perform a traditional Ukrainian antisemitic skit dressed as a Hasid named Zhyd (Kike).[9]

It wasn't long before local Jews' worries were validated. On January 11, a Jew was stabbed near the Podil Synagogue,[10] followed by the stabbing of a yeshiva student on the January 17.[11] In March, the rabbi who spoke in the Maidan was attacked when walking down the street,[12] and a Hasidic couple was chased down the street with sticks.[13] Several incidents of attempted arson against synagogues, as well as graffiti calling for the death of Jews, also appeared during this period,[14] as did antisemitic material on the social media accounts of Ukraine's riot police, a group that played an active part in the violence in the Maidan.[15]

As a result of the mounting threat, security measures were increased at Jewish communal institutions across the capital, and in late February Rabbi Moshe Azman, the leader of a downtown Chabad Hasidic synagogue, warned his congregants to flee the city. "I don't want to tempt fate, but there are constant warnings concerning intentions to attack Jewish institutions," he explained.[16] At the time, Azman said that his primary concern was that "groups of hooligans" would seek to use the conflict as an excuse to attack his community. "We know

---

7 Sam Sokol (@SamuelSokol), "It's not a surprise. You can see a lot of them here," Twitter photo, December 12, 2013, https://twitter.com/SamuelSokol/status/411089492 024377344.

8 See note 6.

9 See note 6.

10 Vyacheslav Likhachev, "Attacks on Jews in Kiev: Facts and Versions," Euro-Asian Jewish Congress, January 19, 2014 (in Russian), http://eajc.org/page18/news42754.html.

11 Sam Sokol, "Jew Stabbed in Kiev on Way Home from Synagogue," *Jerusalem Post*, January 18, 2014, http://www.jpost.com/Jewish-World/Jewish-News/Jew-stabbed-in-Kiev-on-way-home-from-synagogue-338594.

12 "An Attack on Rabbi Hillel Cohen Was Committed in Kiev," Euro-Asian Jewish Congress, March 14, 2014 (in Russian), http://eajc.org/page16/news43878.html.

13 Vyacheslav Likhachev, ed., "Antisemitism in FSU—2014," no. 12 (Kiev/Jerusalem: Euro-Asian Jewish Congress, 2015), http://www.eajc.org/data//file/AntisemitismReport 2014engl.pdf.

14 Id.

15 "Ukrainian 'Berkut' Found Extreme—Jews Turned out to Be Guilty," *Kiev Evreiskiy*, December 22, 2013 (in Russian), http://evreiskiy.kiev.ua/ukrainskijj-berkut-nashel-krajjnikh-12687.html.

16 "Ukrainian Rabbi Tells Kiev's Jews to Flee City," *Haaretz*, February 22, 2014, http://www.haaretz.com/jewish/news/1.575732.

from the past that the first ones to be hit are the Jews," he said, citing the presence of Svoboda members among the protesters.[17] He would subsequently cancel a public menorah lighting ceremony due to such fears.

One Hasidic shopkeeper in central Kiev told me his concern was that the anger manifest in the streets, stoked by the alcohol being imbibed by many protesters, would erupt and that the protesters would turn against his community.

There is ample precedent for such worries. Following the Russian revolution of 1905, pogroms erupted in Kiev, Ekaterinoslav (modern day Dnipropetrovsk) and Odessa, killing hundreds. As Serhii Plokhy writes in his authoritative history of Ukraine, "as the demonstrators attacked the city prison, released political prisoners, desecrated the monument to Nicholas I in front of Kyiv University, removed the imperial insignia from the facade of the university building, destroyed Russian imperial flags and replaced them with red ones, and called for the emperor to be hanged, the conservative public blamed the Jews."[18]

To be fair, antisemitism had not been an issue the last time Ukrainians came out into the streets en masse during Ukraine's Orange Revolution of 2004, but Jews have long memories and there is a history of pogroms in the territories of the former Soviet Union.

Speaking at a press conference on March 3, Russian President Vladimir Putin warned against the "rampage of reactionary forces, nationalist and anti-Semitic forces going on in certain parts of Ukraine, including Kiev." This was later followed by Russian Foreign Minister Sergei Lavrov stating that "it could never occur to anybody that radicals and neo-Nazis could come to dominate Ukrainian politics."[19] The Russian propaganda juggernaut had aimed itself squarely at Ukraine. Such statements became commonplace in the Russian media, with stories about non-existent pogroms and accusations of Ukrainian politicians' secret Jewish backgrounds making the rounds on television, in print, and via Internet outlets.

However, several Ukrainian Jewish leaders shot back, blaming the Kremlin for instigating the incidents.[20] Chief Rabbi Yaakov Dov Bleich was one of the more outspoken figures, lashing out at Putin not only for his statements on anti-semitism but also for his annexation of the Crimean peninsula. This led to a

---

[17] Gil Ronen, "Kiev Rabbi: This is a Revolution," *Arutz Sheva*, December 2, 2013, http://www.israelnationalnews.com/News/News.aspx/174715#.Vf20lSCqqko.

[18] Serhii Plokhy, *The Gates of Europe: A History of Ukraine* (New York: Basic Books, 2015).

[19] Sam Sokol, "Analysis: Propaganda Battle over Ukrainian Jews Is Not Over," *Jerusalem Post*, January 1, 2016, http://www.jpost.com/Diaspora/Analysis-Propaganda-battle-over-Ukrainian-Jews-is-not-over-439057.

[20] Sam Sokol, "Ukrainian Jewish Leaders Blame Russia for Anti-Semitic 'Provocations,'" *Jerusalem Post*, March 16, 2014, http://www.jpost.com/Jewish-World/Jewish-News/Ukrainian-Jewish-leaders-blame-Russia-for-antisemitic-provocations-345516.

harsh war of words between Jewish leaders loyal to Moscow and Kiev, each taking their respective country's side.[21]

In contrast to the Russians, however, other actors in the international community failed to register the same sense of concern. "When they accuse the government of being extreme right, that's wrong," French Foreign Minister Laurent Fabius said at the time. "There are three members of the Svoboda party, that is a party further to the right than the others, but the extreme right is not in the government."[22] The State Department also weighed in, responding to a claim by Vladimir Putin regarding a spate of attacks against synagogues and churches in southern and eastern Ukraine, claiming that "Jewish groups in southern and eastern Ukraine report that they have not seen an increase in anti-Semitic incidents."[23] Speaking to the *Forward*, the State Department's envoy on antisemitism, Ira Forman, went even further, stating that he did not "think President Putin's claims at this point seem to be very credible."[24]

In fact, while antisemitic violence would soon drop precipitously, the coming months actually did see a spike in arson attempts and vandalism across the country, with repeated desecrations of the Babi Yar memorial in Kiev and incidents at synagogues in Zaporizhya, Simferopol, Mykolaiv, Kiev and Khust.[25]

Despite the Jewish community's pitched defense of Ukraine, there was a palpable sense that the Russians might just be right after the announcement of the composition of Ukraine's interim cabinet following Yanukovych's flight to Russia in February 2014. Among the members of the so-called Kamikaze Cabinet were newly appointed Defense Minister and Deputy Prime Minister Ihor Tenyukh and Oleksandr Sych, both members of Svoboda.[26] While Anton

---

[21] Kiril Feferman, "The Crisis in Ukraine: Attitudes of the Russian and Ukrainian Jewish Communities," *Israel Journal of Foreign Affairs* 9, no. 2 (2015): 227-236. See also JTA/Sam Sokol, "War of Words between Ukrainian and Russian Jews Heats Up," *Jerusalem Post*, March 27, 2014, http://www.jpost.com/Jewish-World/Jewish-Features/War-of-words-between-Ukrainian-and-Russian-Jews-heats-up-346721.

[22] Yohann Taïeb, "Ukraine: Pour Fabius, le parti antisémite Svoboda n'est pas d'extrême droite," *Le Monde Juif*, March 13, 2014, http://www.lemondejuif.info/2014/03/ukraine-pour-fabius-le-parti-antisemite-svoboda-nest-pas-dextreme-droite.

[23] "State Department Fact Sheet on Putin's False Claims about Ukraine," *Voltaire Network*, March 5, 2014, http://www.voltairenet.org/article182542.html.

[24] Nathan Guttman and Paul Berger, "Envoy Blasts Russian Effort to Play Ukraine 'Jewish Card,'" *Forward*, March 13, 2014, http://forward.com/news/world/194458/anti-semitism-envoy-blasts-russian-effort-to-play.

[25] Sam Sokol, "Report: Anti-Semitic Vandalism Spiked in Ukraine in 2014," *Jerusalem Post*, May 10, 2015, http://www.jpost.com/Diaspora/Report-Anti-Semitic-vandalism-spiked-in-Ukraine-in-2014-402631.

[26] Daisy Sindelar, "Who's Who in Ukraine's 'Kamikaze' Cabinet," Radio Free Europe/Radio Liberty, February 27, 2014, http://www.rferl.org/a/ukraine-whos-who-cabinet/25279592.html.

Shekhovtsov, an expert on European far right movements, could state in 2011 that Ukraine was unique in that "there has been no overtly nationalist group in the parliament (*Verkhovna Rada*) since independence, and no Ukrainian radical right-wing political party as such has ever been elected to the *Verkhovna Rada*,"[27] now the country's defense establishment was under the direct control of a neo-Nazi. Scary, indeed.

## II. The End of Svoboda

Svoboda's success was not to last, however, proving that while antisemitism may be much more socially acceptable in mainstream Ukrainian discourse than in America and western Europe, Ukrainians were by no means fascists or supporters of the Ukrainian Insurgent Army (UPA) or its parent group, the Organization of Ukrainian Nationalists (OUN). During parliamentary elections in October 2014, Svoboda's public support dropped precipitously, with the party garnering less than the five percent threshold necessary to enter parliament, although several members did gain mandates in single member districts.[28] (Ukraine's electoral system combines both a proportional representation system and direct election of candidates by region.)

A reasonable explanation for Svoboda's dramatic decline is that the cooption of the party's anti-Russian agenda by more mainstream political actors sapped it of its main draw in the post-revolutionary period. While Svoboda's prominent role in the fighting that ultimately led to Yanukovych's flight to Russia could reasonably be expected to have led to further electoral gains, Shekhovtsov has asserted that the party's support was already drying up prior to Euromaidan and that the developments of the revolutionary period proved to be the final nail in the party's coffin:

> Svoboda's relative failure to mobilise its former electorate can be attributed to the demise of former president Viktor Yanukovych's regime: Svoboda was successful in 2012 because it was considered an anti-Yanukovych party, so with Yanukovych ousted, almost half of Svoboda's electorate was gone too. Furthermore, in 2012, Svoboda was also considered almost the only "patriotic" party, but now all democratic parties are patriotic, so Svoboda has lost its "monopoly" on patriotism.[29]

---

[27] Anton Shekhovtsov, "The Creeping Resurgence of the Ukrainian Radical Right? The Case of the Freedom Party," *Europe-Asia Studies* 63, no. 2 (2011): 203-228.

[28] Sam Sokol, "Election Results Buoy Ukrainian Jews," *Jerusalem Post*, October 27, 2014, http://www.jpost.com/Diaspora/Election-results-buoy-Ukrainian-Jews-379969.

[29] Anton Shekhovtsov, "Ukraine's Parliamentary Elections and the Far Right," Anton Shekhovtsov's blog, October 28, 2014, http://anton-shekhovtsov.blogspot.co.il/2014/10/ukraines-parliamentary-elections-and.html.

This assessment is bolstered by a conversation I had with a party supporter in the Kiev municipal administration building in December 2014.[30] We stood in the shadow of the multiple Svoboda banners hanging limply from the gallery above, the yellow hand flashing its eternal victory sign against a blue background, while around us in the grand plenum chamber of Stalinist-Gothic design young men in combat boots and army helmets jostled following a successful battle to repel the Berkut. The Svoboda supporter in question, a linguist by trade, told me that, despite the fears of many in Ukraine's Jewish community, there was no real danger of an outbreak of antisemitism, even with the active participation of the party in the protests. "I've been teased and called a Jew by friends for standing up against antisemitism, and I support Svoboda here," he said, asserting that Svoboda and the other opposition groups had to be supported as an alternative to a leadership that many Ukrainians see as inept and corrupt.

Ironically, the success of Svoboda may have been directly attributable to the pro-Moscow Yanukovych and his dominant Party of Regions. Secret party ledgers recently released by government investigators purport to show a cash payment of 200,000 dollars to Svoboda from the party, adding weight to previously unprovable allegations. Reacting to the news, which broke in mid-August, Max Seddon, the Moscow correspondent for the *Financial Times* tweeted that he "once shared a massive strudel with a soccer hooligan who said the Party of Regions paid for all the Svoboda muscle."[31]

Red flags had been raised previously, with researcher Ivan Katchanovski alleging back in 2012 that "the party and its leader Oleh Tiahnybok undeniably derive considerable benefit from their regular and prominent presence on prime-time TV shows on major national channels controlled by oligarchs from the Yanukovych camp or by the government." Such actions, he continued, "can be regarded as an attempt to tighten [the Yanukovych camp's] grip on power for a long time by turning radical nationalists, unlikely to win national parliamentary or presidential elections, into the main opposition force."[32]

---

[30] Sam Sokol, "Covering Kiev: Jews Fear Opposition's Anger Might Turn against Them," *Jerusalem Post*, December 12, 2013, http://www.jpost.com/Jewish-World/Jewish-Features/Reporters-Notebook-Kievs-Jews-fear-oppositions-anger-might-turn-against-them-334759.

[31] Max Seddon (@maxseddon), "I once shared a massive strudel with a soccer hooligan who said the Party of Regions paid for all the Svoboda muscle," Twitter, August 19, 2016, https://twitter.com/maxseddon/status/766601762354630656.

[32] Ivan Katchanovski, "Ukrainian 'Freedom' Party Should Be Ringing Alarm Bells," openDemocracy Russia (oDR), March 21, 2012, https://www.opendemocracy.net/od-russia/ivan-katchanovski/ukrainian-%E2%80%98freedom%E2%80%99-party-should-be-ringing-alarm-bells.

## III. Trading Propaganda Barbs

In any case, the decline of Svoboda should have put accusations of a fascist coup to rest, but Russian propaganda was, by its nature, less concerned with the facts than with what people were prepared to believe.[33] Rather than peter out, Russia's propaganda efforts against Ukraine intensified in early 2014 as Moscow annexed the Crimean peninsula and began inciting separatism in the country's eastern Donbas region. One of the earliest and most blatant examples of Russian propaganda was broadcast shortly after unmarked Russian troops began the takeover of the Crimean peninsula.

Reporting on attacks against Jews in Kiev and efforts to organize communal self-defense bodies,[34] *Russia Today*, the Kremlin's English-language propaganda arm, reported that "With the lack of peace and stability and the rise of neo-Nazi hardliners many Jews are considering fleeing the country."[35] Among those featured in the segment was Misha Kapustin, the rabbi of Sevastopol's Reform synagogue, who was interviewed while packing up his belongings in preparation for a move away from the recently captured territory. Discussing the appearance of swastikas and other antisemitic graffiti on the walls of his synagogue, Kapustin told *RT* correspondent Paula Slier that he felt that "nobody will do anything wrong to us because we are protected under the law. Ukrainian law. Nowadays, there is no law because everything is changing so fast and I don't expect anybody would protect the Jews if anything happened."

---

[33] While the Svoboda party was defeated at the ballot box, this did not mean that the party was completely gone from the political scene. In December 2015, I wrote an article in the *Jerusalem Post* detailing the election of a Svoboda member as the mayor of the town of Konotop. Unlike many prominent members on the national political scene, this local party apparatchik made no effort to hide his Nazi leanings. According to reports, the new mayor drove around in a car with plates bearing the number 14/88, a numerological reference to the phrases "we must secure the existence of our people and a future for white children" and "Heil Hitler"; he also replaced the picture of President Petro Poroshenko in his office with a portrait of Ukrainian national leader and Nazi collaborator Stepan Bandera and refused to fly the city's official flag at the opening meeting of the city council because he objected to the star of David emblazoned on it. The flag also features a Muslim crescent and a cross. Needless to say, there were those who held up Konotop's new mayor as a sign of resurgent neo-Nazism in Ukraine, despite the fact that he was one of the only Svoboda representatives to manage to get himself elected in the post-revolutionary period. See Sam Sokol, "Local Jews in Shock after Ukrainian City of Konotop Elects Neo-Nazi Mayor," *Jerusalem Post*, December 21, 2015, http://www.jpost. com/Diaspora/Ukrainian-Jews-shocked-after-city-elects-neo-Nazi-mayor-437975.

[34] "Kiev Jews Set up Self-Defense Unit," Jewish Telegraphic Agency, May 8, 2014, http://www.jta.org/2014/05/08/news-opinion/world/kiev-jews-set-up-self-defense-unit.

[35] "'Pushed to leave': Packing Moods among Ukraine's Jewish Minority amidst Far-Right Rise," *RT*, March 15, 2014, https://www.rt.com/news/jews-jewish-ukraine-nationalist-106.

Kapustin's synagogue had indeed been desecrated, but he was less worried about Ukrainian antisemitism than Russian conquest. Earlier that month Kapustin had published an open letter denouncing Russia. "Our town, Simferopol, is occupied by the Russians. Help us, save our country, save Ukraine! Ask your government for help," he wrote.[36]

In a subsequent interview, not all of which I have yet published, Kapustin cast doubt on the putative Ukrainian origins of the graffiti, noting that Crimeans were more pro-Russian than most Ukrainians and that right-wing Ukrainian nationalism was relatively unpopular in his region. "I did not expect anything to be done like that, they just misused my words, they just mislead my words, they just perverted my words," he told me. "In fact it was me, my voice, my words, it was me all the time there, and I must admit they did it professionally, they professionally changed the context so nicely, they do it so professionally."[37]

Russian media reports of a Jewish exodus did not stop. In early May 2014, I reported on preparations being made to evacuate members of the Jewish community of Odessa from the city, especially children in the local orphanage, should violent clashes between pro-government and pro-separatist protesters that left dozens dead continue unabated. This story was picked up by multiple Russian news outlets, promoting a flood or worries calls to local community leaders and compelling them to issue a denial of their earlier statements. A spokesman for the Russian Jewish community explained that the Russian media had exaggerated my initial report and claimed that a mass evacuation of the city's Jews was imminent.[38]

Shortly thereafter, the Russian television news program "Vesti" aired a report claiming that "Jewish organizations and schools are closed without reason" and that as a result of Ukrainian antisemitism thousands of Jews had fled the country. While emigration did rise significantly in the post-Maidan period,[39] over the course of dozens of interviews during the past two years I have yet to come across one Jewish internally displaced person or refugee who cited antisemitism, rather than the Russian-Ukrainian war and the subsequent economic

---

36 Anshel Pfeffer and Marcus Dysch, "Danger Looms in Crimea for Ukrainian Jews," *Jewish Chronicle*, March 6, 2014, http://www.thejc.com/news/world-news/116196/danger-looms-crimea-ukrainian-jews.

37 Sam Sokol, "Analysis: Propaganda Battle over Ukrainian Jews Is Not Over," *Jerusalem Post*, January 1, 2016, http://www.jpost.com/Diaspora/Analysis-Propaganda-battle-over-Ukrainian-Jews-is-not-over-439057.

38 Sam Sokol, "Jewish Leaders Dispute Reports of Odessa Evacuation," *Jerusalem Post*, May 8, 2014, http://www.jpost.com/Jewish-World/Jewish-Features/Russian-Jewish-Congress-disputes-report-of-Odessa-evacuation-351603.

39 Sam Sokol and Yardena Schwartz, "Fleeing Civil War, Thousands of Ukrainians Take Refuge in Israel," *Jerusalem Post*, December 22, 2014, http://www.jpost.com/Israel-News/Netanyahu-links-spike-in-aliya-to-anti-Semitism-in-Europe-385451.

dislocation, as their motivation for flight. The rhetoric used on "Vesti" took a balanced assessment of Ukrainian antisemitism and stretched it beyond its breaking point. "Jewish cultural and historical monuments have already been destroyed more than once by men in uniform with the symbols of volunteer battalions that are fighting in Donbas," it was claimed. "There are criminal slogans appealing for the forced relocation of Jews at mass meetings and demonstrations. The shocking revival of the traditions of Nazi Germany in a modern state is a manifest threat to Europe and European values. It is important that the EU leadership respond to these challenges as soon as possible."[40] Jewish leaders such as Menachem Margolin of the European Jewish Association have been appealing to the West because "Jews are being persecuted," the program added, incorrectly.[41]

However, one of the most blatant examples of Russian propaganda centered not on generic warnings but on specific (and, needless to say, fabricated) incidents in the city of Odessa. In October, concurrent reports in *Pravda*, *Izvestia* and other Russian news outlets claimed that members of Pravy Sektor had "declared war" on the city's Jewish community, beating twenty Jews and prompting local leaders to appeal to the World Jewish Congress to "disarm and disband" the group. The reports quoted community leader Mikhail Maiman as stating that "Pravy Sektor is just destroying us, it is pure militant Nazism."[42]

Both the World Jewish Congress and the local community disputed the veracity of the pogrom reports. Local Jewish leaders also noted that there was nobody in their community hierarchy by the name of Maiman, indicating that reports quoting such a man were fabricated. "There is no question that from the beginning we became a tool," one community leader told me at the time, adding that Ukrainian authorities "realize[d] that any antisemitic attack could reflect badly on them." Knowing the propaganda value of antisemitism to Russia, Pravy Sektor, despite being composed of several neo-Nazi groups, made great efforts to counter its image, promising to protect Jewish institutions[43] and

---

[40] "News at 23:00," Vesti, May 18, 2015, video (in Russian), http://www.vesti.ru/videos/show/vid/645287/cid/1/#.

[41] Sam Sokol, "Ukrainian Rights Group Blasts Russia for Faking Anti-Semitic News," *Jerusalem Post*, June 10, 2015, http://www.jpost.com/Diaspora/Ukrainian-rights-group-blasts-Russia-for-faking-anti-Semitic-news-405608.

[42] Sam Sokol, "Reports of Anti-Semitism in Odessa Highlights Use of Jews in Wartime Propaganda," *Jerusalem Post*, October 12, 2014, http://www.jpost.com/Diaspora/Russian-media-possibly-using-fake-anti-Semitism-reports-as-wartime-propaganda-378664.

[43] Gianluca Mezzofiore, "Right Sector Ultra-Nationalists Back Odessa Jews over Holocaust Memorial Nazi Defacement," *International Business Times*, April 10, 2014, http://www.ibtimes.co.uk/right-sector-ultra-nationalists-back-odessa-jews-over-holocaust-memorial-nazi-defacement-1444276.

bringing on board a Jewish spokesman.[44]

The reality on the ground was obviously quite different from that as portrayed in the Russian media. Speaking with the former editor of Donetsk's Jewish newspaper in Dnipropetrovsk following his flight from the Donbas, I asked if he had experienced any antisemitism during his time in government-controlled Ukraine. His response was surprising. He replied that he had been accosted by a young skinhead shouting racial slurs on a bus but that the attacker had been quickly mobbed and booted off by his fellow Ukrainians. The passengers then apologized to the displaced Jew, distancing themselves from any sort of antisemitic ideology.[45]

That is not to say that such feelings do not exist. According to a 2014 survey by the Anti-Defamation League, thirty-eight percent of Ukrainians harbor views that could be characterized as antisemitic.[46] And during a recent dinner in Kiev, a friend told me that he frequently hears slurs muttered against him by people passing by on the sidewalk.

While spreading these accusations of Ukrainian antisemitism, Russia also attacked the Jews for their loyalty to the Ukrainian state and spread rumors (meant to pander to the Russian Far Right) that Ukrainian leaders were secretly Jewish. The following exchange on Russian television is emblematic of such rhetoric: [47]

Aleksandr Prokhanov: It's strange that these Jewish organizations—European and our Russian ones—support the Maidan. What are they doing? Don't they understand that with their own hands they're bringing a second Holocaust?

Evelina Zakamskaya: They did it the first time too.

Aleksandr Prokhanov: It's an amazing blindness that is being repeated again. Until 1933 many liberal European organizations fed the Führer.

This exchange illustrates the cognitive dissonance inherent in Russian state media's attempts to accuse Ukrainian leaders of antisemitism while simultaneously portraying them as secret Jews collaborating with neo-Nazis. Such parallel propaganda narratives clearly contradicted each other: one was aimed at delegit-

---

[44] Vladislav Davidzon, "Right-Wing Ukrainian Leader Is (Surprise) Jewish, and (Real Surprise) Proud of It," *Tablet*, December 1, 2014, http://www.tabletmag.com/jewish-news-and-politics/187217/borislav-bereza.

[45] Unpublished interview.

[46] "Ukraine," in *ADL Global 100: An Index of Anti-Semitism* (New York: Anti-Defamation League, 2014), http://global100.adl.org/#country/ukraine/2014.

[47] Glenn Kates, "Russian TV Anchor Implies Jews Brought Holocaust on Themselves," Radio Free Europe/Radio Liberty, March 24, 2014, http://www.rferl.org/a/russian-tv-anchor-accuses-jews-of-bringing-holocaust-on-themselves-/25307640.html.

imizing Ukraine among more liberal elements, while the other was intended to mobilize support among members of the Russian Far Right.

In May 2014, *Spiegel Online* reported that a Russian television program "The Chocolate Bunny" had argued not only that Petro Poroshenko was born of a Jewish father but that he "was responsible for radicalizing the Maidan and was tapping the help of right-wing nationalists in order to make the leap to the country's highest elected office."[48] Similar documentaries on politicians Yulia Tymoshenko and Arseniy Yatsenyuk alleged that they were hiding Jewish roots, prompting Russia expert David Fishman to assert a shift in the focus of Kremlin propaganda. "In a nutshell: the Kremlin's attempt, back in late February and March, to paint the new Ukrainian regime as Nazi and antisemitic has failed," he wrote in April 2014. "It didn't pick up much traction in world public opinion. So now the Kremlin is spreading the line that the Ukrainian leaders are Jews. Or at the very least, servants and lackeys of Jews. The intended audience is no longer international; it is domestic."[49]

Subsequent events, such as the Odessa "pogrom," proved that Russia had not given up on its attempts to portray the Ukrainians as antisemites. Accusations of antisemitism and classical antisemitic tropes could coexist in the Kremlin's arsenal of misinformation weapons.

It is naive to think that media reports of Ukrainian antisemitism would be particularly useful in and of themselves in rallying Russian domestic support for action in Ukraine. I believe that the use of Nazi imagery by the Russians served two purposes. First, the instrumentalization of the Jewish issue was key to Putin's goal of awakening Russian national memory related to the Second World War. Known to former Soviet citizens as the Great Patriotic War, the memory of the millions of lives lost in the struggle against Nazism and fascism still resonate in Russia today. By packaging the war as a fight against the modern-day successors of the Nazis, Putin was able to tap into a reservoir of emotion that was incredibly useful in any attempt to mobilize popular support. Second, accusations of antisemitism also provided Putin with a pretext for interference in his neighbor's affairs while supplying a ready-made propaganda weapon to delegitimize the new administration in Kiev in the international arena. Antisemitism is one of the most pressing problems in contemporary Europe, and by linking Ukraine to troubles in France, England, and elsewhere the Russian leadership hoped to influence public opinion abroad.

---

48 "The Chocolate King Rises; Part 2: 'Piss Off, You Jewish Garbage,'" *Der Spiegel*, May 22, 2014, http://www.spiegel.de/international/europe/profile-of-petro-poroshenko-in-the-run-up-to-the-ukraine-elections-a-970325-2.html.

49 David E. Fishman, "The Real Truth about Those Anti-Semitic Flyers in Donetsk," *Forward*, April 22, 2014, http://forward.com/opinion/world/196864/the-real-truth-about-those-anti-semitic-flyers-in/?p=all.

Much ink has been spilled regarding Russia's embrace of hybrid warfare, and nowhere is this approach more readily discernible than in Ukraine. However, the Ukrainians themselves are not without sin when it comes to playing the Jewish card.

In April 2014, several balaclava-clad men were filmed handing out flyers outside Donetsk's synagogue. The flyers called for local Jews to register with the new, separatist authorities. City Rabbi Pinchas Vyshetsky called the flyers a provocation and theorized that it could be the work of "antisemites looking to hitch a ride on the current situation," adding that he had sent someone to the address given for registration to check into the matter but "there was nobody there." The flyers, theorized Dr. Efraim Zuroff of the Simon Wiesenthal Center, appeared to be "some sort of provocation and an attempt to paint the pro-Russian forces as antisemitic," an assessment that Vyshetsky said was not out of the realm of possibility.[50]

In January 2015 the Ukrainian Foreign Ministry announced the imminent formation of the office of a special envoy to combat antisemitism.[51] Nothing was ever done and no further announcements were forthcoming. It may be that the propaganda value of the announcement was all that was desired. Around the same time, the Donetsk Jewish community demanded an apology from the Ukrainian media after reports began circulating that separatists had murdered Yehuda Kellerman, a senior communal figure.[52] Just as Russian reports had "cited" Margolin of the European Jewish Association, the Ukrainian reports "quoted" Viatcheslav (Moshe) Kantor, the president of the European Jewish Congress, as a source. Kantor vehemently denied any connection to the reports.

One of the most blatant lies came in December 2015, when Ukrainian president Petro Poroshenko addressed the Knesset in Jerusalem, telling Israeli lawmakers that the Jews of occupied Crimea should be worried as "the conquerors have started to cultivate the anti-Semitism issue as well."[53] According to

---

50 Sam Sokol, "Jews Cast Doubt on Origin of Anti-Semitic Flyers in Donetsk," *Jerusalem Post*, April 18, 2014, http://www.jpost.com/Jewish-World/Jewish-News/Jews-cast-doubt-on-origin-of-anti-Semitic-flyers-in-Donetsk-349848.

51 Sam Sokol, "Kiev to Appoint Special Envoy to Combat Anti-Semitism," *Jerusalem Post*, January 25, 2015, http://www.jpost.com/Diaspora/Kiev-to-appoint-special-envoy-to-combat-anti-Semitism-388814.

52 Sam Sokol, "Reports of Death of Jewish Leader in Ukraine Greatly Exaggerated," *Jerusalem Post*, January 22, 2015, http://www.jpost.com/Diaspora/Reports-of-death-of-Jewish-leader-in-Ukraine-greatly-exaggerated-388632.

53 Knesset Spokesperson's Office, "Ukrainian President Poroshenko Addresses the Knesset: 'Russia Providing Syria with Weapons Systems That Can Influence the Balance of Power in the Region,'" press release, December 23, 2015, https://www.knesset.gov.il/spokesman/eng/PR_eng.asp?PRID=11839.

Israeli legislator Ksenia Svetlova, Poroshenko also informed her that Jews were "oppressed" in Crimea and were "not allowed" to attend synagogue.[54] This naturally prompted a harsh backlash from the heads of a number of Crimean Jewish institutions and organizations.[55] Despite Ukrainian claims, the Jews of Crimea have been left unmolested, unlike the Tatars. Speaking a month earlier in the Netherlands, Poroshenko had made a similar claim about the self-declared separatist Donetsk People's Republic (DNR) and the Luhansk People's Republic (LNR), claiming that "now there's racism, intolerance, antisemitism" there.[56]

## IV. Separatists and "miserable Jews"

As the separatists began the process of taking over the Donbas, Jewish leaders with whom I spoke stated quite clearly that, while their communities were incredibly shaken by events and a general sense of anarchy prevailed, there was no worry about antisemitism. Death could come in many forms, but antisemitic attacks were not among them. "There is, in general, no anti-Semitism or problems but there is a lack of security," the rabbi of Luhansk said in late April.[57] As far as I have been able to determine, antisemitism directed against members of the Jewish communities of the Donbas is not a problem overall, with one Jewish leader in Donetsk telling me that the separatists "have acted well toward us."[58] However, that does not mean that no incidents occurred.

In April, Luhansk's synagogue came under attack. Chana Gopin, the rabbi's wife, described the incident for the website of the Federation of Jewish Communities of the Commonwealth of Independent States:

---

[54] Ksenia Svetlova, "A brief summary of the conversation with President Petro Poroshenko (I quote his answers)," Facebook, December 22, 2015 (in Russian), https://www.facebook.com/photo.php?fbid=10153914847231414&set=a.10150221290791414.348974.542996413&type=3&theater.

[55] Sam Sokol, "Crimean Jews Angry after Poroshenko Says Russia Instigating Anti-Semitism," *Jerusalem Post*, December 27, 2015, http://www.jpost.com/Diaspora/Crimean-Jews-angry-after-Poroshenko-says-Russia-instigating-anti-Semitism-438513.

[56] "Poroshenko Accused Militants in the Donbas of Racism and Anti-Semitism," Ukrainian News, November 27, 2015 (in Russian), http://ukranews.com/news/393381-poroshenko-obvynyl-boevykov-na-donbasse-v-rasyzme-y-antysemytyzme.

[57] Sam Sokol, "For Jews in Eastern Ukraine Anarchy Is a Concern But Not Anti-Semitism," *Jerusalem Post*, May 12, 2014, http://www.jpost.com/Jewish-World/Jewish-Features/For-Jews-in-Eastern-Ukraine-anarchy-is-a-concern-but-not-anti-Semitism-351949.

[58] Sam Sokol, "Top Rebel Leader Accuses Jews of Masterminding Ukrainian Revolution," *Jerusalem Post*, June 22, 2015, http://www.jpost.com/Diaspora/Top-rebel-leader-accuses-Jews-of-masterminding-Ukrainian-revolution-406729.

There was a lot of tension on the day of the event. I got to the synagogue to check on how things were coming along and to see what I could do to help. And then it happened. A motley crew of vicious rabble tried to get past the wall surrounding the synagogue. A few years ago, thank G-d, we moved to a new building, which shone like a lighthouse of Judaism in Lugansk. But the building wasn't finished, and there was only a temporary wall around it. For a few seconds, I stood mesmerized. A situation that had seemed like child's play had just become dangerous. The building's supervisor, Isana Razinkova, who is very devoted to the activities of the community, tried to scare away the rabble, but they soon toppled the fence and Isana fell on the ground. We called in our security company for backup, and they managed to scatter the hooligans. How did it end? Isana was lightly wounded; one of the community's supporters decided that the community needed and deserved more robust security; and another community supporter, who is a contractor, decided that the time had come to build a more permanent wall. And they did. …

Another serious incident occurred on Friday at 2 p.m., a time when the synagogue is quite busy. Suddenly, unexpected guests appeared. Ten armed ruffians broke in and insisted on searching the premises. Why? They'd heard a rumor that the community had received a shipment of humanitarian aid. (That was the only thing they'd heard that was true.) Some thought that the Ukrainian army was passing arms through synagogue. (That part of the rumor wasn't true, of course.) Explanations did no good. You could have cut the tension with a knife.

They searched the synagogue and disappeared as quickly as they had appeared. But the atmosphere didn't just go back to what it had been. The Rabbi decided to move the supplies we'd received further from the synagogue, and more than that, to wrap the new Torah scroll and another Torah, and hide them in a safe place. Who knew what else the day would bring, and what other surprises were in store for us? That Shabbat, as we read the weekly portion from our old, small Torah, the atmosphere was bitter. Until that day, synagogues had been neutral territory, disconnected from political conflict. One felt the holiness when entering the synagogue and forgot the strife in the streets. Because of this, even more Jews than usual flocked to the synagogue, as if they were running away from the turmoil outside.[59]

Speaking with me the next month, Rabbi Gopin did not raise the issue of anti-semitism. Asked if it was a concern, he replied that "there is, in general, no anti-semitism or problems but there is a lack of security." People are "nervous about war. There is vandalism. There are people going around with guns," he said. However, Jewish institutions in his city were operating normally and the

---

[59] Chana Gopin, "My City is Being Shelled," Federation of the Jewish Communities of the CIS (FJC), n.d., https://fjc.ru/city-shelled.

community had beefed up its security. "We are not in the picture," he concluded.[60]

While antisemitism may not be a daily concern, for the most part, "antisemitic views constantly appear in the separatists' mass media and websites," according to Tel Aviv University antisemitism researcher Irena Cantorovich. "A recent example … is an article claiming that Israel deliberately provides medications containing barbed wire, which kills patients. The article was uploaded on the official page of the Donetsk municipal TV station sponsored by the People's Republic of Donetsk on the "Odnoklassniki" social network," she told the *Jerusalem Post* last November.[61]

The leaders of both people's republics have made public antisemitic comments, with the head of the DNR claiming that "miserable Jews" run Ukraine[62] and the head of the LNR blaming the Jews for launching the Euromaidan:

> "I'd like to ask the historians … or maybe the philologists, can't choose, really, why was it called the 'Euromaidan'? Where did the name come from? From the area [Euromaidan Square in Kiev]? Or perhaps from the people? Those same people who now make up the majority of leaders of what was once our Ukraine?" he asked, intimating that there is a connection between Jews and the revolution because the Russian word for Jew, "Evrei," sounds like "Euro."

> "I have nothing against … Valtzman, Groysman, and many others. [Volodymyr Groysman, a Jew, was then parliamentary speaker and is now Prime Minister] I have nothing against the Jews as a people, as the "Chosen People," we can talk about this separately if we have the time.

> But the crux of the matter is that when we call what has happened a "Euromaidan," we infer that the leaders now are representatives of the people who have been harmed the most by Nazism," the rebel chief asserted.[63]

---

[60] Sam Sokol, "For Jews in Eastern Ukraine Anarchy Is a Concern But Not Anti-Semitism," *Jerusalem Post*, May 12, 2014, http://www.jpost.com/Jewish-World/Jewish-Features/For-Jews-in-Eastern-Ukraine-anarchy-is-a-concern-but-not-anti-Semitism-351949.

[61] Sam Sokol, "OSCE Denies Rebel Claim It Will Attend Donetsk Conference on Fascism and Anti-Semitism," *Jerusalem Post*, November 8, 2015, http://www.jpost.com/Diaspora/OSCE-denies-rebel-claim-it-will-attend-Donetsk-conference-on-fascism-and-anti-Semitism-432407.

[62] Sam Sokol, "Separatist Leader Says 'Miserable Jews' Running Ukraine," *Jerusalem Post*, February 3, 2015, http://www.jpost.com/Diaspora/Separatist-leader-says-miserable-Jews-running-Ukraine-389883.

[63] Sam Sokol, "Top Rebel Leader Accuses Jews of Masterminding Ukrainian Revolution," *Jerusalem Post*, June 22, 2015, http://www.jpost.com/Diaspora/Top-rebel-leader-accuses-Jews-of-masterminding-Ukrainian-revolution-406729.

Gopin responded to that statement, which was made last June, by saying that it "smell[ed] of antisemitism." Other signs of antisemitism in the Russian-backed republics include a rally in which protesters called out "Zionists"[64] and the presence of alleged neo-Nazi and far-right movements among the separatist troops.[65]

Just as Borislav Bereza was used as the Jewish front of Pravy Sektor, the separatists also had a Jewish representative, in their case a foreign minister. Alexander Kofman served as the face of the DNR until February 2016, deflecting criticisms of antisemitism on the part of his superiors and later organizing a conference in Donetsk on combating fascism and antisemitism.[66]

## V. BANDERA, BABI YAR AND THE RETURN OF YUSHCHENKOISM

Despite knowing that much, but far from all, of the antisemitism attributed to Ukraine is Russian propaganda, the Ukrainians still make it incredibly hard to disbelieve the Kremlin. While Jews are not being beaten in the streets, in some ways certain aspects of antisemitism have enjoyed a state-sponsored renaissance.

Last April, the Verkhovna Rada passed four laws, known collectively as the Decommunization laws, which enshrined the Organization of Ukrainian Nationalists (OUN) and the Ukrainian Insurgent Army (UPA) in Ukraine's national pantheon of heroes. Designed to wipe out the stain of the country's Communist past, the laws banned the use of Soviet and Nazi symbols, required the renaming of streets and cities named after Communist figures and banned the denigration of members of armed insurgent groups that fought for Ukrainian independence. The Law of Ukraine on the Legal Status and Honoring the Memory of Fighters for Ukraine's Independence in the Twentieth Century states explicitly that "public denial of the legitimacy of the struggle for Ukraine's independence in the twentieth century is recognized as an insult to the memory of the fighters for Ukraine's independence in the twentieth century, a disparagement of the Ukrainian people and is unlawful," essentially banning anything

---

64 David E. Fishman, "The Real Truth about Those Anti-Semitic Flyers in Donetsk," *Forward*, April 22, 2014, http://forward.com/opinion/world/196864/the-real-truth-about-those-anti-semitic-flyers-in/?p=all.

65 Ibid. See also Sam Sokol, "Alleged Links to Neo-Nazi Groups of Fighters on Both Sides of Ukrainian Civil War," *Jerusalem Post*, September 10, 2014, http://www.jpost.com/Diaspora/Alleged-links-to-neo-Nazi-groups-of-fighters-on-both-sides-of-Ukrainian-civil-war-374981.

66 Sam Sokol, "OSCE Denies Rebel Claim It Will Attend Donetsk Conference on Fascism and Anti-Semitism," *Jerusalem Post*, November 8, 2015, http://www.jpost.com/Diaspora/OSCE-denies-rebel-claim-it-will-attend-Donetsk-conference-on-fascism-and-anti-Semitism-432407.

but an official state-approved narrative of the history of the OUN/UPA.[67]

The driving forces behind the law were MP Yurii Shukhevych, the son of the UPA's wartime commander, and Volodymyr Viatrovych, a revisionist historian and the director of the government-sponsored Institute for National Memory.

The atrocities perpetrated by OUN/UPA were described in an open letter signed by scholars from around the world in which they objected to the law on the grounds that it curtailed freedom of expression and academic inquiry in Ukraine.

> The potential consequences of both these laws are disturbing. Not only would it be a crime to question the legitimacy of an organization (UPA) that slaughtered tens of thousands of Poles in one of the most heinous acts of ethnic cleansing in the history of Ukraine, but also it would exempt from criticism the OUN, one of the most extreme political groups in Western Ukraine between the wars, and one which collaborated with Nazi Germany at the outset of the Soviet invasion in 1941. It also took part in anti-Jewish pogroms in Ukraine and, in the case of the Melnyk faction, remained allied with the occupation regime throughout the war.[68]

Scholars like Jared McBride have repeatedly called out Viatrovych, pointing out that his entire career has been dedicated to whitewashing the record of the twentieth century Ukrainian nationalist movement, rebranding it as a savior of Jews and banishing references to its fascist nature.[69] In Viatrovych's work, McBride writes, "radical right-wing Ukrainian nationalists are depicted as nothing but tragic freedom fighters, occasionally forced to don Nazi uniforms to struggle for independence, liberty, and Western values." Appointed by Poroshenko to head the Ukrainian Institute of National Memory in 2014, Viatrovych has been largely responsible for a resurgence of historical revisionism that had been suppressed under the pro-Russian Yanukovych regime. Explaining his work as the triumph of democratic forces against a repressive Soviet narrative, Viatrovych has also led efforts to rehabilitate Stepan Bandera, the head of the OUN(b), one of two competing OUN factions, which "anticipated the establishment of an ethnic Ukrainian state, without Jews, Poles, Russians and other minorities."[70]

---

[67] Law of Ukraine (No. 314-VIII of April 9, 2015) on the Legal Status and Honoring the Memory of Fighters for Ukraine's Independence in the Twentieth Century, available at http://www.memory.gov.ua/laws/law-ukraine-legal-status-and-honoring-memory-fighters-ukraines-independence-twentieth-century.

[68] David R. Marples, "Open Letter from Scholars and Experts on Ukraine Re. the So-Called 'Anti-Communist Law,'" *Krytyka*, April 2015, http://krytyka.com/en/articles/open-letter-scholars-and-experts-ukraine-re-so-called-anti-communist-law.

[69] Jared McBride, "How Ukraine's New Memory Commissar Is Controlling the Nation's Past," *The Nation*, August 13, 2015, https://www.thenation.com/article/how-ukraines-new-memory-commissar-is-controlling-the-nations-past.

[70] Grzegorz Rossoliński-Liebe, *Stepan Bandera: The Life and Afterlife of a Ukrainian Nationalist: Fascism, Genocide, and Cult* (Stuttgart: Ibidem-Verlag, 2014).

As scholars such as Per Anders Rudling[71] and Grzegorz Rossoliński-Liebe have pointed out, following the end of the Second World War, Ukrainian émigrés to the West created an entire mythology around Bandera, turning him into a Ukrainian national martyr and developing "an entire literature that denied the OUN's fascism, its collaboration with Nazi Germany, and its participation in atrocities, instead presenting the organization as composed of democrats and pluralists who had rescued Jews during the Holocaust."[72] Following the fall of the Soviet Union and Ukraine's emergence as an independent sovereign nation-state for the first time in its history, this new, foreign-grown narrative was ready and available for importation back to the motherland.

However, opinion polls conducted in the period immediately prior to the revolution of 2013-2014 indicate that most Ukrainians do not actually buy into the Bandera myth, nor do all OUN/UPA supporters accept the academic consensus that Ukrainian nationalists killed thousands of Jews and Poles during the war.[73] Under President Viktor Yushchenko (2005-2010), Rudling explains, the Ukrainian state apparatus was turned toward manufacturing what he describes as a "new set of historical myths" through the founding of the Institute for National Memory. At the same time, Yushchenko attempted to present the Holodomor, a man-made famine caused by retributive Soviet collectivization policy in Ukraine, as "the genocide of the Ukrainian nation."

I would contend that this policy, which Rudling refers to as Yushchenkoism, has been revived under Poroshenko, who is desperate to create a unifying mythology in order to rally his people against the Russians. I believe that it was Yushchenkoism and its glorification of the OUN/UPA, which are held in low esteem in southern and eastern Ukraine, that helped prepare the ground for the Russian propaganda necessary to mobilize support for a separatist agenda in the Donbas. If there was already suspicion of western Ukrainians in the east (bearing in mind the historical split between right- and left-bank Ukraine), it would follow that the prominence of Svoboda, the spiritual heir to the OUN/UPA, would be enough to convince eastern Ukrainians of the truth of Russian claims of a fascist putsch in Kiev.

What is certain is that the passage of laws honoring the OUN/UPA and the willingness of Ukrainian leaders to look the other way regarding manifestations

---

[71] Per Anders Rudling, "The Return of the Ukrainian Far Right: The Case of VO Svoboda," in *Analysing Fascist Discourse: European Fascism in Talk and Text*, eds. Ruth Wodak and John E. Richardson (London and New York: Routledge, 2013), 228-255.

[72] Id.

[73] Ivan Katchanovski, "Terrorists or National Heroes? Politics and Perceptions of the OUN and the UPA in Ukraine," *Communist and Post-Communist Studies* 48, no. 2 (2015): 217-228.

of antisemitism indicate an inability to engage in painful historical introspection in the mold of Poland or Germany. Such introspection has not been seen in other post-Soviet states, such as Hungary and Lithuania, and the current conflict with Russia makes it even less likely in Ukraine. It is hard to tear down national heroes who fought the same enemy that is currently at the gates.

In conclusion, I would like to offer three examples of the government's willingness to tolerate antisemitism when conducive to the smooth functioning of the war. The first is the appointment of Vadim Troyan, an alleged neo-Nazi, as head of the Kiev regional police in November 2014.[74] As I wrote in the *Jerusalem Post* at the time, prior to his appointment he was deputy commander of the volunteer Azov Battalion, which has engaged in combat operations against pro-Russian separatists in the country's east. Kiev, while within the district, is an independent jurisdiction.

Azov, which I present as my second example, was one of the only effective fighting forces the government had in the east at the time. Comprised mainly of ultra-nationalists, its flag features a *Wolfsangel*, a symbol associated with neo-Nazi groups.[75] While the authorities likely had little choice but to accept the existence of Azov due to the weakness of its own official military units, the government's collaboration with such a group served to undermine its public statements on combating antisemitism. Last November, Jewish opposition lawmaker and oligarch Vadim Rabinovich accused Kiev of "flirting with radicals" for working with such militant groups. "The government must stop flirting with ultra-radical organizations, which are increasingly gaining ground in Ukraine," he wrote on the website of his Opposition Bloc political party, demanding that the administration of President Petro Poroshenko cut ties with such groups.[76]

Finally, I present the case of Artyom Vitko, the former commander of the government-backed Luhansk-1 Battalion and now a member of Oleh Lyashko's Radical Party. Video of the militant parliamentarian leaked online showing him singing a Russian rock song in honor of Adolf Hitler. As far as I am aware, no condemnations were forthcoming from anyone in power in Kiev.[77] Vitko's

---

74 Sam Sokol, "Kiev Regional Police Head Accused of Neo-Nazi Ties," *Jerusalem Post*, November 12, 2014, http://www.jpost.com/Diaspora/Kiev-regional-police-head-accused-of-neo-Nazi-ties-381559.

75 Sam Sokol, "US Lifts Ban on Funding 'Neo-Nazi' Ukrainian Militia," *Jerusalem Post*, January 18, 2016, http://www.jpost.com/Diaspora/US-lifts-ban-on-funding-neo-Nazi-Ukrainian-militia-441884.

76 Sam Sokol, "Ukrainian Jewish Leader Accuses Kiev of 'Flirting with Radicals,'" *Jerusalem Post*, November 11, 2015, http://www.jpost.com/Diaspora/Ukrainian-Jewish-leader-accuses-Kiev-of-flirting-with-radicals-432723.

77 Sam Sokol, "Ukrainian Legislator Toasts Adolf Hitler," *Jerusalem Post*, December 27, 2015, http://www.jpost.com/Diaspora/Ukrainian-legislator-toasts-Hitler-438561.

actions came to light the week after Poroshenko's Knesset speech in which he apologized for Ukrainian complicity in the Holocaust (without, of course, touching on the issue of the Decommunization laws).

More recently, questions have been raised regarding Ukraine's willingness to grapple with its past, due to controversies surrounding the seventy-fifth anniversary of the Babi Yar massacre. More than 33,000 Jews were murdered at Kiev's Babi Yar ravine in a two-day period in 1941 as part of what has come to be known as the "Holocaust of bullets." Ukraine has come a long way from the Soviet period when mourning over the deaths of the Jews slaughtered here was suppressed, subsumed under the general victimhood of "Soviet citizens," but in the period following the Ukrainian revolution of 2013 renewed efforts at rehabilitating Ukrainian collaborators have stained efforts to come to grips with the nation's past. Kiev came under fresh criticism regarding its policies of national memory in February when it came to light that a government-backed design competition invited architectural proposals to resolve what it sees as a "problem" of a "discrepancy between the world's view and Jewry's exclusive view of Babi Yar as a symbol of the Holocaust."[78]

During official state commemorations in September 2016, held in collaboration with the World Jewish Congress, Ukrainian officials erected a sign honoring members of the OUN/UPA killed at the site,[79] despite the organization's known role in the Holocaust. This, needless to say, ruffled Jewish feathers. Speaking before the Verkhovna Rada prior to the commemoration, Israeli President Reuven Rivlin took the Ukrainians to task for their revisionism. "Many of the collaborators were Ukrainian, among the most notorious the members of the OUN who carried out pogroms and massacres against the Jews and in many cases handed them over to the Germans," he said. "It is true, there were more than 2,500 Righteous Among the Nations, lone candles who shone in the darkness of humanity. Yet the majority remained silent," he continued, asserting that Ukrainians need to "recognize antisemitism as it was and as it is found today, and not rehabilitate or glorify antisemites." Rivlin's statement touched a nerve, with Viatrovych responding by stating that Rivlin was repeating "Soviet myths."[80] Pavel Podobed, an employee of Viatrovych's, went even further, stating that the Israeli president's speech was the same as Poroshenko

---

78 Sam Sokol, "Ukraine Backtracks on Babi Yar Plans amid Accusations of Holocaust Revisionism," *Jerusalem Post*, February 8, 2016, http://www.jpost.com/Diaspora/Ukraine-backtracks-on-Babi-Yar-plans-amid-accusations-of-Holocaust-revisionism-444268.

79 Sam Sokol (@SamuelSokol), "FYI. This is at Babi Yar. Memorial for OUN(b) and OUN(m)," Twitter photo, September 29, 2016, https://twitter.com/SamuelSokol/status/781652152511070208.

80 "Israeli President's Speech Is 'Spit on the Soul'—Ukraine's Nationalists' Leader," 24today.net, September 28, 2016, http://24today.net/open/695956.

flying to Jerusalem to blame the Jews for orchestrating the Holodomor, a popular conspiracy theory.[81] No official condemnations were issued.

The Ukrainian state is certainly far from being overtly antisemitic. It currently has a Jewish prime minister and, during the worst of the fighting, Ihor Kolomoisky, a prominent and pugnacious Jewish oligarch, was appointed governor of the Dnipropetrovsk Oblast and is widely credited with helping limit the spread of separatism in the east. However, Kiev's tolerance of historical revisionism is unacceptable (if unremarkable when placed alongside similar practices in Hungary and the Baltic states), and its willingness to overlook the neo-Nazi affiliations of those involved in its war effort is worrying indeed.

---

[81] Pavel Podobed, "Imagine yourself… The President of Ukraine visits Israel and at the invitation of the Israelis speaks in the Knesset," Facebook, September 27, 2016 (in Ukrainian), https://www.facebook.com/pavlo.podobed/posts/10210289329326193?pnref=story.

# Friends or Foes?
## Attitudes of the Czech Antisemitic Scene toward Islam and Muslims

Zbyněk Tarant*

*The path of obsessively criticizing global Islam often leads to the Wailing Wall.*

—A Czech neo-Nazi[1]

## INTRODUCTION AND METHODS

To what extent does being an antisemite influence one's attitude toward Islam? What are the actual relationships between antisemitic and Islamophobic concepts in the minds of antisemites? Isn't it time to revise the old "enemy of my enemy" concept? This article attempts to tackle the whole "antisemitism vs. Islamophobia" debate from a fresh perspective by means of a case study that analyses the attitudes of the Czech antisemitic scene to Islam and Muslims. By offering such a concrete case study based on primary sources, I seek to provoke a debate that could lead to a refining of security policies vis-à-vis the domestic European scene of political extremism.

As most of the antisemitic content in the Czech language is located on the web,[2] I have focused the main part of my analysis on the electronic realm. Inspired by similar surveys on the Arabic[3] and Iranian[4] blogosphere, I have

---

* Assistant Professor in the Department of Middle Eastern Studies, University of West Bohemia, Pilsen, Czech Republic. This work was supported by the University of West Bohemia under Grant POSTDOC-14.

[1] "'Deislamizátor' a vyznavač rasového promíšení debatuje s arabistou o hrozbě islámu" *Náš směr*, February 23, 2014.

[2] Printed antisemitic journals and bulletins were available in the past, namely the infamous *Týdeník Politika*, banned in 1994 by a court order. Today, there are two antisemitic publishing houses: *Guidemedia* (led by Pavel Kamas) and *Nakladatelství Adam Bartoš* (a personal publishing enterprise established by Adam B. Bartoš).

[3] Bruce Etling, John Kelly, Robert Faris, and John Palfrey, "Mapping the Arabic Blogosphere: Politics, Culture, and Dissent" (Berkman Center Research Publication 2009/06, Harvard University, June 2009).

[4] John Kelly and Bruce Etling, "Mapping Iran's Online Public: Politics and Culture in the Persian Blogosphere" (Berkman Center Research Publication 2008/1, Harvard University, April 2008).

used the method of social network analysis (SNA).[5] The analysis itself can be divided into three main steps: (1) mapping the Czech antisemitic cyberspace; (2) identifying its most important hubs (i.e. the most influential antisemitic websites); and (3) analyzing how the most important Czech antisemitic websites talk about Islam and Muslims. By using this method, I have ensured that the second, qualitative part of my analysis covers the most influential voices of the Czech antisemites. In the final part of this article, some additional thoughts from a non-participant observation in the terrain are added as well.

In the first stage, a general map of the Czech antisemitic cyberspace was created by starting with several well-known antisemitic websites and exploring the links using the "snowball" method. At the time of the analysis (October 2014), there were about fifty websites in the Czech language that could be considered antisemitic according to the EUMC definition.[6] There had to be at least five articles identifiable as explicitly antisemitic on a given website in order for it to be placed on the antisemitic list. While the number of fifty websites may seem fairly high, there are several factors involved. The Czech far-right scene is highly particularistic. Each and every small group creates its own website. Moreover, with the rise of platforms such as WordPress, which are available for free, many abandoned websites continue their existence years after being forsaken by their creators. Once the domain and hosting are available for free, abandoning the website does not cause it to disappear immediately, as occurs with paid hosting. In the end, of the fifty websites and blogs, only about half are really active and less than a dozen are actually updated on a daily basis. Along with the fifty explicitly antisemitic websites, there were about seventy other websites whose content was judged to be "controversial" yet did not cross the threshold. These represented a "grey zone" and were included in the analysis only if they were linked by at least two other antisemitic websites.

The main part of the survey was performed in late October 2014, and one of its first conclusions was the surprising diversity of the Czech antisemitic cyberspace. Antisemitism in the Czech Republic does not end with neo-Nazi and radical nationalist groups. One can also find neo-fascist groups, Catholic traditionalists, and sites dedicated to Neopaganism, pan-Slavism and New Age esoterica. There are also a substantial number of websites dealing with conspiracy theories (since 2016 referred to as "fake-news sites"), some of which are impossible to situate on the left-right political scale.

In stage two of this analysis, the most influential hubs of the network had to be identified. Czech antisemitic websites are still quite diligent in maintaining

---

5 Independently of my survey, Avukatu and Lupač used a similar method to analyze Czech far-right websites as well. Their results were published in Czech. See Jiřina Avukatu and Petr Lupač, "Analýza on-line sítě české krajní pravice," *Rexter*, no. 1 (2014).

6 European Monitoring Centre on Racism and Xenophobia, "Working Definition of Antisemitism."

their dedicated "links" sections, which allow researchers to follow these links and visualize the relationships between the websites. As to the purpose of this second stage, I was interested in knowing how many incoming links an antisemitic website gets from other antisemitic websites. I expect the websites with more incoming links—Indegree (%)—to be more influential and have a larger impact on the scene than the ones with only a few or no incoming links at all. Ten websites that were evaluated as the most influential by this method were put into the third stage of the analysis. Note that the Indegree values in Table 1 are quite low (between 1 and 5 percent), even for the most influential websites, which might point to a low level of connectedness within the network, caused by the highly particularistic nature of the Czech antisemitic scene.

In order to obtain an additional, comparative source of information on the possible impact and influence of the analyzed websites, an Alexa rating was also taken into consideration. While Alexa's controversial rating system is unreliable for the precise measurement of a website's visitors, it is still sufficient for the simple task of selecting the ten most visited websites from a given list, especially when used only as an additional method. It was found that the lists of the top ten websites provided by SNA and by Alexa were very similar. Three websites were present on the first list and not on the second. For the qualitative stage of the analysis, these two top ten lists were combined and merged, producing a total of thirteen websites that can be expected to have the highest influence (see Table 1).

*Table 1: Top 13 most influential Czech antisemitic websites*

| Website URL | Description | Indegree (%)* |
|---|---|---|
| http://deliandiver.org | neo-Nazi / pan-Aryan / neo-Pagan | 4.56 |
| http://www.delnickelisty.cz | neo-Nazi (Workers' party) | 2.66 |
| http://zvedavec.org | Conspiracy theories / anti-Globalism | 2.28 |
| http://freeglobe.parlamentnilisty.cz | Conspiracy theories / anti-Globalism | 2.28 |
| http://protiproud.parlamentnilisty.cz | Conspiracy theories / Catholic traditionalists | 2.28 |
| http://revolta114.blogspot.cz | neo-Nazi / Autonomous Nationalists | 1.90 |
| http://nassmer.blogspot.cz | neo-Nazi | 1.90 |
| http://sarmatia.wordpress.com | neo-Nazi / pan-Aryan / neo-Pagan | 1.90 |
| http://www.hlas.delnickamladez.cz | neo-Nazi (Workers' Party) | 1.52 |
| http://www.nebruselu.cz | Conspiracy theories / Catholic traditionalists | 1.52 |
| http://www.tedeum.cz | Catholic traditionalists | 1.14 |
| https://radicalrevival.wordpress.com | neo-Nazi / pan-Aryan / neo-Pagan | 1.14 |
| https://widerstandstreetart.wordpress.com | neo-Nazi | 1.14 |

* Indegree (%) is a value showing the relationship between the number of incoming links to each website and all the links in the whole network.

In the third, qualitative stage, these thirteen websites were analyzed by conducting a search of all remarks on Islam and Muslims in general. Below, the results for selected Arab and Muslim countries and regimes in particular will also be shown. The analysis was performed by utilizing Google's capability to limit a search within a given website or domain (e.g. "Islám site:www.dsss.cz"). Each of the thirteen websites were analyzed in this way. For the purpose of analyzing general attitudes toward Islam and Muslims, the articles and posts that were found using this method were coded and sorted into three categories: *positive*, *ambivalent/neutral*, and *negative*.

As Table 2 shows, the results are surprisingly diverse. The first interesting point is the diversity with regard to the degree of attention devoted to the topic of Islam by the particular websites. While for some, such as *Zvědavec*, which is devoted to conspiracy theories, or the neo-Nazi *Náš směr* and *Revolta 114*, run by the former Autonomous Nationalists, Islam is one of the more important topics, with dozens of articles devoted to it. Other webs and blogs tend to almost ignore it. For these websites, such as *Sarmatia*, *Dělnická mládež*, *Hlas mládeže*, or *Widerstandstreetart*, Islam is only a minor topic. *Sarmatia* is a pan-Slavic, Neopagan website. *Dělnická mládež* is a youth movement of the neo-Nazi Workers' Party, for which the most important topic is the Romany community, not the Arabs. *Hlas mládeže* is a bulletin published by this neo-Nazi youth movement and follows the same line. *Widerstandstreetart* is a dedicated Word-Press blog for presenting neo-Nazi graffiti and the topic of Islam is almost absent on this otherwise popular website. On the currently most popular neo-Nazi website, the pan-Slavic and Neopagan *Deliandiver*, Islam is also just a secondary topic.

*Table 2: Attitudes of articles containing the keyword "Islam" from the top thirteen most important antisemitic websites in the Czech language*

| Website URL | Positive | Neutral / Ambivalent | Negative |
| --- | --- | --- | --- |
| http://www.zvedavec.org | 35 | 48 | 18 |
| http://deliandiver.org | 4 | 5 | 10 |
| http://www.delnickelisty.cz | 0 | 0 | 9 |
| http://freeglobe.parlamentnilisty.cz | 3 | 17 | 38 |
| http://protiproud.parlamentnilisty.cz | 4 | 8 | 17 |
| http://nassmer.blogspot.cz | 16 | 33 | 12 |
| http://revolta114.blogspot.cz | 7 | 7 | 6 |
| http://sarmatia.wordpress.com | 1 | 4 | 8 |
| http://www.hlas.delnickamladez.cz | 0 | 1 | 0 |
| http://www.nebruselu.cz | 0 | 0 | 7 |
| http://www.tedeum.cz | 1 | 3 | 10 |
| https://radicalrevival.wordpress.com | 0 | 3 | 5 |
| https://widerstandstreetart.wordpress.com | 0 | 0 | 1 |

*Source: author's own analysis.*

## I. Multi-layered relationship

The analysis shows that the general attitude of the Czech antisemites to Islam and Muslims can be described as being highly ambivalent. Positive remarks about Islam and Muslims appear side-by-side with negative ones and sometimes appear in the same articles. This ambivalence is sometimes palpable even within the movements themselves and among their members. Some of the websites (and the movements behind them) simply do not seek any logical consistency in their rhetoric on Islam at all. While the positive remarks are directed toward particular movements, personalities, and states in the Muslim world, the negative ones tend to talk in a general, abstract way. The vast majority of these negative remarks can be found in relation to migration and Islamization.

The initial conclusion is that the discourse of Czech antisemites on Islam and Muslims is generally dominated by two conflicting stereotypes: the first one sees Muslims as noble warriors and an authentic culture, while the second sees them as immigrants to Europe. Paradoxically, the admired value of "authenticity"—i.e. Muslims being valued for keeping their traditions—becomes a problem once they migrate to Europe, since they are seen as a group that insists on maintaining its traditions and refusing to assimilate. An explanation for this phenomenon can be found in the very delicate balance between general Islamophobia and National Socialist racial doctrines of Blood and Soil: Islam is seen as a partner by the neo-Nazis as long as it remains in its own sphere. To quote an example from the *Freeglobe* website: "Islam is not a threat in the Middle East, it is a threat only in Europe."[7] In a later example from the same website, the pattern continues: "Islam is not a problem on a territory connected with Islam, it is a problem only on our territory."[8] In particular, the Czech far right cannot ignore the theme of immigration, especially when anti-immigration rhetoric is proving to have such strong mobilizing potential all around Europe.

The vast majority of the positive remarks were of a minor character and were directed toward particular individuals, movements, regimes, or countries—Iran, as well as Syria, Egypt, and Libya after the Arab Spring—and their leaders. Redirecting these expressions of support to the secular Arab regimes, or moving them into the "ambivalent" category (as they support one side inside a Muslim country and denounce the other), would make the "positive" category disappear completely. Of the generally positive characteristics of Islam only a few were mentioned, but among these we are able to identify authenticity and resistance against Western influences. Some attention is paid to the Palestinians and

---

[7] Lukáš Petřík, "Měla by ČESKÁ pravice podporovat Izrael?," *Freeglobe*, February 17, 2013.

[8] Michal Urban, "Kolik naší krve ještě bude prolito za cizí zájmy?," *Freeglobe*, July 14, 2014.

support for their armed resistance against Israel, yet it sometimes feels that they are mentioned only "as an obligation" and do not represent a significant topic for Czech neo-Nazis. On some websites, especially *Zvědavec*, some attention is devoted to Islamic banking as opposed to the "usury" of Western banks and corporations. If the writers of the articles are actually able to distinguish the differences between Sunni and Shiite Islam and consider them important, Shiite Islam is usually preferred to Sunni.[9] One finds examples of famous Sunni thinkers, such as Yusuf al-Qaradawi, being described as collaborators with the "New World Order."[10] Surprisingly enough, terrorism or the activities of armed groups against Western targets are mentioned only rarely. Moreover, most of the scene adheres to 9/11 conspiracy theories according to which the World Trade Center was destroyed as part of a sophisticated plot involving the Jews and Freemasons in order to obtain support for Israel. In effect, such conspiracy theories deprive al-Qaeda of its "achievements." Terrorist attacks by Sunni groups such as al-Qaeda are mostly played down as mere "false flag" operations or "media creations." Similar attitudes can be seen today in relation to ISIS, with *Zvědavec*, for example, writing that "ISIS is a project of a Secret Group of Obama's advisors."[11] One rare exception from the past is the neo-Nazi National Resistance's obituary for the al-Qaeda leader in Iraq, Abu Musab al-Zarqawi, from eight years ago. This appeared in 2006, after he was killed in a US air strike. The obituary by Petr Kalinovský, entitled "He Was a Real Son of His Culture, He Was a Hero,"[12] was published on the previously most important and currently defunct neo-Nazi website *Národní odpor*. Today this website is only accessible through the Internet Archive's Wayback Machine.[13] Due to its obsolescence, it is not included in the numerical data of this survey.

## II. Negative reflections on Islam: "Stop Islamization!"

While the vast majority of the negative expressions were found on the *Freeglobe* website, this particular website has a special history as a philosemitic movement that became antisemitic and renounced its original anti-Muslim, pro-Israel attitude. This will be dealt with below in the section on ambivalent expressions.

---

9 "Žijeme v Apokalypse? (4) Sunnitský Islám jako cílová alternativa globální non nacionální civilizace?," *Freeglobe*, September 23, 2013.

10 Jaroslav Moučka, "Sunnitský kazatel: 'Rusko je největším nepřítelem muslimů,'" *Freeglobe*, April 15, 2013.

11 "Ruská FSB: Islámský stát je projektem tajné skupiny Obamových poradců," *Zvědavec*, September 29, 2014. Zvědavec took this article from a Russian source and translated it.

12 Petr Kalinovský, "Byl důsledným synem své kultury, byl hrdinou," *Národní odpor*, June 11, 2006.

13 See http://www.archive.org.

As an example of negative expressions, the *Workers' Bulletin* (*Dělnické listy*) website of the neo-Nazi Workers' Party of Social Justice (WPSJ) is chosen instead. With the WPSJ, the choice of targets for its hate rhetoric seems to be very pragmatic. For example, I have not recorded a single antisemitic expression in the party's propaganda in the last three years (the party was severely anti-semitic in 2006-2009).[14] Instead of the Jews, the party prefers to attack Romanies and Muslims. A brief look at the WPSJ's websites reveals articles such as: "No to Islamization and Multiculture!,"[15] which informs readers about the results of the Swiss referendum in 2009 that decided to ban the construction of new minarets in Switzerland. Another example is "Muslim Union," where the author writes about the "Muslim occupation of Europe."[16] A video of Muammar Gaddafi talking about "Muslim women as weapons of the Islamization of Europe" was embedded under the article. Another interesting piece is "Netherlands: More Freedom, Less Islam,"[17] which expresses support for Geert Wilders.

By digging deeper into the history of the *Workers' Bulletin* website, one can find examples of Islamophobia that are strange to say the least. One of these is a review of Johannes Rothkranz's *Wer steuert den Islam?* (Who truly controls Islam?). This book, originally published in German by a Sedevacantist publishing house, *Pro Fide Catholica*, was translated into Czech by Jaroslav Voříšek[18] and published by the Czech neo-Nazi publishing house, Sowulo Press (without the writer's or translator's consent).[19] In the review, which is more of an advertisement than a review, we read:

> Islam comes from a post-Christian (and anti-Christian) Judaism. It wasn't Allah or Gabriel who inspired the "prophet" Muhammad, but a rabbi from Mecca. The original, true Qur'an was nothing more than an Arab translation and refurbishment of the five books of Moses. The true ideological background of Islam sheds light on the true hidden forces behind the process of the Islamization of Europe. It is obvious that, regarding their numbers, the

---

[14] Zbyněk Tarant, "Workers' Party—From Socialist Nationalism to National Socialism," in *Anatomy of Hatred—Essays on Anti-Semitism*, ed. Věra Tydlitátová and Alena Hanzová (Pilsen: University of West Bohemia, 2009).

[15] Rudolf Pikola, "Ne islamizaci a multikultuře," *Dělnické listy*, December 4, 2009.

[16] Jiří Petřivalský, "Muslimská unie," *Dělnické listy*, August 13, 2009.

[17] Martin Zbela, "Nizozemí: Více svobody, méně islámu," *Dělnické listy*, June 10, 2010.

[18] Jaroslav Voříšek was a notorious Czech antisemite of the early 1990s. Together with Josef Tomáš, he edited the first explicitly antisemitic bulletin of the post-communist era, *Týdeník Politika*. Both editors were sentenced to prison in 1994 for inciting racial hatred, which was a crime under both Czechoslovak and Czech Penal Law. Voříšek died in 2017.

[19] In situations like these, one can find neo-Nazis publicly quarrelling about the copyright and quality of typography. See Erik Sedláček, "Satanova synagoga a ostatní brak od Sowulo press," *Odpor.org*, August 2, 2009.

members of the "chosen people" themselves were not able to acquire world dominance alone. Thus, they used (as seen many times before and since) their racially close, much more numerous and even now purely pagan Arabs. And with their real Talmudic slyness, they equipped the Arabs with a religious ideology for a "holy war" in the name of foreign interests. The same ideology would remove them from power in the (highly improbable) case of a realization of Talmudic-Jewish world dominance, because they serve the wrong god and the wrong law. This, and other interesting titles, can be bought at www.sowulo-press.cz.[20]

This is probably the most extreme example of anti-Islamic rhetoric turning into antisemitism. The quote was actually not written by a Czech neo-Nazi. It is just a translated resume of another book, written by Curzio Nitoglia and published by *Pro Fide Catholica*, entitled *Woher stammt der Islam* (Where does Islam come from?).

Considering the small number of articles devoted to it, Islam seems to be a minor topic in relation to the rest of the WPSJ's propaganda. From the dozens of articles that the party publishes every year, only nine of them from the last five years were about Islam. All of them are negative, however. Only after the main part of my survey was completed did the WPSJ's anti-Islamic rhetoric receive a new boost when the national media exposed conflicts between inhabitants of the North Bohemian spa town of Teplice and its Arab visitors in September 2014. The WPSJ was quick to organize a series of political meetings in the town in September and October 2014, while the topic was still hot.[21] Another boost was provided by a "scarf debate" that also started in the country in September 2014 after two Muslim students dropped out of a public school for not being allowed to wear headscarves. The party's *Dělnické listy* bulletin came up with the headline "STOP the Islamization of the Czech Republic."[22] In this regard, the neo-Nazi policies regarding Muslims can be compared to the ones of the European New Right. Some of the Czech antisemitic far-right movements are aware of this similarity, which can also be interpreted as unwanted competition, however.


III. Ambivalent reflections of Islam: neo-Nazis criticizing Islamophobia?

Typical examples of this ambivalent attitude can be quoted from the polemics of the European New Right. For example, the neo-Nazi website *Náš směr* pub-

---

20 "Kdo skutečně řídí islám?," *Dělnické listy*, no. 19 (2008).
21 "REPORT: V Teplicich protestující odmítli islám," *Dělnická strana*, September 28, 2014.
22 Jiří Štěpánek, "DSSS: STOP islamizaci České republiky!," *Dělnické listy*, no. 44 (2014).

lished the following polemic with the "primitive anti-Islam propaganda" of a pro-Israel, right-wing blog (Ondřej Neff's *Neviditelný pes*). The anonymous author of this polemic, which is a remarkable example of cultural relativism in neo-Nazi thought, writes:

> Yes, there is nothing bad about Islam, it just belongs to its original space, where it had been developing for hundreds of years. We do not have a right to judge it there, especially not in the way you [the author of the criticized article] are doing. Different cultures should not intermingle, but they should know how to communicate from their positions! Only then can we keep the mutual respect, understanding of diversity and ergo facto, the peace as well.[23]

The editor of this website, a prominent Czech neo-Nazi amateur historian and Holocaust denier, Lukáš Beer, continued this discussion in the following words, which again express ambivalence quite clearly:

> Islam is not the cause of multiculturalism. Islam in itself is not an enemy of European culture. However, it is not compatible with the traditions and culture of the Central European autochthonous nations, for example, and there is no biologically or culturally conditioned mutual affinity. Islam, as a domestic culture in the non-European East, must be respected instead of spreading hostile attitudes and phobias. Now the hearts and prudence of the Europeans must sensitively and responsibly deal with the mess that was created in Europe by multiculturalism. It is not going to be an easy task.[24]

The neo-Nazis and other right-wing antisemitic movements are fully aware of the mobilizing potential of anti-immigration rhetoric, but they are disturbed by the fact that this Islamophobic rhetoric is, on many occasions, connected to expressions of support for Israel. This is the context of the quote: "The path of obsessively criticizing global Islam often leads to the Wailing Wall."[25] The neo-Nazis, in particular, dispute the movements and parties such as *Vlaams Belang* in Belgium, *Partij voor de Vrijheid* (PVV) in the Netherlands and *Freiheitliche Partei Österreichs* (FPÖ) in Austria, which they criticize for offering Israel as a counterweight to the alleged Islamic threat.[26] In the eyes of neo-Nazis, the European New Right not only "steals" the anti-immigration rhetoric from the "traditional" nationalist movements but actually supports their arch enemy— the Jewish, Zionist state. Trapped in a double jeopardy (we want to utilize anti-

---

[23] Lukáš Beer, "Diskuse: Ke kritice islamizace střední Evropy zásadně nepatří primitivní urážky domácí islámské kultury," *Náš směr*, March 13, 2010.

[24] Lukáš Beer, "Záludná past antiislamismu," *Náš směr*, October 20, 2010.

[25] "'Deislamizátor' a vyznavač rasového promíšení debatuje s arabistou o hrozbě islámu," *Náš směr*, February 23, 2014.

[26] See, for example, Lukáš Beer, "Demaskovaná tvář wildersovského antiislamismu znovu prozrazuje, co je jeho vlastní prioritou," *Náš směr*, February 5, 2011.

immigration rhetoric vs. we refuse to support the Zionist state in any way), Czech antisemites started to portray the pro-Israel European New Right as part of an alleged Zionist conspiracy aimed at mobilizing European support for Israel.

A neo-Nazi website known as *Sarmatia* (formerly *Bratrstvi.net*) published an article entitled "Islamism wins with Zionist support." From this article, accompanied by a photograph of Geert Wilders wearing a *yarmulka* at the Western Wall Plaza in Jerusalem, I quote:

> It seems that the resulting chaos and radicalization of Muslims suits somebody's political goals. Somebody who likes to put himself in the role of a barrier against radical Islamism. Somebody who initiated the massive influx of Muslims to the old continent in order to transfer the […] fear to Europe.[27]

Another article, entitled "Muslims are not the only immigrants," continued in a similar fashion: "But to divert the attention from the deviant existence of the state of Israel is necessary. Whatever the price, others will pay it and those rightly chosen ones will make the profit. The conservative pro-Zionist political right plays nothing more than the role of useful idiots."[28]

The thoughts and concepts of Geert Wilders, Bat Ye'or, and other radical critics of Islam were originally introduced into the Czech discourse in 2005 by a right-wing, conservative website named *EUrabia* (after Bat Ye'or's book).[29] Until that time, the Czech discourse on Islam was dominated by the prudent voices of orientalists and cultural anthropologists. At the time, *EUrabia* was a strongly pro-Israel, sometimes even naively philosemitic website. Some of the polemics, quoted above, come from 2010 and are directed against this particular website, whose hawkish pro-Israel orientation seemed to prove the "Jews-behind-anti-Islamism" image in the eyes of Czech neo-Nazis. The website was founded by Adam Bartoš and Lukáš Petřík. After five years, in late 2010/early 2011, the website switched sides—from philosemitism to antisemitism and from a radical pro-Israel attitude to anti-Zionist rhetoric that does not even attempt to hide its antisemitic content. The switch was accompanied by a series of articles and interviews in which the founders of the website denounced their former positions.

Adam Bartoš, originally writing under the pseudonym Edward Steinský, announced as early as June 2009 that he had "stopped believing the official version of 9/11."[30] At that time, the website still claimed that it "remains pro-

---

27 "Islamismus vítězí s podporou sionistů," *Sarmatia*, January 27, 2012.

28 "Muslimové nejsou jediní přistěhovalci," *Sarmatia*, November 30, 2011.

29 Probably the first content analysis of this website was performed by Martin Hála, "Strukturální a obsahová analýza serveru Eurabia.cz," *Migrace online*, July 27, 2006.

30 Edward Steinský, "Přiznání šéfredaktora: Jak jsem přestal věřit oficiální verzi o 11. Září," *Eurabia*, June 20, 2009.

Israel." As co-founder of the website, Adam Bartoš announced his conversion in an interview with one of the far-right bloggers[31] and founded a brand new branch of the website—a project entitled *Freeglobe*—with the oldest entry dating back to May 25, 2010. The attitude of the *EUrabia* website changed as well. In one of his book reviews for this website, Bartoš writes:

> I was able to free myself from the naïve faith in Osama bin Laden as the initiator of all the evil in the world. The EUrabia.cz server focuses only on the issues of coexistence with Muslims in Europe. This theme is in fact so huge, both in principle and in reality, that it will be able to stand the test of time, even when we throw the war against terror overboard as an American invention. We will still have many topics and problems to point out and write about.[32]

In an article entitled "The Other Clash of Civilizations, or the Jews in the Shadow of Muslims," Bartoš announces that the "New World Order" represented by influential Jewish individuals is in fact much worse than Islamization, which—according to Bartoš—is nothing more than a tool for gaining support for the State of Israel, or even perhaps a means for gaining control over the world, unified under the banner of the struggle against a common enemy. Bartoš writes: "After all, what is the easiest way to shake off suspicion than to divert the attention onto someone else? And what may be a better way of blunting the teeth of antisemitism than by offering another enemy to society (moreover, our own enemy)?"[33] He continues:

> Very often the gravest rivalry seems to be among those who are in fact very close to one another and strive for the same goal. So the idea came to my mind—what if the whole Clash of Civilizations, masked as the clash of the West with Islam, was in fact a clash between Islam and Judaism? And what if the Jews, who have become used to doing things under cover, obliquely and secretly, were manipulating the West into the clash with Islam, partly to get the public opinion on their side and turn their Middle-Eastern conflict into a world conflict (because without this, they cannot succeed in that conflict), and partly because they need to blame someone else for their ambitions for world dominance, in order to distract the attention from their own plans? If it were like this, it would be a brilliant strategy. And, for the Jews, such brilliant strategies are natural.[34]

---

31 "O médiích a politice s bývalým novinářem z iDnes.cz," *D-Fens*, February 7, 2010.

32 Adam B. Bartoš, "Jak zabít civilizaci? Nad knihou Benjamina Kurase," *Eurabia*, May 23, 2011.

33 Adam B. Bartoš, "Střet civilizací trochu jinak, aneb Židé ve stínu muslimů," *EUrabia*, November 20, 2011.

34 Ibid.

Bartoš then proceeds to sum up the basic theses of his *EUrabia* website in relation to Islam, including the ambitions for world dominance and the notion of being "a chosen people," and announces that these phenomena have been discovered in Judaism as well. Bartoš returns to his new topic repeatedly, for example in the articles "Whom should we thank for Islamization"[35] and "What is the major threat: Islamization or the NWO?"[36] Finally, in an article entitled "The European New Right in the Israeli Service,"[37] Bartoš arrives at the exact same conclusions as his neo-Nazi counterparts. He uses antisemitic concepts in order to denounce the very same ideas he himself radically asserted only a couple of years earlier. The formerly neocon philosemitic website had metamorphosed into an ultraconservative antisemitic one, and its discourse became almost identical to the neo-Nazi attitudes quoted above.[38] After the switch, the polemics between neo-Nazis and *EUrabia* quickly faded away. In a couple of years, the *Freeglobe* website, as an offspring of *EUrabia*, gained wide popularity among Czech neo-Nazis to the extent that it is now among the top thirteen antisemitic Czech websites. While most of its content is fiercely Islamophobic, the conclusions from that Islamophobia are different. The focus is not on the New Right's call for increased assertiveness on the part of the West but rather on the constant blaming of the West (and the Jews, the EU, the Freemasons, etc.) for all the wrongdoings of radical Salafism.

## IV. EXPRESSIONS OF SUPPORT TOWARD INDIVIDUALS AND REGIMES

While most of the negative remarks deal with Islam and Muslims in general, the positive remarks tend to be more specific. From the large, abstract mass of Islam, selected individuals, movements, countries, and regimes are singled out for support. Surprisingly, there are some that manage to fit into the complicated patterns that make them acceptable to the Czech far right. Historically, it was possible to find very positive attitudes on the part of the neo-Nazi groups toward Iran.[39] One of the most important groups of the late 2000s, known as *Národní odpor*, asked the Czech president to allow them to join the ranks of the Iranian army in the event of an Israeli attack. Should the president refuse to give them permission, the group threatened they would launch violent attacks within the

---

35 Adam B. Bartoš, "Komu vděčíme za islamizaci?," *EUrabia*, November 17, 2011.

36 "Je větší nebezpečí NWO, nebo islamizace?," *Freeglobe*, September 18, 2011.

37 Adam B. Bartoš, "Evropská nová pravice ve službách Izraele," *EUportal*, September 13, 2011.

38 Bartoš has published a whole book of interviews, in which he describes the alleged reasons for his conversion. See Adam B. Bartoš, *Edward Steinský vs. Adam Bartoš: Zpověď. Jsem antisemita?* (Prague: Adam Benjamin Bartoš, 2014).

39 For example, see the WPSJ's support for Iran: "Koho chcete poučovat?," *Dělnické listy*, September 30, 2009.

Czech republic.[40] This strong affinity with Iran remains unchanged, and the neo-Nazis in particular have repeatedly expressed their support for the Iranian regime, whenever there is a threat of military escalation.[41] I have not found a single article on neo-Nazi or other far-right websites that is critical of Iran. International pressure against Iran is mostly explained as being the work of the Israeli lobby.[42] On other Middle Eastern issues, it seems that the Czech far right even follows the Iranian line. One can see this in the example of the Sunni Gulf monarchies, which are being delegitimized as mere "US puppet governments."[43] In the case of Bahrain, for example, the Czech far right supports the Shiite protest movements. In some cases, articles from the Iranian *Press TV* or *Farsnews* are translated into Czech for this very purpose.[44] The fact that the West decided to strike against Libya while ignoring the Saudi intervention in Bahrain, which took place at the same time, resulted in deep bitterness within the scene.[45]

After the outbreak of the Arab Spring, Gaddafi's regime in Libya was strongly supported,[46] despite the fact that pre-2011 attitudes toward Libya were dominated by quotations regarding Gaddafi's threat to Islamize Europe thanks to the high birth rate of immigrants. Once the war in Libya had started, neo-Nazis were quick to include Gaddafi's *Green Book* in their electronic libraries, side-by-side with the writings of Julius Evola and Otto Strasser, quoting them as an example of a "third position" ideology.[47] After Gaddafi's death, several neo-Nazi websites produced obituaries for the deceased leader.[48] A similarly ambivalent attitude can be found in relation to Egypt, whose pre-2011 leader, Hosni Mubarak, was seen as a servant of the West. His downfall was seen as proof that Mubarak had refused to carry out American and Israeli orders.

As regards the Middle Eastern agenda, the civil war in Syria has become the most important topic, following hard on the heels of the usual anti-Israel rhetoric. In Syria, the whole scene unanimously supports Bashar al-Assad against the opposition and the Islamic militants. While the Czech antisemitic websites despise using labels such as "terrorists," they are not afraid to use them when it comes to the violent acts of Syrian opposition militants. One can thus read pro-Syrian comments by the WPSJ, such as "Syria Fights Terrorism and

---

40 "Žádost o povolení bojovat proti státu Izrael," *Národní odpor*, August 22, 2006.
41 "Na cestě k íránské válce," *Radical Revival*, March 14, 2012.
42 "Rozpoutá Izrael nukleární válku?," *Národní odpor*, January 8, 2007.
43 "Žijeme v Apokalypse? (4) Sunnitský Islám jako cílová alternativa globální non nacionální civilizace?," *Freeglobe*, September 23, 2013.
44 "Bahrajn zabíjí mladé a odstraňuje jim orgány," *Zvědavec*, April 8, 2011.
45 "O změnách v arabském světě," *Délský potápěč*, May 12, 2011.
46 "K plukovníkově smrti," *Radical Revival*, October 24, 2011.
47 "Zelená kniha o národním faktoru," *Revolta 114*, June 27, 2012.
48 For example, "Nekrolog: My všichni jsme Muammar Kaddáfí," *Revolta 114*, October 24, 2011.

the USA,"[49] or even comparisons between the threat of air strikes against the Ba'athist regime and the bombing of Dresden.[50] The *Freeglobe* website, while using strong anti-Muslim rhetoric, also writes that "Assad Fights for Europe as Well."[51] Within the mind-set of the Czech antisemitic scene, the anti-Muslim attitudes that were quoted above are in complete harmony with the pro-Assad position. The far right portrays Syria as a secular, nationalist, authoritarian state (a goal they actually share) that is fighting radical Muslims, who are allegedly supported by the United States and Israel. The Ba'ath party and its ideology are identified as a successful example of the "third position" ideology. One even sees examples on neo-Nazi websites of the collection and publication of photographs of Syrian government officials, as well as crowds of civilians raising their right hands[52] as they hail Bashar al-Assad.[53]

## V. THE EUROPEAN SOLIDARITY FRONT FOR SYRIA IN THE CZECH REPUBLIC

In 2012, Czech neo-Nazis, inspired by similar activities on the part of *CasaPound Italia*, established a Czech branch of the European Solidarity Front for Syria (ESFS).[54] The initiative is widely propagated by neo-Nazi websites, which claim that "The Battle for Europe is Fought in Damascus."[55] The most visible activities of this pro-Assad group include online activism, public lectures, and the organization of several rallies on the streets of Prague. One of its public seminars took place on May 27, 2013 at Revolution Street in Prague. It took place in a room decorated with Syrian flags (see Image 1). It was easy to see that this was a far-right event as, along with the Syrian flags, Bohemian flags were used instead of Czech national ones. The Bohemian flag, depicting the double-tailed lion within a red shield and red and white stripes in the background, is preferred by the neo-Nazis to the Czech national flag, since some adherents of the scene consider the blue triangle in the Czech flag to be a Masonic symbol. With posters and stickers of Bashar al-Assad emblazoned with slogans such as "Hands OFF Syria!" and "Media Lie about Syria!," the attitude of the movement is more than clear. However, the audience, as well as some of the speakers, were not limited only to the far right. While the founder of the ESFS's Czech branch,

---

49 Jiří Štěpánek, "Komentář: Sýrie bojuje proti terorismu a USA," *Dělnická strana*, July 7, 2013.

50 "Vzpomínka na Drážďany," *Radical Revival*, February 14, 2012.

51 Michal Urban, "Assad bojuje i za Evropu!," *Freeglobe*, June 30, 2014.

52 "Jak se zdraví v Sýrii," *Radical Revival*, August 6, 2011.

53 "Sýrie," *Revolta 114*, June 16, 2012.

54 See the ESFS's website at http://solidarita-syrie.info.

55 "U Damašku se bojuje za Evropu," *Revolta 114*, March 20, 2013.

Patrik Vondrák, is a prominent neo-Nazi, other speakers came from the completely opposite end of the political spectrum. In addition to Vondrák, there was Radovan Rybák from the communist *Haló noviny* newspaper, for example. In the auditorium, the neo-Nazis, dressed in black, were joined by crowds of moderate, secular Syrian Arabs, who have formed a small and well-integrated community in the Czech Republic since the communist era. This is where the approach of the ESFS raises some concerns, since it creates common ground between moderate pro-Assad Syrians and radical neo-Nazis, sometimes without the former realizing the true background of the latter. While the activities of the Czech ESFS branch are peaceful, the neo-Nazi websites also express their support for armed action.[56]

*Image 1: ESFS seminar in Prague, May 27, 2013. Photo: Zbyněk Tarant.*

The ESFS has organized several rallies in support of Bashar al-Assad on the streets of Prague. The events themselves have, so far, been peaceful and orderly. During one of them, on August 1, 2013, supporters of the initiative gathered at Wenceslas Square in Prague under the horse and rider statue dedicated to the Czech national patron. They unfurled large Syrian flags and delivered speeches in support of its president. Following the speeches, the crowd, consisting of Czech neo-Nazis, left-wing anti-globalism activists from Germany, and pro-Assad Syrian Arabs, continued in a peaceful and quiet march toward the US embassy, located in Prague's Malá Strana neighborhood (see Image 2). There, in front of the embassy, from behind the riot fence, the national anthem of Syria was played and Syrian flags were flown (see Image 3). The representatives of the ESFS then submitted their petition to the embassy staff and the rally ended.

---

[56] "Černá lilie—řečtí nacionální socialisté bojují za Asada v Sýrii," *Radical Revival*, November 1, 2013.

*Image 2: ESFS march to the US embassy in Prague, July 20, 2013.*
*Photo: Zbyněk Tarant.*

*Image 3: ESFS rally in front of the US embassy in Prague, July 20, 2013.*
*Photo: Zbyněk Tarant.*

While most of the support for the ESFS emanates from the neo-Nazi websites, this rally was also covered and supported by *Haló noviny*.[57]

## CONCLUSION

What patterns can be identified in this complicated and multi-layered image? While Islam, in general, is perceived mostly negatively by the Czech antisemitic scene, there are some specific exceptions. Positive remarks are directed at particular individuals, movements, regimes, and countries in the Muslim world. Czech neo-Nazis are strongly supportive of Iran, as well as of the Ba'athist establishment in Syria, and speak in defense of Gaddafi's Libya. At the same time, Sunni Gulf monarchies are dismissed as Western "puppet regimes." While the Czech far right supports the regime in Syria, it also supports the opposition in Bahrain. The previous section describes a concrete example of a neo-Nazi initiative in support of the Syrian regime. While the neo-Nazis are hostile to immigrants from Arab countries, they are capable of engaging in pragmatic cooperation with members of the Syrian community and in support of the secular, autocratic, Syrian regime. At the same time, the Czech antisemitic scene downplays the activities of al-Qaeda and ISIS, referring to them as mere Western creations.

There are several important points when it comes to formulating security policies vis-à-vis the antisemitic scene in Central Europe and its relationship with the Muslim world. First, in the bipolar struggle between Iran and the Sunni states, the Czech antisemites side with Iran. Second, as the far-right groups prefer to downplay the activities of the Sunni terrorist organizations, or to portray them only as a threat to Europe, the potential for cooperation between the far right and these armed groups seems to be very low for the time being. Third, it seems that antisemitism is not the primary factor for neo-Nazis when choosing friends in the Middle East. Instead, it seems to be a secondary or even tertiary determinant. While some of the Islamist groups in Syria (such as *Jabhat an-Nusra* or ISIS) are more hostile to Israel than the Syrian regime itself, the secular Ba'athist regime is still supported over its radical jihadist opposition. This support is based on a shared ideology of anti-globalism and anti-Americanism, as well on the apparent affinity between the far right's distorted perceptions of Ba'athist ideology and neo-fascist "third position" political ideas.

The relationship of the Czech antisemitic scene to Islam and Muslims is neither simple nor straightforward. It is clear that the discourse of Czech anti-semites on Islam is highly ambivalent and dominated by two conflicting stereotypes. The image of Islam as an authentic culture that resists Western

---

[57] Radovan Rybák, "Ruce pryč od Sýrie, znělo Prahou," *Haló noviny*, July 20, 2013.

influence is overshadowed by the image of Muslim immigration to Europe. Members of the scene tend to resolve this conflict by stating that Islam can be tolerated as long as it stays in the Muslim world. At the same time, Islamophobia can easily become a source of antisemitism. For example, it has become a weapon in the polemics between the neo-Nazi groups and the European New Right, which is accused of "stealing" the anti-immigration agenda for "Zionist purposes." In other cases, the Jews are held directly responsible for Muslim immigration. In other words, they are being blamed for "Islamization" and Islamophobia at the same time. Thus, one can see how a naively philosemitic yet Islamophobic movement or website could become antisemitic over the course of only a couple of years. Under certain circumstances, Islamophobia can thus actually lead to antisemitism. This is a danger that should not be overlooked.

## Author's note

The research for this article was conducted before the 2015 migration crisis in Europe.[58]

## Bibliography and sources

### Unattributed

"Bahrajn zabíjí mladé a odstraňuje jim orgány." *Zvědavec*, April 8, 2011. Accessed October 25, 2015. http://www.zvedavec.org/komentare/2011/04/4309-bahrajn-zabiji-mlade-a-odstranuje-jim-organy.htm.

"Černá lilie—řečtí nacionální socialisté bojují za Asada v Sýrii." *Radical Revival*, November 1, 2013. Accessed October 25, 2015. http://radicalrevival.word press.com/2013/11/01/cerna-lilie-recti-nacionalni-socialiste-bojuji-za-asada-v-syrii.

"'Deislamizátor' a vyznavač rasového promíšení debatuje s arabistou o hrozbě islámu." *Náš směr*, February 23, 2014. Accessed October 25, 2015. http://www.nassmer.blogspot.cz/2014/02/deislamizator-vyznavac-rasoveho.html.

"Islamismus vítězí s podporou sionistů." *Sarmatia*, January 27, 2012. Accessed October 25, 2015. http://sarmatia.wordpress.com/2012/01/27/islamismus-vitezi-s-podporou-sionistu.

---

[58] For additional information on the far-right response to the 2015 migration wave, see Zbyněk Tarant, "Antisemitism in Response to the 2015 Refugee Wave—Case of the Czech Republic" (ISGAP Flashpoint no. 13, New York, January 28, 2016), https://isgap.org/flashpoint/antisemitism-in-response-to-the-2015-refugee-wave-the-case-of-the-czech-republic.

"Jak se zdraví v Sýrii." *Radical Revival*, August 6, 2011. Accessed October 25, 2015. http://radicalrevival.wordpress.com/2011/08/06/jak-se-zdravi-v-syrii.

"Je větší nebezpečí NWO, nebo islamizace?" *Freeglobe*, September 18, 2011. Accessed October 25, 2015. http://freeglobe.parlamentnilisty.cz/Articles/1054-je-vetsi-nebezpeci-nwo-nebo-islamizace-.aspx.

"K plukovníkově smrti." *Radical Revival*, October 24, 2011. Accessed October 25, 2015. http://radicalrevival.wordpress.com/2011/10/24/k-plukovnikove-smrti.

"Kdo skutečně řídí islám?" *Dělnické listy*, no. 19 (2008). Accessed October 25, 2015. http://www.delnicka-strana.cz/ds-listy/final.pdf.

"Koho chcete poučovat?" *Dělnické listy*, September 30, 2009. Accessed October 25, 2015. http://www.delnickelisty.cz/koho-chcete-poucovat_?ank=62&odp%5B0%5D=1.

"Muslimové nejsou jediní přistěhovalci." *Sarmatia*, November 30, 2011. Accessed October 25, 2015. http://sarmatia.wordpress.com/2011/11/30/muslimove-nejsou-jedini-pristehovalci.

"Na cestě k íránské válce." *Radical Revival*, March 14, 2012. Accessed October 25, 2015. http://radicalrevival.wordpress.com/page/21/?archives-list=1.

"Nekrolog: My všichni jsme Muammar Kaddáfí." *Revolta 114*, October 24, 2011. Accessed October 25, 2015. http://revolta114.blogspot.cz/2011/10/nekrolog-my-vsichni-jsme-muammar.html.

"O médiích a politice s bývalým novinářem z iDnes.cz." *D-Fens*, February 7, 2010. Accessed October 25, 2015. http://www.dfens-cz.com/view.php?cislo clanku=2010020705.

"O změnách v arabském světě." *Délský potápěč*, May 12, 2011. Accessed October 25, 2015. http://deliandiver.org/2011/05/o-zmenach-v-arabskem-svete.html.

"REPORT: V Teplicich protestující odmítli islám." *Dělnická strana*, September 28, 2014. Accessed October 25, 2015. http://www.dsss.cz/report_-v-teplicich-protestujici-odmitli-islam.

"Rozpoutá Izrael nukleární válku?" *Národní odpor*, January 8, 2007. Accessed October 25, 2015. http://web.archive.org/web/20100620131731/http://odpor.org/index.php?page=clanky&kat=3&clanek=525.

"Ruská FSB: Islámský stát je projektem tajné skupiny Obamových poradců." *Zvědavec*, September 29, 2014. Accessed October 25, 2015. http://www.zvedavec.org/komentare_6162.htm.

"Sýrie." *Revolta 114*, June 16, 2012. Accessed October 25, 2015. http://revolta114.blogspot.cz/2012/07/syrie.html.

"U Damašku se bojuje za Evropu." *Revolta 114*, March 20, 2013. Accessed October 25, 2015. http://www.revolta114.blogspot.cz/2013/03/u-damasku-se-bojuje-za-evropu.html.

"Vzpomínka na Drážďany." *Radical Revival*, February 14, 2012. Accessed October 25, 2015. http://radicalrevival.wordpress.com/2012/02/14/vzpominka-na-drazdany.

"Žádost o povolení bojovat proti státu Izrael." *Národní odpor*, August 22, 2006. Accessed October 25, 2015. http://web.archive.org/web/20100615191057/ http://odpor.org/index.php?page=clanky&kat=1&clanek=429.

"Zelená kniha o národním faktoru." *Revolta 114*, June 27, 2012. Accessed October 25, 2015. http://revolta114.blogspot.cz/2012/06/zelena-kniha-o-narodnim-faktoru.html.

"Žijeme v Apokalypse? (4) Sunnitský Islám jako cílová alternativa globální non nacionální civilizace?" *Freeglobe*, September 23, 2013. Accessed October 25, 2015. http://freeglobe.parlamentnilisty.cz/Articles/3298-zijeme-v-apokalypse-4-sunnitsky-islam-jako-cilova-alternativa-globalni-non-nacionalni-civilizace-.aspx.


*Attributed*

Avukatu, Jiřina, and Petr Lupač. "Analýza on-line sítě české krajní pravice." *Rexter*, no. 1 (2014). Available at: https://www.ceeol.com/search/journal-detail?id=717.

Bartoš, Adam B. "'Jak zabít civilizaci?' Nad knihou Benjamina Kurase." *Eurabia*, May 23, 2011. Accessed October 25, 2015. http://eurabia.parlamentnilisty.cz/Articles/6172-jak-zabit-civilizaci-nad-knihou-benjamina-kurase.aspx.

Bartoš, Adam B. "Evropská nová pravice ve službách Izraele." *EUportal*, September 13, 2011. Accessed October 25, 2014. http://euportal.parlament nilisty.cz/Articles/8097-evropska-nova-pravice-ve-sluzbach-izraele.aspx.

Bartoš, Adam B. "Komu vděčíme za islamizaci?" *EUrabia*, November 17, 2011. Accessed October 25, 2015. http://eurabia.parlamentnilisty.cz/Articles/6922-komu-vdecime-za-islamizaci-.aspx.

Bartoš, Adam B. "Střet civilizací trochu jinak, aneb Židé ve stínu muslimů." *EUrabia*, November 20, 2011. Accessed October 25, 2015. http://eurabia. parlamentnilisty.cz/Articles/6933-stret-civilizaci-trochu-jinak-aneb-zide-ve-stinu-muslimu.aspx.

Bartoš, Adam B. *Edward Steinský vs. Adam Bartoš: Zpověď. Jsem antisemita?* Prague: Adam Benjamin Bartoš, 2014.

Beer, Lukáš. "Demaskovaná tvář wildersovského antiislamismu znovu prozrazuje, co je jeho vlastní prioritou." *Náš směr*, February 5, 2011. Accessed October 25, 2015. http://nassmer.blogspot.cz/2011/02/demaskovana-tvar-wilder sovskeho.html.

Beer, Lukáš. "Diskuse: Ke kritice islamizace střední Evropy zásadně nepatří primitivní urážky domácí islámské kultury." *Náš směr*, March 13, 2010. Accessed October 25, 2015. http://nassmer.blogspot.cz/2010/03/diskuse-ke-kritice-islamizace-stredni.html.

Etling, Bruce, John Kelly, Robert Faris, and John Palfrey. "Mapping the Arabic Blogosphere: Politics, Culture, and Dissent." Berkman Center Research Publication 2009/06, Harvard University, June 2009. Accessed October 25, 2015. http://cyber.law.harvard.edu/sites/cyber.law.harvard.edu/files/Mapping_the_Arabic_Blogosphere_0.pdf.

European Monitoring Centre on Racism and Xenophobia. "Working Definition of Antisemitism." Accessed October 25, 2015. Available at: http://www.akdh.ch/AS-WorkingDefinition-draft.pdf.

Hála, Martin. "Strukturální a obsahová analýza serveru Eurabia.cz." *Migrace online*, July 27, 2006. Accessed October 25, 2015. http://www.migraceonline.cz/cz/e-knihovna/strukturalni-a-obsahova-analyza-serveru-eurabia-cz.

Kalinovský, Petr. "Byl důsledným synem své kultury, byl hrdinou." *Národní odpor*, June 11, 2006. Accessed October 25, 2015.

Kelly, John, and Bruce Etling. "Mapping Iran's Online Public: Politics and Culture in the Persian Blogosphere." Berkman Center Research Publication 2008/01, Harvard University, April 2008. Accessed October 25, 2015. http://cyber.law.harvard.edu/sites/cyber.law.harvard.edu/files/Kelly&Etling_Mapping_Irans_Online_Public_2008.pdf.

Moučka, Jaroslav. "Sunnitský kazatel: 'Rusko je největším nepřítelem muslimů.'" *Freeglobe*, April 15, 2013. Accessed October 25, 2015. http://freeglobe.parlamentnilisty.cz/Articles/2814-sunnitsky-kazatel-rusko-je-nejvetsim-nepritelem-muslimu-.aspx.

Petřík, Lukáš. "Měla by ČESKÁ pravice podporovat Izrael?" *Freeglobe*, February 17, 2013. Accessed October 25, 2015. http://freeglobe.parlamentnilisty.cz/Articles/2649-mela-by-ceska-pravice-podporovat-izrael-.aspx.

Petřivalský, Jiří. "Muslimská unie." *Dělnické listy*, August 13, 2009. Accessed October 25, 2015. http://www.delnickelisty.cz/muslimska-unie.

Pikola, Rudolf. "Ne islamizaci a multikultuře." *Dělnické listy*, December 4, 2009. Accessed October 25, 2015. http://www.delnickelisty.cz/ne-islamizaci-a-multikulture?ank=62&odp%5B0%5D=1.

Rybák, Radovan. "Ruce pryč od Sýrie, znělo Prahou." *Haló noviny*, July 20, 2013. Accessed October 25, 2015. http://www.halonoviny.cz/articles/view/7661730.

Sedláček, Erik. "Satanova synagoga a ostatní brak od Sowulo press." *Odpor.org*, August 2, 2009. Accessed October 25, 2015. https://web.archive.org/web/20091107044329/http://odpor.org/index.php?page=clanky&kat=&clanek=1013.

Steinský, Edward. "Přiznání šéfredaktora: Jak jsem přestal věřit oficiální verzi o 11. září." *Eurabia*, June 20, 2009. Accessed October 25, 2015. http://eurabia.parlamentnilisty.cz/Articles/3093-priznani-sefredaktora-jak-jsem-prestal-verit-oficialni-verzi-o-11-zari.aspx.

Štěpánek, Jiří. "DSSS: STOP islamizaci České republiky!" *Dělnické listy*, no. 44 (2014). Accessed October 25, 2015. http://www.noviny.dsss.cz/delnicke-listy44.pdf.

Štěpánek, Jiří. "Komentář: Sýrie bojuje proti terorismu a USA." *Dělnická strana*, July 7, 2013. Accessed October 25, 2015. http://old.dsss.cz/komentar_-syrie-bojuje-proti-terorismu-a-usa.

Tarant, Zbyněk. "Workers' Party—From Socialist Nationalism to National Socialism." In *Anatomy of Hatred—Essays on Anti-Semitism*, ed. Věra Tydlitátová and Alena Hanzová. Pilsen: University of West Bohemia, 2009.

Urban, Michal. "Assad bojuje i za Evropu!" *Freeglobe*, June 30, 2014. Accessed October 25, 2015. http://freeglobe.parlamentnilisty.cz/Articles/4127-assad-bojuje-i-za-evropu-.aspx.

Urban, Michal. "Kolik naší krve ještě bude prolito za cizí zájmy?" *Freeglobe*, July 14, 2014. Accessed October 25, 2015. http://freeglobe.parlamentnilisty.cz/ShowArticleMobile.aspx?id=4158.

Zbela, Martin. "Nizozemí: Více svobody, méně islámu." *Dělnické listy*, June 10, 2010. Accessed October 25, 2015. http://www.delnickelisty.cz/nizozemi_-vice-svobody_-mene-islamu?ank=62&odp%5B1%5D=1.